D0948721

Sacred Bonds of Solidarity

STANFORD STUDIES IN JEWISH HISTORY AND CULTURE

EDITED BY *Aron Rodrigue and Steven J. Zipperstein*

Sacred Bonds of Solidarity

The Rise of Jewish Internationalism in Nineteenth-Century France

Lisa Moses Leff

STANFORD UNIVERSITY PRESS

STANFORD, CALIFORNIA

2006

Stanford University Press
Stanford, California

This book has been published with the assistance of
Southwestern University.

Printed in the United States of America on acid-free, archival-
quality paper

Library of Congress Cataloging-in-Publication Data
Leff, Lisa Moses.
  Sacred bonds of solidarity : the rise of Jewish internationalism
in nineteenth-century France / Lisa Moses Leff.
    p. cm. — (Stanford studies in Jewish history and culture)
  Includes bibliographical references and index.
  ISBN-13: 978-0-8047-5251-0 (cloth : alk. paper)
  ISBN-10: 0-8047-5251-6 (cloth : alk. paper)
  1. Jews—France—History—19th century. 2. Jews—France—
Politics and government—19th century. 3. Jews—France—
Identity. 4. Jews—Cultural assimilation—France—19th century.
5. Jewish diaspora—History—19th century. 6. France—History—
1789-1900. 7. France—Ethnic relations. I. Title. II. Series.

DS135.F83L375 2006
305.892'404409034—dc22   2006005161

Typeset by Classic Typography in 10.5/14 Galliard

We do not believe that the Jews are destined to inhabit the ancient land of Jerusalem as a nation once again . . . but we do believe that one day, between the men of all nations, we might see the establishment of such a harmony of belief, morality and doctrine, of political and religious institutions, that this people, dispersed everywhere, will be able to believe that they inhabit a common fatherland.

—LÉON HALÉVY

Contents

Acknowledgments   xi

Introduction   1

1. The Jewish Citizen   17

2. Alliances with Restoration Liberals   40

3. Jewish Identities in the Age of Romanticism   81

4. Secularism and the Civilizing Mission   117

5. The Making of Modern Jewish Solidarity   157

6. The Myth of Jewish Power   200

Conclusion   229

Notes   239

Bibliography   279

Index   307

Acknowledgments

It is a great pleasure to express my gratitude to the many people who have helped me to complete this project. This book began as a dissertation at the University of Chicago, and I hope that this final product bears the mark of that stimulating environment. Above all, I would like to thank my wonderful teachers and advisors, Leora Auslander, Bill Sewell, and especially Jan Goldstein, for their feedback, criticism, and guidance on so many occasions.

Numerous colleagues read parts of what has become this manuscript at various times and offered helpful feedback and advice, and I am grateful to all of them for their suggestions and their generosity. In this regard, I would like to thank Vicki Caron, Eileen Cleere, David Cohen, Nancy Green, Elizabeth Green Musselman, Paula Hyman, Matthew Karush, Alison Landsberg, Nadia Malinovich, Erica Peters, Rebecca Roiphe, Jennifer Sartori, Ronald Schechter, Kimberly Smith, Kenneth Stow, and Lizabeth Zack. I was extremely fortunate to meet Aron Rodrigue when I was still conceptualizing this project; he gave useful research advice, then read and provided feedback on several chapters, and finally, helped bring it to publication. Frances Malino was particularly generous with her time and attention, reading and commenting on the entire manuscript in its dissertation form. The anonymous reader at Stanford University Press provided suggestions that helped enormously in the revision process. Finally, Norris Pope made the publication process flow smoothly and easily.

I also owe a debt of gratitude to the institutions and individuals who offered material assistance as I was thinking about, researching, writing, and revising this book. My research in France, Israel, and

Boston was supported by the Council for European Studies' Pre-Dissertation Research Fellowship, the French government's Bourse Chateaubriand, the University of Chicago's Overseas Dissertation Research Fellowship, the American Historical Association's Bernadotte E. Schmitt Grant, and a Cullen Grant from Southwestern University. My writing was generously supported, in two different stages, by the Woodrow Wilson Foundation's Charlotte W. Newcombe Doctoral Dissertation Fellowship and by Southwestern University's Brown Fellowship. Two additional Cullen Grants from Southwestern helped support the final revisions. I am particularly grateful to my colleagues in Southwestern's history department, whose practical and moral support allowed me to focus as fully as possible on revising when it was most necessary.

In addition, I would like to thank the directors and staff of the libraries and archives where I conducted my research, especially Jean-Claude Kuperminc and Rose Lévyne of the Alliance Israélite Universelle (Paris) and P.-E. Landau and Jean-Marc Lévy of the archives of the Consistoire central (Paris), all of whom offered not only access to their rich collections, but valuable advice and interesting conversations about the history of Jews in France. I also wish to thank the archivists, librarians, and staff of the Bibliothèque nationale (Paris), the Archives nationales (Paris), Brandeis University Archives (Waltham, Massachusetts), the Centre des archives d'Outre-Mer (Aix-en-Provence), the Archives of the Jewish Theological Seminary (New York), the Archives of the Hebrew Union College (Cincinnati, Ohio); the Central Archives for the History of the Jewish People (Jerusalem), Harvard University Libraries, Yale University Libraries, and the University of Texas Libraries (Austin).

Parts of Chapter 2 and 5 appeared in an earlier form in my article "'Jewish Solidarity' in Nineteenth-Century France: The Evolution of a Concept," *Journal of Modern History* 74 (March 2002), and I gratefully acknowledge the University of Chicago Press for permitting me to include this material here.

Some personal thanks are in order as well. Since our days in Chicago, Maureen Healy has offered steadfast friendship, a great eye for detail, and imaginative ways of looking behind the closed door to the past. She also read and commented on much of the manuscript and offered excellent suggestions, as well as much needed moral support. My parents, Arnold and Claire Moses, and my sister, Leslie Moses, instilled me with the love of a good story, a good argument, and a general desire to know more about things. My mother, Claire, is a colleague as well; her professional advice and support have always been invaluable. With their timely arrival, my sons, Adam and Meyer, motivated me to finish this book by making life beyond it seem much more interesting. And most of all, I am grateful to my husband, Benjamin Leff, for his incisive criticism and insights on just about every version of everything that appears in this book, as well as for his love and support during the many years I have been working on it.

Sacred Bonds of Solidarity

Introduction

To speak of Jewish international solidarity before the modern era would be anachronistic. While Jews have probably always felt connected in some way to other Jews living far away from them, solidarity denotes a particular kind of bond that emerged only in the nineteenth century. Jewish international solidarity encompasses a broad set of ideas, including mutual responsibility and unity among dispersed Jews, especially in the face of adversity. In a way that may at first appear paradoxical, Jewish international solidarity grew out of the political, economic, and social integration of Jews into modern nations. This book seeks to explain this historical connection.

The practices of Jewish international solidarity are well known because they became commonplace in the twentieth century. In the name of solidarity, highly assimilated Western Jews have organized on a massive scale to help Jews elsewhere to fight oppression, to gain citizenship in the nations where they live, or if necessary, to emigrate. While Jews have sought to help their fellow Jews in distant lands since antiquity, the scale of this type of Jewish philanthropy increased tremendously after 1840, and Jewish leaders developed a new language to describe their work. The first major venture of this sort occurred in 1840, when Adolphe Crémieux, a French Jewish leader, worked with Sir Moses Montefiore, an English Jewish leader, to advocate for the persecuted Jews of Damascus using arguments designed to gain the support of Western liberal statesmen. Rather than working purely behind the scenes, these Western Jews publicized the plight of their Eastern brothers, decrying the actions of their oppressors as contrary to the enlightened spirit of the age. In the same vein, a group of French Jews established the Alliance Israélite Universelle in 1860, a permanent institution whose goal was to promote Jewish rights around the globe by emphasizing the liberal values of tolerance, equality, and religious freedom. French members of the Alliance worked with English, German, Austrian, and American Jews to help Jews in the Balkans, North Africa, the Middle East, and Eastern Europe by publicizing their plight in the Western press and by appealing to state leaders on their behalf. In the twentieth century, Jewish international solidarity increased even more; one need only think of the Zionist movement; the resettlement of Eastern European Jews in the Americas; the establishment of the American Jewish Joint Distribution Committee and other relief organizations; the efforts to rescue Jews living in Nazi Europe; and more recently, the programs to resettle Ethiopian and Russian Jews in Israel and to combat a rising tide of antisemitism around the world.

The unprecedented scale of modern Jewish international aid has been supported by new understandings of the role of Jews and Judaism in the modern world. Even though the injunction *kol yisrael arevim zeh bazeh* ("all Jews are responsible for one another") comes from the Talmud, modern Jewish advocates described their solidarity not only as fulfilling a religious duty, but also as playing a role in achieving a larger goal of uniting the entire world in a peaceful order. "Solidarity" was not defined by territorial bounds, but rather, as the force binding a community of people who share sentiments of brotherhood. Solidarity has roused Jews to action on each other's behalf, and these actions are meant to bring great benefit to all humanity. Inspired by the ideologies of Enlightenment universalism, nineteenth-century political messianism, and the imperial "civilizing mission," Jewish advocates saw their international solidarity as a means through which a complete global solidarity could one day be achieved. Seeing their work as leading all nations to embrace liberal values like tolerance, equality, and freedom, Jewish philanthropists viewed their solidarity as part of the progress of "civilization" itself.

For Jews in France, Great Britain, Germany, Austria, and the United States, international solidarity was often framed as an expression of patriotism as well, since these nations embraced universalist ideologies and imperial ambitions. Nowhere was this more pronounced than in France, where since the time of the revolution, patriots hoped to extend liberty, equality, and fraternity to all humanity. Because of this ideological connection to the revolutionary tradition, French Jewish leaders got involved in international aid somewhat earlier than other European Jews. This connection also inspired French Jews to be more public about their work, articulating the connection between their actions on behalf of Jews in other countries, their integration into the French nation, and their hopes for a world united under liberal ideals. On the occasion of the 1889 celebration of the centennial of the French Revolution, for example, a number of French rabbis delivered sermons in which they described Jewish international solidarity as a pure expression of French patriotism. In Verdun, Rabbi Emile Lévy said to his congregation,

> As Moses said to the tribes of Gad and Manasseh, "So your brothers will have to struggle and fight, while you sit in peace!" Appropriating these tribes' answer for ourselves, let us swear that we will not forget our unfortunate brothers, and let us not see our mission as finished until we have helped them gain possession of the freedom and security that the Hand of the Almighty bestowed upon all humans. And we are fortunate to realize that this duty has been largely understood by French Israelites, who, with noble hearts and humanitarian feelings, founded the Alliance Israélite Universelle, which has undertaken the task of protecting those who suffer on account of being Israelites, and elevating them from the degraded and reviled state where hatred and injustice have cast them. To support this beautiful and noble institution, to cooperate in its philanthropic and regenerative program is to fulfill one of our most sacred duties, to perform a double act as Israelites and as Frenchmen.[1]

Like Lévy, other French Jewish advocates saw Jewish international solidarity as a fulfillment of a duty to bring "freedom and security" to Jews elsewhere, a duty they identified as simultaneously Jewish and French, and which, they hoped, would ultimately unify and ennoble all humanity.

National Integration and Jewish Internationalism

How can we account for the emergence of Jewish international solidarity among the most highly assimilated French Jews in the middle of the nineteenth century? At first glance, at least, it appears paradoxical that Jewish internationalism and national integration were embraced by the same people at the same time. Indeed, since the end of the nineteenth century, dedicated antisemites and Jewish community leaders alike have portrayed Jewish internationalism as a sign that Jews were not fully integrating into their nations. In this view, Jewish identity is a fundamentally ahistorical identity that is in crucial ways different from national identities (e.g., French or German identity), seen as equally timeless. To take on a national identity would thus necessarily mean to abandon Jewishness. This perspective is apparent in some of the best-known histories of modern French Jewry as well, including Arthur Hertzberg's classic *The French Enlightenment and the Jews* and Hannah Arendt's *The Origins of Totalitarianism*. These books and others like them posit that "assimilation"—beginning with "emancipation" or the acquisition of national citizenship—was an either-or proposition in which Jews were forced to abandon Jewishness in order to integrate into the modern world.[2] Useful as this argument is in understanding some aspects of Jewish modernization, it cannot account for the fact that nineteenth-century Jewish leaders used their international solidarity to demonstrate their fidelity to both their fellow Jews and their fellow nationals. For this, a more nuanced model of Jewish integration is needed.

A closer look, in light of recent scholarship on the path of French Jewish integration, reveals that highly assimilated French Jews affirmed their Jewish identities even as they became French. As historians like Phyllis Cohen Albert, Jay Berkovitz, Michael Graetz, Paula Hyman, and Ronald Schechter have shown in studies using different sources and methodologies, integration did not, in fact, erase Jewish identity. Even though the acquisition of citizenship, the dissolution of the traditional communal bodies, and increased contact with gentile Frenchmen represented cataclysmic changes, French Jews reaffirmed their Jewishness in new terms meaningful in French culture. They transformed their religious practices and education, moved to larger cities and made a living in new ways, and became part of new social networks. In addition, they radically altered their relationship to the state. Yet these scholars have argued persuasively that Jewish identity remained strong and visible.[3]

Recent work in French history on the development of national identity can further deepen our understanding of how it was possible for Jews to "become French" while maintaining a strong identification as Jews. Rejecting older models of national integration that held that one could become French only by casting off prior identities, scholars have painted a more nuanced picture in recent decades. The literature on this topic reveals that Jews were not the only group that "turned into Frenchmen," that is, came to be understood as "French" after centuries of being understood as, say, Jews, Bretons, peasants, or artisans.[4] By identifying and analyzing how members of different social groups understood the ideology and institutions of nationhood and citizenship, scholars have found that each maintained a distinctive identity, even as their members came to see themselves as part of a broader national community of citizens. In part, this was because the terms each group used to understand citizenship were culled from their own distinctive traditions. To take but two examples, William Sewell has argued that workers defined the rights and obligations of citizenship by reusing and transforming the meaning of terms which had been important in their social and political life under the Old Regime. Likewise, in her study of French identity formation among Bretons, Caroline Ford has demonstrated the centrality of conceptual elements pulled from the tradition of Catholic resistance, arguing persuasively that national identity is "a process continually in the making rather than the imposition of a fixed set of beliefs." Examined together, these studies of national integration suggest that "citizenship" was constructed by different groups based on the social language they already used, rather than purely imposed by a single, monolithic group of "revolutionaries" or state policy makers in the nineteenth century.[5] Nineteenth-century Jews were thus far from unique in using familiar language to define what it meant to be a French citizen, thereby affirming their particular identity while becoming part of the national community.

This study builds upon this recent work in both Jewish and French history by looking at how the rhetoric of nineteenth-century international solidarity grew out of the new self-understandings and political commitments that French Jews developed during the revolution and its aftermath. Looking closely at the terms Jews used in their expressions of solidarity, I have found that the purpose of such expressions was far more complex than it may first appear. Not only did French Jews seek to help Jews elsewhere whom they perceived to be in need; they also used the language of solidarity—filled as it was with decidedly republican ideals—to solidify their own position within France. In seeking to help Jews elsewhere, French Jews formed alliances with other liberals and republicans equally committed to reshaping French law, foreign policy, and imperialism. Even more importantly, they helped shape the terms of the struggles.

To fully understand the development of Jewish internationalism, it is essential to keep in mind how long Jews campaigned for equality before the law in France, and how their success depended upon the fortunes of the revolutionary, liberal, and republican movements to displace the Catholic Church from its central role in French politics. Like so many ideals espoused by revolutionaries in 1789, this full legal equality was not achieved in a lasting way with the Jewish emancipation decrees of 1790 and 1791. It would take until 1830 for all remnants of Jews' corporate disabilities, including special taxation, to be removed. Anti-Jewish prejudice remained a persistent problem in France throughout the nineteenth century as well. In addition to occasional outbreaks of anti-Jewish violence (as in Alsace in 1848), Jews were kept out of many professions well into the nineteenth century; the press regularly defamed their religion; and even the most assimilated of Jews had reason to fear that their political rights were not as secure as the rights of gentile Frenchmen of their class.

The alliances Jews forged with other political players in their world formed a crucial part of their response to the problems they continued to face. Though these alliances shifted over time, the Jewish leaders most concerned with securing Jewish rights at home and abroad found that their best allies were those who were committed to equality before the law, religious freedom, a "national" rather than religious understanding of the body politic, and a mission in foreign policy tied to the revolutionary heritage rather than the Church. As we shall see, the inventors of modern Jewish solidarity used their advocacy to express their support for these ideals. Non-Jewish liberals and republicans welcomed the Jewish voice in the debates that were reshaping France's foreign and colonial policy. Jews thus participated as allies in the liberal and republican struggle for state secularism. This struggle involved both limiting the role of the Church in public life and replacing it with a new set of institutions, ideals, and conceptions of community, in which Jews could participate as equal members without abandoning their Judaism.

This study shows that Jewish internationalism was a by-product of national integration in France, aimed simultaneously at helping Jews elsewhere, forging alliances with liberals and republicans at home, and furthering the cause of state secularism—an ideal they and their allies cherished. These findings support the conclusions of Michael Graetz and Jay Berkovitz, who have shown how deeply French Jewish leaders became committed to the revolution and, in its aftermath, to the evolving liberal and republican traditions. It also supports their finding that Jewish identity and even religious sensibility were profoundly reshaped by this commitment.[6] Thus, although the objective of international solidarity was ostensibly philanthropic rather than political, closely examining the terms Jewish leaders used to describe it reveals the same liberal commitments, the same strategies of alliance building, and the same transformation of Jewish religion and identity that these scholars have described. By placing the rise of Jewish internationalism in the context of national integration, this study seeks to add yet another dimension to our already rich portrait of the transformation of Jewish life in nineteenth-century France.

The Construction of Secularism

Although my contention that national integration did not erase Jewish identity in France supports the findings of scholars working in the field in recent years, I do challenge the common understanding that

Jewish political emancipation and social integration in France took place primarily in the national arena. I have found that international identifications and outreach played a remarkably important role as well in the modernization of Jewish life. Indeed, it seems all but impossible to fully separate the national and international aspects, since nineteenth-century French Jews used their work in each arena to justify their place within the other. Accounting for the fact that international advocacy helped Jews to secure their place within the French nation gives us a fuller picture of the transformation of Jewish life in nineteenth-century France. At the same time, it gives us a valuable new vantage point from which to think about some important issues in the national political culture into which French Jews were integrating.

Previous work on Jewish integration in various national contexts has done little to explain why internationalism emerged as part of the process of national integration. Most historians of European Jewish emancipation and integration share a basic perspective that national cultural norms, state policy, and liberal ideology were the most important influences upon how assimilated European Jews understood their relationships to each other, to their gentile neighbors, to their religion, and to the state.[7] Even Michael Graetz's *Jews in Nineteenth-Century France*, which seeks to explain the development of Jewish international activism, sees it primarily as an outgrowth of a struggle for power between different social groups (the "center" and the "periphery") within the French Jewish elite during its process of national integration. Aron Rodrigue rightly posits that the roots of Jewish internationalism lay in continued efforts to defend Judaism, especially in the press, and a commitment to the ideology of "regeneration," the Enlightenment idea that people could be remade through greater civil rights and education, which French Jews first encountered in the late eighteenth century. Yet his study's focus on the Alliance Israélite Universelle's schools in Turkey, rather than French political culture, leaves him little room to elaborate his argument in any detail, and no room at all to explore its implications on our understanding of French political culture.[8]

By taking a closer look at the political issues that most concerned elite French Jews in the nineteenth century, we can understand why internationalism first emerged in this particular context and why it took the form that it did. As we shall see, French Jewish leaders, in an effort to create new policies for France based on their interpretation of the revolutionary heritage, actively forged alliances with liberals in the Restoration era, with utopian socialists in the July Monarchy, and with republicans in the Second Republic and Second Empire. Yet more than their non-Jewish allies, the inventors of modern Jewish solidarity saw their own fortunes as dependent upon the realization of their political ideals in France's policies on the international stage as well as at home. Jews in France were in a unique position that made them particularly attentive to the international dimension of the campaign for state secularism. On the one hand, France had made them citizens and was thus committed to protecting their rights within France's borders. Yet on the other hand, until the 1860s, France remained committed to certain Catholic interests, especially in its foreign policy, and Jews were particularly concerned with the potential effect this might have on their own rights at home. As a result, they worked especially hard to make equal rights for religious minorities a key part of France's agenda in its colonies and its diplomatic work. The history of the forging of modern Jewish solidarity is thus fully intertwined with the history of the struggle for secularism in France.

Accordingly, this book will also trace the history of the construction of French state secularism as it was conceived by its proponents, from the liberals and utopian socialists of the Restoration and July Monarchy to the republicans of the Second Republic and Second Empire. Looking at this history from a Jewish perspective provides a particularly illuminating viewpoint. As the only group of non-Christian citizens whose religion was officially recognized, administered, and supported by the state, Jews were particularly attentive to the state's ambivalent relationship to the Catholic Church, and attuned to the Christian biases of their fellow liberals and republicans. Following this campaign through the eyes of the politically active Jewish elite can thus broaden our understanding of the nature of state secularism in France in a number of ways.

First, this perspective makes it clear that the liberals and republicans who defined the terms of the struggle for secularism before the 1880s were anything but irreligious. Far from seeking to ban all expressions of religiosity from the public arena, anticlerical activists actually encouraged some of them, even as they sought to limit the voice of the Church in state affairs. This is clear in any number of instances that will be examined here: the revolutionaries' welcoming of Jews' use of Judaism as a pedagogy for citizenship; the Saint-Simonians' attempts to construct a new Christianity to serve as a spiritual underpinning of the new world order in the 1820s and 1830s; and Second Empire liberals' unambiguous support for Jewish leaders' blessing of French intervention in the Middle East. Rather than being relegated to the purely "private" world of the home, the heart, or the house of worship, Judaism in nineteenth-century France remained relevant to public life. This finding challenges our basic understanding of what proponents of state secularism in France demanded of religions, as we too often focus only on activists' attitudes and actions vis-à-vis the Catholic Church. Building on recent scholarship that has demonstrated the continued importance of Christianity and Christian imagery beyond the Church in French public life, this study seeks to broaden our understanding of secularism by showing how Judaism's place in the public arena was transformed—but not erased—as state secularism was built in France.[9]

Examining the construction of state secularism from this vantage point also allows us to see the importance of Jews and Judaism to left-wing political symbolism in this period, and the impact this symbolism had on Jewish identity and self-defense. Throughout the nineteenth century, the proponents of a secular state championed Jews' rights in France, and later they did so in the French colonies and around the world. As we shall see, activists vaunted this support as an important sign of their movement's tolerance, high moral standing, and universality in comparison to the Catholicism they hoped to supplant. This was by no means an entirely new strategy for those embattled against Church power. As Ronald Schechter has shown, such symbolism was already used by eighteenth-century writers and, in different ways, had been used by Christian reformers throughout European history.[10] Yet as the nineteenth century progressed, Jews became an increasingly important symbol for the anticlerical movement, so much so that by the end of the century, antirepublican activists would themselves pick up on this symbolism and challenge the republic as a "Jewish conspiracy." Examining how proponents of secularism in all areas of French state policy perceived Jews and Judaism will help us to better understand the goals, strategies, and impact of the anticlerical movement as it developed from the revolution to the Third Republic.

In addition, looking at the construction of secularism from this perspective can help us to see just how broad the scope of this battle was. Far from confined to domestic issues like education, the battle for secularism was understood to be a battle about what France represented in the world. As such, this issue penetrated discussions about colonial and foreign policy as well. Indeed, as Alice Conklin has argued in her work on French colonial discourse, secularism played an important role within France's *mission civilisatrice*, the ideology that served to justify French colonialism. With this ideology, French colonial policy makers were able to see themselves as "bearers of civilization," which meant, in their minds, liberating native Africans and Asians from tyranny and backwardness by bringing a superior form of rule.[11] Championing secularism as a key ingredient of "civilization" also played an important role in republican diplomacy, guiding the French in their approach to the Crimean War and the negotiations of trade agreements with Romania and Serbia in its aftermath. Looking at the international dimension of the campaign for secularism from the perspective of Jewish liberals and republicans, it becomes clear how important the relationship was between the securing of Jewish rights within France and the transformation of French colonial and foreign policy from a Catholic to a republican model. In a way that challenges traditional understandings of how minority integration took place, we will see here how minority rights within France became linked politically to the extension of French imperialism as well as to a nascent international human rights discourse.

Outline of the Book

This book traces the development of Jewish international solidarity in chronological fashion, from the revolutionary era to the triumph of the anticlerical movement in the 1880s. This chronological organization can help us to better understand the relationship between Jewish integration within French political culture, the campaign for secularism in all areas of French state policy, and the rise of Jewish internationalism. The first three chapters examine the period from the revolution to the 1840s. Although Jewish internationalism did not develop until mid-century, these chapters explore its roots by tracing the relationship between Jews' efforts to gain and secure their rights within France and the broader anticlerical movement around them. We will also see how Jews came to function as an important symbol for liberals and utopian socialists in ways that would later shape the rhetoric of Jewish internationalism and contribute to its success.

Chapter 1 examines the roots of solidarity in revolutionary and Napoleonic France, when Jews were first granted equal rights and their semi-autonomous *communautés* were dissolved. Given how tumultuous the revolutionary era was, it would be impossible to identify a single cause that led to Jews' acquisition of citizenship rights in 1790 and 1791. Nevertheless, by the time of Napoleon, Jews' citizenship was cemented not by relegating Judaism to the purely private sphere, but rather, by identifying Judaism with state ideology. Emancipation thus set the stage for the development of Jewish internationalism a half-century later, when a generation reared as French Jewish citizens would come to act in a way that simultaneously affirmed their Jewishness and their Frenchness in the international political arena.

Chapter 2 examines Jewish leaders' quest to secure their equality and free themselves from their remaining corporate disabilities in the Restoration period. In an era when their rights appeared tenuous, French Jews fought against the remnants of corporatism by using the language of the liberals who opposed the regime in the name of the Charte of 1814. Although the Bourbon monarchy had been restored, the Charte nonetheless guaranteed freedom of worship and equality of all citizens before the law, regardless of religion. In their struggles, French Jewish leaders found creative ways to consolidate the gains they had made under Napoleon by further identifying Judaism with the state. At the same time, these struggles became an important site for forging alliances with Restoration liberals in ways that would later shape the political campaign to make French foreign and colonial policy secular in the second half of the nineteenth century.

Chapter 3 focuses on the changing meaning of Jewishness within liberal social networks, where some of the most highly assimilated French Jews had begun to move by the 1830s and 1840s. In this period, a small but highly visible segment of the Parisian Jewish elite touted their Jewishness proudly in all sorts of new arenas, such as courts of law, the arts, and the Saint-Simonian movement. Portraying themselves as exotically Eastern and yet identified with the French revolutionary promise, these Jews played to a wider French audience rather than to a traditional Jewish one. This chapter decodes the meaning of these expressions, and finds that within the Saint-Simonian movement and, to a lesser degree, in broader liberal circles, the presence of Jews came to represent the moral righteousness and universality of the movements themselves, especially as compared to the *ultramontane* Catholic right. This symbolism served to further identify the liberation of Jews with the promise of the revolution in ways that would come into play when the struggle for secularism moved into foreign and colonial policy.

The second half of the book looks at how self-defense and an abiding commitment to the struggle for French state secularism came together in the form of a pioneering Jewish internationalism. Emerging in the 1840s with the Damascus affair and the securing of colonial rule in Algeria, Jewish international solidarity was in many ways a natural outgrowth of the path of Jewish integration since the revolution, in which Jews secured their rights by participating in the liberal struggle to create a secular state. As France expanded abroad, French Jews championed the rights of Jews in the areas under French influence in a way that they hoped would bring the fruits of the revolution to all people everywhere, within and beyond France's borders.

Chapter 4 examines how and why French Jews became interested in the plight of Jews in Algeria and the Ottoman Empire in the period from 1840 to 1860, as France began to expand its influence in those areas. Here, I argue that this interest was fundamentally tied to their stake in building a new, secular foreign and colonial policy that championed a "civilizing mission" rather than France's traditional Catholic mission abroad.

Chapter 5 considers the rhetoric and practices of solidarity that became the hallmark of the Alliance Israélite Universelle from the moment it was founded in 1860. Originating in the discourse of the burgeoning republican movement, Jewish leaders used this rhetoric in a way that linked it simultaneously to Jewish tradition, French republicanism, and the "civilizational" discourse that was taking on increased importance in European diplomacy and imperialism.

The book's final chapter examines how and why this era in the history of Jewish politics came to an end at the very moment that the anticlerical republican movement was finally achieving some of its most cherished goals. Beginning in the 1880s, members of the emerging antisemitic movement, unhappy with the Third Republic's anticlerical measures, targeted Jewish leaders as a conspiracy of cosmopolitan bankers seeking to take over the world, using the organs of republicanism in France and liberalism in the world as a front for their maneuvers. As a result, certain prominent Jewish leaders became somewhat more wary about public expressions of Jewish solidarity, in ways that became apparent during the Dreyfus affair in the 1890s. In the past, this reticence was mistakenly interpreted by many as a sign that French Jews were unable to speak *as Jews* in their own defense in the public arena because of a long-term process, beginning with emancipation, of the erasure of Jewish identity in favor of French patriotism.[12] But as scholars in recent years have shown, this was far from the case. Not only did many Jews speak out against antisemitism, as Pierre Birnbaum has convincingly demonstrated, but whatever reticence certain prominent Jewish leaders may have displayed should be ascribed more to a well-grounded anxiety about the immediate political context rather than to the long history of Jewish integration in France.[13] As we shall see here as well, far from erasing Jewish identity, integration provided new reasons and language for its expression. Throughout the nineteenth century, French Jewish leaders spoke loudly and proudly, in the name of Judaism and the French revolutionary tradition, in defense of Jewish rights. Only with the rise of political antisemitism did new strategies, such as Zionism, emerge to challenge solidarity as the prime means through which French Jews defended themselves.

French Jewish expressions of "solidarity" with Jews elsewhere had multiple valences and meanings, solidifying the position of Jews within

France by embracing its universalist vision, and attempting to extend this vision to the rest of the world. These expressions developed because French Jews had a distinct status as citizens who were subject to continued social discrimination for religious reasons. As a result, they became invested in prioritizing a broad, universalist vision of the bounds of the social and political order. To secure their own position within France, they fought to define France as the defender of Jewish interests everywhere, and helped to forge alliances with other nations on these grounds. French Jews could not and did not think only of the national arena as the site of the acquisition of their citizenship; securing their rights by seeking to make foreign and colonial policy secular was just as important. While Jews were in a unique position in France, this part of the story of their integration has implications for how we understand social and political modernization more broadly, testifying to the importance of international issues in the national arena.

One   The Jewish Citizen

Like so many developments in modern France, the roots of Jewish internationalism can be traced to the revolutionary era. Recent studies of Jewish emancipation during the French Revolution and its reaffirmation under Napoleon have convincingly disproved the once conventional wisdom that in becoming citizens, Jews had to relegate their Judaism to the purely private sphere and become just "a man on the street, a Jew in the home." Most scholars now agree that although Jewish identity was radically transformed, it was by no means destroyed during the revolution or under Napoleon. With emancipation, Jews were forced to abandon their semi-autonomous communal institutions, like all other Old Regime corporate bodies. In spite of Napoleon's professed religious tolerance, he demanded that Jewish leaders defend themselves and their religion against charges of usury and immorality, and accordingly, Jews feared that they might be expelled from France altogether. Yet despite these radical changes and threats, Judaism survived, and with the establishment of the consistories, state agencies whose task was to regulate Jewish life, the groundwork was laid for its transformation. As Phyllis Cohen Albert, Jay Berkovitz, and Michael Graetz have argued, the founding of the consistory system would eventually give French Jewry its distinctive character by unifying the previously separate Sephardi, Ashkenazi, and *avignonnais* (southeastern French) communities, and by providing an ideological framework borrowed from revolutionary rhetoric that would guide its work for generations to come.[1]

In order to understand the emergence of solidarity, we begin with its earliest roots in Jews' experience of emancipation in the revolutionary and Napoleonic eras.[2] Some scholars have already noticed a connection between Jewish internationalism and Jews' emancipation in France. As Aron Rodrigue has noted, the very ideals that French Jewish philanthropists sought to bring to Jews elsewhere were shaped by the experience of emancipation. It was in the period of emancipation that Jews first encountered the language of "regeneration," which would come to play such an important role in French Jewish philanthropy, both at home and internationally. In Berkovitz's words, this term referred to the act of "restoring to its original state something that had become corrupted or decadent." On the eve of the revolution, Jews encountered this language when Enlightenment theorists applied it to them as a warrant for removing their legal disabilities and making them citizens. In the nineteenth century, Berkovitz has shown, regeneration became a "systematic program" for consistory leaders intent on reforming French Jewry. And as Rodrigue has shown, this same ideology undergirded French Jewish educational programs abroad.[3]

The similarity between the rhetoric of emancipation, as applied to one generation of French Jews, and the rhetoric of international aid efforts, as conceived by another, is intriguing. To understand why this later generation, reared as French citizens equal to their Christian neighbors in most respects, came to see their Frenchness and their Jewishness as fundamentally interdependent in a way that would give rise to this kind of international philanthropy, we will have to examine, of course, developments far beyond the revolutionary era. But, as we shall see in this chapter, the roots of this identification can be traced to the way that secularism was conceived by revolutionaries when Jews received their citizenship rights, and, more importantly, to the way secularism was construed by Napoleon, who reaffirmed those rights in 1808. As a religious minority group fearing possible expulsion, Jews were not in a position to reject the terms of the new relationship the revolutionaries and Napoleon sought to establish between religions and the state. The acquisition of citizenship rights was made possible precisely because Jewish leaders were willing to embrace the model of secularism envisioned by Napoleon, in which religions were granted a new, but still important role in public life.

Although Jews received their citizenship in a series of decrees in 1790 and 1791, it was only under Napoleon that the terms of Jewish citizenship were set. As we shall see, in the revolutionary era, many different warrants for Jewish emancipation were advanced. Amid the cacophony of voices, no single argument emerged as the primary reason for Jewish emancipation, and no consensus was reached on the question of what, if anything, should be demanded of the Jews in becoming citizens. While Jews were indeed declared active citizens while their *communautés* were dissolved, their detractors remained vocal and their status—like so many other elements of French society—remained unstable until the Napoleonic era, when a lasting framework was finally erected that subordinated Judaism to the state. Indeed, Napoleon ultimately associated Jewish religious tenets with state ideology. Building on revolutionary theories of Jewish citizenship, Napoleon and the Jewish leaders he consulted turned Judaism into a system to educate Jews in civic virtue, as well as a sacred force that would legitimize state power and ideology in the eyes of its adherents. Far from erasing expressions of Jewishness in the political arena, the new role assumed by Judaism would lead, in later years, to many new forms of expression, including Jewish international solidarity.

The Revolutionary Era: A Cacophony of Arguments for Emancipation

Jewish emancipation was a subject of frequent discussion among lawmakers in the first years of the revolution, even though the French Jewish population, at forty thousand, represented only 0.1 of 1 percent of the total French population. Yet despite the rich record of discussion, no single reason can be identified for lawmakers' decision to grant citizenship to the Jews starting in 1790. Indeed, different Jewish *communautés* were emancipated at different times, following different discussions, which further complicates the problem of understanding why Jews were made French citizens. In their insightful analyses of why revolutionaries devoted so much time to what might have been a relatively minor issue, historians Gary Kates and Ronald Schechter have pointed to the strong symbolism Jews carried in eighteenth-century France, which made discussions of their status important sites for working out the limits of revolutionary ideology.[4] This symbolism was quite potent, and as Schechter convincingly argues, it was multivalent. Far from representing merely one thing, Jews presented a "rich menu of symbolic choices" for arguments about all sorts of difficult issues that the revolutionaries were confronting as they attempted to craft a workable notion of what it meant to be a citizen.[5] Talking about Jews thus had widely varying implications, depending on the context. Moreover, no clear, single ideological reason was given for the revolutionaries' decision to emancipate the majority of France's Jews on September 27, 1791, other than the desire to remove a glaring exception from the new Constitution's provisions defining active citizenship.

The arguments revolutionary lawmakers put forth about Jewish citizenship in the years 1789–91 in debates over Jewish citizenship were a cacophonous mix. Furthermore, the years between Jewish emancipation and Napoleon's reorganization of Jewish life in 1808 were a chaotic period in which Jewish religious life, Jews' citizenship rights, and even Jews' security in France remained precarious.[6] Despite contemporaries' lack of consensus on Jewish citizenship, examining some of the more important arguments put forth in the revolutionary period is useful, since that is where we will find the ideological roots of Napoleon's model for secularism, and his corresponding reorganization of Jewish life.

One important set of arguments for Jewish emancipation predates the revolution. Building on the Enlightenment concept of "regeneration," proponents argued that relieving Jews of their traditional legal disabilities would make them more "useful" to the French economy. These arguments pertained particularly to the Ashkenazi communities of Alsace and Lorraine, since they included the poorest Jews in France and their legal disabilities were the most onerous. With 30,500 inhabitants, these communities comprised three-quarters of the French Jewish population in the late eighteenth century.[7] Their legal disabilities effectively barred them from trades other than money lending, the cattle trade, and the trade in old clothes, and, according to their detractors, they were hated by their gentile neighbors. The concept that it would be possible to "regenerate" the Ashkenazim by lifting their legal disabilities was rooted in the idea that Jews were men like all other men, and that their apparent difference was merely a result of the years of oppression they had suffered. Give them rights, proponents of regeneration argued, and Jews would surely contribute to the common good.

This perspective comes across clearly in the essays submitted for the 1787 Metz Royal Society of Arts and Sciences contest, whose topic read, "Are there means to render the Jews more useful and happy in France?" Prizes were awarded to three authors: Claude-Antoine Thiéry, a Protestant lawyer; the Abbé Henri Grégoire, a Catholic clergyman from Lorraine; and Zalkind Hourwitz, a Polish Jew who had immigrated to Paris by the 1770s.[8] The three essayists agreed that the best thing to do about the Jews, for their own sake and for the sake of the nation, was to grant them civil and economic rights. For Thiéry, it was gentile society's fault that Jews had developed strange customs, for it had excluded them. If they were allowed to practice the *arts et métiers*, Jews would easily integrate without being converted.[9] Grégoire argued that authorities should treat Jews like Christians because reforming them was a Christian duty, and because it would enrich the public fortune.[10] Hourwitz agreed that allowing Jews the freedom to integrate economically would make them "happy and useful." He defined the rights of citizens as the rights to own property, to practice agriculture and skilled crafts, to trade and travel freely, and to be schooled together with Christians.[11] Hourwitz rejected the notion that Judaism required that Jews see themselves as a nation unto themselves. In response to the charge that Jews were waiting for their homeland to be restored, and thus constituted a nation, he wrote:

> The Jews are foreigners neither by nature nor by their religion but only as a result of the injustice of regarding them as such. Grant them the rights of citizenship and you will see that they are French just like all other subjects of the Kingdom. It is true that they do not believe they will remain permanently in the country they inhabit and that they await the arrival of the Messiah who will re-establish them in Palestine, but they await death with even more certitude and this

does not prevent them or for that matter anyone from sowing or planting wherever permitted.[12]

As Hourwitz's imagery in this last sentence reveals, he believed that Jews, like any other men, would become rooted in French society, were they allowed by law to "sow and plant wherever permitted." Jews were "foreign" only because of their legal disabilities, not because their religion required they be treated as a nation unto themselves.

Once the revolution was underway, however, the argument that Jews were oppressed individuals who could be regenerated through citizenship did not garner enough support to result in their immediate emancipation. In the first major debate on the subject in late December 1789, Count Stanislas de Clermont-Tonnerre declared that Jews should be considered citizens based on the abstract provisions of the Declaration of the Rights of Man and Citizen. The declaration, after all, held that "all men are born and remain free and equal in rights; social distinctions cannot be found but on common utility"; and that "no person shall be molested for his opinions, even such as are religious, provided that the manifestation of these opinions does not disturb the public order established by the law." Clermont-Tonnerre addressed concerns about Jews' money lending and foreignness with a rhetoric of regeneration, claiming that Jews' economic profile and national identity could be changed by bestowing citizenship rights. But just to be certain, Clermont-Tonnerre argued that the Jews should be required to give up their separate political institutions in becoming citizens, and perhaps money lending as well:

> Every religion must prove but one thing—that it is moral. If there is a religion that commands theft and arson, it is necessary not only to refuse eligibility to those who profess it, but further, to outlaw them. This consideration cannot be applied to the Jews. . . . Men who possess nothing but money cannot live but by making money valuable, and you have always prevented them from possessing anything else. [They are] insatiable, one says. This insatiability is [however] not certain. The Jews should be denied everything as a nation, but granted everything as individuals. . . . Every one of them must individually become a citizen; if they do not want this, they must inform us and we shall be compelled to expel them. The existence of a nation within a nation is unacceptable to our country.[13]

In contrast, the opponents of Jewish emancipation in these debates clearly saw Jews as irredeemably menacing outsiders, whose usurious practices threatened their neighbors. Led by the Alsatians Jean-François Reubell and the Abbé Maury, the opponents argued that Jews, particularly in their role as moneylenders, were a menace to local society.[14] This argument was clearly compelling to many of the deputies; at the conclusion of the debate, the National Assembly voted by a margin of 408 to 403 to table the question of Jewish citizenship.[15]

The emancipation of the Sephardi Jews of southwestern France was achieved on the basis of an entirely different reasoning, having to do with their pre-revolutionary privileges. Unlike the Ashkenazim, on the eve of the revolution these Jews already possessed a certain number of civil and economic rights. One thousand nine hundred and fifty Jews lived in the Bordeaux region, as the "Nation Portugaise," under French law and with relatively extensive economic rights, having been admitted to France as "New Christian" *conversos* from Spain and Portugal.[16] Twenty-five hundred Jews lived in the Bayonne area, with rights much like those of their *portugais* brethren in Bordeaux.[17] By the early eighteenth century, the descendants of the Portuguese and Spanish *conversos* who comprised the Nation Portugaise had begun to practice Judaism openly. Though restricted from the guilds and the chamber of commerce, and forbidden to live in the city of Bayonne proper, they lived under French jurisdiction, and many were granted bourgeois rights and became successful merchants, bankers, and army suppliers. In 1776, the king issued new *lettres patentes* that granted the Sephardim the full freedom to acquire, sell, and bequeath property, to make contracts, and to live "according to their custom," that is, as Jews, in the region where they resided.[18] After the debates of December 1789 ended in stalemate, the Portuguese Jews argued for their citizenship based on these preexisting civil rights, which the Ashkenazim did not possess.[19] In January 1790, the Assembly considered the Sephardim alone and declared them eligible for citizenship rights. As Isaac-René-Guy Le Chapelier said, "There is no connection between the Jews of Bordeaux and those of Alsace; for the former, the issue is to conserve their rights; for the latter, to give them something they do not have."[20]

Another set of warrants for citizenship had to do with Jews' displays of patriotism and virtue during the revolution itself. The small and diverse community of Parisian Jews was the most successful in gaining support for their cause based on such arguments. In a speech before the Paris Commune on January 28, 1790, Jacques Godard, a Parisian lawyer devoted to the Jewish cause, emphasized the "civic zeal" of Parisian Jews, citing the participation of one hundred of them (representing a fifth of their total number, in his estimation) in the National Guard. He singled out Zalkind Hourwitz for his exemplary virtue, as Hourwitz had donated a quarter of his salary to the "patriotic cause."[21] The next day, the Carmelites district of Paris voted to extend active citizenship to the Jews (though the Constituent Assembly would grant Parisian Jews citizenship only in September 1791). Because most Parisian Jews lived in this district, the representatives said, "We have had an opportunity to observe the behavior of the Jews, and to get to know their principles and to judge their morality. . . . [We are thus] the first to render public homage to their patriotism, their courage and their generosity." Representatives applauded the Jews' "love of order and justice," their "acts of charity towards the poor," as well as their willingness to contribute money to the district.[22]

A similar argument can be seen in the appeals made by members of the Jewish communities of the Lorraine cities of Lunéville and Sarreguemines. Making explicit reference to the recent arguments in the Paris Commune, Jews in these cities sent an appeal to the Constituent Assembly on February 26, 1790, arguing for their right to citizenship on the basis of their patriotic bequests. The Jews of Lunéville reported that on August 3, 1789, after having been turned away from the local militia, they were the first to make a patriotic bequest to their city.[23] When they came before the Constituent Assembly with their petition in February, they were able to present a certificate of *civisme* and they reported that because of their contribution, they had been declared the town's "most zealous citizens." Thus, they argued, "since we serve the *Patrie* like other citizens, she should grant us the same rights as them."[24] As Schechter has observed, these Jews were following an old tradition, in which Jews purchased their rights, "[serving] the *patrie* as providers of specie."[25]

Perhaps the most important warrant for Jews' emancipation had little to do with the Jews at all, but, rather, with revolutionaries' broader conception of national sovereignty, in which religions were to be subordinated to the state. Here too, however, revolutionaries had different visions, and applied them differently to the question of Jewish citizenship. In one approach to the issue, religion was to be relegated to the private arena. Under this view, Judaism was irrelevant to Jews' citizenship. This perspective was voiced by Clermont-Tonnerre in the December 1789 debates when he argued that the generality of the law placed it above religion, which was particular to individuals. "The law is the general will, to which the individual will of each member of the social body submits. Conscience is the one thing that cannot be put into society," he argued. With these words, Clermont-Tonnerre linked Jewish emancipation to the larger issue of defining national sovereignty as residing in the "general will." Following Rousseau, revolutionaries saw the nation's "will" as sovereign only insofar as it was general and unified; any particularization or dissent was understood as threatening, and increasingly so as the revolution progressed.[26] For Clermont-Tonnerre, the generality of the nation's will was implicitly challenged when anti-Jewish activists sought to exclude Jews from it on the basis of their particular beliefs or practices. In other words, if the state were to adopt a particular dogma, it could not represent the general interest. It was human nature to disagree on matters of religious opinion, but the law was to sit above such disputes, and to include all members of society rather to adjudicate between opinions:

> There is no middle ground possible: either have a National Religion[,] . . . cast out of your society the men who profess another religion, and thus erase the article [guaranteeing freedom of religious opinion] from your Declaration of Rights, or allow each man the right to his own opinion, and do not exclude from public service those who make use of this permission. This is justice, this is reason, so too will politics tell you: attach men to the Law. The Law must therefore be detached from that which divides men and which has no social utility.[27]

As numerous historians of Jewish emancipation have pointed out, Clermont-Tonnerre's vision of secularism involved forging a clear opposition between "Jew" and "man," relegating Jewishness to the private realm and making the abstract individual "man" the basis for citizenship.[28] Yet we must be wary of reading these words as clear evidence of the demands placed on Jews in exchange for citizenship. Clermont-Tonnerre failed to convince the Assembly to grant Jews citizenship in late December 1789, so his propositions bore no fruit. Nonetheless, it does point to something important: that the question of Jewish emancipation was embedded in a larger, highly charged debate among revolutionaries about the place of religion—or religions—in public life.[29] Indeed, Clermont-Tonnerre's vision for remaking the relationship between religions and the state was not shared by all his fellow revolutionaries, or even by his fellow supporters of Jewish emancipation. While Clermont-Tonnerre saw religion as "divisive" and lacking in "social utility," and sought to relegate it to the private sphere, other revolutionaries sought to use religions in the service of state power. While the revolutionaries who articulated this vision originally had the Catholic Church in mind rather than Judaism, they later applied their ideas to the question of Jewish citizenship as well. It was this vision that moved the Constituent Assembly to adopt the Civil Constitution of the Clergy on July 12, 1790, a measure that aimed at bringing the clergy within the institutional structure of the state without changing Church dogma. The decree drew new clerical territorial districts, confirmed the 1789 acts abolishing the tithe and nationalizing Church property, and held that Church officials would henceforth be elected by their parishioners and paid by the state. The clergy were also to be loyal to France and its Constitution, rather than to any foreign power (such as Rome), and were required to reside in the district they served. In effect, the Civil Constitution of the Clergy affirmed the primacy of the nation and severed the tie binding the French clergy to Rome. Yet at the same time, it affirmed religion's central role in French public life.

Radical as the Civil Constitution of the Clergy was, the summer of 1790 saw no major stirrings of revolt against it. Rather, as historian Nigel Aston has pointed out, on July 14, the clergy participated actively in the Festival of the Federation with blessings, masses, Te Deums, and sermons that served to legitimate and even more importantly, to consecrate the revolutionaries' construction of a new temporal order. In April 1791, however, the pope publicly condemned the Civil Constitution of the Clergy, as well as the November 1790 decree requiring all clergymen to take an oath of loyalty to the state. As Aston has argued, this condemnation led to a "parting of the ways" between the Church and the revolution, and an end to the hope for the reform of the Gallican Church within the new state apparatus.[30] The revolutionaries' approach to reforming the relationship between religions and the state provoked fierce opposition from Catholic Church leaders, long before the revolutionaries brought the question of Jews' status into the debate. The king's aborted attempt to flee France in June 1791 only compounded the problem. Long associated with the absolute monarchy, the clergy—especially those reticent to take the oath—were viewed with increasing suspicion by revolutionaries as they finished writing France's new Constitution in the summer of 1791. And the mistrust was mutual.

Finally completed and made public on September 3, 1791, the Constitution's vision of secularism was more like Clermont-Tonnerre's than like that of the Civil Constitution of the Clergy. It made no mention of the Church, nor did it confer any status whatsoever on Catholicism as a religion. In addition, lawmakers made no provisions restricting citizenship to adherents of any particular faith. The Constitution thus embraced the same abstract language as the Declaration of the Rights of Man in defining sovereignty as emanating directly from the nation without the intermediary of Church or monarch, and issued no definitive answer to the question of Jewish citizenship.

It was only after the promulgation of the Constitution of 1791 that the Jews of Alsace, Lorraine, and Paris were finally granted citizenship rights. Yet even then, no clear, single reason can be identified for the decision, although some larger vision of secularism clearly played a role in lawmakers' thinking. As Malino has pointed out, this September 1791 debate was quite different from earlier ones on the subject, perhaps because many of the opponents of the Jews had emigrated and the remaining deputies were understandably wary of creating exceptions to the Constitution they had just promulgated. Reubell still voiced strong objections to considering the Jews citizens, yet most deputies seem to have agreed with Regnault that "all who speak against this proposition are fighting against the Constitution itself," which they were exceedingly loathe to do given the circumstances.[31] As such, lawmakers voted on September 27 to consider all Jews citizens, provided that they met the requirements for citizenship as laid out in the Constitution of 1791.

While it is hard to identify what principle, if any, guided deputies in supporting this final emancipation decree, the September 28 discussion over an amendment to it suggests that some larger vision of remaking the relationship between religions and the state played a role. The amendment stipulated that by taking the oath, Jewish citizens were "to be seen as formally renouncing any civil and political laws to which they had been particularly subject" in the past. This meant, in effect, that as with the Catholic Church and other corporate bodies, the formal institutions of the Jews were to be dissolved, but that the Jewish religion would remain legal. This amendment was not about relegating Judaism to private life, but rather, about making a distinction between Jewish corporations and Judaism as a religion. As Deputy Prugnon specified in the debate, "Instead of saying [that taking the oath will] 'be seen as a renunciation of their civil laws, etc., we [should] say, 'be seen as a renunciation of their privileges'; because the laws of the Jews are identified with their religious laws, and it is not our intention to force them to abjure their religion." Significantly, this rewording was adopted in the final redaction.[32]

The fact that the deputies found a wording that conveyed their intention to keep Judaism legal, even while destroying Jewish civil and political institutions, was significant to Jewish leaders. Their public response to emancipation shows that unlike Clermont-Tonnerre and the other deputies who shared his vision of secularism, they saw their religion as playing an essential role in their citizenship. This perspective is clear in the open letter written in French by the enlightened Jewish leader Berr Isaac Berr of Nancy (1744–1828), to his fellow Ashkenazi Jews, on September 28, 1791. The letter was ostensibly designed to persuade less enlightened Jews to be good citizens, stop thinking of themselves as a *corps*, defend France, serve in the military, and extend friendship to all their fellow citizens. (Of course, the fact that it was written in French, which most Jews in eastern France did not read, suggests a different audience—in all likelihood, non-Jewish revolutionaries interested in how Jews understood what citizenship entailed.) Berr wrote that the best way to assure that Jews would become good citizens was to establish schools that would teach both French and Hebrew, studying the Bible and the French Constitution. The Bible was to be the basis for this education, for it was the source of all truth and morality. "This way," he argued, "they will be penetrated by the holiness of our religion's true principles, and can be simultaneously good citizens and good Jews."[33] Berr saw a seamless relation between Judaism and French constitutionalism. Even though he believed that Jews were in need of reform, especially when it came to their professions, he did not think Judaism needed to be reformed, nor did he see it as a purely private set of beliefs. Rather, Judaism could be the basis for teaching Jews about national sovereignty. For Berr, the general will was God's will, before which all men were equal and in which all men participated. In such a perspective, there could be no question of excluding the Jews from citizenship, since Judaism was a guarantor of civic virtue.

From this brief tour of the different arguments revolutionaries advanced in favor of Jewish citizenship, it is clear that no single ideology stood alone as its foundation. Yet we can nonetheless speak of a cluster of important ideas. First, many (but not all) revolutionaries seemed concerned that Jews were in need of some transformation, especially in their professional lives and in their understanding of their national identity, in order to become citizens. And second, Jewish emancipation was linked to the creation of a new relationship between religions and the state. While revolutionaries certainly had different visions for this new relationship, the concept that religions should be made subordinate to the state and used to teach their adherents the values associated with citizenship was already present. Under Napoleon, this vision would be applied systematically to each of France's religious groups, including the Jews.

The Napoleonic Era:
Judaism as a Guarantor of Citizenship

By creating official Jewish institutions within the broader French state apparatus, Napoleon cemented and strengthened the ideological link between Judaism and French citizenship that some revolutionaries imagined already in the 1789–91 period. In a series of meetings convened by the emperor in 1807 and 1808, Jewish leaders were asked to explain how the religious and civil aspects of their life in France were mutually dependent. Based in part on their answers, Napoleon created the consistories, state institutions whose task was to teach these ideas as religious doctrine to all French Jews. The creation of the consistories gave official sanction to Judaism, articulated as a set of unchanging moral principles fully in line with French citizenship. Even more importantly, Napoleon declared the state itself to be the administrative apparatus through which the "dogma" of Jewish citizenship would be diffused. The Constituent Assembly's vision of particular religions serving the dual function of teaching morality to citizens and legitimating state authority was thus realized in this period.

Although revolutionaries had emancipated the Jews in 1791, Jewish rights remained tenuous throughout the revolutionary period, especially in eastern France. In the minds of anti-Jewish agitators, the fact that Jews were considered citizens did not settle the issue of their money lending, nor had it resolved the question of the morality of the Jewish religion. In the countryside of Alsace, anti-Jewish sentiments remained strong, and after Napoleon came to power, a new wave of pamphlets appeared, attacking Jews as usurers and demanding that they be stripped of their citizenship.

In addition, Jewish leaders were unhappy that revolutionaries had dissolved their communal organizational structure. The old *communautés* were still deemed responsible for the collective debts they had owed before the revolution; but now there was no official body to collect tax money from Jews to pay off those debts. Lacking a legal organizational structure, Jewish leaders also found it difficult to appoint rabbis, fund synagogues, or administer Jewish schools. Emancipation had settled nothing in any permanent fashion.[34]

In 1806, Napoleon addressed these problems by convening an Assembly of Jewish Notables from all the areas of the empire to answer a set of questions about the relationship between Judaism and French citizenship. On the basis of their answers, he created a new institutional structure to administer Jewish religious life. This was in line with Napoleon's broader religious policy, in which citizens had the freedom to practice their religions, but religious administration was reorganized and brought much more strictly under the control of the state. Under the Concordat of 1801, the state took fiscal responsibility for the Catholic religion, paying for church maintenance and clerical salaries. In return, the pope agreed to let bishops be appointed by the government, to have the clergy take an oath of obedience to the state, and to allow ecclesiastical geography to be remapped onto the newly rationalized secular political geography of France. Then, in 1802, the Protestant denominations were reorganized into consistories, state agencies that paid for the maintenance of churches and pastors' salaries and placed the religious hierarchy under the control of the government.[35]

Jews appealed to Napoleon for a similar organization to solve the problem of paying for Jewish worship.[36] But not until 1806, when complaints against Jewish usury in Alsace once again reached a fevered pitch (this time, activists demanded that Jewish usury be outlawed altogether), did Napoleon formally address the question of how the Jews of France were to be organized. Moreover, because agitators proposed stripping the Jews of their citizenship, Napoleon's response involved reopening the question of Jewish civil status that had seemingly been resolved in 1791.[37]

Napoleon addressed these issues by issuing a decree that called Jewish notables from each town in the empire with a population of more than one hundred Jews to meet in Paris in July 1806. As Simon Schwarzfuchs has pointed out, these notables had reason to be worried about the emperor's intentions. Not only did the decree make explicit reference to Jewish usury in eastern France, and the need to remind Jews of their civic duties; it also placed a one-year hold on all mortgage and loan contracts signed by Jewish creditors in eastern France, and strictly limited Jewish immigration. Furthermore, the first meeting was set for a Saturday, even though the state officials who called the meeting knew that Jewish law forbade working on the Sabbath.[38] Along with the proposals circulating in the capital that aimed to limit the rights of Jewish citizens, this decision made it clear that the notables were expected to subordinate their religious interests to state interests. This expectation was confirmed when the notables were presented with a list of twelve questions—about Jewish marriage law, relations between Jews and gentiles, rabbinical authority, and the money lending—formulated in a way that suggested that Jews were not worthy of citizenship. The situation itself thus demanded that Jewish leaders affirm that they belonged to the French nation and polity.

As Paula Hyman has suggested, although the notables had no real choice about whether to affirm that they no longer considered themselves to be a separate people, they did choose what arguments they marshaled to that end.[39] They asserted their claim to citizenship based on three fundamental principles, all of which had been advanced already in the revolutionary era. First, they argued that Jews were religiously bound to observe the laws of the country in which they lived. In this vein, they held that their equal subjection to the law made them members of the nation, and thus entitled to citizenship. Second, they argued that since their emancipation, they were already French, and they had proven their national belonging through displays of love for their fellow citizens. And third, they explicitly defined the role of Judaism in the lives of Jewish citizens. Judaism, they argued, taught civic values appropriate for French citizens. The institutions that administered Judaism should not *represent* Jews politically; they should rather be seen as educational institutions.[40] All three of these arguments recapitulated arguments made by Jews and their supporters in the revolutionary era. Yet now, the notables were seeking not only to reaffirm their civil and political status, but also to obtain a legally recognized administration for their religion, since they deemed it necessary for citizenship. In this situation, their greater emphasis on the third argument—that Judaism was a crucial component of Jews' citizenship—makes perfect sense.

Their first argument for citizenship was apparent already in the preamble to the notables' answers. Here, they explained that the general principle underlying their answers was the Jewish legal principle *dina d'malkhuta dina*, according to which "the law of the land is the law" in civil life. If religious law and civil law ever conflicted, the French Code would reign supreme. Judaism was thus an inferior body of law, necessarily subordinate to the greater authority of the law of the sovereign. This meant, for example, that for French Jews, polygamy was forbidden, divorce valid religiously only if valid civilly, and intermarriage legal, even if rabbis objected to it on religious grounds. The rabbis were more than willing to subordinate religion to state authority. They proclaimed that modern rabbis had no jurisdiction as police among the Jews, but in ancient times, a body of seventy-one judges called the Sanhedrin had had such authority.[41] Under this principle, then, the notables accepted the subordination of religion to state and the relegation of religious authority to the nonpolitical realm.

The notables' second warrant for citizenship similarly hearkened back to arguments made in the 1789–91 period. Like the Jews of Paris and the Lorraine cities of Lunéville and Sarreguemines, they stated that they were already citizens who had displayed great loyalty to their nation. Jews and Christians in France were all brothers, they argued, because they lived under the same government, enjoyed the same rights, and called the same land their *patrie*.[42] The Jewish notables thus understood and accepted the revolutionary principle that all citizens were brothers, in spite of the differences between them in private or personal beliefs. They affirmed their belonging to the national community with ancient as well as modern examples, thereby demonstrating that Jews had a history of integration into the nations. In Babylon, they said, the Jews had lived under non-Jewish law, made it their home, and so loved it that even when Cyrus allowed them to return home, most chose to stay. Likewise, the modern French Jew loves France so much, they said, that he "considers himself, in England, as among strangers, although he may be among Jews; and the case is the same with English Jews in France." French Jews felt this way so strongly, they added, that in the recent war, Jews died at each others' hands fighting for different nations.[43] Recognizing that loyalty to France might come into conflict with the brotherhood Jews might feel toward non-French Jews, the notables assured Napoleon that their distinctiveness would always be secondary to their patriotic feelings and duties.

The third argument the notables advanced was by far the most extensively developed. Judaism, they claimed, was a set of teachings appropriate for instilling French Jews with the social values necessary for citizenship. Here, the Jewish notables built the revolutionary vision of secularism articulated in the Civil Constitution of the Clergy and in Napoleon's compromises with the Catholic and Protestant Churches, in which religions would be used as a support for state authority. They began with a defense of Judaism as a universalist religion preaching love for one's fellow men rather than merely love for other Jews. Jews and Christians, they asserted, worshipped the same God and were equally subject to the Noachide laws, the seven laws of Noah that Jews believe to be common to all civilized men.[44] This equal subjection to God's law as well as to state authority made Jewish and Christian Frenchmen brothers. With this argument, the notables reiterated their belief that the Bible was the source of this revolutionary ideology, a perspective articulated by Berr Isaac Berr in 1791. They also suggested that Judaism's teachings were commensurate with Christian teachings. They cited Hillel's summation of Judaism in the precept "do not unto others what thou shouldst not like done to thyself."[45] In effect, Jewish notables indicated here that Judaism, like Christianity, preached love for all mankind, and thus justified their participation in the polity by virtue of their religious law.

Judaism's universalism was stressed even more fully in the section where notables discussed the doctrine of "loving the stranger." Judaism, they explained, does not acknowledge a legal difference between brother and stranger:

> When the Israelites formed a settled and independent nation, their law made it a rule for them to consider strangers as their brethren. With the tenderest care for their welfare, their lawgiver commands to love them, "Love ye therefore the strangers," says he to the Israelites, "for ye were strangers in the land of Egypt." . . .

[A] religion which makes a duty of loving the stranger, which enforces the practice of social virtues, must surely require that its followers should consider their fellow citizens as brethren.[46]

Note that the Jewish notables were not claiming that there was no difference between brothers and strangers, only that the law compelled them to love both alike.[47]

This claim also figured strongly in their answers to the three questions about usury. First, the notables established that Jews are forbidden to lend at interest to a brother asking for assistance. Rejecting the implied opposition between "usury" and "charity," they used the more neutral term "lending at interest." Since the ancient Hebrews were an agricultural people, lending was never a way to earn a living, so the biblical passage forbidding them to take interest from each other did not refer to money lending as commercial speculation. Instead, they depicted the law against taking interest from one another as "a lesson in reciprocal benevolence," a "principle of charity," meant "to draw closer between them the bonds of fraternity."[48] Now that Jewish and Christian Frenchmen were brothers, they added, Jewish law forbade them to lend at interest to "their fellow citizens of different persuasions, as well as to our fellow-Jews" for needs which should be covered by charity. They included a generous mechanism for determining need: merely by asking for assistance, the recipient was entitled to a loan without interest from a Jew who had the means.[49]

In discussing whether Jews were allowed to take usury from strangers, the notables carefully distinguished between charity and commercial speculation. They stated that Jews were permitted to lend money at interest to each other, as well as to non-Jews, in commerce. This lending was permitted because since the dispersal, Jews had ceased to be an agricultural people and thus, the biblical laws meant to regulate them as such could no longer apply. How then, should modern Jews, who recognize their fellow citizens of all faiths as their brothers, lend? Did the biblical permission to lend at interest to strangers apply to anyone at all? Yes, the notables reasoned. Since God loved his people, and did not want to "impoverish the Jews to enrich foreign nations," the ancient Jews were permitted to lend at interest in their relations with strangers, which were the only commercial relations they had. In the modern world, this was taken to mean that Jews were permitted to lend at interest in any commercial enterprise, as long as the rates of lending were not oppressive to the borrower.[50]

This argument about usury constituted not only a defense of the Jews as a charitable people; it was also a defense of the right to earn a living at commercial speculation, a livelihood much under attack by anti-Jewish activists as well as by proponents of "regeneration." This defense was later elaborated by Abraham Furtado, the president of the Assembly of Jewish Notables, in a separate publication that addressed the suspension of Jewish loans in the decree of May 30, 1806. Stressing the fact that the ban made it impossible for Jews to borrow as well as lend money, Furtado argued that Jewish "regeneration" would be impossible under this ban. For Jews to become property owners, he argued, they needed credit. Credit was thus a necessary and implicit part of property rights, which were sacred and inviolable, and curtailing them was to deny Jews the right of existence in France, tantamount to banishing all Jews from the country.[51]

Though Napoleon was largely satisfied with the answers provided by the assembly, he was unhappy that the notables' status did not compel all Jewish citizens to adhere to their responses. However, the answers the notables submitted gave Napoleon an idea for how to deal with this problem. They had stated that the only body capable of legislating in the name of the Jewish people was the Sanhedrin, the body of judges in ancient Israel. Thus Napoleon decided to reconvene this body and empower it to place a stamp of approval on the notables' answers.[52] From Napoleon's perspective, the Sanhedrin was the religious equivalent to the pope, capable of validating Judaism's submission to the state. The Sanhedrin was to issue a "second legislation of the Jews, which, while keeping the essential character of that of Moses, will adapt itself to the present situation."[53]

While permitting the notables to determine how the Sanhedrin's meetings would be structured, Napoleon left nothing to chance as to its rulings, dictating the dogma the Sanhedrin was to formulate into Jewish law. Judaism was not to be considered a separate body of law; it was a set of teachings commensurate with civic values. In addition to ruling on issues of dogma, the Sanhedrin was also to determine how rabbis would be appointed, trained, and paid; to define the duties of rabbis; and to establish an institutional structure for Judaism. Departmental consistories, in charge of maintaining the Jewish religion, would be elected by the Jewish notables in each area of the empire. These consistories would answer to a central consistory in Paris, which was to be supervised by the Ministry of Worship. Modeled on the Protestant consistories, this structure would teach that religion is subservient to state authority.[54]

In the minds of the notables, the convening of the Sanhedrin represented a legal recognition of Judaism as a valid and protected religion in France. Any new rulings it would issue would not constitute reform, but a return to "the practice of our ancient virtues," as Furtado wrote in an open letter addressed to the synagogues of Europe.[55] Abraham de Cologna, an Italian Rabbi who would later serve as chief rabbi of France, implied as much in his opening remarks to the Sanhedrin's first meeting on February 7, 1807, charging his listeners to "reconcile the duties of civil life with religious duties; show the harmony of their principles; do this so well that each supports the other . . . in short, develop the maxims of true *sociabilité*, upon which our belief is based."[56] By involving rabbis in the establishment of a new organization for Judaism, and by giving them the power to legislate Jewish dogma, Napoleon accomplished two key tasks. First, he protected Judaism by bringing it into the fold of state organization. Second, he assured that this religion, now under the ultimate authority of the state, would emphasize the common values between French citizenship and Mosaic law.

Even though the Sanhedrin met only a few times between February 1807 and March 1808, the very fact of its existence, which its members publicized by writing to Jewish communities across Europe, was even more important to the establishment of modern French Judaism than emancipation itself had been. Napoleon and the Sanhedrin turned revolutionary rhetoric into lasting institutions by turning the arguments for Jewish citizenship into religious law, and by creating an official body with the power to teach all Jews this doctrine. By 1809, all rabbis throughout the empire had sworn an oath pledging adherence to the nine articles that comprised the doctrinal decisions of the

Sanhedrin and promising to teach nothing contrary to those decisions.[57] The Sanhedrin had the power to create an official French Judaism within the state, and the teaching of Judaism was considered
necessary for the task of regenerating the Jews into good citizens. Far
from relegating their Jewishness to a private realm, Napoleon made
Judaism a permanent state institution that would teach social virtues.

Conclusion

Although revolutionaries had dissolved the Old Regime Jewish corporations, Judaism and organized Jewish life survived because they
were deemed essential to the creation of citizens. This link between
Judaism and the state was already imagined by some in the revolutionary era, but became a reality only under Napoleon, when Jewish
leaders turned the new interpretation of Jewish citizenship into religious doctrine, and diffused that doctrine through the consistory system, a permanent hierarchical structure within the growing French
bureaucracy. The Jewish citizen was an abstraction created in a particular discursive context: the establishment of a secular state upon the
"eternal principles of justice and reason," rather than upon church and
king.[58] This vision for a secular state, however, was not irreligious.
Rather, as this examination of Jewish emancipation reveals, under
Napoleon, the state incorporated the religious institutions of its citizens within its bureaucracy to varying degrees, and sought to use the
teachings of these religions to form good citizens. This was particularly true of Judaism, because unlike Catholicism, its leaders—who
were in a far weaker and more tenuous situation than Catholic leaders—did not publicly offer any wholesale alternative to the revolutionary and Napoleonic model.

An important result of emancipation was that the Jewish citizen
was tied to the state and its ideological project much more tightly
than to the local Jewish community to which he belonged. This Jewish citizen was at once French and universal. Tied not to the local
community in bonds of mutual responsibility, but instead to an ever
expanding, centralized bureaucracy, the post-revolutionary Jewish cit-

izen could exist anywhere in the lands under French sovereignty. As Napoleon brought administrative reform to areas outside territorial France, he brought citizenship to the Jews in these areas as well. Rabbis and lay leaders were sent from Germany and Italy to the Assembly of Jewish Notables and the Sanhedrin; after 1808, consistories were established and rabbis appointed in all the areas of the empire. Even in the Assembly of Jewish Notables, where all discussion had to be translated back and forth among three languages, Jewish leaders never indicated that they understood the Jewish citizen to be any different in the different contexts of Germany, Italy, or France. Napoleon's goal regarding the Jews was indeed universal, if somewhat pernicious in its tacit devaluation of Jewish tradition. He wrote, "The . . . project is to lessen, if not to cure the tendencies of the Jewish people, who have such a great number of practices contrary to civilization and to the maintenance of order in society, in all the countries of the world."[59]

The way in which future generations of French Jews would come to think about the condition of Jews elsewhere was profoundly shaped by the ideology of secularism that undergirded the establishment of the consistories. First and foremost, this was because it was this ideology of secularism that had given them a new, more secure place in French public life. For that reason, French Jewish leaders would remain deeply committed to its full realization, siding with its proponents in the decades-long battle against Catholic legitimists, wherever that battle was fought. Second, this was because through the consistories, French Jewish life became linked to the French state and its ideological project. This, as we shall see, would mean that as France sought to extend its dominion to areas beyond its borders, so too would Jews extend this function for Judaism, tied as it was to French revolutionary ideology and the expanding French bureaucracy.

Two Alliances with Restoration Liberals

The transformation of French Jewish life from corporatism to citizenship was as protracted a process as the establishment of state secularism, with which its history is fundamentally intertwined. Emancipation may have been the work of the revolution, but it was under Napoleon and the Restoration that a lasting institutional structure was built to replace the old semi-autonomous *communautés*, and it was only under the July Monarchy that all vestiges of Jewish legal disabilities were removed. From 1808, when Napoleon established the consistories, until 1830, when the government finally annulled the special tax for Jewish citizens, Jewish leaders fought to achieve the equality guaranteed by the emancipation decrees and reaffirmed in the Charte of 1814, which deemed all citizens equal before the law, regardless of their religion.

For French Jews, the achievement of full legal equality involved a greater identification of their religion with the ideology and constitution of the state, as well as greater incorporation of Jewish religious institutions into the state apparatus. In keeping with the Napoleonic heritage, the conception of secularism that ultimately made Jewish legal equality possible was one that considered Judaism, Protestantism, and Catholicism equally dignified, equally universalist moral codes appropriate for civic education and for public expressions of religious sentiment, and thus equally worthy of state support. Far from making religion a wholly private matter, conceived as the responsibility of individuals or private associations, Jewish institutional life in France was transformed under a model of secularism in which religions were public and identified with the state.

As we saw in Chapter 1, Jewish leaders had become committed to this model of secularism by the time of Napoleon. And yet even with the establishment of the consistories in 1808, this vision for Jewish institutional life was not yet a reality. Although Jews had become citizens and their old *communautés* were replaced by the consistories, Restoration Jewish leaders saw Jews' legal position in France as irregular and fought to change it. Jews' remaining legal disabilities were less burdensome than those of the Old Regime, but they were nonetheless irksome, expensive, and restrictive. Another set of problems revolved around the role of the consistories in Jewish life. These institutions were nominally analogous to the Protestant consistories, state agencies rather than separate political bodies. Yet synagogues (unlike churches) remained self-supporting until the early 1830s, and as a result, the consistories remained in this respect more like the old *communautés* than like the agencies managing Protestant and Catholic worship. Furthermore, unlike Protestant consistories, Jewish consistories were involved in identifying, taxing, and policing Jewish citizens—functions that harkened back to the Old Regime corporations.[1] Jewish leaders' struggle against the remnants of corporatism was ultimately a struggle to build a new institutional structure that would guarantee legal equality, national status, and religious freedom for individual Jews.

This chapter examines the arguments Jewish leaders used to free themselves from the remnants of corporatism. These struggles were self-defensive, aimed at regularizing the equal status Jews had nominally achieved in the revolution under the restored monarchy, which had once again declared Catholicism the official state religion. In their work, Jewish leaders resolutely affirmed their commitment to the form of citizenship in which individuals, not corporate bodies representing different social groups, were the main category subject to the law. They also went to great lengths to make Jewish religious life more public in key ways, most notably, by seeking to get the consistory system itself more fully incorporated within the state administration, claiming that Judaism had an important public role in the moral education of individual citizens.

As we shall see, in articulating this perspective, French Jewish leaders aligned themselves with the revolutionary and Napoleonic heritage and thereby began to make a place for themselves in the emerging liberal networks of the 1820s, where the ideas that would come to constitute nineteenth-century French secularism were being defined. The liberalism apparent in Jewish leaders' arguments testifies to their growing participation in wider French political battles, itself a product of the rapid social integration of members of the Jewish elite in Paris that historian Christine Piette has documented for the period from 1808 to 1840.[2] A broad commitment to the liberal cause is apparent not only in these arguments, but also in many of their personal choices, such as the increasingly common decision to send their children to *lycées* and *collèges* known for their liberal teachers. By the 1820s, the Jewish leaders who led the fight against the remnants of corporatism had become remarkably fluent in the liberal lexicon, and worked tirelessly to win prominent liberal politicians and writers to their cause. Influenced by such liberal political, social, and religious ideals, Restoration Jewish leaders extended and solidified the gains of the emancipation period, breaking the last chains of communal solidarity to achieve full legal equality.

Restoration Jewish leaders were interested in liberal ideas as more than just a means to secure their rights. They also sought to contribute more broadly to contemporary discussions about the place of religion in modern life. This was especially the case after 1825, when a range of liberal thinkers—from the *doctrinaire* François Guizot, to *Le Globe* editor Charles de Rémusat, to the Saint-Simonians—began to embrace the idea that post-revolutionary French society needed a new kind of theocracy based not on outdated Catholicism, but on a new kind of religion.[3] Adding their voices to these discussions, Jewish writers like Elie and Léon Halévy and Joseph Salvador redefined Judaism as a universal moral code that, like the new forms of Christianity celebrated by liberals in their world, they identified with the French constitutional state. Their commitment to building this model of secularism would have long-lasting effects, coming to serve in later decades as the foundation for French Jewish leaders' expressions of solidarity with Jews in other countries.

Collective Burdens as a Challenge to Citizenship

In this era of reaction, Jewish leaders faced important challenges to their hard-won status as citizens. Unlike members of other Old Regime corporations, individual Jews remained responsible for paying off the debts contracted by the Old Regime Jewish *communautés* which had been dissolved by the emancipation decrees, a responsibility that passed to their children when they died. Another disability was reserved for the Jews of eastern France alone, who were barred from borrowing or lending money for ten years by the "Infamous Decree" of 1808. In addition, in courtrooms across France, Jews were often required to take a special, humiliating Jewish oath, the *more judaïco*, before testifying.

In defending their rights against these challenges, Restoration Jewish leaders affirmed their commitment to legal individualism, an ideal inherited from the revolutionary era. As the emerging Jewish leader Adolphe Crémieux (1796–1880) argued, the 1814 Charte granted citizenship to all individual Frenchmen in exactly the same terms, and religion—like all other forms of social difference—should not be recognized in any way within the law. "All titles, all statuses, all religious denominations are erased before the majesty of the law; sovereign master, the law rules over all citizens equally, and it must be applied equally to all," he argued.[4] Although Catholicism had once again become the official state religion, Jews in this period stressed the Charte's liberal provisions to continue their fight to solidify their legal status as individual "citizens," with rights indistinguishable from those of other citizens. Although their main motivation for fighting this battle was, of course, self-defensive, in the process they sought out allies in the liberal camp, which was then emerging as the dominant voice opposing an increasingly reactionary regime.

Jewish leaders' view that the collective burdens they faced were fundamentally illegal was built on their interpretation of the Charte of 1814. Since the destruction of the feudal order in 1789, French legislators and courts had upheld the principle that citizens were subject to the law as individuals rather than as part of legally defined corporations or as members of a particular religious sect. This guiding vision was not altered under Napoleon, and in the Charte promulgated by Louis XVIII in 1814, religion was once again deemed irrelevant to an individual citizen's legal rights, unlike age, sex, wealth, or nationality. Yet in spite of the Charte's assurance that religion was irrelevant to an individual's legal rights, Jews still found themselves treated differently before the law than their fellow citizens in a number of ways. During the Restoration period, as they saw German Jews lose the citizenship they had gained under the Napoleonic occupation (and in 1819, fall victim to the notorious *Hep! Hep!* riots as well), and saw Catholicism reinstated as the official state religion at home, French Jews were determined to solidify the Charte's promise that they would no longer be singled out for special burdens as "Jews" in the law.

Jewish citizens' responsibility for the debts of the former *communautés* was an important concern. This burden primarily affected Jews connected to the *communautés* that had owed large debts to outside creditors before the revolution and their descendants. For them, the debts represented a financial burden that did not pertain to citizens of other faiths. Moreover, the legal issues at stake were important for all Jewish citizens in France. As historian Zosa Szajkowski has shown, the communal debts of other dissolved corporations, as well as much of the debt of the Catholic Church in France, were assumed by the state in 1793, and the decision to hold Jews responsible for their communal debts was an exceptional measure taken later, in 1797.[5] Jews objected to the reasoning behind the decision to hold them accountable for these debts, for it was based on a conception of the former Jewish *communautés* as non-French. This holding, Jews felt, was a dangerous misreading of the history of Jewish status in France that might have repercussions on their national status in the future. In important ways, the issue of the debts raised broader questions about whether the revolution's destruction of the corporate order and the 1814 Charte's proclamation of religious liberty and equality would be upheld under the Restoration.

The Jews' responsibility for the debts of their ancestors was a throwback to Old Regime corporatism. In post-revolutionary France, few groups had such a high degree of legally binding mutual responsibility, especially vis-à-vis a dissolved corporate body. The fact that this was a corporate concept squeezed into the new legal framework of Napoleonic France is illustrated by the very fact that the legal term used to describe it, *solidarité*, was itself a neologism introduced into the French language in the Civil Code of 1804.[6] This term's juridical meaning was older than the political meaning that is now more common; in 1839, Pierre Leroux would be the first writer to systematically use the term *solidarité* in this latter sense.[7] In the code, *solidarité* denotes a status defined previously in Roman law (in Latin, *in solidum*), in which a person is legally accountable for another's debts, in such a way that each party individually is fully responsible for the whole amount. The authors of a recent French legal textbook write that *solidarité* is based on the principle "unity of object, plurality of ties." For example, if a group of people contract a debt together, they owe a single amount to one creditor (unity of object); but if the debt is not repaid, the creditor has a legal claim against each and every debtor individually (plurality of ties).[8] Juridical *solidarité* is thus a relationship in which people can be held accountable for other people's promises and transgressions.

The jurisprudence of *solidarité* was new in Napoleonic law in that for the first time, it could not be presumed except in a very limited set of cases. Under the Old Regime, each of the legally recognized corporate bodies, such as municipalities, artisans' corporations, and Jewish *communautés*, was treated as a single entity before the law, and its members were *solidaires*, or collectively responsible for each others' debts or wrongdoings. When legislators abolished the system of privileges in the first years of the revolution, corporate *solidarité* was abolished as well, at least nominally. Jews may have been the only group whose communal *solidarité* survived Napoleon in certain respects, but a few other noncorporate types of juridical *solidarité*—between husbands and wives, for example—survived as well, if only in limited form. Article 1202 of the Civil Code stated that *solidarité* "cannot be presumed; it must be expressly stipulated," either by contract or by entering into a relationship that the code defined explicitly as *solidaire*. The code was sparing in what relationships it defined as *solidaire*: spouses under certain stated circumstances; coexecutors of a will; tenants in a same building if the cause of a fire cannot be found;

and shareholders vis-à-vis their agent or proxy.[9] The code's limitation of *solidarité* fit well within the general framework of imperial jurisprudence, which stressed individual freedoms over and against the power of associations, and thereby embodied and reinforced Napoleonic notions of citizenship.[10]

The Jews' struggle against their creditors centered in the regions where there had been the highest communal debts, Metz and the former Papal States. These *communautés* had incurred their debts in order to pay the special taxes that had given them the right to live in their respective regions. In Metz, the heaviest burden had been the Brancas tax, an annual sum of twenty thousand *livres* owed directly to the Brancas family, established as a personal favor in 1715 by the regent Philippe d'Orléans. In addition to this sum, the Jews of Metz had been required to pay heavy taxes to the city, and they had also spent a large amount in bribes to Church and state officials. By July 20, 1790, when the National Assembly abolished the Brancas tax, the Jewish *communauté* of Metz owed about half a million *livres* to Christian creditors.[11] The Jews of the Papal States, emancipated just two weeks after the region was annexed to France on September 14, 1791, were in a similar situation. These communities had to pay special taxes to the Church to protect themselves from regular humiliation and violence. Yet here, the Church itself functioned as a creditor to the Jews, and thus, when Church property was nationalized, so too were some of the communal debts. By 1818, descendants of the members of the former Jewish *communautés* of Carpentras, Avignon, L'Isle-sur-Sorgue, and Cavaillon owed about 165,000 *livres* to the French government for communal loans incurred before 1791.[12]

Other Jews also suffered under the weight of debts of the former *communautés* too. The rural Jewish *communautés* in Alsace owed Christian creditors smaller amounts that had been contracted for communal expenses.[13] In 1810, the government assessed these Alsatian debts at 182,645 francs, and decreed that this sum was to be collected from the Jewish population in special taxes by the consistories of the Upper and Lower Rhine.[14] In addition, the enormous Metz debt came to affect much of the French Jewish elite through marriage. Adolphe Crémieux, for example, was from Nîmes, but nonetheless became responsible for a share in it in 1824 when he married Louise-Amélie Silny, who was originally from Metz. Even though Jews were citizens, shares in communal debts became personal property that all descendants of Jews in Old Regime France inherited, an obligation from which even converts to Christianity were not released.[15] The worst burden was reserved for those individuals descended from a *syndic*. Because the *syndics* had personally guaranteed communal loans, their descendants could be held responsible for the entire debt.[16]

As soon as the *communautés* were dissolved, Jews asked that the government nationalize the communal debts. Because the Jewish emancipation decrees had made no mention of the debts, it was unclear whether or not the laws that dissolved all corporations and liquidated their debts applied to the former Jewish *communautés* as well. In the eyes of the Jews of Avignon, who submitted a petition to the National Convention in 1794, however, there should have been no confusion at all. Since they no longer had any communal existence, they argued, and since they themselves had become citizens, their debts had to be nationalized as well. Likening themselves to the inhabitants of cities, whose debts had been forgiven when their corporate structures were dissolved, they saw the dissolution of their corporation as annulling its debt. "The National Convention cannot recognize the Jews," they wrote. "There are no more Jews in France. In France, there are no more Catholics, Protestants, Anabaptists, Jews, or confessionals of any sort; there are only Frenchmen."[17] The Jews of Metz used similar arguments in legal briefs submitted to municipal courts on the issue, but met with the same failure.[18] In 1807, representatives of the Italian Jewish communities argued to the imperial government that since the debts had been a result of immoral taxation, the new regime should not honor them; this argument also failed.[19]

At the time of emancipation, local authorities in Metz, at least, probably favored the dissolution of the Jewish debts, since they saw dismantling the entire administrative structure of the Jewish *communautés* as a necessary part of reforming Jewish morals.[20] But when the national government finally considered the issue in 1797, the result was not what the Jews had hoped. Even though the special commission established to study the problem recommended nationalizing the debts, the Council of Five Hundred ruled that Jews would remain responsible for them.[21] Still later, in a follow-up to this first commission's report, François-Marie-Joseph Riou de Kersalaun warned against bringing together a class of citizens in an administrative structure, even if this structure had the sole role of repaying old debts, because to do so would be tantamount to forming a corporation once again.[22] Still, the Council of Five Hundred and local authorities refused to treat Jews like other former French corporations. In 1801, the Moselle Prefecture ruled that the dissolution of the Jewish *communauté* was not retroactive, meaning that past debts were still owed because the community had in the past constituted a recognized political entity.[23]

In deciding not to nationalize the Jewish communal debts, the Council of Five Hundred adopted the position that Jews could not be likened to other old corporations because before emancipation they had been foreigners, not Frenchmen, who were then naturalized by the emancipation decrees.[24] Like the French nation as a whole, which remained responsible for its pre-revolutionary debts, Jews were responsible for the debts incurred by their "nations" in the past, even though the "nations" no longer existed in any formal sense. The council's writings on the issue made no mention of the fact that Jews in the Old Regime had several times been considered French subjects (*régnicoles*). Thus Jews were held responsible for them, and began the long process of paying them off. Special Jewish communal commissions were first established to collect the necessary funds by selling communal properties and collecting special taxes established for this purpose. Later, in some areas, the consistories were made to serve this function.[25]

In 1821, a group of creditors from the Vaucluse submitted a petition to the Chamber of Deputies stating that because so many wealthy Jews of the region had moved away since the revolution, it was becoming quite difficult to collect the money they were owed by the former members of the region's four *communautés* and their heirs. In their appeal, the creditors argued that the Jews who had lived in the area, together with their heirs, were responsible for the debts because the loans had been contracted with the understanding that they were guaranteed by the borrowers' children and their fellow Jews by an implicit communal bond of *solidarité*.[26] The following year, the Marquis

Forbin des Issarts, a returned émigré then serving as a deputy from the Vaucluse, took up the creditors' cause and explained before the Chamber of Deputies why this *solidarité* was so important to the contract between them and the Jewish communities. Only because Jewish *solidarité* was understood to be perpetual, he argued, could loans have been made to the Jews, who, as foreigners everywhere, had no guarantee to offer but the eternal tie binding the community, forged by faith and reinforced by the Jews' political position. The fact that these Jews were now citizens in no way released them from this *solidarité*.[27]

From his home in Nîmes, Adolphe Crémieux wrote to the influential liberal deputy Benjamin Constant, himself a Protestant, for his support in this matter. Constant replied that while he and other liberals eagerly awaited the day when their views would be in the majority, other forces currently held sway in the Chamber. "Israelites, Protestants, liberals, friends of religious and political rights: we are all hit with the same horror. I am consoled to find myself together with you in this," Constant wrote.[28] Crémieux had rightly identified an important ally on this issue, yet Forbin des Issarts' argument nonetheless prevailed and the Jews remained responsible for their predecessors' debts.[29] The debts thus became a burden for at least one more generation, as is clear from an 1845 case involving a Mr. Dreyfuss, who was sued by two tax collectors for nonpayment of his share of the Metz communal debt. Dreyfuss's case was argued—unsuccessfully—by Crémieux in Paris.[30]

Although the Jews never managed to convince officials to annul or nationalize the debts of the former *communautés*, they were somewhat more successful in their efforts against another remnant of corporatism, the 1808 Infamous Decree. This decree forbade all the Jews of eastern France (and specifically *not* the Jews of Bordeaux or Bayonne) to lend or borrow money for ten years, whether or not they had ever lent money in the past.[31] Though the decree appears not to have been enforced strictly by police officials, Central Consistory members nonetheless saw it as economically harmful and socially stigmatizing for the Jews of eastern France, most of whom lived in poverty.[32] That this decree was not renewed when it expired in 1818 was in part due to the efforts of Jewish leaders, worried at least as much about its impact on the political rights of all French Jews as its deleterious economic effects on the Jews of eastern France. As in their protests against the communal debts, these leaders saw the decree as reminiscent of the Old Regime's legal system and fought it as an illegal remnant of corporatism, a form of communal *solidarité* that held all members of a group accountable for the actions of a few.

The first publication opposing the ban on Jewish money lending came from Abraham Furtado, president of the Assembly of Jewish Notables, soon after the temporary ban was decreed in 1806. Not only did this decree impinge on the civil rights of Jewish citizens, Furtado argued, it was contrary to the administrative spirit of the revolution, which had outlawed all privileges or special legal status of particular groups of citizens. Sharing a religion should not condemn Jews to what Furtado called a "*solidarité* of punishment," for opinion was a private matter, not to be represented politically.[33] To forbid Jews to borrow or lend money was essentially to expel them from the nation, he added, since it denied them fundamental rights. "Either the existence of Jews in France is a curse, in which case they should be banished; or it is not a curse at all, and thus we should see in them not Jews, but Frenchmen," he wrote.[34] In his pamphlet, Furtado made use of the neologism *solidarité* to explain how the decree created a kind of collective oppression illegal in the framework of post-revolutionary jurisprudence. Holding one group of citizens collectively responsible for the crimes of a few, by creating special, restrictive legislation, was tantamount to treating them as a foreign nation. Furtado—like the Jewish leaders who struggled against responsibility for the communal debts—saw this enforced *solidarité* as worse than restrictions in the Old Regime, since corporations no longer existed. Here, Furtado returned to the definition of citizenship that he, like Clermont-Tonnerre, had espoused in 1789: inclusion in the nation meant subjection to the same laws and institutions.

In 1817 and 1818, consistory leaders in Paris and in the eastern *départements* affected by the decree petitioned the government against its renewal, and the ban on Jewish money lending was not renewed when it expired in 1818.[35] However, the struggle was not yet completely over; in 1820, some deputies from Alsace suggested that the decree be reinstated. In response, the outraged Central Consistory members penned a letter to the minister of the interior that restated Furtado's claims from 1806. "The decree of March 17, 1808, placed the Israelites outside of the common law (*droit commun*) and outraged all friends of justice," they wrote. "If Frenchmen, regardless of their religion, participate in an illicit trade, the law is there, may it be exercised against them in all its rigor. But by what right can a great number of citizens be struck with an exceptional measure, which puts the innocent together with the guilty?"[36] For Jewish leaders, *solidarité* was contrary to the very spirit of the new regime's justice system, which treated all citizens the same before the law.

As with the Infamous Decree and the communal debts, Jewish leaders saw the imposition of the *more judaïco* in courtrooms across France as a challenge to Jews' rights as individual citizens. Jewish witnesses were required to take this oath on a Torah scroll, usually in a synagogue. The oath was administered by a rabbi, who held the scroll open to the words, "You shall not take the Lord's name in vain," and was also expected to list the curses that would fall upon the oath taker should he fail to tell the truth. In 1792, the minister of justice had directed courts to drop this custom, seeing it as contrary to the principles of equality and religious freedom. "The law does not distinguish between Jew and Christian, Protestant and Catholic, Conformist and Dissident," the directive explained. From then until its reimposition, Jews testifying in court had simply said, "I swear," as all other Frenchmen did in courts.[37] The Napoleonic Code required all witnesses to swear to tell the truth in court, but did not specify the form the oath would take; an imperial decree of October 10, 1808, specified that all witnesses were to swear in court with one hand on a printed Bible.[38] The fact that the Jewish oath did not originate in the mind of Napoleon or his ministers in Paris is clear from the fact that neither the members of Paris Sanhedrin of 1807, nor David Sintzheim, the first chief rabbi of France (selected in 1809), were sworn into their offices with this special oath. Furthermore, the imperial decree of October 19, 1808, specified that the members of the consistories were to be sworn in with the same oath as all other public servants, not a special Jewish oath.[39]

The question of what oath Jews were to take in courts emerged in the decidedly hostile environment of the Upper Rhine *département* in

1807, a time, as we have seen, when numerous pamphleteers were calling for Jews' expulsion from France on account of their "immoral" money-lending practices. The *more judaïco*'s reemergence clearly began as a local affair related to the question of whether Christian debtors would be held accountable for loans they had contracted from Jewish moneylenders prior to 1806, when the temporary ban on Jewish money lending was first promulgated. Indeed, the Upper Rhine Consistory wrote to the Central Consistory in 1809 that the oath was used to intimidate Jews so that they would not testify in civil cases, since Jews were not accustomed to taking oaths and were terrified of the prospect.[40] Indeed, in at least one case, a Jewish defendant was willing to pay a six-hundred-franc fine rather than submit to the oath. More often, it appears that Jewish defendants merely refused to take it, losing cases as a result.[41]

The legal justification for the oath was as much a breech of Jewish citizens' rights as the use to which it was put. In 1809, the Colmar Appeals Court ruled on the matter in a case between a Christian debtor and his Jewish lender. The court held that Jews had to swear in court "according to the custom common in Germany," and based its holding on the fact that this was the practice specified in the royal *lettres patentes* of 1784. Such reliance on Old Regime law is surprising, especially since privileges such as these had been given to corporations, not individual citizens. In addition, the Colmar Appeals Court added a factually inaccurate historical reason to further support its decision: "The Jews of the Rhine Department are of German origin, and thus they must take the oath *more judaïco* in the Synagogue . . . with the ceremony in usage in similar cases in Germany."[42] The decision thus represented a challenge to Jewish citizenship in a number of key ways. First, it challenged Jewish nationality by depicting Jews as "Germans." This was false information as well; as historian David Feuerwerker points out, Alsatian Jews were no more "from Germany" than Protestant and Catholic residents of Alsace, which had become French only in 1648.[43] Equally problematic in the framework of imperial law was the court's decision to deem "German custom" the appropriate usage for French citizens of "German origin." This created a legal category based on a group's descent, which was otherwise anomalous in Napoleonic jurisprudence, as a way of translating Old Regime corporate privileges into the individualistic framework of the Civil Code. From the moment it reappeared, then, the use of the *more judaïco* was justified with claims about Jews' special status as former "foreigners" still governed by provisions granted to them collectively before the revolution.

Slightly different reasoning was provided by the Commercial Court in Mainz in the occupied Rhineland, which justified its use of the Jewish oath based on the principle of religious freedom. Arguing that while Christians understood their obligation to tell the truth merely by taking an ordinary oath, a Jew would have to swear before "the Tablets of his Law, the altar of his God, his priests, and the books of his belief," in order to feel bound to tell the truth.[44] In the eyes of the Mainz Commercial Court, the oath was a religious, not a political act, and thus, each witness must be "permitted" to swear according to his faith. Based largely on the reasoning of the Mainz Commercial Court, the minister of justice accepted the *more judaïco* as a protection of Jews' religious freedom.

In response, local rabbis on both sides of the Rhine waged a campaign of staunch opposition, many of them refusing to administer the oath when they were called to do so. The Central Consistory mobilized as well. The renowned Rabbi Ezekiel Landau from Prague, French Chief Rabbi Sintzheim, the members of the Central Consistory, and the members of the local consistories in the regions it was used (Upper Rhine, Mont-Tonnerre, and soon, the Lower Rhine as well) wrote letters objecting to the oath, explaining that Jews would feel themselves obligated to tell the truth by taking the ordinary oath on a printed Bible in the courtroom, the form prescribed for all witnesses in the imperial decree of October 19, 1808. Although not all judicial bodies followed the ruling of the Upper Rhine court—the Turin Appeals Court, for example, ruled in 1809 that the oath was illegal on the grounds that it did not appear in the Civil Code—courts in Alsace and the Rhineland nonetheless continued to use it, with the approval of the minister of justice. The practice continued under the Restoration as well, in spite of the numerous protests by Jewish lay leaders and rabbis.[45]

The legal battle against the oath took a different turn in southern France in 1827, when the Nîmes Appeals Court declared it illegal in two separate cases. Both cases had first been heard by a trial court in nearby Uzès, and Adolphe Crémieux handled both appeals. The first involved a creditor, Alphandéry, who was attempting to collect a sum owed from the heirs of his debtor. The defendants claimed that Alphandéry had fabricated the agreement he produced as evidence of the debt. For this reason, the Uzès judge ruled that the loan contract was itself not enough to support Alphandéry's claim; an oath was also needed, on the grounds that the oath "makes the party who takes it a judge in his own case . . . [and thus] lends authority to the thing judged," because its religious "solemnity" makes the witness's statement "credible" to the court. The Uzès judge went on to hold that as a matter of religious freedom, Alphandéry was to take the *more judaico* rather than the ordinary oath; this was a protection rather than an attack on his religion, since "nothing prevents a judge from obligating a Catholic Christian to take the oath on the holy Gospel."[46]

Crémieux, then thirty years old and already known as one of the best lawyers in the region, represented Alphandéry on the appeal. He not only won the case, but on the basis of this success, achieved national fame as a liberal interpreter of constitutional law and emerging leader of French Jewry. Crémieux argued that in its rulings in both cases the lower court had misused the notions of religious freedom and equality. The law, he argued, protects religious liberty properly by protecting its ministers, administrators, and edifices (churches and synagogues) from attack. Individual believers, by contrast, are citizens, and are equal in that the law considers them all to be the same; they thus have no religion before the law. Were the law to recognize individual citizens' religion, it would be an attack on an individual's religious freedom. This was because in order to find out what an individual citizen's religion was, the law would have to peer forcibly into the citizen's heart—an act of force that was ultimately as impossible as it was illegal. Thus, according to Crémieux, the Uzès court had not protected religious liberty, but had rather violated it by undertaking an "*inquisition* into the religion of each citizen."[47] Crémieux argued that the ruling also compromised legal equality by creating "laws particular to each sect" in a country whose Charte affirmed the unity of the nation under a common code of law. In his estimation, "equality" in article 1 of the Charte ("All Frenchmen are equal before the law") meant "the absence of all difference of any sort between individuals."[48]

Convinced by Crémieux's arguments, the Nîmes court held that the *more judaïco* was illegal because it compromised the equality of a certain class of citizens by placing them outside the common law. They equivocated somewhat on the question of whether the oath was a religious or civil act, suggesting that it made no difference in this case, since the rabbinic evidence presented in the case proved that Jews were religiously bound by the ordinary oath.[49] Although courts in eastern France would continue to use the Jewish oath until the Cour de Cassation ruled it illegal in 1846, French Jewish leaders clearly felt triumphant; the Paris Consistory wrote to congratulate Crémieux, calling him "the pride of the Nîmes bar, the hope of French Jews."[50]

Crémieux's victory in Nîmes owed much to the liberalism of the court that heard the case and the issues at play in the local context. Nîmes was a city with a large liberal Protestant minority, and Crémieux's reputation had been made by representing Protestants in their cases for restitution for damages incurred during the White Terror of 1815, which had been particularly brutal there. His reference to the Inquisition is particularly telling in this context—as were the numerous times in his brief where he made reference to theoretical instances in which Christians could be and had been persecuted for their beliefs. The Nîmes bar itself was known in this period for its liberal positions on freedom of speech and the abolition of the death penalty.[51] The reception of the case in the national arena further illustrates how much Crémieux's ideas about religious freedom and legal equality were shared by non-Jewish liberals. The *Gazette des Tribunaux* reported that Crémieux's arguments reached "the highest philosophical level," especially where he demonstrated that religious liberty was compromised when the state asked individual citizens what religion they professed. In addition, André Dupin (1783–1865), already one of the country's best-known lawyers, who would become a major political figure during and after the 1830 revolution, supported Crémieux in the second of the two cases, and soon after, brought him in to work with him on cases involving press censorship.[52] Here, unlike in his private efforts to get help from Constant in his campaign against the communal debts, Crémieux's liberal interpretation of Jewish status under the constitutional monarchy was presented in a more favorable setting.

Jewish leaders' legal battles in this period thus followed the same strategy consistently in these three very different types of cases. From the perspective of Crémieux and other Jewish leaders, emancipation meant that it should now be considered illegal to have any laws that define a class of citizens and treat them differently than any other. They understood the cases where they were defined as Jews—in one case, as former members of a particular corporation; in another, as of purported foreign origin; and in yet another, as citizens professing a particular minority faith—as attacks on their citizenship. Within the new legal framework, they surmised, one could not be a citizen and be subject to special particular laws, no matter how that group was identified. Jewish leaders' commitment to this new radical legal individualism also shaped their view of what it meant for the law to protect an individual's religious belief. A private matter, religious belief was located in an individual's conscience, and was thus something the state should not recognize in its legal codes or its courtrooms.

The Consistory: A New Kind of Jewish Institution

Despite this strong commitment to excising the category of "Jew" from the law, Jewish leaders in Paris were nonetheless committed to building Jewish institutions with a strong public presence and, they argued, a crucial role in the formation of Jewish citizens. For Jewish leaders, these were two parts of the same goal of creating a new, more just relationship between religions and the state, thereby establishing true equality between citizens of different faiths. Efforts to make the consistory system less like the former *communautés* and more like other arms of the French state played a crucial role in this transformation. Jewish leaders' efforts in this regard pulled from arguments about the proper relationship between church and state from the revolutionary and Napoleonic eras. They were also inspired by a whole host of ideas popular in the liberal networks of the time, including new ways to finance large-scale projects and new conceptions of state administration, such as those of the *doctrinaires*, who argued that the best way to stabilize the French state was to coordinate its power with institutions of civil society, such as learned societies, chambers of commerce, and councils of experts in arts and industry.[53] Their arguments in these struggles, as in their legal battles against other remnants of corporatism, testify to Parisian Jewish leaders' growing level of integration within French liberal networks.

In theory, there was a world of difference between the consistory systems and the *communautés* they were meant to replace, and yet in practice, the consistories of the Restoration period were saddled with many responsibilities reminiscent of the old corporations. The consistory system bears the telltale mark of its founder, Napoleon: hierarchical centralization. By decree of March 17, 1808, one consistory was established in each *département* with more than two thousand Jews; each of these departmental consistories answered to the Central Consistory, located in Paris, which in turn answered to the minister of the interior's section of non-Catholic sects. Jewish consistory members were chosen from the ranks of the Jewish notables of each *département*, itself composed of men who met specific qualifications of wealth, age, and merit. Initially, the notables selected four of their members to serve on the consistory, two rabbis and two laymen; the Central Consistory, headed by the chief rabbi of France, was to have three rabbis and two laymen, selected from the ranks of the Jewish notables of Paris. In 1823, a decree expanded the number of laymen to seven, one representative for each departmental consistory (the decree also expanded the number of laymen on departmental consistories from two to seven).[54]

This hierarchical centralization distinguished the Jewish consistories from the Protestant consistories, which had been established in 1802, and made it easier to regulate Jewish dogma and religious practice than French Protestantism, which, lacking a central regulatory body, retained a much higher degree of doctrinal diversity.[55] For the Jews, decisions about religious practice and teachings were to come from the top down. The *ordonnance* of 1823 specified that all books taught in Jewish primary schools had to receive the approval of the Central Consistory. Other issues as well, like reforms to circumcision methods, discussions about Sabbath observance, changes to prayer melodies, and eventually, the fusion of the Ashkenazi and Sephardi rites into a single French rite would be the responsibility of the Central Consistory.[56] These regulations made French Judaism more like traditional Catholicism than traditional Judaism, especially in France, where differences in ritual, Hebrew pronunciation, and sacred music between Sephardim and Ashkenazim were quite pronounced.

Even though it took time before the consistories were understood as truly different from the Old Regime representative communal bodies, this hierarchical, centralized organization gave Central Consistory leaders the power to implement their vision of reform. As Phyllis Cohen Albert has persuasively argued, consistory leaders themselves had an important voice in shaping these institutions over time, successfully petitioning state authorities for changes they saw as necessary in many different instances.[57] Since all members of the Central Consistory were required to be residents of Paris, the Central Consistory's leaders all hailed from that city's Jewish elite, a group in many ways distinct from the rest of French Jewry. Most Parisian Jewish families between 1810 and the end of the 1820s were recent immigrants to the city from very different places, including Alsace, Lorraine, the former Papal States, Bordeaux, Bayonne, and central Europe. Yet in spite of great differences in their backgrounds, they were nonetheless bound to each other socially and professionally. The situation for this first generation of elite Parisian Jewish leaders was complicated. On the one hand, the city offered economic, educational, and social possibilities that were unavailable elsewhere; yet on the other hand, the persistence of anti-Jewish prejudice limited them to the professions of banking and commerce, with some noteworthy exceptions entering the liberal professions and the military. They were concentrated geographically as well, living in the neighborhood near the Bourse, north and northwest of the traditional Jewish neighborhood near the rue Saint-Avoye.[58]

The leaders of the Paris Consistory and the Central Consistory included such important bankers and merchants who had come to the city around the time of the revolution or shortly thereafter, such as Olry Worms de Romilly (b. 1759), Benjamin Rodrigues (b. 1769), Simon Mayer-Dalmbert (b. 1776), Isaac Rodrigues (b. 1771), Berr Léon Fould, Salomon Halphen (b. 1773), and Jacques Javal (b. 1781), to name only a few.[59] Although some of the men in this generation—young adults during the revolution—had little formal education themselves, many sent their children to Paris's *lycées* and *grandes écoles* in increasing numbers, beginning in the Napoleonic period. Some members of this younger generation, born between 1790 and 1810 and thus part of the well-studied "Generation of 1820," began serving as Paris and Central Consistory leaders in the 1820s. Among the children of prominent Restoration Jewish leaders who came of age in Paris in the 1820s were Olinde (b. 1795) and Eugène Rodrigues (b. 1797?), Benoît (b. 1792) and Achille Fould (b. 1800), Max (b. 1795) and Alphonse Cerfberr (b. 1797), Fromenthal (b. 1799) and Léon Halévy (b. 1802), and Léopold Javal (b. 1804). As was the case with Adolphe Crémieux (b. 1796), some provincial Jewish leaders came to Paris as young *lycée* students. Still others of this second generation of elite Jews, such as Michel Goudchaux (b. 1797), Emile (b. 1800) and Isaac Pereire (b. 1806), were children of provincial Jewish leaders who moved to Paris in the 1820s. In the capital, through their social and professional connections to elite Jews raised in Paris, these men too eventually came to play an active role in liberal social and political networks and, in the case of Goudchaux, consistory leadership, during the July Monarchy.[60]

Throughout the Restoration period, Central Consistory leaders sought to achieve a status equal to that of the Christian sects by making Judaism more fully incorporated into French public administration. This was no easy task, considering that the imperial decrees of 1808 charged the consistories with many functions reminiscent of the old *communautés*. The consistories were responsible for governing Jewish citizens in certain ways, including preparing an annual budget for religious expenses, compiling an annual tax roll listing how much each Jewish family should be taxed by the state, controlling Jewish immigration, establishing and running schools for Jewish children, building and maintaining synagogues, nominating and paying rabbis, regulating kosher slaughter, and submitting demographic information to the Ministry of the Interior about the Jewish population.[61] Moreover, because members of each departmental consistory were elected by a college of notables named on the basis of community standing and wealth, they came from the same wealthy elite families who had represented the old Jewish *communautés*.

Indeed, although the national administrative structure of the consistory system was supposed to reflect the new uniform administrative structure of the *départements*, a closer look at its fiscal organization shows astonishing continuities with the old corporate system. In spite of the Central Consistory's regular protests, until 1830 religious expenses (schools, rabbis, synagogues, etc.) were funded out of a special tax that state officials collected from the Jews living in each locality.[62] Protestants and Catholics did not have to pay an analogous tax, as their clergymen were salaried by the state and their churches owned by municipalities. This inequality only worsened over the course of the Restoration, a period in which the state doubled the budget for Catholic schools, clergy, seminaries, and church buildings.[63] Though Jewish leaders no longer collected the taxes themselves, as the administrators of the old corporate *communautés* had, they nonetheless maintained responsibility for compiling a budget of expenses, assessing the net worth of each Jewish household, and dividing the tax burden between the households by percentage. Once the total amount needed was divided among the households of the community according to their means, the list, called a *rôle de répartition*, was submitted to the local prefect, who would collect this special Jewish tax along with the regular taxes Jews owed as citizens of France. Unlike the consistories themselves, which were to map onto the political geography of the new rather than the Old Regime, the *rôles de répartition* treated each old *communauté*, rather than each department, as a fiscal unit. For example, the Marseilles Consistory compiled separate budgets and *rôles de répartition* for each of the old *communautés* under its control, such as Avignon, Carpentras, and L'Isle-sur-Sorgue, instead of dividing expenses and taxes among members of the entire department.[64]

Likewise, the Bordeaux Consistory compiled separate lists for Bordeaux, St. Esprit, Clermont, and Narbonne; and the Strasbourg Consistory compiled lists for twenty-five different communities.[65]

As a means for dividing the tax burden, the *rôle de répartition* was itself a holdover from the days of the *kehilla* and preserved the plutocratic structure of the Jewish communal life. Even the most cursory comparison of the *rôles de répartition* with the members of the departmental colleges of notables makes clear that the richest were saddled with the greatest share of the tax burden and also held the positions of leadership. With the exception of the smaller rural communities of Alsace, where there was less power to share, power remained concentrated in the wealthy elite, as it had been before the revolution.[66] The system of notables itself reinforced this continuity. These fiscal arrangements not only set Jews apart from their Christian neighbors, they also kept them organized—at least fiscally—as *solidaire* communities, who owed a single amount to an outside collector. The Jews themselves were responsible for dividing this amount within the community however they saw fit. The *rôle de répartition* created a tight social bond in which the group figured less as an association of equals than as a collective functioning toward an outside creditor as a single entity.

In keeping with the spirit of French administration, many Jewish leaders—even the wealthy ones who occupied positions of power in the Central Consistory—objected to the fact that power rested in the hands of the wealthy, regardless of merit, due to this system of taxation as well as to the two-tiered system of election. As a very young and ambitious Crémieux, not yet a member of the consistory himself, complained in a letter to a friend in 1821, "Oligarchy kills off everything it touches; it is the mother of all abuses, of all privileges, the source of all injustice. . . . I agree that we need a new religious organization. I have an idea for a new Israelite organization, so that we can abolish our indecent consistories, those useless, rodent-like bodies whose powerlessness is the least of their evils."[67] Crémieux's assessment was somewhat unfair, since Central Consistory leaders were already in the process of modernizing a number of administrative practices. First, lay leaders were selected according to new criteria. Although in practice the notables who elected members of each local consistory came from a small number of wealthy elite families, in theory participation was based on merit rather than birth. In the more cosmopolitan areas of the Napoleonic empire, like Paris and Amsterdam, Ashkenazim and Sephardim served side by side, neither group claiming domination over the administration. In an 1812 letter to the newly established consistory of Amsterdam, the Central Consistory explained how the local college of notables should choose its consistory members: "To make your choice, you should not concern yourself with whether one of our brothers spent his western sojourn in the North or the South, but only if he practices the private and social virtues and if he possesses the talents necessary for an administrator, the qualities of the heart and spirit that characterize the truly good men."[68] One's parentage was also deemed less important than merit. In 1819, when Mardochée Mévil complained to the minister of the interior that it was his right to inherit his father's place among the notables of Paris Jewry, the consistory successfully selected the more intellectual David Singer instead, arguing that notability, unlike nobility, was not inherited and was based on personal qualification.[69] This change, initiated by Central Consistory leaders, was formalized by the 1823 *ordonnance* that reformed the consistories; article 15 took steps to break the concentration of power in the hands of families. Fathers and sons, brothers, fathers- and sons-in-law, and brothers-in-law, were forbidden to serve together on a consistory.[70]

The centralization of power was another process common to both the consistory system and other parts of the French public administration. This progressively reduced the power of historically important provincial families, and at the same time served to link Jewish religious administration to the state more fully. The consistories evolved from something like a federation of communities at the time of their establishment, to a system in which all power emanated from Paris. Partially, this had to do with the government's legal categories. Though the state recognized Judaism as a legal religion and protected the religious freedom of its Jewish citizens, it made no distinction between Jews from different localities, having legally dissolved the local communities in favor of a national administrative structure. As the Central Consistory explained to the Amsterdam Consistory, "the French Government recognizes only Frenchmen of the Mosaic faith (*des français professant le culte mosaïque*)," not Sephardim, Ashkenazim, or Jews of any particular local community.[71]

The fact that the consistories were administrative bodies rather than semi-autonomous corporate entities was another factor in this process of centralization. In 1810, the Central Consistory wrote to the Strasbourg Consistory to support its efforts to "regenerate" Jews in the area by encouraging them to practice charity, and even more importantly, to enter the manual trades rather than money lending or sale of secondhand goods. The Central Consistory applauded the leaders' goals but admonished them for their rhetorical techniques, which seemed too political. The Strasbourg Consistory's tone, they said, "was more like a legislative act than an appeal to the generosity and religion of those under your administration." A "pastoral exhortation" would have been more fitting for a religious administration than this "tone of authority."[72] The Central Consistory not only expected local consistories to use a softer tone; it was also quite concerned that the vocabulary the Strasbourg Consistory used to describe itself be altered. The word *synagogue*, Central Consistory leaders explained to the Amsterdam Consistory, referred at once to "*culte*, or . . . beliefs, and to religious administration, and sometimes to the edifice in which meetings of the faithful were held," and it should not be used in a political sense, like the word *kehilla* had been.[73] Consistory administration was merely religious, and though its teachings could help Jews become better citizens, it did not represent them in the political sense.

Even clearer was the directive sent out the same year in a letter from the Central Consistory to all departmental consistories. Although the consistories were supposed to maintain order, members of the Central Consistory wrote, they were not allowed to levy fines or impose penalties on Jewish individuals, because consistories were not courts. Consistories could watch over Jewish citizens, they could instruct them and even report or bring delinquents to higher authorities, they could set rules in the synagogue and maintain order preventatively, but they could not judge or punish them. Furthermore, neither rabbis personally nor the consistories as institutions were allowed to collect taxes from Jewish citizens, even for purposes like education or charity, since consistories were only intended to regulate Jewish religious life, not supplement the Jewish tax by collecting extra money from the congregants.[74]

This last clarification points to a major problem the consistories faced until the 1830 revolution. With neither the power to collect taxes nor the right to state support for their rabbis and charity, consistories simply did not have the funds to meet their needs, much less "regenerate" the Jews of France through religious education in schools and public worship, as they were expected to do. From the fact that this letter itself was printed rather than handwritten, and that it synthesized a whole set of related questions from several different consistories, it is likely that the letter was intended to be read not only by members of the departmental consistories but also by administrators in the Ministry of the Interior as a way of calling attention to their plight.

Central Consistory members raised the issue of their need for greater support more directly to various officials and legislators on several occasions. In 1816, they wrote to the minister of the interior to complain that the King's plan to "reestablish public morality" by making primary education available to all did not provide for Jewish children as well as Christian children, and this, like the refusal to pay the rabbis' salaries, violated the Charte's promise of legal equality for all citizens regardless of religion. "It is . . . in the highest interest of the state to take its subjects of all classes out of the miserable condition of ignorance and irreligion in which they find themselves, for these are the most fertile sources of depravity, the worst scourge of society," they wrote.[75] In 1819, they raised the issue before the Chamber of Deputies, arguing that the Jewish tax was not only insufficient to cover religious expenses; it was illegal because it identified a certain class of citizens as "Jews" in the law, which was an assault on their religious freedom and their legal equality. Much to the Central Consistory members' chagrin, the majority of deputies saw otherwise and refused to cover Jewish religious expenses in the state budget, on the grounds that if Jews were too indifferent to cover their expenses personally, this was not the state's concern.[76] This response must have been particularly insulting to consistory leaders, since it implied that Jews, unlike Christians, were outside the common order. As was clear in their

1816 letter regarding education, Central Consistory leaders agreed with the king that religiosity was a cornerstone to civic life and thus something that needed to be fostered by the state through proper support of religious education and public worship. To deny such support to the Jews would be to define them as a community apart. The issue would never be resolved to Jewish leaders' satisfaction under the Restoration; only with the establishment of the July Monarchy in 1830 were Central Consistory members finally able to convince the Ministry of the Interior to include its expenses on its annual budget.[77]

Consistory leaders' creative response to the practical financial problems they were facing in the Restoration period sheds additional light on their changing conception of Jewish institutions. Between 1810 and the end of the 1820s, consistory leaders in Bordeaux and Paris devised a new method—the sale of interest-bearing bonds, to be repaid from the Jewish tax funds—to generate the large amounts of money needed to build new synagogues that the government refused to fund directly. The fund-raising plan represented a departure from common practice of the eighteenth-century French Jewish *communautés*, in which a wealthy community leader (or group of leaders) might have purchased the land in his own name and built a synagogue upon it as an act of charity, or even more often, built a communal prayer room in his own house.[78] This plan was quite different. It was first proposed by the consistory of Bordeaux in 1809 in order to raise eighty thousand francs to build a synagogue, and was carried out after the minister of worship approved it in 1810. Under the plan, the Bordeaux Consistory created bonds (*actions*), in the amounts of four thousand, three thousand, two thousand, one thousand, and five hundred francs, for the initial capital. These bonds would earn 5 percent interest each year, the legal rate of interest established by Napoleon.[79] The Bordeaux Consistory used the tax money collected by *répartition* to pay the interest and buy back two of the bonds—selected by lottery—each year until the entire amount was repaid. This method essentially guaranteed that the creditors would earn back at least the amount of money they had invested plus 5 percent per year; potentially, if their bond was the last reimbursed, they could double their investment.[80]

Although the investment was a decent one, it was mainly Bordeaux Jews and not investors at large who participated in the financing of the synagogue. Buying shares was probably understood as a duty of faithful synagogue goers rather than as a way to increase one's wealth. Names of the wealthiest Jews of Bordeaux, primarily concentrated in long-distance trade and banking, filled the long list of bond holders. Among them were the three lay members of the Bordeaux Consistory, Lopès-Dubec (the president), Rodrigues aîné (Benjamin Rodrigues, b. 1769, who would soon relocate to Paris and serve on the Central Consistory), and David Gradis, as well as other wealthy notables including Alexandre, Fonsèque, Dacosta, Astruc, Furtado, and Raba. When additional bonds were issued in February 1810, a number of Sephardi Jews living in Paris bought shares as well, bringing the total value of bonds issued to 114,000 francs. Interestingly, in this February round, a large number were purchased by Rachel Pereire in the name of her recently deceased brother, Isaac Rodrigues Pereire (1771–1806), whose sons Emile (b. 1800) and Isaac (b. 1806) would eventually move to Paris and use a similar kind of strategy (minus the lottery), by then a common practice in industrial development, on a much larger scale to finance railroad development beginning in the 1830s.[81]

The use of bonds does not represent a complete shift in Jewish practices, since the Bordeaux Consistory still relied on its wealthy members to supply the initial capital, and later relied on the *rôle de répartition* to pay off the bond debt. Nonetheless, it is a clear departure from eighteenth-century practice and speaks to the involvement of Bordeaux Jews in the greater world of French finance, where this kind of transaction was typical. The sale of *actions* was less common for financing public works like this one. Yet it was not unheard of. Although the Jewish *nation* of Bordeaux had relied on charity for communal expenses of this sort, the eighteenth-century French state had used *rentes* (government bonds), and in some cases, had repaid the bonds through lottery, an arrangement meant to appeal to the contemporary taste for games.[82] Financing public works in France with bonds would become standard practice during the July Monarchy and the Second Empire, when railroads and canals were built in this way.[83] Associated with French public works and private financing rather than with traditional Jewish communal practices, the Bordeaux synagogue fund-raising plan represented an important step in transforming Jewish institutional life and rooting it more fully in the French context.

In addition, using this new fund-raising method allowed the Bordeaux Consistory to meet its goal of elevating the place of Judaism in French public life. The fact that many of the bond holders were clearly wealthy enough to have given this money as charity is a key factor to consider here. Why did they not donate the money outright, as an act of charity, as had been common practice in the old *communautés*? The key difference may be that this financing plan allowed the synagogue to be paid for, ultimately, through tax money. Though many of the Bordeaux Jews were wealthy privately, the consistory was poor, since it relied on Jewish tax money for its expenses, and as the complaints of the consistories in the northern regions in 1810 suggest, these taxes were insufficient to cover rabbis' salaries, charity, and synagogue maintenance. Thus, the bond sale was a kind of loan that made it possible to build an expensive building that was truly public—paid for by taxpayers—rather than privately owned or even the charitable donation of a wealthy person. In addition, it effectively made the synagogue the property of the Bordeaux Consistory, while preserving that body's role as an arm of the state rather than a separate institution with its own funds. Thus this fund-raising method kept the consistories from a task they were reluctant to assume: collecting taxes themselves. By meeting all of these goals, the plan testifies to their desire to give Judaism a greater place in public life without having separate institutions, and also speaks to their belief that Jewish religious life was the responsibility of the state rather than of private charity.

This interpretation can help us to understand what was at stake in the Paris Consistory's travails surrounding the financing and ownership of its synagogue. Inspired by the Bordeaux Consistory's synagogue finance plan, the Paris Consistory proposed a similar plan to finance its new consistorial synagogue on the rue Notre-Dame de Nazareth in the Saint-Avoye neighborhood. In 1819, when the landlord failed to renew the lease on its existing space, the Paris Consistory was granted royal permission to build a new synagogue through the sale of interest-bearing bonds to be repaid though a yearly lottery; the new building was completed in 1822.[84] Unfortunately, the Paris Consistory could not have predicted the problems that were to arise after 1830, when the special Jewish tax was abolished and the Jewish budget was incorporated into the state budget. In this first year, the consistory received only a paltry sum from the state, and additional money came only from charitable contributions, the sale of synagogue honors, and membership dues (*location de places*, or seat rental). With this, the synagogue could cover its basic needs, but could not continue to pay either the interest or the capital on the 131,500 francs worth of bond debt it still owed. As early as December 1830, the Paris Consistory and the Central Consistory wrote to the minister of worship to remind him of the outstanding bond debt and to ask for help in repaying it, but they received no response.[85] In February 1831, they asked the minister of worship to continue to impose the special tax on the Jews of the Seine department for seven years until the debt was paid; again, they were ignored.[86] Without the help of the government, the synagogue administration was left to its own devices to raise the money. Throughout the 1830s, it unsuccessfully asked synagogue goers for charitable contributions to this end, but with no success, and by 1837, some bond holders were threatening to initiate legal proceedings to recover the interest they were owed.[87] Finally, in 1839, the Central Consistory turned to the Seine prefecture, offering the city ownership of the building, along with responsibility for its debts. Although this plan was by no means inconceivable, since the city already owned Catholic and Protestant churches, it was nevertheless rejected.[88] Only in 1840 did the government finally decide how to handle the problem. It included three thousand francs in its 1841 budget for the express purpose of paying off the synagogue's outstanding debt; the amount increased each year, and the debt was finally paid off in 1846.[89] In 1849, with no bonds outstanding, the Paris Consistory donated the synagogue building to the city of Paris.[90] Like the creation of the bond plan itself, the consistory's attempts to have the bond debt paid by the state rather than through charity, as well as the eventual decision to donate the building to the city, serve as further evidence that Jewish synagogues were increasingly considered the property and the responsibility of the state, rather than of the Jewish "community" as a separate entity.

The Central Consistory's efforts to have its administrative budget absorbed by the state represented an opposition to corporatism, much as the campaigns to achieve full legal equality had been. This incorporation into the state administrative apparatus, including its budget, Central Consistory members were quick to point out, was guaranteed by the principle of equality before the law. "Frenchmen are Protestant, Catholic, or Jewish before God," they wrote in one such protest, but "they are Frenchmen before the law. The law cannot oblige certain Frenchmen to pay a religious tax."[91] In theory, the new organization of the consistories would facilitate regeneration by teaching Jews the civic values of the new state. In practice, it unified and redefined French Judaism, involving provincial elites in the administration of the Jewish religion while progressively centralizing the decision-making process. Through this institutional overhaul, Judaism was becoming identified with the state, an agency whose task was to provide Jewish citizens the moral education and opportunities for worship that the king himself had said that all citizens needed.

Although the Jewish consistories always remained to some degree anomalous in French public administration, the way that Restoration Jewish leaders conceived them shows the influence of Restoration liberal theory. In the 1820s, the *doctrinaires* François Guizot, Prosper Barante, and Pierre-Paul Royer-Collard elaborated a theory that they believed would solidify the gains of the revolution by assuring both a stable form of state power and individual liberties. The influence of Guizot is particularly apparent in the final form the Jewish consistories would take. After the July Monarchy incorporated Jewish expenses into its budget, the consistories truly became less like Old Regime corporations and more like the official bodies of state-sanctioned "experts" who worked with the state on matters related to some field of social life, without such responsibilities as taxation and policing. These institutions, which Guizot had been imagining as potential pillars of social stability since the early 1820s, included a range of groups, some already in existence and some created only in the 1830s, including chambers of commerce, *conseils supérieurs* (teams of experts in agriculture, industry, and other fields officially named to work with the state on policies related to these areas), and learned societies. These institutions were meant to function as teams of experts lending a voice to the state's "direct" governance of its citizens. In this model of governance, power is both centralized and diffuse, since it is grounded in a network of associations that recapitulate some of the functions of the old corporations without, however, compromising individual freedoms by representing citizens in their relations with the state.[92] Much as in this *doctrinaire* conception of administration, Jewish leaders sought to have their social power recognized, without taking on the task of identifying, policing, representing, or taxing a designated subgroup within the broader community of citizens. The story of the transformation of Jewish institutional life is thus part of the broader story of the establishment of French liberalism in the same period.

The Impact of Liberalism on Jewish Thought

Jewish leaders' struggles to have Jewish institutions fully incorporated within the state rested on their view of the proper relationship between religions and the state in a constitutional monarchy. Like other liberals, Restoration Jewish leaders envisioned a society in which the authoritarian Catholicism celebrated by the *ultras* would no longer be a political force. Yet religiosity was nonetheless important in the education of citizens, in the maintenance of social stability, and in the legitimization of state power. Like other liberals of their day, these Parisian Jewish leaders saw religion as playing an important social role, teaching respect for the constitution and the individual liberties it guaranteed without causing social fracturing. Adding their voices to the struggle against the *ultras*, Jewish leaders portrayed Judaism as a religion with a dignity and a beauty equal to Christianity, and a universal moral code appropriate for educating citizens. Typified by the Central Consistory's 1816 letter seeking state support for their schools, Jewish leaders' arguments about the role of Judaism in public life thus served not only to reform the consistories and regularize Jews' legal status in France, but in addition, a small but significant number of Parisian Jewish leaders used this issue to contribute their voices to the larger effort of building a liberal model of state secularism.

Throughout the Restoration, liberals and *ultras* alike agreed that religion was needed for political and social stability; yet the two groups strongly disagreed on the question of whether ultimate authority lay with the Church or with the Charte. Thinkers and politicians in the *ultra* camp were not satisfied with the return of Catholicism to its former place as the official religion of the state; they also sought to reunite Throne and Altar, bringing temporal power back to the Church. In this quest, *ultra* politicians cited such works as Joseph de Maistre's *Considerations sur la France* (1796), Louis de Bonald's *Théorie du pouvoir politique et religieux* (1797) and his *Législation primitive* (1802), and Félicité de Lamennais' *Essai sur l'indifférence en matière de religion* (1817), all of which argued that Catholicism alone provided a firm basis for social and political life. Lamennais' book, which argued that a solid social foundation could be found only under the strict authority of the Church, was particularly influential, since it appeared just as a new concordat with the pope was being negotiated.[93] For their part, liberals also saw religiosity as an important backbone of social stability. However, they argued that true religiosity was stifled by authoritarian Catholicism, and that the Charte's guarantee of freedom of conscience would allow religious expression to flower and thereby improve society by providing a firm moral foundation for public life. The Protestant Benjamin Constant was perhaps the most influential and persuasive of liberals in the first years of the Restoration to advance arguments of this sort, and his views were widely shared.[94]

Jewish publications in French between 1815 and 1820 are consonant with the perspective of Constant and his allies. The writings of Elie Halévy (1760–1826) are particularly illustrative in this regard. A scholar, journalist, cantor, and composer, Halévy was the son of a rabbi from Fürth, Bavaria, who moved to Paris in 1798 by way of Metz, where he married Julie Mayer (1781–1819). In Paris, the couple had two sons, the composer Fromenthal and the writer Léon, as well as three daughters, Esther-Zélie (b. 1801), Flore (b. 1805), and Mélanie (b. 1813).[95] In 1817 and 1818, Halévy and Central Consistory member Simon Mayer-Dalmbert published the first French-language Jewish newspaper, *L'Israélite Français*. Its timing, short run, and tone suggest that the journal's purpose was connected to the Infamous Decree; the journal was designed to show that Jews were upright citizens and that there would thus be no need to renew the decree when it expired in 1818. To this end, Halévy depicted Judaism as a universalist religion and argued that allowing it full freedom would guarantee social stability. Emphasizing that both Jews and Christians worshipped the same God, Halévy showed that it was possible to be Jewish *and* to be a citizen of a modern Catholic state based on universalist values laid out in a written constitution. This argument drew heavily on the insights of *maskilim* of the previous generation such Moses Mendelssohn, whom Halévy had known in Germany.[96]

Halévy emphasized the value of Jewish education in instilling civic virtues in Jewish youth, making them good citizens, much as Berr Isaac Berr had in the emancipation period. In one article, Halévy wrote, "In all parts of the civilized world, religion is highly tied to instruction. . . . Rarely does a man with a religious education become a dangerous citizen; perhaps more rare in fact is the man who, educated without religious principles, becomes a good citizen, useful to his state and his neighbors."[97] Elsewhere, he analyzed the basic principles of the Jewish religion in greater depth to show exactly why a Jewish education would produce good citizens: "The entire vast edifice [of our religion] . . . ," he wrote, "is constructed on love alone. 'Love your God, love your parents and your neighbor,' this is the law, this is the sublime law that guided our fathers, that still guides us today, and will always guide us, whatever our destiny may be."[98] In 1820, Halévy wrote a book for Jewish children's education entitled *Instruction religieuse et morale à l'usage de la jeunesse israélite*, which the Central Consistory adopted as its official catechism. Printed in Hebrew and French, the text was aimed at the new generation of French-speaking Jews. Halévy, like the members of the Paris Sanhedrin, stressed fraternity and compassion toward all others as the fundamental morality of

Judaism, and even included the Sanhedrin's answers to Napoleon's twelve questions as an appendix.[99]

Largely inspired by the ideas of the German-speaking *maskilim*, it is important to note that Halévy's depiction of Judaism also resembled Catholicism as Lamennais described it in *Essai sur l'indifférence en matière de religion*. As described in their respective works, both religions could be boiled down to the precepts of love for the neighbor and submission to authority. In addition to emphasizing the commonality between the basic principles of the two religions, Halévy also demonstrated that he agreed with the Catholic king's belief that a civil society needs religion to hold society together. Religion, he wrote, "is the indissoluble tie between the Creator and the reasonable creature; it is the eternal law which conserves human societies."[100] Not only were Catholicism and Judaism teaching the same law; they were both social religions necessary for the well-being of a modern state. This engagement with Lamennais' book suggests that Halévy was not merely repeating arguments made in a previous generation; his rhetorical strategy of likening Judaism to Lamennais' Catholicism was meant to persuade readers that Catholicism was not the only religion worthy of dignity and official status in France.

Arguments such as Halévy's not only supported the Central Consistory's work to achieve fuller state support; they also contributed to the broader struggle of Restoration liberals to build a new relationship between religions and the state. As the clerical party sought and received greater support for the clergy and Catholic education, liberals looked for ways to describe constitutional rule and free inquiry in equally commanding ways. In 1821, Guizot went so far as to claim that "freedom of conscience is itself the religious idea of our day."[101] As part of the *Société de la morale chrétienne*, he also worked to bridge the divide between Catholics and Protestants on the basis of his belief that the true spirit of Christianity fostered religious liberty.[102] In arguing that Judaism taught civic virtues just as well, Restoration Jewish leaders participated in the quest to find alternative, but nonetheless religious, grounds for the legitimating constitutional rather than divine-right governance in France. Given this shared vision, it makes perfect sense that their struggle to have the consistories' budget incorporated in the state budget was finally successful following the revolution of 1830, when the opposition liberals from the 1820s came to power.

Even more overtly than Elie Halévy, the writer Joseph Salvador contributed to this greater liberal cause. The son of a Jewish man and a Catholic woman, the Montpellier-born Joseph Salvador (1796–1873) probably had little Jewish education, using French and Latin translations of Hebrew texts in his writings. Graduating from the medical school of Montpellier in 1816, Salvador soon moved to Paris, where he pursued a career as a writer.[103] Salvador's originality of vision was unmatched; throughout his career, he wrote works that systematically tied the question of Jewish status to the broader question of the relationship between religions and the French state. In his first two books, a preparatory study, *Loi de Moïse* (1822) and a much longer work, *Histoire des institutions de Moïse et du peuple hébreux* (1828), Salvador analyzed the ancient Jewish state and its legal foundations, arguing that ancient Jewish law was the first social code. For Salvador, the Jews were historically important because they were the first people to develop the philanthropic and just social legislation that modern social theorists sought to create in the wake of the French Revolution. In his discussion of the ancient Jewish state, Salvador claimed that the law was a creation of Moses—perceiving what was best for the public—rather than coming from God.[104] In its rejection of revelation, Salvador's argument represents a major departure from Mendelssohn. While Mendelssohn—in the spirit of rabbinical tradition—had maintained that the source of Jewish law was divine and revealed, Salvador explained it with reference to Rousseau's social contract theory. He wrote, "Moses said 'there is only a people where there is a law,' and to give birth to the law, a general will is necessary, a general agreement freely and clearly expressed." The "génie israélite" for Salvador was that they had the most "sublime pact" of any nation, whose "sole imperfection was that it did not include humanity in its entirety."[105]

From its reception in the liberal press, it is clear that Salvador's work was understood to be about more than just Judaism. Liberal readers in the 1820s saw Salvador's work as making a strong case for the primacy of constitutionalism over divine-right monarchical government. In its review of the *Loi de Moïse*, for example, the liberal newspaper *Le Constitutionnel* argued that the book proved that constitutional rule was older and thus more authoritative than Catholicism, and that the book thus represented an ideological triumph of the liberal camp.[106] *Le Globe*, the liberal journal founded by Pierre Leroux and, in this period, edited by Charles de Rémusat, gave a warm reception to Salvador's work, lauding it as remaining true both to Judaism and to the Enlightenment. Rémusat, in the process of making a name for himself as the defender of religious liberty in all its forms by defending even the Jesuits' religious freedom, went so far as to push Salvador's argument in an even more radical direction. Characterizing Salvador's intention as identifying the republic of Hebrews with a republican or constitutional France rather than a theocracy, he criticized this goal as overly facile. Instead, he urged him to imagine that some theocracies might in fact foster liberty: "The dominant thought in Salvador's work is to have seen that the Republic of Hebrews was never a theocracy. But is a blind and empty despotism the inevitable consequence of a theocracy? No; no more than freedom is necessarily produced by republican forms."[107]

In this critique, Rémusat was not rejecting Salvador's work; rather, he was attempting to push his argument in a more radical direction, toward the new kind of theocratic thinking that he and others on the left were beginning to articulate. By the late 1820s, a range of men in the overlapping circles around the *Globe* newspaper and the Saint-Simonian movement were experimenting with reclaiming the concept of theocracy from the divine-right clerical party for their own liberal political agenda. Pierre Leroux, Rémusat's collaborator at *Le Globe*, would eventually develop a democratic political agenda fully grounded in a nontraditional Christianity redesigned for the modern age. Such theocratic thinking on the left became commonplace in the 1830s, and was especially powerful in movements that involved the working class.[108]

Saint-Simonians were the first left-wing group to counter the clerical party with a fully articulated new theology meant to add spiritual legitimacy to the gains of the revolution; their ideas about the relationship of religions with the state also resonated with those of Jewish leaders. The movement was founded in 1825 by a group of students and recent graduates of the Ecole Polytechnique at the time of the death of their revered mentor, the Count Henri de Saint-Simon.[109] Beginning in the late 1820s, this cluster of young men envisioned a new religion for France, a "New Christianity," that would teach all humanity social values, as Christianity had attempted to do in the past.

In spite of its name, the "New Christianity" of the Saint-Simonians had much in common with the kind of French state secularism that Jewish leaders envisioned. Indeed, Olinde and Eugène Rodrigues, who played key roles in developing the movement's theological outlook, were the sons of the banker Isaac Rodrigues ("Rodrigues fils" in consistory documents), who had been the secretary of the Paris Sanhedrin and had taken an active role in the consistory's campaign against the renewal of the Infamous Decree in 1818.[110] Other Jews involved in the Saint-Simonian movement in its early years were also connected through family or work to the consistory leadership, including Olinde and Eugène's sisters Amélie and Mélanie, their cousins Emile and Isaac Pereire, Léon Halévy, Gustave d'Eichthal (b. 1804), and Edouard (b. 1797) and Henry Rodrigues (b. 1799?).[111]

Saint-Simonian theology was based on the teachings of Saint-Simon, but it was more fully elaborated by his prolific followers in their newspapers *Le Producteur* and *L'Organisateur*, and later, *Le Globe*, which Leroux turned over to the movement in 1831, as well as in numerous speeches and pamphlets. In the late 1820s, the followers most involved in elaborating this theology included, in addition to the Rodrigues brothers, Etienne Bailly, Emile Barrault, Saint-Amand Bazard, Philippe-Joseph-Benjamin Buchez, J. B. Duvergier, Barthélemy-Prosper Enfantin, Léon Halévy, P. M. Laurent de l'Ardeche, and Emile Pereire. These religious ideas were explicitly designed to replace Catholicism in the new age, which had been ushered in by the French Revolution. As Catholicism had served as the spiritual foundation for the Old Regime's system of inheritance, the New Christianity was intended to serve as the foundation for a new temporal world order. Like the Catholicism it was meant to replace, the New Christianity was built on the ideals of love, hierarchy, and the emancipation of the oppressed. The temporal system built upon it was industrialized, centralized, and hierarchical, but this hierarchy was based on merit rather than inheritance. The new order was to be run through a divinely legitimated state, which, by controlling industry, credit, and faith in a single administration, would, in Saint-Simon's words, "bring the greatest good to the greatest number."[112] Saint-Simonians were explicit about the kinds of political and economic institutions they saw as most important. State administration, railroads, and credit institutions were all crucial for creating good social relations and breaking down the old barriers that the system of inherited power had erected.

Saint-Simonians theologians agreed with the Restoration Jewish leadership on a number of crucial points. Indeed, not only were several young Jews connected to the consistory leadership involved in articulating its platform; consistory leaders themselves seem to have been interested in the movement before 1830. Olry Worms de Romilly, Central Consistory president and one of Paris's wealthiest Jews, had even bought shares in the movement's first newspaper, the *Producteur*, in 1825.[113] This support is understandable given the consistory leaders' outlook on a number of key issues, including the role of the state in society; the opposition to the system of inheritance; the place of traditional Catholicism in French politics; and the relationship between religions and the state. Like consistory leaders, the Saint-Simonians saw the French Revolution as a distinct point in world history, after which the religious boundaries that divided people had begun to erode. In place of these old distinctions and the Catholicism upon which it was based, a new ideology would be established, in which people of different faiths would be treated equally by a new kind of state apparatus which embodied religious ideas. Saint-Simonians and consistory leaders alike saw the inclusive ideology emerging in France since the revolution as dependent upon practical structures that would teach new social values.

The 1820s saw a flowering of liberal theories on the relationship between religions and the state that may, in certain respects, appear strange to readers today. Far from excluding religiosity from the public arena, they sought to ground the new order in a new religious system that gave spiritual force to its social, economic, and political goals and would educate a new generation of citizens and thereby bring lasting peace to a society recently torn apart by revolution. In this way, the *doctrinaires*, the Saint-Simonians, and Restoration consistory leaders shared a basic view of how religious life for Jews as well as Christians would be changed in the nineteenth century. At last, both groups believed, a world order was being established in which Jews and Christians would be equal before the law, free to worship as they wished, and to learn, through their different religious traditions, to show their feelings of brotherhood toward each other. This new system did not entail barring religion from the public arena, but rather, creating a new ideology and state apparatus that supported and incorporated both Judaism and Christianity.

Conclusion

Jewish emancipation in France was a much slower process than a study of revolutionary discourse alone would ever reveal. It took almost forty more years of consistent appeals by the consistory leadership before French Jews would finally be free from some of the most pernicious forms of communal solidarity, such as the inherited communal debts, special legislation, and special taxation. The Central Consistory saw its battle to eradicate these forms of corporatism as part of the larger transformation liberals and other groups emerging on the political left were trying to effect in France as a whole, where new principles of organization were beginning to replace inheritance.

It would be a mistake to read the story of French Jewish leaders' commitment to emancipation as the establishment of a strict separation between private realm of faith and public realm of abstract citizenship. In the struggle to free themselves from the remnants of corporate organization, French Jews affirmed that their religious beliefs and practices were private and without legal standing; and yet at the same time, they argued that Judaism as a religion was of great public importance and as such, the fiscal and administrative responsibility of the state. At the heart of this campaign was a notion that in the post-revolutionary state, Judaism and Christianity alike had a social purpose, and that the administration of both religions should thus be seen as part of the state. Based on this belief, Jewish leaders worked to make the consistories distinct from the Old Regime *communautés* and more firmly rooted in the French state.

As the Central and Paris Consistory leadership conceived it, the new organization of Judaism was a national organization, in which local centers were no longer meaningful except as administrative units. The Parisian Jewish elite who controlled the consistory system thought of Judaism as a single set of beliefs rather than as a set of differentiated communities each with their own representatives and ways of life. The system of financing new synagogues by the sale of bonds rather than charitable donations fit well within the framework of the nationalization of Judaism. This new practice shows that Jews had begun to free themselves from the solidarity of the old *communautés*, without abandoning their religion. The synagogue they helped finance ultimately became public property, because they believed that Judaism's purpose was fundamentally tied to the state that governed them.

In addition, through their struggles to free themselves from these last remnants of corporate solidarity, this group of Parisian Jewish leaders participated in a broader discussion among liberals about how to establish a new relationship between religions and the state that, unlike authoritarian Catholicism, would guarantee individual rights without compromising social stability. The influence of liberal ideas, which Parisian Jews encountered in their process of integration, can be seen clearly in Crémieux's legal battles, the synagogue finance plans, the campaign against the Jewish tax, as well as in the writings of Halévy and Salvador. Even more remarkably, through these battles, some of these Parisian Jewish leaders began to make their voices heard in the discussions taking place in liberal circles. As the reception of Crémieux's legal arguments and Salvador's scholarship suggests, Jews' contributions to contemporary discussions about religion were met with interest by liberals seeking to replace authoritarian Catholicism with a new set of religious ideals. This interest would grow in the 1830s, as Jews and Judaism came to take on important symbolic meaning in liberal and utopian socialist discussions about how to establish a new relationship between religions and the state.

Jewish leaders' commitment to this evolving model of secularism would play an important role in the construction of Jewish international solidarity in the second half of the nineteenth century. While during the Restoration period, French Jewish leaders centered their efforts on regularizing Jews' legal status within France, in later decades, as the French state began to exert greater influence beyond its borders, Jewish leaders would seek to have the French state treat Jews equally in its foreign policy as well. In this move from the domestic to the international arena, Jewish leaders would rely on strikingly similar rhetorical and practical strategies to achieve their goals.

Three   Jewish Identities in
the Age of Romanticism

> I am not arguing here for a trifle: my client's cause is that of all
> Jews; it is my cause. Yes, it's a Jew before you, fighting for his home
> and hearth, for his faith, for the most precious of all his freedoms.
> Why then am I without fear? Why then am I so full of hope? It's
> because I am arguing for what's right, and because you are my
> Judges!
> —Adolphe Crémieux, before the Royal Court in Nîmes (1827)[1]

> As a Jewish girl, my origin gives me the power that made the weak,
> young Judith the liberator of a people; it gives me the inspired love
> that made the beautiful Esther a wise and courageous Queen. I am
> a child of the Orient; the sun that burns our countries and formed
> my heart endowed me with an instinct that makes me fight the cold
> calculations of a world in which you manage life only by shrinking
> back from it. What a trustworthy guide my conscience is! And I
> have but one feeling for the false proprieties of a society guided by
> interest: pity!
> —Eugénie Foa, in her novel *La Juive* (1835)[2]

In quotations such as these, highly acculturated French Jews born
around 1800 proclaimed their Jewishness proudly and theatrically on
the French public stage, assuming the sympathy of their intended audiences. Rather than hiding their Jewishness or making it irrelevant to
their professional lives, many members of this first generation of Jews
educated in French schools, entering new professions, and participating in mainstream political movements made their Jewishness a
key element of the public personae they crafted for themselves. Path-
breakers like Adolphe Crémieux, the writer Eugénie Foa (1796–1853?),
the composer Fromenthal Halévy (1799–1862), the writer Léon Halévy   81
(1802–83), and the Saint-Simonians Olinde Rodrigues (1795–1851) and
Gustave d'Eichthal (1804–86) affirmed their Jewishness proudly in such

places as the courtroom, Saint-Simonian meetings, and the pages of liberal newspapers, romantic novels, and popular operas and plays. Acculturated as these young Jews were, they claimed to belong to a long-suffering race whose origin lay far from France and which was now dispersed all over the globe. Crafted to be meaningful to the French reading public of the 1830s, the Jewishness claimed by these young innovators was an innate moral sensibility, felt deeply and personally; it was decidedly exotic and oriental, ancient and strong, yet French and modern as well. As the quotations above illustrate, these characteristics were not portrayed as in conflict with one another. Above all, their Jewish identity was expressed as an abiding sense of justice connected at once to the French Revolution—which they defined as having liberated the Jews from oppression—and to a revelation more ancient than Catholicism.

More fully rooted in secular social networks than their parents had been, many of the young and economically privileged Parisian Jews who forged this identity had been socialized and educated from a very young age—often before reaching the age of ten—in Parisian *lycées* rather than in separate Jewish schools. As a result, they were far better integrated into French social and political life than their parents, even though, due to the persistence of anti-Jewish prejudice in other professions, they were still concentrated in banking and finance. With their high level of integration, these young members of the Parisian Jewish elite were by no means representative of the majority of French Jews, who remained culturally and socially separate from their gentile neighbors. Yet distinct as they were, acculturation did not make these young Jews break from their own families. On the contrary, their parents had sent them to these schools and supported them in their later endeavors.[3] Among the children of prominent Parisian Restoration Jewish leaders who comprised this small but dynamic cohort were Foa, the Halévys, Olinde Rodrigues and his brother Eugène; July Monarchy deputy and Second Empire senator Achille Fould (1800–1867); *Gymnase* theater manager Alphonse Cerfberr (1797–1859); his brother-in-law and cousin, July Monarchy deputy and Central Consistory president Colonel Max Cerfberr (1795–1876); and Léopold Javal (1804–72), the banker largely responsible for the development of the Parisian *om-*

nibus. As was the case with Crémieux, some of them had been sent to Paris from the provinces to attend a *lycée*, living as *internes* in boarding houses and spending their days off from school with school friends or relatives in the capital. Still others—Second Republic finance minister Michel Goudchaux (1797–1862) and the Crédit Mobilier founders Emile Pereire (1800–1872) and his brother Isaac Pereire (1806–80)—came as young adults to Paris, where, through their social and professional connections, they too eventually came to play an active role in liberal, republican, and socialist circles. As a result, these innovators shared the tastes, social attitudes, and the political perspectives of the Generation of 1820, whose utopian sensibilities provided both the intellectual backbone and the personnel for the revolutions of 1830 and 1848.

This chapter examines what expressions like Crémieux's and Foa's meant in the particular contexts in which they were uttered, because as Michael Graetz's work shows, it was Jews speaking in similar terms in these same integrated contexts who would forge the new form of Jewish internationalism that would emerge after 1840.[4] More influenced by the political and cultural currents around them than by Jewish tradition, the Jews who crafted the identity this chapter will examine were well integrated into the French "Generation of 1820." Following Alan Spitzer, I use this term to refer to the world of prominent, intellectually and politically active, *lycée*-educated youth, born between 1790 and 1810, who came to dominate French public life beginning in the 1820s. As Spitzer shows, members of this social network may not have had uniform political views or literary tastes, but they did have a strong sense of themselves as a distinct group, living lives very different from those of earlier generations. In important ways, these men and women thus felt more connected to each other than they were to their ancestors. Among the ranks of this group were Romantic literary stars like Victor Hugo, Alphonse de Lamartine, and Alfred de Vigny; political visionaries like Prosper Enfantin and Pierre Leroux; intellectuals like Victor Cousin, Jules Michelet, and Auguste Comte; and politicians like Adolphe Thiers. In part because of their rejection of the social conventions of past generations, the contributions of Jews and Protestants were met with great interest in this group's political movements, newspapers, creative endeavors, and social gatherings.

The images Jews projected of themselves in these settings were intended to serve as symbols in the debates that were taking place in this period. In the 1830s, liberals and utopian socialists remained concerned about the role of religion in public life, seeing the new political, economic, and social world they inhabited as needing a new form of spirituality to replace the authoritarian Catholicism of traditional France. In that context, Jews presented themselves in such a way as to glorify the revolutionary tradition and its contemporary self-proclaimed heirs, by depicting their very presence in the arenas where they were speaking as testament to the universally liberating spirit of the new order. Critical of traditional religious institutions, but wary of atheism and individualistic liberalism, the Jews of the Generation of 1820 wanted to help craft a religiosity that could include everyone without compromising their freedom or their racial distinctiveness, unlike the separatist Judaism or the oppressive Catholicism of the past. To this end, they showcased their Jewishness as a sign of the universality and moral righteousness of the new ideology they helped to construct. The cosmopolitanism of this new Jewish identity was also meaningful, signifying that although the new world order was born in France with the revolution, it was intended to be extended everywhere. Reframing their Jewishness in this way, the Jews of the Generation of 1820 set the stage for the rise of Jewish internationalism by imaginatively connecting their own emancipation to that of Jews everywhere, and by seeking to make the amelioration of the position of Jews all over the world a central concern for the French liberal and utopian socialist agenda.

The Jewish Presence in the Saint-Simonian Movement

Of all the sites of secular sociability frequented by the members of the Generation of 1820, the internationalist, utopian socialist Saint-Simonian movement was the first in which Jewish members expressed a form of Jewish identity comfortably and proudly, making it relevant to the group's overall agenda. Because of their education, the Jewish Saint-Simonians were highly integrated into secular social networks, but they also maintained close ties to their families, who were among the Parisian Jewish banking elite. Proud as they were of being Jewish, these Saint-Simonians defined their identities in a way that made far more sense to others in the Generation of 1820 than it did to Jews in a more traditional setting. Defining their Jewishness as an inborn, racial identity that linked them at once to both ancient revelation and modern financial knowledge, the Jewish Saint-Simonians described their equal participation in the group as an important sign of their movement's moral superiority to the Catholicism it sought to supersede, as well as of the global scope of the world order they sought to construct. Crafted initially to glorify the movement in the eyes of the liberal reading public of the 1830s, this same symbolism would appear in later decades in left-wing rhetoric about the French state itself, as former Saint-Simonians and those influenced by this movement made their way into positions of power in mainstream French political life.

It is perhaps because the Saint-Simonians as a whole welcomed their Jewish members' expressions of Jewish identity and saw them as meaningful in light of the movement's overall purpose that the group has so often been characterized as "Jewish" by both admirers and detractors, even though in sheer numbers Jews comprised only a tiny fraction of its total membership. Founded in 1825 by Olinde Rodrigues following the death of Henri de Saint-Simon, the Saint-Simonians sought to transform European social, political, economic, and religious life by elaborating their master's ideas systematically, spreading them to all who would listen, and attempting to put them into practice. Rodrigues and his neighbor and former classmate Léon Halévy had been disciples of Saint-Simon when he was alive; after his death, the inner circle also included a handful of other Jews: Olinde's brother Eugène and his sisters Amélie and Mélanie, their cousins Emile and Isaac Pereire (in addition, Emile married Olinde's sister Rachel) and their friend Gustave d'Eichthal (whose father Louis had worked for decades with Olinde's father Isaac Rodrigues, Olry Worms de Romilly, the Foulds, and Abraham Mendelssohn). A few others were also involved, but in a much more limited way.[5]

Given their education and socialization, it is not surprising that the Jewish identity these young Jews crafted was more legible to an audience fluent in utopian socialist and liberal language than it was to a more traditional Jewish one. Even though they all hailed from the Restoration Jewish elite and enjoyed the support of their families in their endeavors, the Jewish Saint-Simonians were educated in secular institutions and appear to have known little about traditional Jewish life.[6] Olinde Rodrigues' background is a case in point. The son of Isaac Rodrigues (1771–1846), the wealthy banker and Central Consistory leader originally from Bordeaux, Olinde reported that his father "wanted to make [him] a man of the future and not of the past; never did [he, Olinde] practice Jewish rituals."[7] Olinde, a graduate of the Lycée Charlemagne who worked for a time as a tutor at the Ecole Polytechnique, was a brilliant mathematician who met Saint-Simon through contacts made at the *école*. Olinde's involvement in the world of the Ecole Polytechnique in the 1820s did not mean a break from his father's world, however. Although he never became a major leader of Parisian Jewish institutional life or the head of a Jewish bank, Olinde's Jewishness made it impossible for him to enter the Ecole Normale Supérieure and obtain a teaching post, so instead, he worked for his father.[8] Far from seeing his son's decision not to take a leading role in the family bank or in Jewish institutional life as a betrayal, Isaac Rodrigues supported his son's endeavors until 1832 (when the group embraced a radical stance against traditional marriage) by buying *actions* to support the founding of the Saint-Simonians' first newspaper, *Le Producteur*. As we saw in Chapter 2, Olry Worms de Romilly, Central Consistory leader and close friend and business associate of the family, also bought shares. A former deputy mayor of the Fifth Arrondissement of Paris in 1799–1800, Worms de Romilly's support likely reflected a shared anti-Restoration political outlook as well as friendship with the young Jewish Saint-Simonians.[9]

Gustave d'Eichthal's parents were from the same milieu, and like Olinde Rodrigues' parents, they encouraged him to integrate into French society, and supported him, at least to a point, in his involvement with the Saint-Simonian movement. His mother was born Fleurette Lévy, the niece of Berr Isaac Berr, the eminent Jewish revolutionary from Nancy, and his father was born Louis Seligmann, a second-generation banker from Fürth, Bavaria, who changed his name to d'Eichthal when he came to France. Gustave's parents taught him only French, sent him to the Lycée Henri IV, and had him, his sister Annette, and his brother Adolphe baptized in 1817. In 1822, Gustave reluctantly went to work in Isaac Rodrigues' bank; but this was by no means the end of his contact with secular liberal circles, since it was there that he became close to Isaac's son Olinde, who in turn introduced him to the philosopher Auguste Comte and numerous students from the Ecole Polytechnique. Briefly, d'Eichthal studied with Comte, but upon his paternal grandfather's death in 1824, he left for Germany to help reorganize the family bank. The trip did not pique his interest in the family business, however; instead, he spent his time talking about Comte's philosophy, romanticism, and how to improve society with Félix and Bethsy Mendelssohn, the children of his father's associate Abraham Mendelssohn.[10] By 1829, d'Eichthal left banking altogether to devote his time entirely to the Saint-Simonian movement, and in 1832, he and Olinde Rodrigues were among those who moved to the communal retreat in Ménilmontant.

The Jewish Saint-Simonians enjoyed the support of the movement's leadership, especially Prosper Enfantin and Emile Barrault (whose wife and mistress, according to d'Eichthal, were both Jewish).[11] These two non-Jewish leaders added their voices to the Jewish Saint-Simonians' in celebrating the "Jewish element" in the group. The centrality of this issue dates back to Saint-Simon's friendship with Olinde Rodrigues. Rodrigues later wrote that the master believed that their partnership itself symbolized the beginning of a new spiritual era, for it represented the reconciliation of Judaism and Christianity: "On the day when the Jew met Saint-Simon and saw in him a new Father, the universal family was founded . . . the feudal Christian gave a paternal kiss to the persecuted Jew who had crucified Jesus Christ."[12]

Claims such as these placed the issue of Jewish involvement in the movement at the very heart of its goals. Ultimately, the Saint-Simonians sought to replace the Old Regime's hereditary, property-based socioeconomic system with an international, credit-based meritocracy. Believing that each new era had its own distinctive spiritual order that supported and legitimated a corresponding temporal order, the movement's theorists saw their socioeconomic and theological goals as mutually interdependent. Seeing each new era as growing out of the previous one, improving on it in some ways, repeating it in others, they argued that just as the Old Regime had been supported by Catholic theology and rituals, the new regime should have a "New Christianity" that improved upon Catholicism without rejecting it entirely. As they conceived it, the New Christianity was thus neither Catholic nor the complete rejection of Catholicism (as some liberals might have wanted), but rather, a theology fully rooted in Christian revelation, designed to supersede Catholicism and to expose the injustices committed in its name. Only by grounding their new material order in a theological system built on the foundation of previous systems, they believed, would they be able to improve "the moral and physical existence of the biggest and poorest class."[13]

The Saint-Simonians influenced other left-wing political thinkers to use a Christian theology to support their political agenda in the 1830s. The immense popularity of writers who championed Christianity was another important influence; these ranged from the conservative François-René de Chateaubriand to the enigmatic Félicité de Lamennais, who, by the 1830s, had abandoned his former unwavering support of the pope's authority and had embraced a much more liberal, but still thoroughly Christian political perspective. Throughout the 1830s and 1840s, a wide array of utopian socialists used images of Jesus and the early Christians, reinterpreting the Gospel in such a way as to connect early Christianity to French revolutionary ideals. These included former Saint-Simonians Pierre Leroux and Philippe Buchez, but also men who had never associated with the movement, like Pierre-Joseph Proudhon and Charles Fourier. The figure of Jesus Christ in particular played a central role in the egalitarian and fraternalist rhetoric developing on the left in the July Monarchy period, and was especially powerful in reaching the popular classes.[14]

The Saint-Simonians were thus at the forefront of a wider trend in their use of religious terminology. Their strong emphasis on a Jewish element in their midst as proof of their legitimacy made them somewhat unique, but its symbolic meaning would have been easily understood by other liberals in their world in the late 1820s and early 1830s. Likening themselves to the early Christians, they saw themselves as bringing all humanity together in a shared belief system and a single, unified temporal organization. Eugène Rodrigues, the group's most important theologian until his untimely death in January 1830 at the age of twenty-four, argued that the New Christianity, unlike the oppressive Catholic Church, would bring universal brotherhood to the temporal as well as the spiritual realm.[15] This was a decidedly messianic goal; as Isaac Pereire wrote, *now* was the era of temporal reunification predicted by Jesus when he said, "My Kingdom is not *yet* of this world."[16] Since the New Christianity sought to hasten the messianic age by spreading its message to all people, its ability to convert Jews was central. "Is not all humanity the people of God, and the whole globe the promised land?" wrote Eugène Rodrigues.[17] Saint-Simonians like Pereire and Rodrigues saw the presence of Jews in their midst—themselves included, of course—as proof that their religion superseded the Catholic Church on its own terms: it was more universal, more authoritative, and more able to address social ills.

The reading public of the Restoration and July Monarchy would certainly have understood the Saint-Simonians' use of the image of the Jew to legitimate their movement. Since the 1820s, the image of Ahasverus, the wandering Jew depicted in European Christian tradition since the sixteenth century, had become a familiar figure in French literature and theater. Before the nineteenth century, its appearances had been largely confined to German-speaking areas. A mythic character cursed by Jesus for not offering him rest at the time of the crucifixion, Ahasverus was understood to be condemned to wander the earth until the second coming. The myth thus tied the Jew symbolically to the messianic age, when he would finally be redeemed. His popularity in nineteenth-century France among liberals is apparent beginning in the 1820s. In 1822, the young historian Edgar Quinet wrote a first-person version of the story that ended with an indictment of Restoration *ultras* as preventing the dawn of the messianic age with their intolerance and the limits they sought to place on individual liberties.[18] The popularity of this image is clear from the fact that Quinet returned to the topic in 1833 with his well-known poetic work *Ahasvérus*, from the appearance of Merville and Maillau's play *Le Juif Errant*, on the stage in 1834, and from the popularity of Eugène Sue's serialized novel *Le Juif Errant*, which began to appear in 1844, and was later turned into a play and then an opera.[19]

Given this broader cultural context, in which Jews' redemption signified the coming of the messianic age, it makes sense that the Saint-Simonians would depict the actual existence of Jews in their midst as of great symbolic importance. Prosper Enfantin raised the issue at some of the movement's most important junctures as a means to maintain his authority over the group when faced with challenges from Saint-Amand Bazard at the end of 1831 and Olinde Rodrigues in early 1832. Both men threatened to leave the group over issues including, most importantly, Enfantin's radical position on monogamous marriage, his growing authoritarianism, and a host of financial issues. For a short time, until his death in April 1832, Bazard formed a new group which included Leroux and Jean Reynaud; Rodrigues did return to the group in time to join Enfantin and those who had stayed with him at the Ménilmontant retreat. In the absence of Bazard and Rodrigues, Enfantin announced that Bazard represented "the old Christian morality" and Rodrigues "the old Jewish morality" too much to play a useful role in the movement.[20] Enfantin's authority thus derived in part from his claim to reconcile Judaism and Christianity into a new religion, symbolically accomplished by the presence of Jewish and Christian people in the group.

For the Saint-Simonians, the meaning of having a Jewish element in their midst was derived not only from their historic place in the Christian imagination, but also, from Jews' diasporic condition. This is particularly apparent in Gustave d'Eichthal's writing, but indeed, Saint-Simon himself had already argued that Jews' internationalism was significant. In one unpublished theological manuscript, d'Eichthal reminded the Saint-Simonians that the master himself had written:

> The people of God, who received Revelation before Jesus appeared, the people most spread out over the surface of the globe, have always felt that Christian Doctrine, founded by the Church fathers, was incomplete. They have always proclaimed that another great era would arrive, an era they called *messianic*, an era in which religious doctrine would be presented in the most universal way, and that this doctrine

would have both temporal and spiritual power, and that in that age, the entire human species would have but one religion and one organization.[21]

Concerned as he was with the temporal world, Saint-Simon saw Jews' internationalism as particularly important. Their conversion to the New Christianity would help spread the new doctrine everywhere, hastening the arrival of the messianic age.

In this spirit, d'Eichthal sought to include more Jews in the movement and to integrate some of their teachings and practices as well. In September 1832, he led Barrault, Charles Lambert, and Félicien David to meet with a series of Parisian Jewish leaders individually, including Marchand Ennery, the chief rabbi of France, and Samuel Cahen, teacher at the Paris Jewish boys' school, to find out more about Jewish rituals, bringing back books about the topic to the group. They also attended Yom Kippur services at the Paris consistorial synagogue in the full regalia they had adopted as "apostles." This was the first time d'Eichthal had ever been in a synagogue, and it made a lasting impression on him. The purpose of these visits was, at least in part, to proselytize; d'Eichthal recorded that they announced to Rabbi Marchand Ennery that they were there "to rehabilitate the Jews" when they arrived at his home.[22] But they were also interested in learning about Jewish rituals and beliefs to incorporate into their own. For d'Eichthal, this was essential; he never ceased reminding Enfantin that Saint-Simon himself had written that the authority of the new moral system derived from the Jews' acceptance of it.

For Saint-Simonians, giving symbolic significance to the Jewish element in their ranks served not only to give authority and purpose to their theology; it was also important in their endeavors to transform the material order. In this vein, the Jewish Saint-Simonians spoke out about their Jewishness in discussing how credit could better human existence and foster brotherhood. If they wanted to replace the property regime with new practices and a new morality, Jewish Saint-Simonians argued, the group should examine Judaism and Jewish economic practices. The claim seems to have appeared first in Léon Halévy's 1825 *Résumé de l'histoire des juifs anciens*, written when Halévy was still associated with the movement (he, like many others, would leave within a few years). In this book, Halévy claimed that in ancient times, Jews had invented the social legislation that could serve as the universal law of the new era. When the Romans sent them into exile, he argued, the Jews brought their law with them and remained faithful to it. Their love of peace inspired them to practice occupations like commerce, the "true power of modern times." They also gave a great gift to the world by inventing credit, "that immense power that today governs humanity."[23]

To some degree, this claim echoed the rulings of the Napoleonic Sanhedrin, since they described Jewish credit as a form of philanthropy, a way of binding society together. Halévy was certainly familiar with these rulings, which he would later include as an appendix in the second volume of his history. He may also have been influenced by Joseph Salvador's 1822 *Loi de Moïse*. As we have seen, this book presented ancient Jewish law as the first form of a truly philanthropic social order which could serve as a model for what modern theorists sought to create in the wake of the French Revolution. Salvador's second work, the 1828 *Histoire des institutions de Moïse*, argued that Jews invented credit and long-distance commerce, peaceful and associative systems which operated according to the same philanthropic principles as ancient Jewish legislation. "A tribe dispersed among all the tribes of the globe, they continued to work . . . toward the formation of that unity which comprises the entire thinking of their law: they connected Europe, Asia, and Africa; they transported to each the products of the others, and showed the Europeans about industry and commercial ties," he wrote.[24]

It is not entirely clear whether it was Halévy or Salvador who first advanced the idea that Jewish commerce and credit embodied Jewish law; as we saw above, Halévy had made such a claim in the preface to his 1825 *Résumé de l'histoire des juifs anciens* and returned to it in his *Résumé de l'histoire des juifs modernes*, published the same year as Salvador's *Histoire des institutions de Moïse*. Together, these books likely served as the basis for the claims made by Olinde Rodrigues and d'Eichthal in Saint-Simonian meetings and publications. In 1831, Rodrigues wrote that the Jewish religion had taught humanity about "political and moral unity" in ancient times, and, after their exile, the Jews, "dis-

persed, united and persecuted all over the earth, began the emancipation of the workers by creating credit."[25] In the same vein, d'Eichthal
argued in 1832 that the Jews were the first to protect workers from being exploited by their employers, and in modern times, could use
credit to bring peace to all Europe and all humanity.[26]

In the context of the movement, these claims were used to support
the goal of glorifying the institution of credit as the bearer of a new international social law that would bring prosperity and social peace to
the whole world. This was a remarkable perspective given the heritage
of eighteenth-century French liberal economic thought, which was notoriously hostile to credit, and the fact that France was to some degree
still shaking from the failure of John Law's system and the collapse of
the revolutionary *assignats*. Yet the Saint-Simonians saw public credit
not only as a means to enrich the world, but also as a way to destroy
the regime of property, which in their view was the backbone of feudalism. This issue was central in the public lectures, newspaper articles
and propaganda of 1828–29, much of which was published as *The Doctrine of Saint-Simon, First Year*. In these articles, Saint-Simonians called
for the establishment of a regime whose major task would be to manage public credit, administered by an organization of bankers who
would redistribute wealth by lending money to the capable. Eugène
Rodrigues argued that inheritance was an immoral system for trans-
mitting wealth, and should be replaced by what he called "investiture
by capacity," a system in which the capable of each generation would
occupy the positions of power.[27] The public credit system would ultimately replace profit-driven private banks; this transformation, they
believed, had already begun with the establishment of the Bank of
France and especially its work under Jacques Laffitte, but banks still
had to centralize and merge with the state to better society.[28]

The Saint-Simonian argument for establishing a system of public
credit was moral as well as economic. According to d'Eichthal, an expansion of credit would allow men to feel more connected to one another by affirming a common goal and a shared morality. Bankers,
uniting to issue credit to worthy industrialists, would reconnect the social order. This bank would be like an ideal government, creating "con-
fidence, faith in others."[29] In his private correspondence to his brother

Adolphe, he made his hopes even clearer: "Imagine a completely organized Credit, that is, a banking system, spreading over the country, accrediting or discrediting everyone according to their merits . . . and you will see how close we are to abolishing inheritance."[30] After the Saint-Simonian movement fell apart, d'Eichthal held to this belief, claiming that the movement's greatest legacy was to have popularized the idea of credit as a social institution.[31] The Pereires and Olinde Rodrigues also remained deeply committed to the extension of public credit long after the dissolution of the Saint-Simonian movement. Rodrigues returned to the world of finance and industrial development and advocated the extension of public credit in 1848, and the Pereires founded the Crédit Mobilier bank in 1852, as a means to achieve Saint-Simonian goals.[32]

How are we to understand Jewish Saint-Simonians' claim that the Jews had "invented credit," especially the kind of credit the Saint-Simonians advocated, highly organized, wealth-producing, and liberating? Various forms of this myth are, of course, still powerful among both proud philo-semites and venomous antisemites, as historians Derek Penslar and Mitchell Hart have explored elsewhere, yet it is nonetheless historically inaccurate.[33] Its roots are hard to determine for the Jewish Saint-Simonians. Certainly, the Rodrigues and d'Eichthal families were bankers and many of the Jews they knew were involved in that profession. They would also have known about the "court Jews" of central Europe, and knew that many European Jews had historically earned a living in the money trades. Yet the claim that Jews "invented credit" does not follow from any of these historical facts. Moreover, as Bertrand Gille has shown, the movement's ideas for a new system of public credit were largely derived from those advanced during the Restoration period by Jacques Laffitte, the non-Jewish former head of the Bank of France and later a key player in the 1830 revolution. Laffitte himself had supported the Saint-Simonian movement in the early days and had been an *actionnaire* in the *Producteur*. He and the majority of his associates were not Jewish, although alongside the more famous names of bankers who worked regularly with him such as Ardoin, Blanc, Vital-Roux, and Ternaux, one can also find the names of Isaac Rodrigues, Olry Worms de Romilly, Louis d'Eichthal, Berr

Léon Fould, Abraham Mendelssohn, and James de Rothschild, a new-comer to the city, having arrived from Frankfurt only in 1812.[34] Per-haps the exaggerations of the Jewish Saint-Simonians were based on the fact that the Jewish world from which they came was filled with progressive bankers interested in precisely the kind of reform these young men were championing. Still, the men had to be aware that their parents, like themselves in the Saint-Simonian movement, were but a visible, disproportionately numerous, but still small minority in the broader world of high finance.

It is more likely that the Jewish Saint-Simonians did not intend their claims to be taken as literal *fact*. The claim that Jews "invented credit" appears in these texts as a kind of colorful, dramatic outburst, and its truth seems to depend largely on its readers' preexisting asso-ciation of Jews with money lending. The miserly, misanthropic Jew-ish banker was one of the most predominant stereotypes of Jewish men in the literature of the day, at least as popular as the image of the wandering Jew, if not more so.[35] In this sense, the claim was probably a rhetorical strategy designed to emphasize a larger point about the movement's goals. The association of public credit with the Jews—rather than, say, with Great Britain, where experiments with new sys-tems of public credit were in fact taking place—added force to the movement's claim to be advancing a radically new economic system, entirely distinct from the Old Regime and based on a new Christian theology that was capable of redeeming humanity. Imaginatively harnessing the Jews' secret to accumulating wealth was a powerful symbol of this material transformation; praising Scottish or English bankers, as d'Eichthal did in his private papers, would have been much less effective rhetorically.[36]

Furthermore, the Jewish Saint-Simonians' claim that the Jews in-vented credit can be linked to their theological efforts to rehabilitate the Jew. A parallel can be established here between this claim and Saint-Simon's assertion that the Jews had "crucified Jesus" but now accepted the New Christianity. Here too, the Saint-Simonians mobi-lized a well-known, essentially negative stereotype: that of the self-interested, foreign, heavily-accented Jewish banker of the sort that Balzac sketched in his recurring characters Gobseck and Nucingen and that Shakespeare and Scott had painted in equally repugnant terms in works popular in France in the 1820s.[37] Like the image of the deicidal Jew, the Saint-Simonians rehabilitated the Jewish banker's image by portraying his activity as potentially beneficial to all humanity if the new system were fully established. As with their theological claims, then, the function of the image of the Jew here was to demonstrate the movement's ability to overcome divisions that once seemed insurmountable in such a way as to bring about a new, messianic age of universal happiness, peace, and prosperity. Rehabilitating the Jew in the material realm as in the spiritual realm testified to the novelty, the radicalism, and most of all, the higher level of morality possible through Saint-Simonianism as opposed to its predecessor, Catholicism.

With such importance placed on their presence qua Jews within the movement's ranks, it is not surprising that the group's overall goals informed its Jewish members' conception of Jewish identity. The Jews most integral to the group's leadership—Halévy (who left the group early on), the Rodrigues brothers, and d'Eichthal—used their Jewishness to provide rhetorical force and fuller meaning to some of the movement's most fundamental goals. As they defined it, Jewishness was important in the contemporary world, and the presence of Jews within the movement was a sign that a better material and spiritual world was on the horizon. Jewishness was identified as bearing practical as well as moral lessons, and their participation in the Saint-Simonian endeavor was meant as a sign of the movement's modernity and its high moral standing. Furthermore, the fact that the Jews were dispersed internationally was significant to the Saint-Simonians, who hoped to transform not only France, but the whole world with their new system. The fact that the new system could rehabilitate the Jews was a key element of its legitimacy.

As defined in the movement, this Jewishness was quite distinct from previous forms. It was not tied to membership in a community, be it formal or informal, nor was it grounded in knowledge or observance of Jewish rituals, customs, or texts. And yet this Jewishness was depicted as moral. Not a learned morality, to be sure; it was a substance in the bodies of individuals born to Jewish parents. As d'Eichthal wrote: "As you said, Barrault: the Jew is the only one who may glorify his *race*, because he alone has never intermixed; thanks to the women, the blood of Israel still flows in his veins."[38] As these words suggest, Jewishness was an embodied identity, carried in the blood, connected to an ancient past, once persecuted but now on the brink of redemption. It therefore makes sense that d'Eichthal always identified himself as Jewish, even though he had converted to Catholicism at the age of thirteen and knew little if anything of Jewish observance. As his remarks in his diary over the course of his lifetime reveal, d'Eichthal saw his body—marked by circumcision, reflexively revolted by the taste of "pig and oysters" (as he noted in one diary entry)—as the source of his Jewishness and as such, of his mission to humanity.[39]

The Jewish Saint-Simonians' conception of Jewishness as located in the body was made possible by the novel situation in which they and other Jews in this generation found themselves. Unconnected to traditional Jewish communal structures, education, and worship, they were nonetheless identified as Jews in the circles in which they moved. In this context, the emergence of a new form of Jewish identity, using terms meaningful in the circles in which they moved should not surprise us. In addition, the Jewish Saint-Simonians' choice to adopt a racial form of self-identification was an expression of their political views, as is clear from an examination of the origin of this language, which was first used systematically in the contemporary academic historical works of the Thierry brothers, François Guizot, Jules Michelet, and Edgar Quinet, all of whom were associated with left-wing causes over the course of their careers, especially anticlericalism. In academic historiography, the language of race emerged as a way to define France's history in a way that glorified the revolution for uniting the diverse people of France together in a single order without fully erasing their distinctiveness from one another.

Augustin and Amadée Thierry, in their respective studies of Britain and France published during the Restoration, were the first to use race as the analytic key to history. Change in human societies, they argued, took place because of conflicts between migrating and warring racial groups, who each brought with them identifiable and distinct forms of culture and politics. Once conquest was secure, they argued, some part of the dominant racial group mixed with the dominated group, yet nevertheless, a strong degree of racial difference remained present even in contemporary Britain and France. Racial differences were visible as differences in temperament as well as physical appearance, and national variation in political forms and ideas evolved due primarily to their influence. Amadée Thierry argued that in France, the "Gauls" displayed the character traits of loving freedom, disobedience, fickleness, and gallantry, and that it was due to their enduring "national pride" that they developed the modern concept of national political independence.[40]

Although the Thierry brothers' racial theory can be read as a view that might makes right, it also contains an important political statement about the right to social difference. The Thierrys asserted that France was made up of distinct racial groups, all of whom were initially from elsewhere, and all of whom possessed enduring characteristics, protected by natural right.[41] This perspective was shared and further elaborated by the eminent historian (and later statesman) François Guizot. In his "Course on the History of Civilization in France," delivered at the Sorbonne in 1820, Guizot argued that the French Revolution had finally brought an end to the long-standing struggle between the races in France. This was not done by the elimination of one of the races, but rather, by establishing a legal and institutional framework that mediated between them.[42]

Seen through this lens, the Jewish Saint-Simonians' use of race language can be read as an assertion of the right to difference. In his history of the Jewish people, Léon Halévy described Jewish distinctiveness as a "particular physiognomy," and claimed that it had endured intact throughout the time of their dispersion.[43] For Halévy, it was their *racial* character that endowed Jews with a penchant for long-distance commerce and credit, occupations that fostered international peace and prosperity. Decades after their emancipation in France, Halévy concluded, the "vitality of this race" was still clearly visible, most notably in their morality but also in their professional knowledge. With the era of Christian persecution finally drawing to a close, he predicted that the Jews "will still play an important role in the history of the world," bringing peace and prosperity to a world in desperate need of both.[44] It is not surprising that Halévy would have adopted the Thierrys' analytic lens for history, given their common background: he and Augustin Thierry had both been associated with the Ecole Polytechnique and worked with Saint-Simon in the early 1810s. Saint-Simon himself had used a similar racial framework for understanding historical development in such works as his 1813 *Mémoire sur la science de l'homme* and his 1823 *Catéchisme des industriels.*[45]

Halévy's assertion that Jews were distinctive by their race—rather than their religion or legal status—was an argument that Jewish difference was legitimate and dignified in a way that skirted the old theological questions dividing Christians and Jews. It also used the racial model developed by the Thierrys to provide a new framework for understanding how Jews, as bearers of a distinctive morality, could be incorporated into France, and gave a sense of why this inclusion was beneficial. The Jews, like the Gauls or Franks, could be understood as a once wandering tribe, settled in France, with distinctive and admirable moral and physical characteristics, living alongside other races in peace under a single set of institutions and laws. Race theory thus provided a statement of the natural right to difference and the concept of the modern state as a mediator between racial groups of unequal strength.

Beginning in Ménilmontant and continuing in certain respects for decades after the movement's formal end, d'Eichthal developed Halévy's ideas further, bringing them to bear on the question of the role the Jewish race could play in building the new international order. To this end, in the mid-1830s d'Eichthal wrote a poetic theological tract called "Le Chant d'Ahasvérus" (which was never published), meant to publicize the idea that although in the past Jews had crucified Christ and denied his divinity, now they were on the brink of rehabilitation and were destined to unite the world. The Jewish race, he claimed, was to reconcile East and West because Judaism was the "father" of two "daughters," Islam and Christianity. D'Eichthal seems to have meant this as an argument about Jews' collective biological makeup rather than purely about the historical relationship between the three monotheistic faiths. He wrote that because Jews were dispersed, they had come to embody elements from races all over the earth, and their law and social and economic practices were designed to mediate between them with justice.[46]

D'Eichthal's definition of race makes no sense if we fail to take into account the contemporary understanding of "race" as an embodied set of traditions and beliefs. For d'Eichthal, culture and morality, carried in the body, unified and defined Jews in their diversity. In his 1839 *Lettres sur la race noire et la race blanche*, d'Eichthal further theorized that all the races in the world could live in harmony if they had a law, a religion, and other peaceful practices to mediate between them, as the Jews did. The Jewish race, he argued, was in a special position to mediate between races and religions, precisely because it offered a law that had administered justice between diverse people for millennia.[47]

D'Eichthal's view that different races had different moralities but were on the verge of coming together in an unprecedented way was by no means esoteric. This utopian belief was broadly shared among left-wing Romantic historians working in the July Monarchy period, whether or not they had associated formally with the Saint-Simonian movement. In this sense, d'Eichthal assigned Jews a central role in a global transformation understood to be imminent by a whole range of political thinkers in the social network in which he moved. A similarly utopian, messianic quality is evident in the way Jules Michelet used racial terminology in his historical works, and indeed, he and d'Eichthal were close friends and exchanged work throughout their lives.[48] In the 1830s and 1840s, Michelet published numerous studies embracing and elaborating the Thierry brothers' idea that races were moral types and that multiple races were visible in contemporary French society. In his works, Michelet described the particular "génie" each race had to contribute to humanity. In his *Introduction à l'histoire universelle* (1831) and *Histoire romaine* (1831), Michelet followed the Thierry brothers in using the category of race to understand the process of political domination, describing the ancient "races" as the ancestors of modern-day national groups.[49]

The vision of an impending reconciliation of the races of the world continued to play an important role in academic historical writing and left-wing politics in the 1840s. In this period, Michelet argued that because of the revolution, the races were now on the brink of a new moment in history, in which they would at last unite and the cycle of conquest and submission would end. Like his friend Edgar Quinet, Michelet saw the Romantic nationalist movements emerging across Europe as racial yearnings finally taking political form. Rather than seeing nationalism as erasing racial specificity within nations, Quinet and Michelet described nationalism as the peaceful flowering of racial spirits. For Michelet, the history of the French Revolution was a model for a global future: democratic institutions would form to mediate between the races, allowing them to live in peace alongside one another.[50] Similarly, Quinet argued that like the Catholic Church before it, contemporary France's mission in the world was to make "an alliance between the human races," or "to reconcile one day the spirit of the north with the spirit of the south" through spreading its morality and its science.[51] By the 1850s, race theory in mainstream public discourse thus was embraced by thinkers committed to anticlericalism and to supporting the democratic movements emerging across Europe. The language seems to have been used primarily as a way of describing diverse groups coexisting harmoniously, each contributing something particular to the world, a "holy alliance of peoples," intended to replace the Christian Holy Alliance.[52]

The way that the Jewish Saint-Simonians described their Jewishness thus resonated with contemporary academic historical writing, Romantic literature, and left-wing political discourse, and had little in common with more traditional forms of Jewish identity. The Jewish Saint-Simonians defined the Jews as a distinguished, ancient race with an unyielding moral code and impressive financial knowledge. The internationalism of Saint-Simonianism and of other contemporary forms of democratic political messianism (such as that of Michelet and Quinet) was also reflected in the new form of Jewish identity crafted in this setting. Intending their words to be meaningful in this conversation, these Jews stressed the cosmopolitanism of the Jewish "race" in spite of the fact that they themselves were quite assimilated. This was intended to give the Jews an important role in the process of world reconciliation that they and those in their milieu believed to be at hand. At once French and foreign, Jews were depicted as a universal, timeless people, who bore in their religion and their commercial practices the elements of a new material and moral law that could be used to unite all humanity. The new Jewish identity that the Jewish Saint-Simonians expressed reflected the fact that in the left-wing circles they frequented in the 1830s, the status of Jews was an extremely meaningful issue. Their participation in the Saint-Simonian movement itself was a sign of the movement's superiority to Catholicism, and their liberation in the modern era, beginning in France, was a sign that world unity was close at hand. Far from demanding that Jews abandon their distinctiveness or even their foreignness in order to participate fully in the movement, the Saint-Simonians saw Jewish difference as symbolically important and encouraged its expression, even as they supplied radically new terminology for defining it.

The Literary Context: Eugénie Foa's *La Juive*

In the 1830s, new images of Jews were also common in Romantic literature, theater, and opera. As in the context of left-wing politics, a small set of Jewish artists made their voices heard in this artistic context as well, similarly showcasing their Jewishness in a way that resonated with liberal aspirations. In doing so, they simultaneously advanced their own careers, helped to push a liberal political agenda, and identified Judaism with that agenda in much the same way that Christian socialists were identifying Christianity with it. Moreover, as in Saint-Simonianism, the Jewishness they defined was at once French and foreign, so as to emphasize both the novelty and the universal promise of the liberalism they championed.

Among the young, assimilated Jews making a name for themselves in the arts in the 1830s were writers like Léon Halévy, Heinrich Heine (1797–1856), and Alexandre Weill (1811–98); composers like Fromenthal Halévy, Giacomo Meyerbeer (1791–1864), and the brothers Henri (1806–88) and Jacques Herz (1794–1880); and the actress Elisa-Rachel Félix (1821–58). Félix's choice to go by the unmistakably Jewish stage name "Rachel" by the time she made her debut at the Comédie-Française in 1838 testifies to the degree to which Jewishness in the arts had become not only acceptable, but a selling point in the increasingly money-conscious world of the arts.[53] Just as Adolphe Crémieux had carved a legal career in the 1820s by branding himself a defender of Jews and Protestants in the name of religious liberty, so too did Jewish writers, composers, and performers find their own paths to success in their equally competitive professions by stressing, rather than hiding, their Jewishness, and using Jews as a symbol of the French Revolution's promise to liberate all humanity.[54]

Like her Saint-Simonian friends, the writer Eugénie Foa contributed to shaping these new images of Jews before the French reading public. The first Jewish woman to support herself fully from her writing, Foa initially made her mark by writing about Jewish topics, only later switching genres to the children's literature for which she is best remembered. Her early works—*Le Kidouschim; ou, L'Anneau nuptial des hébreux* (1830), *Philippe* (1831), *Rachel; ou, L'Héritage* (1833), and the two-volume tragic novel *La Juive: Histoire du temps de la Régence* (1835)—all provided richly detailed descriptions of Jewish religious practices and family life to a reading audience with a proven thirst for such images, and her "exotic" Jewish heroines show the unmistakable influence of contemporary favorite Romantic authors like Chateaubriand, Madame de Staël, Lamartine, and Musset.[55]

Like the Jewish Saint-Simonians, Foa embedded her representations of Jews within a recognizably left-wing political agenda. These images provided a symbolic language through which she outlined a moral framework that was meant to be read as original but also grounded in an ancient wisdom. More successfully than Gustave d'Eichthal, Foa integrated Jewish teachings and practices into the liberal moral framework she was constructing, in much the same way that left-wing Christian thinkers were doing at the time. Grounded as it was in secular political concerns, Foa's representations of Jewish identity built on those of other Romantic writers and artists. The Jewish characters in *La Juive* are depicted as insider/outsider figures, racially distinct, yet connected to the fulfillment of the promises of the French Revolution. Foa portrayed Jews as insiders in that they represented a kind of moral essence identified with such French virtues as brotherly love and care for the weak. Yet her Jewish characters were also cultural outsiders—marked with accents, exotic clothing, foreign names, and more often than not, explicitly identified as having a special connection to Jerusalem. Such images resonated with representations of the Wandering Jew in contemporary culture, showing Jews as culturally distinct and downtrodden, but on the brink of integration and rehabilitation under a new regime that respected personal freedom, romantic love, and charitable action. In this way, Foa's portrait of the Jewish world was quite obviously crafted to support the liberal cause, legible to those fluent in the language of French liberalism rather than for Jews less familiar with French literature and politics. Yet more than other representations of Jews and Judaism in this context, Foa used Judaism itself as a building block of the new moral system she described.

Not only did Foa resemble the Jewish Saint-Simonians in how she used images of Jews, but she hailed from a similar social background as well. The daughter of the banker Isaac Rodrigues-Henriquès (1765–1836; of the Bordeaux banking house A. Rodrigues et fils; not to be confused with his namesake, Olinde's father), and Esther Gradis (d. 1859), Foa could hardly have come from a more important French Jewish family. Her father had represented the Gironde *département* at the Napoleonic Assembly of Jewish Notables in 1806 alongside her paternal uncle Benjamin Rodrigues (b. 1769). Her paternal grandfather Abraham Rodrigues (b. 1735) and maternal great-uncle David Gradis had represented the Bordeaux Jews in 1790 before the National Assembly. Along with her mother and young brother Hippolyte (1812–98), Eugénie followed her father from Bordeaux to Paris shortly after her brief, unhappy marriage to Joseph Foa ended in 1814, and her youngest sister Léonie was born in the capital in 1820. Although in the 1840s, Eugénie became estranged from her mother and converted to Catholicism, she probably wrote *La Juive* and her other works on Jewish topics while still living in her parents' apartment on the rue Monthalon in Paris.[56] There, the family was surrounded by other Sephardi Jews like the (Olinde) Rodrigues and the Pereires; the Pereires had trained in the Gradis family bank in Bordeaux before coming to Paris. Also in this circle were Foa's first cousins, the brothers Henry and Edouard Rodrigues (b. 1797), Benjamin Rodrigues' sons. Edouard's daughter Cécile (1823–77) converted to Catholicism and married Gustave d'Eichthal in 1842.[57] The Halévys were also part of this world; Eugénie's sister Léonie (1820–84) was a sculptor who married Fromenthal Halévy in 1842; their daughter was the Dreyfusard *salonnière* Geneviève Halévy Bizet Strauss (1849–1926), immortalized by Marcel Proust.[58]

Of her early works, Foa's novel *La Juive* was the best known, and by far the most complex. The novel tells the story of a doomed pair of lovers—the Christian André and the Jewish Midiane—set against the backdrop of political intrigue and financial experimentation during the period following the death of Louis XIV, when the Duc d'Orléans was regent. Together with her family, the heroine Midiane comes to Paris from Syria for her father Schaoul's banking business, and while they are there, Schaoul becomes involved in helping John Law build his legendary system. Although her father attempts to hide her away, Midiane nevertheless meets André, an orphaned painter who lives with his uncle, an individualistic *philosophe*. Midiane and André are immediately drawn to one other, but Midiane's tyrannical father has other plans for her future. Long before she was born, he had arranged for her to marry Daniel Samla, the son of a deceased Jewish business associate. Daniel is a kind, hunchbacked doctor who has spent his life passing as a Christian and by the time the story takes place, he is coincidentally André's best friend. Out of friendship, Daniel agrees to let Midiane and André follow their hearts, much against Midiane's father's wishes; this entails breaking the engagement contract (*kiddushin*) that his father and Schaoul had signed long ago. But although Midiane is able to escape her family to be with her love, the couple does not find happiness together. As a mixed couple, the Church will not marry them, the Duc d'Orléans refuses to help, and his daughter, the Duchesse de Berry, is sympathetic but powerless. Unable to marry, Midiane and André are outcasts, they grow poor and ill, and finally, they die, leaving an infant daughter behind. Midiane's two maiden aunts, Lia and Angélique, filled with the true altruism lacking in both the Church and the Jewish home, take in the orphan and raise her.

The novel ends with the aunts telling Midiane's orphaned daughter, "You will marry whomever you like, Jew or Christian . . . once you have heard the story of your mother, my niece."[59]

In its thematic content, *La Juive* was a plea for personal freedom against the constraints of religious intolerance and patriarchal authority. These themes were already popular in Romantic literature in the 1830s, the genre's earlier conservative orientation having given way to a new political outlook associated with the Generation of 1820. In Victor Hugo's words, by 1830, Romanticism had become *"liberalism* in literature."[60] The revolution of 1830 had brought the Duc d'Orléans, Louis-Philippe, to power, and with him, a new Charte that declared Catholicism "the religion of the majority of Frenchmen" rather than the official religion of the state. Over the next decade, artistic works dramatizing the issue of religious freedom attracted attention from newspapers and audiences alike. Clerical intolerance was the main theme of a whole set of new works on Martin Luther by Leon Halévy, Heinrich Heine, and Jules Michelet in the mid-1830s. It was also the central issue in popular operas like Giacomo Meyerbeer and Eugène Scribe's *Les Huguenots* (1836) and Fromenthal Halévy and Eugène Scribe's *La Juive* (1835), which shared a title but not a plot with Foa's novel. The setting for Halévy's opera is the Council of Constance in the early fifteenth century, where Jan Hus was burned as a heretic; it is a story of clerical persecution of a Jewish father, a banker named Eléazar, and his beautiful daughter Rachel, who falls in love with a Christian prince but cannot marry him. The opera culminates in the tragic martyrdom of Rachel and Eléazar. As Diana Hallman has argued, all these works bear the imprint of Voltaire, whose criticisms of both clerical oppression of religious dissenters and political tyranny were widely read in this era, and had enormous influence on contemporary debates about the monarchy and the role of the Church in state affairs.[61] Foa's novel too linked the familiar issue of freedom from tyranny (in this case, romantic freedom from paternal tyranny) to the issue of religious intolerance, in that the central conflict of the novel is the refusal of a Jewish father and Christian society to accept a freely chosen interfaith love as legitimate.

In addition, Foa used familiar Romantic tropes to depict Jewishness as exotic and enticing in a way that clearly built on readers' familiarity with the "Orient" from contemporary French literature and English literature in French translation. Here, as was so often the case in Romantic literature, the exotic oriental world is a setting for extreme patriarchal despotism. The Jews in the novel are unmistakably "oriental"; their clothing, their garden, and especially their beautiful women, kept captive in a "harem" by a strong father, are described in terms that resonated with well-known Romantic travel literature written by men like Chateaubriand and Lamartine. This resonance was clearly intentional, given that almost every chapter of *La Juive* begins with an epigram from a well-known Romantic writer, including these two authors.

Descriptions of the riches hidden in the protagonist Midiane's father's counting house and his strong, turbaned black servants were similarly informed by Romantic literature. Edward Said's analysis of Romantic orientalism as depicting a world enticing through its hidden riches and beautiful hidden women certainly applies here, although Foa is depicting a Jewish world within Paris rather than a Muslim world in a far-off "Orient."[62] For example, chapter 9, entitled "Orgy," includes this tantalizing description:

> You all know Schaoul's house . . . his office is adorned with mirrors, one of which is encircled with a gold circle made up of gold nails. One of these nails is bigger than the others, and if you press it with your thumb, the mirror turns, a staircase appears, and a vault, and a charming, delicious harem, where two women live alone, practicing their religion; they can only get air and exercise by walking in their immense garden, surrounded by high walls.[63]

The world inside Schaoul's home is meant to be hidden, but the words used to describe it invite the reader inside to taste its hidden treasures. This description resonated with contemporary Romantic art. Delacroix's *Femmes d'Alger*, presented at the Salon of 1834, featured seated bejeweled women (the Algerian models were, in fact, Jewish) with their black servant in a strikingly similar oriental harem. In William Vaughn's estimation, this painting was read at the time as suggestive of both sensuality and ennui—exactly the themes Foa depicted with her bored, beautiful, confined Jewish women in Paris.[64] Drawing on this emerging orientalist tradition added a kind of flair to her novel probably designed to sell books, a real concern for a new writer; Delacroix's paintings of Algeria and Morocco after his 1832 trip were well known, and had also inspired other depictions of Jews in the period. Most notably, Halévy's opera *La Juive* pulled its costume ideas for its Jewish characters from Delacroix's paintings of Algerian and Moroccan women.[65] Despite their very different story lines, Halévy and Foa's works shared a basic aesthetic sensibility as well as the same liberal political message.

La Juive depends on its readers' familiarity with the stereotype of Jews as fanatical and tyrannical to support its narrative as well as its aesthetic sensibility. Because she mobilized these stereotypes, her readers could understand the story as contributing to the liberal critique of patriarchal and religious extremism. Her portrayal of the key tension in the novel, for example, follows a tradition easily recognizable to her readers, in which a Jewish father, usually a banker, is overly tyrannical with his family and is "intolerant," refusing to let his daughter marry her Christian lover. This motif would have been familiar to readers from similar works like Halévy's opera *La Juive*, Scott's *Ivanhoe*, Shakespeare's *Merchant of Venice*, and others. Schaoul's actions are depicted as restrictive and harmful, observing the letter of the law without understanding the true spirit of religion. The depiction thus harkens back to eighteenth-century tropes, themselves built on an ancient Pauline critique of Judaism. It comes across clearly when Midiane pleads with her father to let her follow her heart, even if it means breaking a contract, arguing that the Jewish religion—and all religions, for that matter—should be understood as encouraging love, even between Jews and Christians. "Religion, true religion, shouldn't it unite men, rather than keeping them apart?" she asks. "God, sovereign master of everything, makes no distinction between his children, why then do we tear ourselves apart from one another?"[66] This Enlightenment argument fails to convince Schaoul, who holds fast to his understanding that Judaism demands that Midiane honor the engage-

ment contract. Readers would easily understand the political statement: fanaticism perverts religion's true message of unity and personal
freedom.

The tragedy of the novel thus comes from Schaoul's rigid religious
adherence, coupled with his iron rule over the women in his household. This is apparent in how the drama unfolds. After failing to convince her father that "true religion" would allow her to follow her love
even if it meant breaking a contract, Midiane attempts to get out of
the engagement by appealing to Daniel, the kindly hunchback to
whom she had been promised, in a letter where she explains her love
for André. Daniel, moved by her letter and ashamed of his physical
deformity, breaks the contract himself. Schaoul is outraged. The tragedy is set in motion: Schaoul sets the house on fire, places a curse
upon Midiane, and locks her in a room as the house burns down.
With the help of her mother, Midiane escapes the fire and is left to her
own devices, alone, cast outside of the Jewish world completely. The
vengeful violence so typical in literary representations of Jewish men
(as in the opera *La Juive*, for example) appears here in the form of paternal tyranny.

Yet, there is clearly a tension between Foa's use of these stereotypes
to contribute to the contemporary liberal critique of intolerance and
paternal tyranny, and her desire to defend the Jewish religion from
such attacks. Far more than Halévy's opera, Foa depicts Judaism as a
rich culture with beautiful and virtuous religious practices and beliefs.
In the context of French literature, in which Jews were often depicted
as miserly and their religion as hateful of Christians, Foa used her
voice to defend Judaism in the terms most important to liberals, in
much the same way that the members of the Napoleonic Sanhedrin
and, later, Léon Halévy had. In chapter 5, she explains that Jews are
obliged to give charity to gentiles; in chapter 16, she describes the
beauty and dignity of Daniel's bar mitzvah ceremony; and in chapters
18 and 19, she describes a Passover Seder in rich detail as the celebration of freedom from slavery (a similar scene with a similarly liberal
emphasis appears in Halévy's opera as well). In another colorful inter-
lude, two rabbis appear at Schaoul's house to collect money for the

poor Jews of Jerusalem. "My brothers," says Schaoul, "come by my bank tomorrow. God made my harvest, my business, prosper; according to our holy customs, I have put aside one portion for the foreigners and one for our poor; I will give you the portion for our poor."[67] As in her earlier works on the Jewish practices of engagement, marriage, redemption of the first-born (*pidyon ha-ben*), and divorce, Foa's descriptions of Jewish rituals in *La Juive* were unusually detailed, emphasizing their consonance with values like individual and collective freedom, public responsibility for the welfare of the poor, the protection of the weak, and parental pride.[68]

The portrayal of Judaism as altruistic was unusual in the context of contemporary literary representations. For example, although Halévy's opera *La Juive* is, in essence, a harsh critique of Catholic intolerance, culminating in a cardinal's refusal to grant mercy to the two Jewish characters who meet their end in a horrific auto-da-fé, it provokes the audience's sympathy for its Jewish characters primarily in that they become martyrs. This sympathy is accentuated by the fact that the protagonist Rachel turns out to have been the cardinal's own daughter—not a Jew by birth at all—adopted long ago by the Jewish banker Eléazar. In this portrayal of the *belle Juive* as sympathetic because she was born a Christian, Rachel in Halévy's opera resembled others popular in the day, such as the secretly Christian-born Jewesses in Maria Edgeworth's *Harrington*, Scott's *Ivanhoe*, and Lessing's *Nathan the Wise*, among others.[69] The fact that Foa's Midiane—who in most other respects resembles these other Jewesses—is born a Jew, expresses pride in her heritage, and never renounces her Judaism is unusual and represents a statement of the religion's worthiness.

Even the portrait of the patriarch Schaoul, which pulls so heavily on traditional anti-Jewish Enlightenment stereotypes, is unusually complex, suggesting that a form of Judaism teaches a morality useful for building a good society. Unlike Shakespeare's Shylock, Foa's Schaoul is not depicted as a misanthropist. Schaoul's most abiding character trait, Foa explains in the novel, was not so much fanaticism but steadfast reliability and loyalty: "She knew that, a banker in all his actions, in his family as in his office, one word from Schaoul was as good as a contract, as good as his signature on a *lettre de change*, he never said anything by accident."[70] Following the holdings of the Napoleonic Sanhedrin, Foa shows that Judaism is a religion that demands that its adherents practice charity toward non-Jews. Schaoul's problem, as Foa paints it, is thus not that he is Jewish, but that he does not understand the underlying wisdom of his religion, which teaches its adherents to be charitable, to care for the weak, and to understand their connectedness to all people.

Foa's attempt to make a form of Judaism an integral part of the new morality she was advancing is not just a critique of religious intolerance (be it Schaoul's rigid tribalism or clerical oppression), it is also a critique of extreme individualism. In the novel, Foa uses what she clearly sees as the essence of Judaism as a basis for creating a moral framework that was religious without being narrow or rigid, and charitable without compromising individual freedoms, especially romantic freedom. Critical as she was of the Jewish world as overly patriarchal and stifling of its children's happiness, Foa was equally critical of the extreme individualism of Enlightenment philosophy. This critique comes across in her characterization of the rather comic Honoré de Prezel, André's uncle and guardian. De Prezel is described as a classic *philosophe*: he is working on a systematic philosophy called *Traité sur les matières*. With his seemingly boundless set of interests—including Judaism—one might think de Prezel would provide ideas for forming a new world. Yet he is far too ardent an individualist to help the young lovers—or anyone, for that matter. One telling moment comes when André approaches his uncle to ask for a loan to help Daniel, his best friend, who is in prison until he can pay back his late father's debts. André reminds his uncle that Daniel was the doctor who once set his broken leg, hoping that the fact that Daniel had helped him in the past would inspire his sense of charity. This does not work, however; de Prezel merely responds that he has already paid for that service and thus has no reason to be concerned for Daniel. André then reveals that he himself has signed for Daniel's debt, and will be jailed if he fails to find the money by morning. Still, de Prezel remains unmoved. Before giving up, André tries evoking his uncle's pity: "Poor Daniel," he says, "no parents, no fortune, a poor orphan . . . ," and the uncle answers cynically, "Orphan, orphan. . . . Who's *not* an orphan? You are André, and so am I."[71] The uncle is a caricature of Enlightenment individualism: not only does he refuse to help Daniel, he also refuses to help his own nephew. For de Prezel, whose motto is *chacun fait comme il peut* ("you do what you can"), every person is alone, at the mercy of his own individual fate.

Foa's moral message in *La Juive* stresses the importance of charitable action over and against extreme individualism. This comes across in the resolution of the saga of Daniel's debt. Daniel's problem is solved when Schaoul, fulfilling his religious obligation to give charity to gentiles, throws the money from his carriage which André catches and then uses to get Daniel out of jail. Foa thus tells her readers that Schaoul's strict religious observance is charitable, and limited as it is, it is still preferable to André's uncle's individualism. Even better than Schaoul's charity is André's, because he, unlike Schaoul, has freely chosen to take on this responsibility for friendship's sake, and fully understands its meaning. For André, being friends or receiving charity from someone was the start of an ongoing relationship in which each friend took responsibility for the other's welfare. Throughout the novel, Foa celebrates compassion for the weak, brotherly acts of self-sacrifice, and freely chosen bonds of friendship and love over and against selfish individualism, rigid adherence to religious doctrine, and even familial bonds.

In *La Juive*, Foa places representations of Judaism and the Jewish family within an important left-wing political debate of the time by staging the conflict between too much paternalism on the one hand (the Jewish woman's family who won't let her choose her own mate), and social apathy on the other (the non-Jewish world's lack of charity for the outcast couple). Numerous groups across the political spectrum in the 1830s remained concerned with the question of how citizens could be taught to honor both freedom and social interdependence, and how lasting social bonds could be formed after tyrannical authority, propped up as sacred, was delegitimated and destroyed. As we have seen, this issue had formed the basis for the Saint-Simonians' elaboration of New Christianity in the early 1830s, and later, became a major preoccupation for Christian socialists like Proudhon, Fourier,

Leroux, and even anticlerical democratic thinkers like Michelet and Quinet. It also took center stage in the writings of other July Monarchy romantics like Hugo, Lamartine, and George Sand.[72] Foa's novel thus engaged with increasingly important contemporary discussions about building a new religion or reforming an ancient one in order to sanctify the fundamental unity of all people, encouraging them to take responsibility for one another, and at the same time, not to act in such a way as to compromise each other's personal freedom.

Foa's tragic story can be read as using Judaism in much the way that some of her socialist contemporaries were using Christianity. She too built new models for modern morality and politics on the grounds of an ancient revelation, but hers are drawn from Jewish history and religious teachings rather than from Christianity. In contrast to both the extreme individualism of André's uncle and Schaoul's patriarchal tyranny, Foa poses a few examples of true charity and religiosity that respect freedom and universal human interdependence. Daniel's decision to respect Midiane's wish to follow her heart is a good example of this; another is in André and Daniel's friendship, which involves many acts of self-sacrifice for the sake of the other. Similarly, the two maiden aunts, Lia and Angélique, are perhaps the most altruistic characters in the entire novel. Foa explains that as young women, the two aunts had both fallen in love with the same cousin. To decide who would marry him, they drew straws; but when Lia won the draw, she was moved to pity by her sister's unhappiness and refused to go through with the marriage. The two sisters resolved never to marry or to separate from each other, and were growing old together in a house on the "rue de la Poule Mouillée" on the Ile Saint-Louis. The story of the two aunts is clearly inspired by the biblical tale of Rachel and Leah, though of course, with a different ending. With such a well-developed feeling of love and obligation toward each other, it's no surprise that it is they—with the help of the hunchback Daniel—are the ones who wind up raising Midiane's daughter at the end of the story.

A final example of admirable moral behavior is found in Midiane herself, who finds inspiration for her courageous behavior in Jewish tradition, as she interprets it. In her letter to André, bravely telling him that she is willing to forsake her family for his love, she writes:

> As a Jewish girl, my origin gives me the power that made the weak, young Judith the liberator of a people; it gives me the inspired love that made the beautiful Esther a wise and courageous Queen. . . .
>
>   I love; my God, my religion, it's all there. I love, this love makes up my whole life, my whole existence; I love, this word makes me tall and strong, opens my eyes and my mind; the air seems purer to me, the earth lighter, nature sweeter; like celestial harmony, this word spreads a charm around me; it changes my being; from a child with vague and frivolous ideas, it has made an exalted, passionate woman.[73]

Like the maiden aunts, Midiane finds a model for modern virtue in ancient Jewish heroines, and declares that her love is the fulfillment of her religion rather than a betrayal of it. Far from the narrow Judaism of Schaoul, this rehabilitated Judaism is open to the world. Most importantly, it celebrates a freely chosen romantic love rather than stifling it. Even as Foa encouraged Jews to integrate into French society, and advocated reform within the family, she affirmed her faith in Judaism and especially its philanthropic practices. Unlike other popular authors using these tropes—Shakespeare, Scott, Lessing—Foa depicts Midiane's Jewishness as central to her courage. At her most admirable, she is identified with an ancient, exotic race as well as with moral teachings celebrated within the French revolutionary tradition. Moreover, in envisioning a new moral order as including Jews, she affirms that the new morality she advocates is not so much about overcoming Judaism as it is about forming a world in which Jews and Christians can interact freely. Midiane's Jewishness is no obstacle to this; in fact, it serves as a sign that though this new morality is not Catholic, it is nonetheless grounded in an ancient, dignified revelation.

Like the writings of the Jewish Saint-Simonians, Foa's novel accomplished an important goal by finding terms to make expressions of Jewish identity relevant within contemporary French aesthetic and political discussions. Setting *La Juive* in a Jewish family—depicted as patriarchal, traditionalist, and oppressive but ultimately, capable of being rehabilitated—served to add rhetorical force to her liberal political agenda, in much the way that it did for the Saint-Simonians. It served to endow legitimacy and superior moral standing to her vision of a new moral order because it proved that love, equality, and personal freedom could be recognized as fundamental rights without compromising religiosity. Advocating a new religion of friendship and charity to all did not set Foa apart from other liberals in her world. But in presenting models for this from Jewish tradition, Foa's novel connected Judaism to liberalism in much the same way that socialists and democrats were connecting a decidedly non-Catholic form of Christianity to liberalism in the same era.

Conclusion

Pulling on well-established arguments about the consonance of Judaism and French civic virtues, the Jews of the Generation of 1820 redefined Jewish identity as something found in a set of personal, deeply felt emotions, an exotic racial heritage, and an unwavering sense of justice that they connected to the French Revolution and its liberal and utopian socialist heirs. This Jewishness was located within the individual rather than in belonging to a community, passed through heredity rather than learning, and practiced through acts of brotherly kindness rather than religious observance. In some of these representations, images of the Jew represented a new France, liberated from oppression, moral but not Catholic, free but concerned with the welfare of others, ancient but yet tied to the messianic age. This Jewishness, as they defined it, thus bore the mark of the political discussions unfolding in the secular, liberal enclaves for which it was constructed. As these progressive, acculturated Jews saw it, their presence as proud equals in contemporary France was a sign of the success of liberals in the contemporary struggles against religious intolerance, political tyranny, and extreme individualism.

Acculturated as they were, the Jews of the Generation of 1820 nonetheless emphasized their exoticism and their imagined connections to Jews elsewhere in their expressions of identity before the broader

French reading public. Several reasons can be given for this choice. First, given the cultural vogue for things exotic in the age of Romanticism, these young Jews appear to have been able to gain a very positive kind of attention with these representations, especially in the arts. Second, for the Jews involved in contemporary utopian socialist movements, Jews' imagined connectedness in their dispersal served as a model for thinking about how the new global system they hoped to establish might function. Finally, some representations of Jews as outsiders in this context served to glorify liberalism itself as having an important role in world history, painting it as the ideology that could liberate this historically oppressed people everywhere. Indeed, some Jewish writers, like Eugénie Foa, used elements of Judaism itself as conceptual building blocks for the new liberal morality they envisioned for the modern age.

For these young Parisian Jews, cultural and political factors within the milieu in which they were integrating thus provided important reasons for asserting an exotic identity despite their high level of acculturation. The new identity they forged for that audience would play an important role in shaping the form of Jewish international solidarity that was to emerge after 1840, because it laid the groundwork for thinking of the French liberal state as having a mission to "liberate" Jews all over the world.

Four   Secularism and the Civilizing Mission

After 1840, French Jews began to take a heightened interest in the Jews they referred to as "Eastern" or "oriental," that is, who lived in the Ottoman Empire, the Middle East, and North Africa. French Jews' interest in Eastern Jews was multifaceted—simultaneously aesthetic, historical, philanthropic, and political. At its heart was a concern that Eastern Jews' basic human rights were being compromised in the places where they lived because of their religion. In their emerging political advocacy, French Jews portrayed Eastern Jews as mirrors of their own history, oppressed brothers in need of modern education, rational governance, and most importantly, equal rights before the law. Although they often described them as degenerate and backward, French Jews portrayed the Eastern Jews as playing an important role in the modern world as potential conduits through which the fruits of the French revolutionary tradition could be spread. These representations clearly resonated with the politically potent images of Jews that acculturated liberal French Jews had begun to create in this period, which we examined in Chapter 3. At once familiar and exotic, Eastern Jews were portrayed as capable of linking the modern West and the timeless East in a new world order that French Jews, together with their liberal allies, called "civilization."

Why did French Jews begin to reach out to Eastern Jews at this time, and how did these efforts affect their struggle for full equality under a secular state at home? Early French Jewish advocacy on behalf of Eastern Jews seems to have served multiple functions simultaneously. One was directly self-defensive. By the middle of the July Monarchy, French government officials had come into contact with Eastern Jews in Algeria after the conquest of 1830 and in the Middle East following the 1840 Eastern Crisis. In the early 1840s, French Jews were worried about reports that French consuls in the Middle East and French army leaders in Algeria were treating the Jews they encountered abroad with disdain and prejudice. Worse, these officials' slanderous statements about the Jewish religion were beginning to make their way into the French metropolitan press. The most simple reason that French Jews began to defend the rights of Jews abroad was thus to protect Judaism's reputation in France.

Yet in attempting to change the goals and language of French foreign and colonial policy, French Jewish leaders were not acting solely out of defensive self-interest. Defending Jewish rights abroad also provided a way for French Jews to affirm their faith in emancipation and to articulate their commitment to spreading "civilization." In their lexicon, "civilization" included a whole set of political ideals connected to the French Revolution, including religious tolerance, equality before the law, and the protection of individual freedoms, as well as more contemporary liberal economic ideals meant to increase material prosperity, such as free trade and industrial development. In their work on behalf of Jews elsewhere, French Jews expressed their belief that the extension of "civilization" to areas beyond France's borders was a transcendent good and an obligation incumbent upon France, because it would complete the important work of establishing universal freedom, tolerance, and equality begun by the revolution, and would bring material prosperity as well.

Defending Jewish rights abroad in the name of a French "civilizing mission" thus also became an important site for strengthening the alliances between acculturated Jewish leaders and liberals in the 1840s, an increasingly vast group then coalescing into a republican movement. This group included reformist deputies on the left, former Saint-Simonians, university professors, lawyers, and a wide array of journalists and politicians, many of whom would emerge as leaders in the Second Republic of 1848. In the 1840s, members of this network remained committed to limiting the role of the Catholic Church in setting state policy; for this reason, they too took a strong interest in advocating that France embrace secularism in its foreign and colonial policy. Indeed, like education, foreign policy was an important battle-ground in the struggle between *ultramontane* Catholics and anticleri-cals throughout the nineteenth century. This struggle was particularly heated in the early years of the Second Empire, when, as our examina-tion of the Crimean War shall reveal, Emperor Napoleon III was most clearly committed to furthering Catholic interests in foreign policy. Continuing work begun under the July Monarchy, anticlerical liberals struggled in the 1850s to define the "mission" of French policy abroad in terms explicitly connected to the revolution rather than the Catholic Church, and by the 1860s, their arguments would have a significant im-pact on Napoleon III's foreign policy. After the fall of the Second Em-pire in 1870, the concept of a secular "civilizing mission" would shape the Third Republic's colonial and foreign policy even more markedly. As historian Alice Conklin has shown, the Third Republic's colonial civilizing mission was an extension of a particular set of liberal values, including resistance to tyranny, slavery, and feudalism; economic pro-ductivization; a belief in science and progress; hygiene and medicine; private property; and anticlericalism.[1] In the context of this broader struggle between liberals and the clerical party, Jewish leaders' advocacy for Jewish rights abroad was understood as a contribution to a broader effort to wrest control over the power to define France's mission away from the Church in the name of the revolution.

This chapter examines how, through their work on behalf of Jews elsewhere, Jewish leaders cemented their alliances with anticlerical lib-erals, and so helped build a new vision for French foreign and colonial policy that used "civilization" rather than Catholicism as a rallying cry. Examining Jewish contributions to the debates on French foreign and colonial policy in the 1840s and 1850s can help us to understand what was at stake for French Jews in advocating for the rights of Eastern Jews in the name of the French Revolution. In so doing, this chapter also sheds light on the relationship between the battles for secularism and the historical construction of the liberal "civilizing mission" in French foreign and colonial policy in the mid-nineteenth century. As Lucien Febvre and R. A. Lochore have shown, although the term *civ-ilization* was used by a variety of political groups in the first half of the nineteenth century, by the 1850s it became more fully identified with the liberals, who used the term as a secular alternative to the values embraced by *ultramontane* Catholics.[2] In its name, a coalition of liberals, including Jewish leaders, sought to limit the influence of the Church in foreign and colonial policy, and simultaneously, sought to spread the fruits of liberalism to other parts of the world.

The Damascus Affair of 1840

Jewish leaders' commitment to framing France's mission in the world as that of "civilization" has roots in Restoration-era Jewish political rhetoric, but emerged fully only during the Damascus affair. In February 1840, a Sardinian Capuchin friar named Father Thomas disappeared with his servant in Damascus. Although it is clear that the Damascus Jews had nothing to do with his disappearance, they were accused of abducting the two men and killing them in order to use their blood for ritual purposes. A long inquiry ensued, in which Muslim and European Christian officials—especially the French consul, the Comte de Ratti-Menton—worked together to extract "confessions" from leading members of the Jewish community. The methods they used included torture, and resulted in numerous deaths. Meanwhile, Ratti-Menton sent stories about the events to the European press, enraging British and French Jewish leaders who saw the reports as inciting traditional European Christian anti-Jewish beliefs.

In the summer, Adolphe Crémieux, then vice president of the Central Consistory, traveled to Egypt with Sir Moses Montefiore of England to meet with Mohammed Ali and seek his help in defending the Damascus Jews—and Judaism—against the charges that had been leveled against them. In their meeting, they asked Mohammed Ali to issue a *firman* clearing Jews of the charges entirely and declaring the ritual-murder accusation itself to be a "calumnious declaration"; Crémieux also wanted him to abolish altogether the use of torture in interrogations.[3] Though unsuccessful in obtaining any such declarations about Judaism or abolishing torture, the accused were pardoned, and perhaps even more importantly, Montefiore and Crémieux sent back news reports to European newspapers that provided an otherwise absent defense of the Jews and their religion. Even though he failed to achieve many of his goals, Crémieux was greeted as a hero by the liberal press and the Jewish leadership upon his return home for having defended Judaism in the name of the "civilized" world.[4]

The Damascus affair showed Jewish leaders just how important foreign policy was for their own sense of security at home. According to a series of treaties dating back to the seventeenth century, Roman Catholic clergy, and the Capuchins in particular, were protected in Ottoman lands by the French consuls, who answered to the French foreign minister, a post occupied in 1840 by Adolphe Thiers.[5] In this case, Ratti-Menton was not dealing with the rights of Jewish citizens of France, but with Damascus Jews accused of killing a man whose safety he was bound to protect. In this case, then, there was an opportunity for the French official's prejudices against Jews and Judaism to inform his actions. If Ratti-Menton, as an agent of the French state, acted on his belief that the Talmud demanded that Jews kill Christians, then similar accusations might surface once again in France. This was all the more conceivable because Ratti-Menton was also responsible for sending news to European newspapers about the events as they unfolded. Especially in newspapers like the *ultramontane* Catholic *Univers*, Ratti-Menton's reports gave credence to popular Christian fears about the Jewish religion at a time when Jewish rights in France were still somewhat insecure.[6]

Because of the situation's gravity, French Jewish leaders had to be extremely careful about how they responded. Though they believed Ratti-Menton to be in the wrong, criticizing a French official for mistreating foreign Jews was tricky business. Furthermore, as historian Jonathan Frankel has shown, the Damascus affair had reopened the debate about the morality of the Jewish religion in the German states and in Britain, where government leaders had begun to consider expanding the rights of Jews.[7] In France, the situation seemed dangerous as well. In the Chamber of Deputies, Thiers supported Ratti-Menton when more liberal deputies like the antislavery activist François Isambert and the Jewish deputy Benoît Fould criticized the consul for his actions and his obvious prejudice. In a move that greatly disturbed French Jews, in a speech he made in the Chamber, Thiers even went so far as to describe an opposition between French interests and Jewish interests:

> You protest in the name of the Jews of Damascus and I protest in the name of a Frenchman who until now has carried out his duties with honor and loyalty. . . . When the facts were known, [the Jews] were aroused all over Europe and they brought an enthusiasm and heat to this affair which in my eyes do them profound honor. And, if I may be permitted to say so, they are more powerful in the world than they have pretensions to be. At this very moment they are putting forward their claims in every foreign chancellery. And they are doing so with an extraordinary vigor and with an ardor which can hardly be imagined. It requires courage for a minister to protect his agent under attack. . . . Gentlemen, you should know, and I repeat, the Jews at this very moment are in the chancelleries about this affair and our Consul has no support except in the French Ministry of Foreign Affairs.[8]

By criticizing Ratti-Menton directly, French Jews would only make it appear as though they were part of a conspiracy against French interests. Crémieux challenged this view by identifying his work on behalf of the Damascus Jews with French state ideology. He and his colleagues on the Central Consistory identified France with "humanity, civilization, and religion," terms which for them denoted freedom of conscience, the equality of Jews and Christians, and the understanding of Judaism and Christianity as sharing a set of fundamental values. In this framework, the Jews of Damascus, wrongfully accused, were portrayed as needing the protection of "civilized" France from barbaric oriental despots. Armed with this rhetorical strategy, the Central Consistory wrote to Thiers in July:

> The Israelites of all countries, whose ancient and holy beliefs seem incriminated, are protesting with energy. Generous men outside of their faith have shared their indignation. In the English Parliament, in the French Chambers, voices have been raised in favor of the accused . . . a distinguished lawyer of the Paris bar, a member of our consistory, and an Israelite, former magistrate of the city of London, have just left to help the accused with counsel and devotion. . . .
>
> France, the first country to abolish torture in criminal trials, does not want to perpetuate its use in the countries where it favors

the progress of civilization. We do not ask any favors for the accused, in spite of what they have been through; we demand only an enlightened and regular justice, which does not use violence. If they are guilty, may they be left to the rigor of the country's law, if they are not, may their innocence be proclaimed. . . . Say a word, one single word, and the truth will be revealed, and we will thank you in the name of humanity, civilization and religion.[9]

Frankel has shown that Crémieux's reports in the liberal French press portrayed France as the defender of "civilization"—which necessarily included religious tolerance and equality—against fanatical, barbaric accusations.[10] This rhetorical strategy proved effective before the liberal reading public, then highly interested in the issue of religious tolerance, as we saw in Chapter 3. The reports also appeared in several new Jewish newspapers, like the German *Allgemeine Zeitung des Judentums* and the new *Archives Israélites de France*, founded in the wake of the affair. Crémieux linked his defense of the accused Jews of Damascus to the global propagation of the ideals of the French Constitution, especially equality, religious tolerance, and abolition of torture in legal proceedings.

Crémieux's rhetorical strategy in the Damascus affair represents an extension of his vision of secularism to the realm of foreign policy, a vision developed initially in conversation with other opposition liberals in the Restoration era, as we saw in Chapter 2. In so doing, he followed in the footsteps of the Jewish liberal writer Michel Berr, son of the Jewish revolutionary Berr Isaac Berr. In 1814, Berr had argued that the Restoration constitutional monarchy was based not on particular Catholic principles, but as the "defender of religious ideas" in the world, including "freedom of conscience and the civil liberty of religious practice [*la libérté civile des cultes*]." Post-Napoleonic Europe, he contended, should also embrace the true "religious" spirit, affirming "equality and justice for all inhabitants of all the nations" at the upcoming Congress of Vienna by protecting the citizenship rights of German Jews, under threat because of the end of French occupation.[11] In much the same way, during the Damascus affair, Crémieux too depicted France as the champion of religious liberty, and would argue that state policies that discriminated against Jews were "barbaric," and

that France stood for its opposite, "civilization." Like Berr's, Crémieux's language was modestly religious in that it defined religious
freedom and equality as protecting religion rather than harming it. As
we saw above, the Central Consistory had written to Thiers that the
principles of religious liberty and equality were "religious."

Some of Crémieux's non-Jewish supporters, in contrast, went
much farther in their use of religious language. In the new, messianic
religious spirit that had gripped the left since the early 1830s, one
anonymous author published a poem in the *Observateur des Tribunaux*
about Crémieux's trip to the East as a sacred mission for liberal legal
principles. This excerpt illustrates just how "religious" this cause was
understood to be by supportive friends in the legal community:

> . . . Crémieux, your mission is holy;
> It is worthy of you.
> Neither gold nor fear
> Has ever frightened or tempted you away from your faith.
>
> You don't sequester your faith away in the narrow sphere
> Of sects divided, nor of Hebrews rites;
> Your faith lives in these words, "All men are brothers;
> Let them be equal with one another!"
>
> Yes, since Judea, dispersed in the world,
> Is once again banned from this equality,
> Run to Damascus; there, let your voice plant
> Seeds, the fate of legality!
>
> Go, unveil the error, and confound the imposture
> Put the flame back in the hands of the innocent
> Go tell Mohammed that torture
> Puts the judge behind the executioner.[12]

Identifying Mohammed Ali with the Prophet Mohammed, calling him
an "impostor" and painting Crémieux's trip as a mission against "error"
appealed directly to these liberal readers' ideas of a holy crusade. Yet
though the mission Crémieux was undertaking was depicted as religious, it was certainly not identified as Christian; rather, it was a crusade
of universally applicable legal principles. In addition, Crémieux is unmistakably Jewish in this poem; the use of the term *banned* (*mise . . . au
ban*) even alludes to the oppression Jews suffered under the Catholic

Inquisition. Crémieux's Jewishness was represented as a voice of pure morality that speaks out against intolerance, greed, and oppression, much like Foa's depiction of the heroine in her 1835 novel *La Juive*. As such, it served as a vehicle for this anonymous author to glorify French legal principles as a kind of sacred crusade of revolutionary principles by using terms that resemble and replace the Catholic conception of France's mission.

French Jews' strategy of replacing Catholic language with that of "civilization"—itself increasingly deemed religious by its liberal champions—was not abandoned after the resolution of the Damascus affair. In part, this was because the affair reverberated throughout the 1840s. New ritual-murder accusations against Jews in the Ottoman Empire surfaced in the French press in 1843, 1844, and 1847, and the anti-Jewish press continued to publish documents from the Damascus affair itself throughout the 1840s.[13] On these occasions, the French Jewish press called on its government to protect accused Jews in the name of its most cherished humanist values, which, French Jews argued, took priority over the traditional mission of French Middle Eastern policy to protect Christians. In response to the 1843 case, Samuel Cahen (1796–1862), editor of the newly founded *Les Archives Israélites*, followed Crémieux's rhetorical strategy closely, with a clear appeal to anticlerical allies: "The representatives of the most civilized nation must make civilization prevail everywhere. France proclaims herself the protector of the Catholics of the Orient. Here is what politics dictates: France must be the protector of humanity everywhere."[14] Similarly, in response to the 1844 case, Cahen called upon the Foreign Ministry to abandon the protection of Christians over and above the goals of civilization, which Cahen defined as "tolerance and legality."[15] Cahen knew as well as Crémieux did how well such language fit with the liberal agenda of the day; he himself was an avid reader of the liberal press, as can be seen in *Les Archives Israélites*. In addition, his son Isidore (1826–1902) was a brilliant philosophy student at the time; through him, Samuel too would likely have been acquainted with the anticlerical ideas of Jules Michelet and Edgar Quinet.[16]

Jewish leaders' willingness to take a stand about this issue publicly was transformed by the Damascus affair, and particularly, by the support Crémieux had received from liberals for his mission to Egypt. In the midst of the events of 1840, the Jewish deputy, Benoît Fould, had hesitated before challenging Thiers in the Chamber at the risk of seeming to represent particular "Jewish" interests. In stark contrast, once Crémieux himself was elected to the Chamber in 1842, he made frequent allusions to this event and to his Jewishness, even when it was not necessarily relevant.[17] Reminding his fellow deputies of his Jewishness and his connection to the Damascus affair seems to have provided a means to emphasize his credentials before others similarly committed to the revolutionary tradition, and to anticlericalism in particular. One telling moment in this regard came on February 5, 1846, when members of the Chamber of Deputies were drafting a document supporting Polish nationhood. When Henri Monier de la Sizeranne proposed the wording, "In the name of the rights of nations, in the name of Christian civilization and humanity," Crémieux objected, demanding that the document read simply "civilisation tout court [just civilization]." Murmurs broke out in the Chamber; one voice exclaimed, "It's an allusion to the persecution of the Syrian Jews!" Monier de la Sizeranne responded with a clarification: "Since M. Crémieux . . . asks me why I insist on the words Christian civilization . . . I mean any civilization that takes the basic precepts of Christianity as its foundation and line of conduct, that is, which proclaims tolerance and freedom." Crémieux, long a supporter of the Polish nationalists, was not objecting to supporting their movement; rather, he was taking the opportunity to promote secularism, as conceived within the French revolutionary tradition, in foreign policy.[18] Monier de la Sizeranne himself certainly understood this, gauging from his response. Crémieux's outburst pleased the increasingly acculturated Jewish reading public. Reporting on the matter in the Jewish newspaper *L'Univers Israélite*, editor Simon Bloch commented, "The chamber did not adopt M. de la Sizeranne's version; the members probably thought that tolerance and freedom in France date back to our revolutions and not at all to the birth of the Gospel. Before '93, were our *rois très-Chrétiens* (good Christian kings) particularly tolerant toward Jews and Huguenots?"[19] For Bloch as for Crémieux, foreign policy was increasingly important terrain not only for defending Judaism, but also, for defending the anticlerical tradition of the revolution.

The Jews in Early Colonial Algeria

Crémieux and other Jewish leaders embraced a similar political strategy in another crucial setting in the 1840s: the relatively new colony of Algeria. Here too, they defined France as having a mission of "civilization" rather than Christianity, and "civilization" was identified as including the extension of religious liberty and equal treatment for all religions formally recognized under the law. Unlike in the Damascus affair, however, French Jews were extraordinarily effective in shaping French policy regarding Algerian Jews. With the help of policy makers from the university and the Ministry of Worship, French Jews were able to provide the initial contours for shaping a "civilizing mission" in French colonial policy in Algeria, guided by the conception of secularism they had developed in the 1820s.

As in the Damascus affair, French Jewish interest in the Algerian Jews first emerged in response to the anti-Jewish prejudice displayed by the French officials in the region. The conquest of Algeria was still insecure in the early 1840s, and as such, the colony remained under the control of the War Ministry. French Jews' concerns about the War Ministry were strikingly comparable to their concerns about the Foreign Ministry, and the facts of military rule seemed to warrant this concern. In the 1830s and 1840s, the military administration based in Algiers was largely autonomous from metropolitan authorities. General Thomas-Robert Bugeaud, the most important French leader in Algeria until 1847, was widely known to harbor anti-Jewish sentiments, and furthermore, his secretary in the early 1840s was the notorious Jew-hater and *ultramontane* activist, Louis Veuillot, who later returned to Paris to edit the Catholic *Univers*.[20] The diverse population of the new colony included a significant minority of over twenty thousand Jews, who were in a rather tenuous situation under Bugeaud's control.[21] Bugeaud believed that these Jews were working against the French in their attempts to secure control in the colony, even though some of them had served the French army as interpreters, money-changers, and guides. In a series of writings about the Jews, Bugeaud argued that the French had made a great mistake in treating Jews and Arabs alike, for this equal treatment made them seem less trustworthy in the eyes of the Arabs. Jews, he wrote, were "parasites" and "spies for our enemies who exploit us scandalously . . . who corrupt our soldiers in buying them clothes, and who, in times of great danger, will betray us." He recommended expelling the Jews and seizing their property, or perhaps sending them to France where they could be properly "regenerated."[22]

Bugeaud was not the only administrator in the Division of Algerian Affairs to see the Jews as useless members of colonial society, nor was he alone in wanting to govern Algeria separately from metropolitan France, and by ideological principles distinct from those embodied in metropolitan government and its Charte. In Algeria, unlike in France, the Jews were treated as a corporate entity. The War Ministry allowed Jews to maintain their own religious law in civil matters like inheritance, marriage, and divorce, and to administer their own system of taxation. Furthermore, all government dealings with the Jews were mediated through the community's leadership.[23] In 1844, C. E. Guyot, an official in the Division of Algerian Affairs who later became governor-general, addressed the question of whether Jews should serve in the local militias. Given the need to break the Jews of the "esprit de caste," he wrote, Jews theoretically should be asked to serve. However, he went on to specify, only those who wore European dress and spoke French should be allowed to do so. Recognizing that this would mean that almost all Algerian Jews would thus be exempt, he went on to suggest that the community be required to pay a heavy tax for their exemption. This final proposal suggests that Guyot's plan was designed less to encourage acculturation to European norms than to justify heavy communal taxation in the name of Jewish "backwardness" and "clannishness."[24]

French colonial administrators' attacks on Algerian Jews were disseminated in the French press and some writers used them to show that Judaism was fundamentally immoral. In 1845, Marseilles Consistory president Isaac-Jacques Altaras (1786–1873), a vocal advocate for the Algerian Jews, reviewed the ways in which Algerian Jews had been slandered since the conquest. He reported that even the liberal *Journal des Débats* had described the Algerian Jews as "half-barbarian." In the more conservative *Courrier de Marseille*, he reported, they were depicted in even more ominous terms:

> We energetically protest the epithets of barbarians, half-barbarians, ignorant, brutish, and so on, which are given to our Algerian co-religionists by men who do not even know them. Because some miserable Africans have been seen dragging their tattered rags through the streets of Marseilles, five hundred thousand Jews who live in that part of the world are condemned! Everyday, we see the unfortunate of all countries walking the streets of our capital in even more hideous poverty, and certainly, no one would ever get the idea to judge entire peoples by these sad specimens. May it be well known: when one is an ISRAELITE, living in any country whatsoever, one cannot be barbarian, nor brutish; one can be oppressed, persecuted, misunderstood by sincere writers, slandered by intolerant lunatics, but one can never lose the divine intelligence that the Jewish faith has lit in our soul.[25]

With the War Ministry blatantly discussing expelling Jews from Algeria and the French press suggesting that Judaism was "uncivilized" at the very time of the Damascus affair, members of the Central Consistory were alarmed. In addition, since the late 1830s, a vocal group of Catholics in Marseilles had been pushing the War Ministry to begin to convert the Algerians (Jews and Muslims both) to Christianity.[26] In response, the Central Consistory wrote to the members of the Marseilles Consistory—many of whom had personal and business contacts with North Africans—imploring them to suggest ways to improve the conditions of Algerian Jewry.[27] The two men who responded were well qualified: Marseilles Consistory president Isaac-Jacques Altaras was a Syrian-born entrepreneur and president of his local chamber of commerce, fluent in Arabic as well as French, and Joseph Cohen (1817–99) was a lawyer and amateur Jewish historian from Aix.[28]

In 1842, after a short trip to examine conditions in the colony, Altaras and Cohen submitted a report advocating direct governance by metropolitan agencies rather than by army officials on the spot, the legal dissolution of the formal *communautés* and the establishment of consistories to regulate Algerian Jewish religious life and education.

At the heart of their report was an implied criticism of army administration as reminiscent of Old Regime feudalism. Direct governance
from Paris, they argued, was the only way to fulfill France's obligation
to establish a rational legal system and to defend freedom of conscience and religious equality. They suggested that the army's treatment of Algerian Jewish *communautés* as legal entities was tantamount
to feudalism. Although they recognized that this policy was to some
degree consistent with those of the Turks before the French conquest,
they argued that the policies of the Division of Algerian Affairs that
treated Jews as legally distinct were fundamentally unconstitutional,
and left open the possibility of abuses and arbitrary governance that
the French, as "civilized" rulers, were obligated to oppose.[29] Altaras
and Cohen's report argued forcefully that corporatism had no place in
a French colony. In interesting ways, this argument foreshadowed the
Third Republic's colonial policy of combating native systems of governance in the name of eradicating "feudalism."[30]

Altaras and Cohen saw France's purpose in the colony as a "sublime"
mission to "initiate the fallen races to modern civilization," by bringing
a new political system, French education, and commerce to its inhabitants.[31] Their report is filled with references to France's colonial mission as a sacred one; yet the means through which it was to be achieved
were not churches or synagogues, but rather, secular state institutions.
The first step in dealing with Algerian Jews, Altaras and Cohen suggested, was to incorporate them into the body politic by bestowing political rights and obligations upon them.[32] In their minds, Algerian
Jews were essentially stateless, and the communal institutions that military officials treated as sovereign bodies were, in fact, corrupted religious institutions. They argued that native rabbinical courts should at
once be abolished and replaced by French ones and that Algerian Jews
should be subject to French law in all matters. In addition, they advocated radical fiscal reform on a metropolitan model. Jewish communal
leaders should no longer collect taxes, since this led to corruption, and
the community treasury should be nationalized and Jewish religious
administration should be incorporated within the state budget.[33] Furthermore, Altaras and Cohen advocated replacing Algerian rabbis and
religious teachers with French schools and French rabbis under the

control of the Central Consistory, in order to assure that "civilization" would progress without compromising freedom of conscience. Consistorial schools would "enlighten" Algerian Jews by teaching them "useful" vocational skills as well as the duties and fruits of modern citizenship. They described these schools as a "baptism to be spilled on the head of the people" to teach them good morals, good work habits, and agricultural knowledge.[34] Here, to emphasize that the bestowal of the rights and obligations of citizenship was uplifting and transformative, Altaras and Cohen adopted the language of Christian conversion for the French colonial mission. Instead of bringing them into the Church, this "baptism" would introduce them into a new life as French citizens, changing and uplifting them without compromising their religious freedom.

Altaras and Cohen's suggestion to establish colonial consistories thus rested on their understanding of the proper relationship between religion and the state, based on the model that Central Consistory leaders had fought so hard to establish in the Restoration period. They argued that religious bodies should be transformed into educational and spiritual bodies, whose main task should be to teach the proper values for good members of society. In replacing Algerian rabbis and teachers with French schools and French rabbis, Judaism would be elevated, not threatened. Moreover, by bringing religion into the public budget, the French state would assure that Jews could return to the central values of Judaism—fraternity and philanthropy. Thus, using the logic developed in the French Jewish experience, Altaras and Cohen saw incorporating Judaism within the French state as the means to elevate Judaism to a higher form, and at the same time, to create good citizens and thereby secure French rule in the colony.[35]

Implementing Altaras and Cohen's suggestions for colonial religious policy would never have been possible had Central Consistory members in Paris not found allies among officials in the Ministry of Worship, the university, and the War Ministry administration in Paris. These allies shared an understanding of what France's "civilizing mission" in Algeria should be, and how religious policy could be used to achieve those ends. Agreement over these issues was clearly apparent by February 1843, when the War Ministry formed a commission to propose a new organization for the Jews of Algeria. The deputy Eugène Janvier presided over the commission, which included three members of the Central Consistory (Philippe Anspach, Colonel Max Cerfberr, and Crémieux), a War Ministry official (Fellman), a representative from the Ministry of Worship (Charles-Frédéric Cuvier, a Protestant serving as head of the Ministry of Worship's division of non-Catholic sects), and a university official (Nicolas Artaud, a collaborator on Pierre Leroux's *Revue encyclopédique*).[36] Commission members immediately reached a consensus that the French had a duty to "civilize" the Algerian Jews, and that this was best achieved by bringing them under French jurisdiction, establishing schools, and abolishing communal leadership. Cuvier stated that this was the best way for France to begin to fulfill her mission to "civilize" Algeria, since the Jews were "closest to us."[37] Building on established liberal arguments about the consonance of Judaism with French civic virtues, the commission members thus implicitly distinguished Judaism from Islam, which most colonial policy makers perceived as conflicting with French civic virtues.[38] This distinction set the stage for governing the two groups of native Algerians in very different ways.

The transformation of Algerian Jewish life envisioned by the commission was to be effected by a set of changes in civic life: defining rabbis as "religious" leaders rather than political representatives, bringing religious organization under the control of the Central Consistory, and establishing schools to teach Algerians the morality of citizenship. Education, in the hands of consistorial rabbis, was at the very center of the commission's idea of how Algerian Jews could be "civilized." Artaud, who in 1848 would be given the task of organizing French schools in Algeria, described the colony as a "country under tutelage."[39] Like Altaras and Cohen, he thought consistorial schools could help Algerian Jews—whom he believed to be quite intelligent and lacking only a decent education—to realize their potential. Janvier agreed, pointing out that with new teachers, the young would learn new ways, as Frenchmen had after Napoleon Bonaparte reorganized the university system. All the members agreed that French schools should be established immediately, under the direction of the consistories and the inspector of public education, like their counterparts in

France. The three Central Consistory members were adamant that these schools, like the rest of the consistorial budget, be funded by the French government. Consistory president Max Cerfberr, who, like Crémieux, had been elected to his first term as deputy in the French Chamber the previous year, even went so far as to argue that the government should allocate funds to encourage children to go to these schools, but Janvier struck down his motion as impractical.[40] Although the consistory members were interested in more state fiscal involvement than the gentile commission members, all believed that religion should be used as a pedagogy for citizenship, as it was for Jews in France.

The commission's decisions were submitted to the king, who formalized them in the *ordonnance* of November 9, 1845. Although Algerian Jews were not made citizens and thus, still retained a special status under French jurisdiction, they were no longer considered a nation apart, living by their own law with their own communal leaders and courts, as the Muslim communities were. To regulate Algerian Jewish religious life, three departmental consistories were established in Algiers, Oran, and Constantine. As with the departmental consistories in metropolitan France, the Central Consistory was given the power to appoint rabbis and lay consistory members. These rabbis and lay members would exercise a great deal of control over the native population, which would otherwise be stripped of any legitimate institutions of government until 1870 when Algerian Jews were made French citizens.[41]

In the late 1840s, French rabbis were sent to administer Algerian Jewish worship and establish schools. Their work in the colony shows that they too saw the transformation of religious life on a metropolitan model as a crucial element of France's "civilizing mission" in Algeria. Two principal changes concerned them most upon their arrival: first, to teach new values to Algerian Jews through sermons and schooling; and second, to dismantle all indigenous communal institutions, which they saw as largely responsible for the "degeneracy" of Algerian Jews. These concerns reflected their metropolitan biases. As we saw in Chapter 2, French Consistory leaders perceived the consistories as neutral state institutions acting solely in the public interest.

In contrast, separate communal Jewish institutions were viewed with suspicion as corporate entities reminiscent of feudalism.

This perspective is clear in the early reports compiled by the leaders of the three Algerian consistories—Rabbi Lazare Cahen in Oran, Rabbi Michel Weill in Algiers, and Marx Gugenheim, a French businessman and lay president of the Constantine Consistory—who arrived from France in the late 1840s. In 1850, these leaders were asked to submit reports about the conditions of the Jews in their areas. Once completed, these reports were reprinted in *Les Archives Israélites* and thus diffused among French Jewish leadership. Each of the reports began with a critique of the communal institutions in place, which they (like Altaras and Cohen) described as corrupted and corrupting because they were administered by individuals rather than by a state acting in the public interest. In Oran, Rabbi Cahen reported that since synagogues were privately owned, religion itself was in danger. The owner was an "absolute master" of his synagogue, and anyone unhappy with how he did things would not be able to complain; instead he would leave the synagogue and form his own. Furthermore, the proceeds from the sale of synagogue honors went directly to the owner. Cahen saw this as wholly unacceptable, and a cause of moral degeneracy among Oran's Jews. He wrote, "You understand, Messieurs, all the indignity and sacrilege that makes up this sort of organization. A house of prayer, created out of discord, hate, and vengeance, meant to satisfy personal vanity, and winding up as an object of speculation, I ask you Messieurs, is this a holy place, a house of God?" Instead, Cahen proposed that the Oran Consistory build a "single, vast temple, proportionate to the size of the population and in harmony with the sacred needs of the religion," to be supported entirely from the budget of the Ministry of Worship.[42] Cahen described the French model of religious administration as unified and rational, as opposed to the tyrannical and arbitrary rule of illegitimate leaders.

Consistories were in charge of much more than houses of worship, and in every domain, the French rabbis proposed changes that effectively extended the metropolitan model of secularism to the colony. Michel Weill (1814–89), chief rabbi of Algiers, believed that Algerian Jews were good-hearted but lacking modern instruction. Their education centered only on religious forms rather than what their religion could teach them about morality and especially, the crucial value for citizens, fraternity.[43] Weill focused on this larger project of *moralisation* in both his educational programs and his sermons, in which he portrayed Judaism as embodying individual values like perfectibility, courage, self-control, and social values like charity, fraternity, sympathy, and foresight, qualities that in his mind, formed the basis for good citizenship.[44]

The reforms Weill proposed depended on important fiscal support from the state, since he was essentially advocating that the local community no longer support its own charity and other services. Weill was particularly committed to modernizing charity, which he believed would eventually solve the problem of Algerian Jewish poverty. His solution to this problem mirrored Cahen's solution to the problem of private synagogues in Oran. He believed that only by making charity a public program rather than a matter of individual choice would the problem of Jewish poverty in Algiers finally be resolved. Although he found the Algerian Jews particularly hospitable and generous, he saw their charity system as unproductive, offering no long-term solutions to the problems of the poor. Using a language familiar to metropolitan readers, Weill called for the establishment of charity institutions which would be not only generous, but could prevent future ills. He wrote:

> The sole defect of their charity, a defect found among all uncivilized people, is its shortsightedness. It is reparative but not providential; it seeks ardently to diminish the sufferings of poverty, but it cannot prevent them; it extends its hand to he who has fallen, but it shows itself unable to prevent the fall; it opens its purse to any passerby, to the beggar, to the sick, to those without work and without resources, but it is incapable of reducing begging, to comfort the infirm, to cure illnesses, to teach work skills for the unemployed to use in the future.[45]

In reforming Algerian Jewish charity, Weill sought to teach the sick, the poor, and the unemployed the same moral lessons he was teaching the young in his schools. In 1847, he created a consistorial charity committee, which he hoped would replace the preexisting charity institutions entirely. Eventually, he sought to reform all the financial practices of the community by having all religious expenses—including the administration of charity, synagogues, and schools—paid directly by the state. By taking these services out of the hands of the community, he though they would be administered in a more "providential" manner.[46]

The reform program of the Algerian consistories differed from those of the metropolitan consistories only in that the people whose religious life they administered were not French citizens. Otherwise, the aim of educating the Jews through religious and professional instruction and the reform of charitable institutions was similar.[47] This change in charity practices fit well with new metropolitan policies which saw the problem of poverty as public rather than individual, and saw the state, not the Church, as obligated to provide the solution. As historian Lee Shai Weissbach has shown, the transformation of Jewish charity in this period corresponds to a larger shift in French charity practices. Gérando's 1820 classic, *Le Visiteur du pauvre*, had inaugurated a new era in French charity which accompanied the industrial revolution: a secular form of charity in which the elite felt themselves responsible for the "social regeneration" and "moralization" of the lower classes. This form of charity sought not only to relieve the pain and poverty of the needy, but to transform their morality by teaching them values like domestic religiosity, thriftiness, discipline, cleanliness, and work.[48]

French Jews' campaign on behalf of the Algerian Jews was rooted in an understanding that the Charte obliged the French state to extend its religious policy to all places under its control. Based on a shared notion that France had a mission to "civilize" those who fell under its jurisdiction, Central Consistory members and their liberal allies embarked on a gradual program to reform Algerian Jews by administering their religion and education, extending the metropolitan model of religious policy to the colony. Religious bodies, they agreed, had an important public purpose: they were to educate citizens, not to represent, nor to collect taxes, nor to adjudicate between members of society. Making these changes was incumbent upon France, as the heir of the revolutionary tradition. "France never forgets that she is the fertile mother of civilization and freedom," Samuel Cahen wrote in *Les Archives Israélites*. "She found Jews in Algeria oppressed and miserable, downtrodden by slavery and humiliation . . . she took on the glorious task of rehabilitating them, of breaking the chains of their ignorance and prejudices, of reawakening the feelings of dignity and honor within them. And she gave this noble mission to eminent men, chosen from among the French Israelites, entrusting them with the education of these disinherited pariahs."[49] Cahen's view of French Jewish action in Algeria is clear here: it is a "noble" work of tutelage, conducted in the name of the French revolutionary tradition that liberates people from the bondage of barbarism, feudalism, and religious fanaticism. Together with these allies similarly committed to secularism as conceived within the liberal tradition, French Jews helped transform the situation of Algerian Jews, and at the same time, secured a position for themselves within the agencies of French policy making.

The range of issues French Jews confronted in the 1840s show how essential it had become for French Jews to contribute to redefining French policy abroad. In order to stem the tide of negative publicity about their religion, and instead, to affirm Judaism's consonance with the basic civic morality of France, French Jews advocated advancing the principles of the revolution in colonial and foreign policy, principles that they called, with increasing frequency, "civilization." Indeed, by the time Crémieux opposed *civilisation chrétienne* to *civilisation tout court* in the Chamber in 1846, the difference between these two concepts had become relatively clear to French Jewish leaders. Foreign policy, like domestic policy, should be free from religious prejudice, advancing "civilization" rather than Christianity. So too did colonial policy represent an extension of metropolitan religious policy to the colony—as least as it concerned Jews. In the colonial context, "civilizing" Algerian Jews meant transforming their systems of governance, education, charity, and worship, all under the supervision of French Jewish consistory officials, with the ultimate goal of eradicating communal autonomy and making Algerian Jews French citizens, a legal status they would attain formally only in 1870.

The Crimean War

During the Crimean War of 1853–56, and especially at its conclusion, French Jewish leaders began to advocate for equal rights for Jews in Ottoman lands, arguing that France had a mission to promote equal treatment for religious minorities before the law everywhere. To this end, members of the Central Consistory wrote to Emperor Napoleon III urging him to make sure that Jews as well as Christians would soon be treated as legal equals in the Ottoman Empire. The philanthropist Albert Cohn, a member of the Paris Consistory and employee of the Rothschilds, embarked on a trip to assess the condition of Jews in the Ottoman Empire and established schools for them. The Jewish press published numerous articles on Ottoman Jewry, informing the public of their living conditions and the dangers they currently faced, and calling on readers to express sustained support for their "civilization."[50]

The rhetoric French Jewish leaders used to advocate for the rights of Jews in the Ottoman Empire strongly resembled their advocacy on behalf of Algerian Jews in the 1840s. Here, however, allies were found much more easily, since the Crimean War had occasioned an extensive public discussion about whether France's mission in foreign policy should be a Catholic or a secular "civilizing" mission. Indeed, unlike in Algeria or in the Damascus affair, in this case, French Jews' advocacy was not so much directly self-defensive as designed to add their voices to a larger liberal campaign already underway. The politics of this liberal campaign were decidedly anticlerical, and pulled strongly from ideals articulated by Saint-Simonians in the 1820s and 1830s and the republicans of 1848, and were clearly informed by the movement for secular education in the 1840s. Taking place in the aftermath of Louis Napoleon's coup d'état that formally established the Second Empire, the Crimean War raised crucial issues about the new emperor's agenda in foreign policy, and this issue was debated at length in the press throughout the conflict. In this context, French Jewish leaders' advocacy during the conflict gave them a place within this broad coalition of liberals interested in limiting the role of the clerical party in shaping

French policy. Far more than in the 1840s, French Jewish leaders' support for a secular foreign policy during the Crimean War served to solidify their alliances with former Saint-Simonians, anticlerical professors, and republicans similarly committed to a "civilizing mission," which they defined as necessarily including freedom of conscience, equality before the law, championing the rights of the oppressed, and limiting the role of the Catholic Church in determining matters of state policy.

Because of the issues involved, the Crimean War was a crucial moment in forging the liberal ideological foundation of France's "civilizing mission" to the world. The war grew out of a diplomatic crisis between Russia and Turkey that began in 1850. By the end of March 1854, France and Britain had come to Turkey's aid, sending troops to meet the Russians in battle in southeastern Europe. A primary cause of this war was the long-standing "Eastern Question," the tensions and rivalries among the European powers (Austria, France, Great Britain, and Russia) over the withdrawal of Ottoman control from portions of its empire.[51] The conflict erupted following the so-called "quarrel of the keys," a dispute between Catholic and Orthodox monks, beginning in 1849, about which group had the right to control the Church of the Holy Sepulcher in Jerusalem. Because the Catholics were protected by the French and the Orthodox Christians by the Russians, the monks' dispute became an international incident, further exacerbated when, in 1853, Russia attempted to intervene on behalf of Montenegro, an Orthodox Christian nation, in its border dispute with Turkey. In response to this Russian attempt to expand into its territory under the pretext of protecting Orthodox Christians, Turkey declared war in October 1853, and solicited the support of Britain and France. After the Russians and the Turks failed to reach a peace agreement, France and Britain declared war against Russia at the end of March 1854.[52]

In the minds of some historians today, the religious issue between the Catholic and Orthodox monks in Jerusalem was but "a petty and absurd affair of only local relevance."[53] This issue ignited a fire long in the making, not entirely or even fundamentally centered on the sectarian concerns apparent in the quarrel of the keys. Yet the centrality of religious questions in guiding French foreign policy in the conflict was the subject of an intense debate in the domestic press during the conflict itself. As numerous historians have contended, Napoleon III became embroiled in the Crimean conflict for domestic reasons as well as diplomatic ones. Sending troops to the Crimea appealed to the same diverse group of Catholics—ranging from moderate republicans like Monsignor Marie-Dominique-Auguste Sibour, the archbishop of Paris, to *ultras* like Veuillot—who had supported the 1849 Rome Campaign, undertaken when Louis Napoleon was president of the Second Republic. In the early years of the Second Empire, the emperor needed this kind of support to maintain his power, and it was for this reason that he framed France's involvement in the conflict as based in the long-standing French duty of protecting Catholic interests in the Ottoman lands.[54]

The declaration of war was well received by numerous French Catholic leaders. Since the 1840s, Catholic leaders in France (like Protestant leaders in England and Switzerland) had been calling on their congregations to put pressure on their governments to help the beleaguered Christians of the Ottoman Empire.[55] Their views were widely publicized at the outset of the conflict. César Famin, the French consul in Jassy, Romania, and editor of the *Encyclopédie catholique*, published a book in 1853 reminding readers of the French legal obligation to protect Christians from the Muslim Turks (whom he called "infidels"), who did not allow Christians to own property or build churches. Explicitly invoking the memory of the crusades, Famin asserted that in the current crisis, the main issue was whether Russia or France would emerge as the protector of Christian rights in the Ottoman Empire, and patriotically called on France to uphold its historic duty in this regard.[56]

Although Famin argued that France should protect Jews in the East as well—their rights, he wrote, were also compromised under the Turks—other leaders were more focused on defining France's mission as exclusively Catholic.[57] According to reports in the Jewish press, Archbishop Sibour led public prayers for the troops engaged in what he saw as a new holy war, fighting for "the cause of civilization and our holy religion." Sibour, who had been a staunch supporter of the Second Republic, had also played an important role in the clergy's struggle for greater control in education. The blessing he offered in the name of both "civilization" and Catholicism mirrors his attempt to embrace liberalism while also strengthening the role of the Church in public life.[58] More conservative Catholic writers were reported to have called the war a "holy crusade" waged purely on behalf of the Church.[59] In the eyes of those embattled against the clerical party, Church leaders at home seemed to be using this opportunity to push for a greater role in policy making and national self-definition.

For this reason anticlerical writers sought to define France's mission in the conflict in purely "civilizational" rather than Catholic terms. Still supporting the war, liberals defined the war as a struggle between "barbarism" and "civilization," rather than between Catholic and Orthodox Christians or between Christians and Muslims. In adopting this strategy, liberals did not oppose protecting Christians in Ottoman lands, but rather claimed that only advancing liberalism within Turkey would truly protect Eastern Christians. Journalist Emile de Girardin, former deputy and founder of the liberal newspaper *La Presse*, was particularly articulate in putting forth this perspective. As he saw it, France should pursue a policy that would bring religious tolerance, the liberation of oppressed nations, as well as the development of science, technology, industrial production, commerce, and credit in the Ottoman Empire. Only this, he claimed, would strengthen Turkey and thus resolve the Eastern Question. Girardin contrasted this goal of "the civilization of Turkey" to a number of other writers' proposals, all of which he saw as either impractical or barbaric. For example, John Lemoinne, an editor of the *Journal des Débats*, had suggested supporting a Greek takeover of the Ottoman Empire, thereby Christianizing it. This, Girardin contended, was a throwback to the medieval crusades, based in *ultramontane* superstition and intolerance, which went against nineteenth-century France's most fundamental notions of freedom and "civilization." Still other writers, according to Girardin, had suggested dividing the Ottoman Empire among the European Christian powers; this, he asserted, was impractical and unjust, since it would involve either a massive population transfer of Muslims to Asia, or even worse, their extermination. Furthermore, he contended, a new crusade on the medieval model would do nothing to protect the holy sites in Syria; on the contrary,

any war around those sites would certainly destroy them.[60] "Civilization" was thus an overarching goal that would simultaneously advance
modern governance, industry, finance, science, and technology, and
also protect Christian holy sites and the rights of non-Muslim subjects
in the Ottoman Empire. Girardin was not attacking Catholicism here;
rather, he was putting forth an argument for state secularism recognizable to others in his orbit by claiming that particular religions, including the Christian confessions, were best protected and even up-
lifted by establishing a liberal legal and economic system.

Girardin's religious politics were crucial to his argument, particularly since they resonated with, and thus drew support from, ideas being articulated by others committed to state secularism along this same
model in the mid-nineteenth century. University professors who had
opposed the return of the Jesuits to French education since the 1840s
were particularly good allies in this regard. Historian Edgar Quinet, a
republican in exile following Louis Napoleon's coup d'état of December 1851, had advanced a similar perspective in two different works in
the 1840s. In his 1845 *Le Christianisme et la Révolution française*, Quinet
had argued that the French Revolution represented a new moment in
which particular sectarian concerns were replaced by a broader "religious" system characterized by its democratic principles. In the revolution, Quinet asserted, France had superseded the Catholic Church as
the bearer of the "religious" mission to form an "alliance of the human
races" by extending democratic principles to the world.[61] In appropriating the terms "religious" and "Christian" to describe revolutionary
principles, Quinet defined democratic beliefs and practices as a set of
transcendent values that incorporated and thus protected particular
ways of worshipping. In contemporary discourse, using these terms in
this way also signaled a strong opposition to the clerical party.

Quinet's view of religion and politics was made even clearer in 1849,
when he published a tract provocatively entitled *La Croisade autrichienne, française, napolitaine, et espagnole contre la république romaine*, in
which he criticized the Rome Campaign. When France sent troops to
protect the pope against the insurgent Roman republic, Quinet restated his position that France's mission in the nineteenth century was
liberal rather than Catholic. The republic should not launch Catholic

crusades as it had in the Middle Ages, he argued, nor should it support the pope as a temporal ruler by "torturing" the Roman people like medieval inquisitors. "Men of good faith," he wrote, "tell me how you expect to establish order by toppling all notions of human conscience . . . destroying nationality, using religion as a mask . . . dismissing a freely elected national assembly with the sword, waging a religious war without faith, a crusade without Christ, which will turn religious freedom into a friendly nation's auto-da-fé."[62] Quinet argued that France needed instead to be true to the basic "religious" principles of the revolution by championing oppressed national groups like the Italians, as well as freedom of conscience, teaching (*enseignement*), and religious belief.[63] The terms Quinet used here—freedom of conscience, teaching, and religious belief—were the rallying cries of the contemporary Liberté de Penser movement, and served to connect international politics to recent struggles within the university. Under the leadership of philosophy professors Amadée Jacques and Jules Simon, an entire spectrum of intellectuals had united in 1847 to limit the role of the Church in education, and their work continued throughout the Second Empire.[64]

Girardin's views on religion in his *Solutions de la question d'Orient* were also similar to those advanced by the Saint-Simonians in the 1820s and 1830s. Though long defunct by the time of the Crimean conflict, many of the movement's former members remained committed to its basic tenets, and by the 1850s, some of them occupied important professional positions, including noted journalists (Charles Duveyrier, Adolphe Guéroult), government officials (Michel Chevalier), engineers (Fernand de Lesseps), and capitalists (the Pereire brothers). The way that Girardin understood the issue, particular religions, including the Christian confessions, Islam and Judaism, would best be protected if "civilization"—as an internationally connective set of values—were advanced. For former Saint-Simonians, advancing "civilization" resonated with some of their earliest goals, designed to transform post-revolutionary France's foreign policy. In fact, one of the group's members may have been first to dub France the "eldest son of civilization," a play on the traditional expression "the eldest daughter of the Church," which would later be used by such liberal luminaries as

François Guizot, Charles de Rémusat, and Quinet.[65] This foreign policy goal was but one part of their broader utopian aim to bring coher-
ence, rationality, and progress to both the material and moral aspects
of modern life by establishing an international banking system, building global transportation networks, emancipating women and workers, eradicating the power of the traditional aristocracy, improving the
economic position of the poor, and establishing a new dogma that
would unite Christians, Muslims, and Jews in a new spiritual order.
By the 1850s, a broad spectrum of liberals, including Girardin, shared
the Saint-Simonian understanding that in order to foster world integration, Catholicism needed to be replaced by a new, more universal
religious perspective.

Indeed, Girardin's 1852 book shares many of the same policy suggestions advanced by Gustave d'Eichthal, ever faithful to Saint-Simonian
goals, in the previous decade. In a text entitled *De l'unité européenne*,
written during the 1840 Eastern Crisis, d'Eichthal argued that as the
"cradle of the religious thought of so many peoples," Syria could be
used for reunifying Europe in the nineteenth century.[66] Instead of
fighting wars for control of the Holy Land, the European nations
should work together to develop commerce and transportation networks in the Middle East, and pressure Turkey to emancipate its non-
Muslim subjects. By working together to "regenerate" Syria, d'Eichthal
argued, Europe could itself be regenerated. But, he stressed, in order
to forge this unity, Europe needs to make sure Turkey holds to its recent promise that "all religions (*cultes*) based in the Bible [will] have
the right to worship freely." Only this, he concluded, could bring
about "the association of all the modern peoples and the two major elements of their civilization: in the material domain, freedom and reg-
ularity of movement between the farthest removed parts of the globe;
and in the moral domain, union of faith with religious tolerance."[67] In
his use of the terms *civilization, regeneration*, and *tolerance*, Girardin
was thus recapitulating this earlier Saint-Simonian argument.

Girardin's book resonated with Saint-Simonian economic goals
even more than its religious perspective. Though he staunchly opposed waging holy war on a medieval model, or extending French
sovereignty formally to the Middle East, he was by no means against

France's greater involvement in Middle Eastern life. He advocated a long process of transforming Turkey through capitalist development, under the tutelage of Western capitalists (who would, of course, also benefit from the endeavor) and legal advisors. One important set of reforms could be achieved by using European capital and technological expertise to establish banks; build railroads, canals, and factories; and establish international houses of commerce. This economic development, he argued, did not mean forcing the Turks to abandon Islam. Long portions of his book were devoted to explaining how favorable Islam was to commerce and credit, so favorable, it seemed to him, that Turks could make it seem as though religion itself was the source of economic development.[68] Girardin also thought that the Turks needed the advice of French and British lawmakers and legal experts, who would help them to transform their legal system on a Western European model. The areas most in need of reform were the tax system—which Girardin saw as irrational, draining manpower with required military service rather than helping build capital with a monetary income tax—and the judicial system, which was so complicated and irregular that foreign commerce was stymied rather than encouraged.[69] These legal reforms, like the economic reforms, were clearly designed to bring foreign investment to Turkey. For Girardin, capitalism itself was a transcendent good that brought moral and material benefits such as "peace, exchanges, credit, circulation, reason, publicity, freedom, reciprocity."[70]

Jewish journalists and consistory leaders in the early 1850s supported arguments like Girardin's in order to express their own liberal views. More directly than Girardin, writers in *Les Archives Israélites* and *L'Univers Israélite* spoke out against the Catholic leaders' views on the war. When Archbishop Sibour blessed the troops in 1854, *L'Univers Israélite* editor Simon Bloch objected, reminding his readers that there were Protestants and Jews among the French troops, and reclaimed the mission for the cause of "civilization." He wrote, "We too call on Heaven to bless our brave troops, not for the good of the Pope or Mohammed, or for Latin or Greek orthodoxy, but in the interest of French national glory, justice for all men, the civilization of all the empires, the moral emancipation of all humanity. For this holy crusade, we can say, God wills it!"[71] Here, Bloch was contrasting a new, universalist religiosity with a Catholic one. A similar perspective was voiced in *Les Archives Israélites* by Isidore Cahen, son of the editor Samuel Cahen (whom Isidore would replace in 1859), who had joined the journal's staff after being barred, because of Catholic prejudice, from taking the philosophy teaching post he had obtained in Brittany in 1849. A former student of the anticlerical philosopher Jules Simon, Cahen's experience in Brittany only served to strengthen his commitment to limiting the role of the clerical party in setting state policy.[72] In 1854, he, like Bloch, objected to Sibour's blessing with clear, anticlerical reasoning that defined tolerance as truly sacred: "To evoke in such a case memories of the crusades, this anachronism is more ridiculous than dangerous," he wrote. "Have they forgotten that the first exploits of the crusaders of the eleventh and twelfth centuries were massacres of Jews?" Crimea was not a "religious war, a war of one sect against another," Cahen argued, "but a truly holy war, that is, a duel between humanity and justice against barbarism and iniquity."[73] The influence of his mentors is apparent here in his distinction between Catholicism and the cause of "justice and humanity," claiming the latter as the truly transcendent "holy" ideal, and the former as having no place in state policy.

Jewish leaders also adopted a liberal perspective on how the "civilization" of the Ottoman Empire should be achieved. Focusing on how to improve the condition of Jews in the empire, French Jews argued that a long-term solution could only be reached with the extension of Western European education, science, technology, industry, and commerce to the region. Isidore Cahen suggested that bright young Turkish Jews be brought to Europe for training in the fields of "teaching, commerce, manual trades, medicine, surgery, architecture, and other sciences." In addition, young Turkish Jews would also "become familiar with the customs, industry, and relations of Europe," which were necessary for establishing lasting relationships with Europeans through which "civilization" could be spread to the entire region.[74] Like Girardin, Cahen saw the creation of global networks of capitalist production and trade as a crucial element of the civilizing process.

Suggestions for legal reform were also just as common in French Jewish discourse as in other liberal discourse. Often, these suggestions were framed in terms reminiscent of the French Revolution. For example, in their petition to the emperor at the outbreak of war, Central Consistory members described Ottoman Jewry as living under "feudal tyranny." They argued that France's war should be waged not on behalf of Christians, but against the "intolerant laws" that discriminated against both Jews and Christians. Just as France had established equal rights and duties for all men on its own soil, and had brought "freedom of conscience" to Africa by "liberating" Algerian Jews from "savage fanaticism," so too should the French establish religious equality and freedom in the Ottoman Empire in the Crimean War.[75] This same liberal perspective is clear in Jewish responses to the 1856 Congress of Paris. Among the numerous internal legal reforms the Turks made at the conclusion of the war was the *hatti Humayun*, promulgated before the congress but included in the treaty as well, which granted members of all religious confessions greater equality in school admission, conscription, and civil service employment.[76] "The Turkish government has fulfilled its duties," Isidore Cahen wrote; "as long as it executes these rules, freedom of conscience is guaranteed from now on in Turkey, and a regime of oppression, iniquity, and antagonism is toppled completely . . . from now on in Turkey, there are no more privileges!"[77] Cahen's language here is telling; as in Jewish leaders' views on the French colonization of Algeria, he was describing the *hatti Humayun* as the destruction of a feudal order.

Although Jews' support of the "civilizing mission" in French foreign policy was not self-defensive in any direct way, it is clear that Jewish leaders felt that in some indirect sense, their own rights were at stake in the construction of a new mission for French foreign policy. Evidence that Jews saw French foreign policy aims as linked to their own struggle for equality can be seen in the Jewish coverage of the Crimean War. In one especially telling article, Isidore Cahen argued that France's championing of equal rights at the peace conference was a sign that "civilization" was making headway in France as well as in Turkey. He suggested that while the troops were fighting in the East, an equally important war had been waged between liberals and the clerical party in the pages of the French press. Initially, he reminded his readers, the war was seen as a kind of crusade undertaken to protect Christian rights in the East. Yet by the end, liberals had won the day. Far from the narrow politics of defending Christians, French diplomats at the peace conference framed France's mission as the pursuit of "universal justice," "rights of conscience," "religious equality [*égalité des cultes*]," "tolerance," "civilization with its arts, teaching, and generosity," and the "cause of the oppressed."[78] For Cahen, French foreign policy had itself been civilized when France had embraced a mission to civilize the rest of the world.

The "Civilizing Mission" as a Liberal Crusade

Isidore Cahen was in many ways correct to see liberalism as triumphant in the Crimean War. By the 1860s, Napoleon III had embraced a *politique des nationalités* in foreign policy and the term *mission civilisatrice* had become commonplace in the press.[79] One telling moment came in 1858–59, when Napoleon III took action on behalf of an Italian Jewish boy, Edgardo Mortara, who had been abducted by papal authorities who insisted that the family had no right to raise him, since he had been secretly baptized by a Christian servant. Though the emperor's actions in this affair alienated many Catholics, the liberal press heartily applauded the cause of the Mortara family.[80] The emperor's actions in the case testified to the shift in his foreign policy, which had come to prioritize freedom of conscience over the interests of the Church.

As liberalism became a more powerful force in foreign policy, it nonetheless bore the stamp of the earlier battles with the clerical party in defining French national identity. Like the Catholic mission in opposition to which it had been constructed, the term *the civilizing mission* was based in a set of ideals that defined a community of believers and obligated them to spread the ideals to the world. The term *civilization* had developed from a largely academic concept, explored by historians like François Guizot and Edgar Quinet, to a political concept meant to be the basis for French action in the world.[81] Among mid-nineteenth-century intellectuals, there was an increasingly strong disagreement over whether there was a single, ever expanding civilization or if in fact, it was more appropriate to speak of multiple "civilizations" developing simultaneously.[82] Yet the journalists and policy makers who developed the political concept of the "civilizing mission" were clearly committed to Guizot's notion that there was but a single "civilization" which was spreading from its European birthplace to the rest of the world. Liberals understood this concept to include a legal system guaranteeing religious equality and freedom of conscience, an international system that recognized the right to national self-determination, an economic system based in capitalist production and trade, and a commitment to the progress of science, technology, and the arts. These ideals were treated as transcendent, sacred, and universal, and those who espoused them assumed that if they were embraced everywhere, a peaceful global system would be created which would allow humanity to realize its fullest potential.

Jewish leaders in the mid-nineteenth century were particularly committed to this unitary, expansive conception of civilization. In assessing the gains of the Crimean War, Isidore Cahen wrote the first of many articles in which he measured the "degree of civilization to which a society had arrived" by the level of equality between its citizens. He stated provocatively that with the *hatti Humayun*, Turkey had achieved a greater level of "civilization" than Switzerland, since many Swiss cantons still had laws discriminating against Jews.[83] In another article, Cahen declared that Sweden had not yet achieved the degree of "civilization" it claimed to have, since Catholics there were still burdened with civil disabilities. He called on the people of Great Britain and France to dedicate themselves to "the diffusion" of tolerance to all the countries of Europe by pressuring Sweden to guarantee equality to members of all religious confessions.[84] Civilization, in Cahen's view, was thus something that could be spread through public outrage and diplomatic pressure from the more advanced nations.

What distinguished the Jewish perspective on France's civilizing mission before and after Crimea was not so much the liberal language in which it was expressed, but rather, the degree to which Jews took independent action in its name. Whereas before the conflict, Jews called on French leaders to understand their activities in a liberal framework, now Jews themselves took steps of their own to fulfill the civilizing mission. In 1859, Cahen called for an international organization to be constituted through democratic election, to maintain international peace and justice. Such a body, he wrote, would bring "civilization" by supporting such endeavors as the building of railroads, the improvement of the postal and telegraph systems, the abolition of slavery and piracy, the protection of trade in wartime, and the protection of national rights. Last but not least, of course, this body would make freedom of conscience an "international dogma," sacred and protected everywhere.[85] Europe had a special responsibility in this regard, Cahen argued, in order to prove it was truly "civilized." "How can Europe insist on the equality of the sects [*cultes*] in the East, in spite of the opposition of Muslim fanatics, if she herself continues to exhibit signs of inequality? What mission can France fulfill in North Africa, and England in the Indies, if not a mission of civilization? How can this mission be fulfilled, if not by scrupulously respecting the beliefs of the conquered races, and intervening only in the practices against which outraged humanity imperiously demands intervention?"[86] The concerns Cahen voiced here demonstrate the degree to which economic liberalism, human rights, and colonialism were intertwined in his mind. Taking the colonial "civilizing mission" as an unquestioned good and an essential part of the liberal agenda, Cahen placed particular stress on the notion that minority religious rights should always be included within it.

These kinds of arguments were developed in conversation with other liberal writers, and were designed to convince allies of the importance of religious equality. In this regard, Jewish writers seem to have been remarkably successful. For example, in 1859 Léon Plée wrote in *Le Siècle* that improving the lot of Jews around the world was a collective duty of the European sovereigns.[87] Similarly, in an 1857 study entitled *La Libérté de conscience*, Cahen's former teacher Jules Simon used equal rights for Jewish citizens a kind of litmus test for the progress of civilization, which he believed to be moving toward greater tolerance.[88] Using the level of Jewish rights to measure the progress of civilization would quickly become commonplace among liberals and Jews. By 1869,

Jewish publicist Léon Hollanderski presented the practice as almost commonsensical, requiring no explanation: "The Jews have become a sort of barometer of civilization and universal progress," he wrote. "If you want to know if one country or another is prospering, look into the status of Jewish rights there."[89]

Liberal Jews found another perfect opportunity to turn their rhetorical commitments into action in 1860, when French public attention was turned once again to the problems facing the beleaguered Christians of the Ottoman Empire. Civil war between Maronite Christians—still protected by the French—and the Druses broke out in late April 1860 on Mount Lebanon in what was then Syria. News of massacres of Christians reached the French press in June, provoking widespread public outrage. Seeing the conflict as exacerbated by the actions of Ottoman authorities in the area, European troops—half of them French—were sent to the region in the fall.[90] Undoubtedly, Jewish leaders felt a degree of trepidation about the clerical party's response to these massacres, remembering the Damascus affair all too well. Seizing the moment to press forward with their campaign to forge a liberal mission for France, a diverse group of Jewish leaders publicly declared their support for the Syrian Christians in the name of religious freedom and equality. Adolphe Crémieux, the Jewish leader best known in liberal circles in France, wrote a letter that appeared in *Le Siècle* of July 12, 1860, calling on French Jews to donate money to the cause. "French Israelites, let us be the first to come to the aid of our Christian brothers; let us not wait for the results of diplomacy, which are always so slow. . . . Let us not lose a day, not an hour. Let the signal of an immense rescue be sounded from a meeting of Jews, here in this capital of civilization."[91] Jewish groups around the country showed their support with impressive donations. Money flooded in from the Central Consistory, the departmental consistories, philanthropic groups, and Jewish schools. The cause drew support from rich as well as poor Jews; in Paris, for example, the wealthy newspaper magnate Jules Mirès gave a thousand francs while others gave only one franc.[92]

This action on behalf of the Syrian Christians was also an opportunity for Jewish leaders to announce that they had founded a new organization, the Alliance Israélite Universelle. The Alliance had, in fact, been formed in April of that year by a group of young liberal republicans, including Isidore Cahen, Jules Carvallo (a former Saint-Simonian), Eugène Manuel (a professor, poet, and, like Cahen, a former student of Jules Simon), and Narcisse Leven (a lawyer working for Adolphe Crémieux).[93] The organization was dedicated to working on behalf of Jews in need around the globe, through advocating for their rights and establishing schools. Making the campaign for the Syrian Christians its first publicized activity, its leaders believed, would prove from the outset that Jews were interested in religious liberty for all, and not just Jews. As Isidore Cahen would write of the campaign, "Mr. Crémieux's idea is great and generous; the clerical party is dumbfounded."[94] In a sense, the Alliance was but putting into action the liberal and anticlerical ideals long embraced by its founders. More than a publicity stunt, choosing this cause as the way to announce their existence helped Alliance leaders to define themselves as the defenders of religious equality and freedom in the broadest possible sense.

The campaign was greeted with applause in the liberal press, from Léon Plée at *Le Siècle* to the liberal newspaper *L'Opinion Nationale*, founded by Adolphe Guéroult, a former Saint-Simonian who had recently left *La Presse*. "Is it not a sign of the times," wrote Guéroult, "that this appeal on behalf of the Christians would come from France, that is, the only country where custom, in accord with the law, has granted Jews complete equality?"[95] Clearly an ally in this cause, Guéroult too framed the campaign as a universal, sacred (though by no means Catholic) work of "civilization." True to his Saint-Simonian roots, Guéroult depicted Jewish action on behalf on the Syrian Christians as a sign that the old religions were finally being replaced by a new religious system:

> Our era is great and truly religious, and those who deprecate it are wrong and misunderstand it. While all the established religions seem to be in decline, with their official representatives attacking one another in a war of persecution and intolerance; while Protestants, persecutors in Ireland and Sweden, are unable to pray in Rome or Spain; while Rome is stealing Jewish boys from their parents and Jewish wives from their husbands under the pretext of religion; while fanaticism is oppressing Jews in Tunis and Christians in Lebanon;

while Russia is oppressing Catholics in Poland and Muslims in the Crimea; we are proud and happy to see that one country alone, and it is our country, France, is protecting the Church, the temple, the synagogue, and the mosque equally, and proclaims loudly, in all its laws, that all men are brothers and that everyone is everyone else's neighbor. Is this not the pure tradition of the Gospel?[96]

Alliance leaders and liberal writers saw an inextricable link between the progress of religious tolerance, human rights, colonialism, and the French revolutionary tradition. As in the Damascus affair, liberal writers used religious terminology to define Jewish leaders' efforts, calling upon readers to understand the civilizing mission as analogous to the Catholic religious mission, only better suited to the modern age. Guéroult's view that the civilizing mission was "the pure tradition of the Gospel" was not a unique turn of phrase. In a book advocating the colonization of Indochina, writer Francis Garnier said that France had "received from Providence a higher mission, that of the emancipation, enlightenment, and liberation of the races and peoples still in the slavery of ignorance and despotism."[97] Léon Halévy lauded the 1860 Syrian expedition with an ode containing the lines, "Crusade of the consoling God / You bring together all believers / The Jew has made his contribution / Just as he will give his children!"[98]

As this poem suggests, using the term *crusade* in order to sanctify action carried out in the name of human rights and especially minority religious rights had become surprisingly acceptable among Jews by the 1860s. Although Cahen and Bloch both objected vociferously to Catholic invocations of the crusades (for example, in the Crimean War), both published articles using the term to describe liberal action in the international arena.[99] The German Jewish writer Moses Hess, living in Paris since the 1840s, was so taken with the term that he described the Syrian expedition as a new crusade paving the way for a Jewish national revival in the Holy Land.[100] This strange intellectual leap was only possible in a discursive context where *crusade* was used to sanctify the extension of liberalism. Hess may have been extreme in advocating a return to Palestine, but he was not alone in using the term *crusade* to replace Catholic concepts with sacred ideals of his own.

Conclusion

The "civilizing mission" of French imperialism and diplomacy thus emerged from the liberal struggles to limit the influence of the Church and Catholic concerns in state policy. However, as we have seen, its visionaries were anything but irreligious. Formed in opposition to Catholicism, "civilization" was described by nineteenth-century liberals as a transcendent, sacred ideal rooted in revolutionary revelation, and they argued that those who were "civilized" had a sacred duty to bring these ideals to the rest of the world. While the content of the civilizing mission was markedly different from the Catholic mission, the basic form was the same. Recognizing it as such forces us to reevaluate our widespread assumption that the "secularism" of nineteenth-century France was an irreligious force of modernization. An extension of the revolution, the civilizing mission reflected the decidedly religious worldview of its architects.

The religious perspective of anticlericals is clear in their support for the Alliance Israélite Universelle's activities, and its remarkable identification of Judaism, the French revolutionary tradition, and the civilizing mission. Hostile as they were toward Catholic attempts to define France's mission abroad, liberals applauded expressions of religiosity that came from Jewish leaders. In part, this was possible because Jewish leaders consistently avoided any religious particularism and even embraced Christian terms such as *baptism* and *crusade* in consecrating the civilizing mission. Still, given the efforts of some Catholics such as Sibour to reconcile liberalism and Catholicism in this same period, the disparity between Catholics and Jews is remarkable. Whereas anticlerical activists came increasingly to describe Christianity and the revolutionary tradition as irreconcilable in the 1850s and 1860s, they were clearly more welcoming of Judaism. Perhaps the clearest early expression of this rejection of Christianity as a whole can be found in Michelet's work on the French Revolution; other anticlerical activists would remain open to incorporating Christianity in some form for a longer time. However, anticlerical support for *Jewish* liberal religiosity remained constant, and in this sense, mirrors the philo-Protestantism of anticlericals like Quinet.[101]

The reason for this disparity seems clear. Liberals in this period were not antireligious; they were anti*clerical*. With the widening gap between *ultramontane* Catholics and liberals in the 1850s, exacerbated by the hardening of the pope's position against liberalism, French liberals appear to have found in the kinds of Jewish expressions we have seen here a language to sanctify their political agenda.[102] As in the July Monarchy period, Judaism continued to appear authentically "religious" to these liberals, and yet, accepting expressions of religiosity from Jews could never be confused with openness to Catholicism, since the *ultramontane* camp under the leadership of men like Louis Veuillot was so decidedly anti-Jewish. Thus, embracing Jewish consecration of the civilizing mission could have provided liberals with a language clearly understood to be irreconcilable with the Catholicism of the clerical party, but which nonetheless remained recognizably religious. Acceptance of this language would have served to grant a degree of credibility to their efforts to replace the religiosity of Catholicism with an obviously different kind of religiosity.

Jewish leaders' support for the liberal "civilizing mission" for French foreign and colonial policy formed an integral part of the project of securing French Jewish rights in France. As Crémieux argued on numerous occasions, French "civilization" was based on the notion that all people should be treated equally by state institutions, regardless of their religion. French agencies had to treat Jews equally whether they were at home or abroad, and in extending French control to new areas, this same policy had to be applied. What Crémieux did not explicitly state, but is apparent, is that French Jewish rights depended upon France's adherence to secularism in all its policies. Believing strongly in the need to secure Jewish rights, and also in the universality of the ideology underpinning them, French Jewish leaders mobilized to advocate for Jews elsewhere. Linking "Jewish interests" to "civilization" effectively rooted the question of Jewish rights in the extension of a religious policy based on ideals affirmed in 1789, but actualized only gradually over the course of the nineteenth century.

This development in French Jewish thought speaks to the real optimism French Jews felt about the set of policies and ideals that, by the 1850s, comprised state secularism. Religious tolerance, equal political rights for all individuals before the law regardless of religion, and the destruction of all corporate bodies designated by religion were understood to be the basis for freeing Jews from the oppression they had suffered for centuries. French Jews believed that the extension of French secularism abroad would transform Jewish life everywhere, and this optimism inspired them to develop new forms of philanthropy and advocacy. Yet French Jewish mobilization in the name of the *mission civilisatrice* also speaks to the continuing tenuousness of Jewish status in France. Oppression of Jews in the East at the hands of French consuls and with the approval of French ministers, or in the colonies at the hands of French generals, inspired fear among French Jewish leaders because they perceived such acts as directly threatening to their own position. In this sense, Jewish international advocacy was a defensive response to the widespread Western cultural prejudice against Jews, which continued even as the French state progressively limited the role of the Catholic Church in state affairs. In linking Jewish interests to the general progress of "civilization," French Jews effectively tied their cause to the anticlerical movement that in this period, as during the Restoration, welcomed their involvement as a sign of their movement's tolerance, modernity, and universality.

Five   The Making of Modern Jewish Solidarity

With the foundation of the Alliance Israélite Universelle in 1860, French Jews began to express what they called "solidarity" with Jews elsewhere in the world. Reclaiming a term from the past and using it in a distinctly new way, the French Jewish leaders of the Alliance used this rhetoric to promote Jewish rights on a global scale with the active support of thousands of Jews across Europe and in the Americas. The "solidarity" they expressed was far from the oppressive corporate "solidarity" that French Jews fought to eradicate in the early decades of the century. It was also distinct from the "solidarity" they had expressed in their work on behalf of the Jews of Damascus and Algeria, because it was not aimed at convincing their own government to apply policies of religious tolerance in the areas where French agents had jurisdiction. This new "solidarity" was independent of any particular state, and yet it was based in the same modern ideals that French Jews had embraced in their earlier campaigns to achieve legal equality themselves in the Restoration period and for Jews elsewhere under French jurisdiction in the 1840s and 1850s. It represented an affirmation of their commitment to state secularism and of their belief that "civilized" nations should advance the cause of religious equality in their political and economic negotiations with other countries. The foundation of this international organization thus grew out of French Jews' acculturation to republican values, and especially, their belief that France had a special duty to work for the progress of "civiliza- 157 tion," a hallowed ideal that included equal rights for Jews everywhere.

The solidarity that Alliance leaders created represents a new moment in the history of Jewish self-defense. As they used it after 1860, the term "Jewish solidarity" denoted a feeling of mutual responsibility among Jews dispersed all over the world in the name of shared liberal values, and their work in its name on behalf of Jews elsewhere was understood as a good for all humanity. Solidarity provided a warrant for mobilizing the Jewish leadership on a level never before seen, and with it, Alliance leaders were much more successful than ever before in persuading French policy makers to make the rights of Jews in other countries an issue in their diplomatic efforts. Let us keep in mind that in 1840, when Adolphe Crémieux embarked on a mission to advocate for the Jews of Damascus, he found himself at odds with his own government, and Jewish leaders measured his success by his ability to clear the name of Judaism in the French liberal press. Yet under his leadership in the 1870s, the Alliance won the support of Jewish leaders throughout Western Europe and the Americas in their campaign to compel the Romanian government to grant citizenship to its Jewish inhabitants, and for a moment, at least, their quest gained the support of the Great Powers, and particularly France, as well.

This chapter examines the emergence of the French Jewish rhetoric of international solidarity in the work of the Alliance Israélite Universelle. To better understand its meaning and its effectiveness, we will also examine how the rhetoric was received by its various intended audiences—Jews, French republican policy makers, and world diplomats—in one of the organization's most important early political advocacy campaigns, conducted on behalf of the Romanian Jews in the 1860s and 1870s. As we shall see, although Alliance leaders often stated that Jewish solidarity was an ancient sentiment rooted in Jewish tradition, in fact, the organization's rhetoric was clearly inspired by the contemporary political theories of French revolutionary universalism, Saint-Simonianism, and the democratic liberalism of the 1850s and 1860s. As such, using this rhetoric served several functions at once. First, for French Jewish members of the organization, this rhetoric served to root republican ideals in Jewish tradition, and thereby provided a way to affirm their distinctiveness even as they became better integrated into French society. Second, using this rhetoric was a strategy for gaining the support of French republicans. As historian Philip Nord has shown, the highly acculturated members of the French Jewish elite who founded the Alliance had established a firm place for themselves within the networks of democratic opposition to Napoleon III by the 1860s, and their rhetoric of "solidarity" found support within this milieu.[1] Jewish leaders' successes in the Romanian campaign in the 1870s were inextricably linked to the rise of the French republican movement in this same period, which placed anticlericalism as a central item on its agenda for political change at home and in its policies abroad. Finally, Alliance leaders hoped to persuade world diplomats to make Jewish rights a central concern by using the rhetoric of "civilization." As we shall see, they were not as effective here as they were in the French context. Although in the late 1870s, Alliance leaders believed that their rhetoric had won world diplomats to their cause, their initial success proved fleeting, as realpolitik and economic interests triumphed over liberal ideological concerns in the international arena.

The Alliance Israélite Universelle

In a certain sense, it was the Alliance Israélite Universelle that made international Jewish solidarity a central component of modern Jewish life. Founded in May 1860 by a small group of acculturated young republican Jews in Paris, the Alliance was the first permanent and self-contained institution with no connection to any legally defined Jewish community whose specific purpose was to help Jews around the world to obtain national citizenship, achieve material security, and make "moral progress." In its early years, the Alliance focused on two major tasks: advocating for Jewish rights in other countries and establishing the educational programs for which it is now best remembered. Both activities were based in its leaders' belief that Eastern Jews were backward but could be "regenerated" through gaining political rights and education on a Western model. As historians Aron Rodrigue and Michael Laskier have argued in their studies of the Alliance schools, all of these programs were made possible by the growth of French influence abroad.[2] Indeed, even though the Alliance was an international organization and the vast majority of its members lived outside of France, the organization was nonetheless firmly controlled by French Jews, who shaped its rhetoric to fit within the French political context where they had been educated and socialized.

The ideology undergirding all of the Alliance's work was a modern one that resonated with French liberal and republican ideology. The organization's leaders shared a faith that modern means—such as the press, education, and citizenship—would help protect Jews persecuted in other countries. Moreover, in naming the bond they fostered among dispersed Jews "solidarity," Alliance leaders appear to have found a word that connected modern notions of international connection to ancient ones. By embracing and mobilizing traditional Jewish ideas of mutual responsibility and justice, they gained support and strength from Jews across the world for their distinctly modern projects. At the same time, they generated and disseminated new ideas about what bound Jews living in different countries to each other and to their gentile neighbors. Their focus on advancing "civilization," as they understood this term, made them especially committed to the reform of state legal systems, advocating that countries grant the same rights to all citizens regardless of their religion rather than granting particular rights to Jews. Without advocating that the French state extend its own sovereignty in the areas where they worked, Alliance members were committed to democratic institutional forms and liberal legal systems, and thus nonetheless sought to ensure that new states would establish the same sort of secular legal regime that France had.

From the start, the Alliance embraced publicity as its central strategy for bringing Jews and their allies together in common cause in the name of shared liberal values. Six of the seventeen founding members formed a subcommittee to elaborate the new organization's statutes, and to pen an "Appel aux israélites" announcing the society's creation and inviting other Jews to join them, which was quickly distributed to Jews throughout Western Europe and America. The six men were all Parisian liberal professionals of the same generation: Elie-Aristide Astruc (1831–1905), chief rabbi of the Paris Consistory, who in 1865 would be named chief rabbi of Belgium; Isidore Cahen (1826–1902), who that very year succeeded his father as editor of *Les Archives Israélites de France*; Jules Carvallo (1820–1916), an engineer employed by the Bridges and Highways Ministry, cofounder of the liberal *L'Opinion Nationale*; Narcisse Leven (1833–1915), a lawyer and protégé of Crémieux's; Eugène Manuel (1823–1901), a noted poet and professor who, like Cahen, had studied philosophy at the Ecole Normale Supérieure with Jules Simon in the 1840s; and Charles Netter (1828–82), a businessman who would later set up Mikveh Israel, the first Jewish agricultural society in Palestine.[3]

Their statues and their "Appel" announced the organization's threefold intention to "work for the emancipation and the moral progress of Israelites everywhere," to "lend effective support to those who suffer on account of being Israelites," and to "encourage any publication which would lead to this result."[4] To this end, the Alliance quickly began to publish a *Bulletin de l'Alliance Israélite Universelle* to publicize its efforts and to recruit new members. The first issue contained the "Appel," a stirring call for cooperation that described the spirit of solidarity which would become the hallmark of the organization:

> If, dispersed to all the corners of the globe and mixed with the nations, you remain attached with your heart to the ancient religion of your fathers, however weak the link. . . . If you detest the prejudices from which we still suffer . . . the lies that are repeated. . . . If you believe that the most ancient and simple of spiritual religions must keep its place, fulfill its mission, proclaim its right, manifest its vitality in the ever more active great movement of ideas. . . . If you believe that a large number of your coreligionists, overwhelmed by twenty centuries of misery, can recover their dignity as men, conquer their dignity as citizens. . . . If you believe that it would be an honor for your religion, a lesson for the peoples, progress for humanity, a triumph for truth and universal reason to see concentrated all the living forces of Judaism. . . . If finally you believe that the influence of the principles of '89 is all powerful in the world, that the law which flows from them is a law of justice . . . that the example of peoples who enjoy absolute religious equality is a force . . . [then] Israelites of the entire world, come . . . give us your membership, your cooperation.[5]

As this call to arms illustrates, the Alliance's claim to "universality" rested on its founders' belief that French revolutionary values, and especially religious equality and freedom, were universal, sacred values that underpinned "civilization." This notion, as we saw in Chapter 4, had already been articulated by Jewish intellectuals and consistory leaders and was disseminated in the press in the decades preceding the Alliance's foundation.

Alliance leaders created a practical network of international cooperation that stretched across the Jewish world with impressive breadth. Although the organization did not officially distinguish between its members by nationality, as the years progressed, different national groups were designated to direct particular projects, making the organization more international than transnational. This division of labor developed for both pragmatic and ideological reasons. International organization provided a way to manage the inevitable conflicts that divided Alliance members along national lines. It also helped to facilitate work by directing projects from the countries best situated (geographically or politically) to make a difference in particular areas. Ideologically, this internationalism reflected the members' commitments to their own nations. Members of the Alliance never sought to turn the organization into a politically representative body for the Jewish people. On the contrary, they were committed to contributing to the formation of state policy in their own nations and sought to find common ground between national policies in the name of "civilization" and minority rights.

Rather than a body representing world Jewry, the Alliance was imagined by its leaders as a vast network of Jews in different countries, centered practically and symbolically in Paris, but without any explicit national affiliation. This is clear in how the leaders spoke about their international fundraising efforts, where national language, be it Jewish or French, was studiously avoided. The Alliance's leaders wanted to describe a network of people who gave money for a common moral purpose, rather than a geographically, culturally, biologically, or linguistically defined community. They suggested that a network, rather than a nation, could bring about peaceful world reconciliation. Crémieux said:

> Imagine yourselves, in the middle of the kingdoms, the empires stretching over so many diverse countries, to be a little kingdom in a confined corner of the world: that people will be the Jewish nation; that kingdom will be the Kingdom of Judah, with David

and Solomon, we will see it grow and develop like the rivers whose source cannot be seen but that become magic plains of water that fertilize vast countries.[6]

Even while speaking of the ancient "Kingdom of Judah," Crémieux was not suggesting that Jews were a national body in the contemporary world. Rather, using the metaphor of a river system, Crémieux described the Jewish people as a network whose connections with each other were "fertilizing" the whole world.

The image of a vast international network also applied to the Alliance's schools, the first of which was founded in Tetuan, Morocco, in 1862, and this network was controlled from the Parisian center as well. By the end of the nineteenth century, the network was quite large, extending from Morocco in the West to Persia in the East. With the support of local, Westernized elites, Alliance schools were established for both boys and girls. Their curricula emphasized religious and secular subjects, and instruction included both French and Hebrew. Vocational education was also offered. As Rodrigue has shown, the schools were built upon the same ideology of "regeneration" that developed initially in the French context and that had already been mobilized by Algerian Consistory leaders. With this ideology, Alliance teachers assumed that the Jews in the areas served by the schools were backward, but that schooling could improve their lives by transforming them in the same way French Jews' lives had been transformed in the early part of the nineteenth century.[7] Initially, the teachers for the Alliance schools were French, but with the establishment of the Alliance's Ecole Normale Israélite Orientale in Paris in 1867, teachers were recruited among recent graduates of the Alliance schools themselves, brought to Paris for teacher training, and then assigned to a post, often far from the teacher's country of origin.[8] Paris was thus the center of the Alliance schooling network in terms of both ideology and direction, even though the school personnel were drawn from across the world.

Just as important as the network of schools was the network of local committees that comprised the Alliance membership. Local chapters of the organization were established throughout Europe, the Americas, North Africa, and the Middle East, and members there as

well as in France received the *Bulletin* and were asked to send regular
donations for the projects the Central Committee decided to under-
take. The speed at which the network was built was impressive, made
possible by improved systems of communication and travel and a climate favorable to international cooperation in the cultures where
most of the members lived. By May 1861, 850 people had joined the
organization; 261 additional members joined by 1862; and by 1863, an
additional 274 members added their names. In 1864, there were 2,878
members worldwide. The numbers continued to climb over the next
few decades: in 1865, there were 3,900 members; in 1870, 13,370; and
in 1881, 24,176.[9] While not all members joined through local committees (one could join by writing directly to the Paris office), a vast number of local committees were also founded in the organization's early
years. From 1862 to 1880, 345 local committees were founded in Europe, the Americas, and the Arab lands. These included 55 committees
in France, 114 in Germany, 15 in Austria-Hungary, 4 in Bulgaria, 1 in
Crete, 5 in Gibraltar (including Corfu), 1 in Luxembourg, 15 in the
Netherlands, 1 in Portugal, 1 in Rhodes, 35 in Romania, 1 in Scandinavia (based in Copenhagen), 2 in Serbia, 6 in Switzerland, 5 in Algeria, 4 in Egypt, 2 in Libya, 7 in Morocco, 1 in Tunisia, 2 in Iraq, 3 in
Palestine, 26 in Turkey (including Roumelia, Albania, parts of Bulgaria, and parts of Syria), 2 in the Western Antilles, 2 in Brazil, 2 in
Colombia, and 8 in the United States. In addition, 2 local committees
were established in Great Britain before the Anglo-Jewish Association
was founded in 1870. Italy had 21 local and regional committees which
were directed by an Italian central committee based in Vercelli.[10] Thus,
of the 345 committees founded before 1880, France was home to only
64 (55 in metropolitan France, 8 in Algeria, and the Central Committee), or 18.5 percent of them. Broken down by membership rather
than by committee, Frenchmen (including Algerians) occupied a
larger but still small portion of the total membership in 1881, with
5,711 out of 24,176 members, or 23.6 percent.

   The Alliance helped foster Jewish international connections by contributing to the exchange of news about world Jewry. The *Bulletin de
l'Alliance Israélite Universelle* was sent to every member twice yearly
(and for a period in the 1870s and 1880s, monthly as well), and this

helped Jews in different countries to learn about each other. The *Bulletin*'s articles focused on the legal restrictions, popular violence, and poverty that made Jewish life difficult in places such as Serbia, Turkey, Persia, Palestine, Iraq, North Africa, Romania, Russia, Switzerland, and Galicia. In addition, the *Bulletin* presented reports on the lives of Jews in "exotic" places, even if they were not facing persecution. For example, in 1862, an article appeared on the Jews of China; in 1865, the first of many articles on the Abyssinian (Ethiopian) Jews appeared; and in 1867, a piece on the Jews of Central Asia appeared.[11] With such articles, members of the Alliance not only learned about Jews in other countries; they were also exposed to the explicit and implicit moral and cultural values of the French Jews who wrote the *Bulletin*. The membership and publicity structure of the Alliance played an important role in disseminating the liberal values of citizenship, education, "productive" charity and work, and modern religiosity in an ongoing way to Jews living in different places.

French Jews were clearly in control of the Alliance's leadership, the decision-making process and the creation of the ideology which it diffused in its *Bulletin*, even though they comprised less than a quarter of the total membership. The Central Committee's six officers were always French, a fact which was practically guaranteed since the officers met in Paris. In addition, these officers were elected by a unanimous vote of the committee members, and most committee members were themselves French. While people of any nationality and from anywhere in France could and did join the Alliance, the Parisians maintained firm control over its direction, since it was they who founded it, they who lived close to its headquarters, and they who nominated each other to the Central Committee. Indeed, only twenty-three non-Parisians were elected to the Central Committee in the first five elections, as compared to forty-seven Parisians.[12] The fact that all meetings were held in Paris and that the *Bulletin* was written in French further strengthened the power the Parisians exerted in the organization.

Yet this is not to say that the mentality of the leadership was narrow. Let us keep in mind that in 1872, almost a quarter of the Paris Jewish population was foreign-born.[13] Even among the French-born Jewish residents of Paris, many worked in international business and had occasion to travel outside France on a regular basis. This was certainly true of the Alliance's founders, all of whom were French but most of whom spent time traveling and working outside France, and had strong personal and professional connections to Jews in other countries. For example, Jules Carvallo had friends and a large family in Spain whom he visited regularly, and he worked with friends in Madrid on extending the Southern Railroad across the border.[14] Charles Netter ran an international business with one office in Prague and the other in Paris.[15] As a close associate and former secretary of Crémieux's, the lawyer Narcisse Leven made frequent trips to Oran.[16] Finally, as an editor of a major Jewish newspaper, a significant portion of Isidore Cahen's time was spent reading about Jews in other countries and publicizing their achievements and problems.

These international contacts shaped the Alliance's work from the very start. They not only helped the founders to build their membership, they also helped them to carry out most of their projects in the organization's first decades. This can be seen as early as 1860, when Leven took advantage of a business trip to Algeria to shore up support for the Alliance, and at the same time, Carvallo and Cahen traveled to London where they spoke before a banquet of British Jews and encouraged them to join.[17] Contacts such as these were also important in the Alliance's efforts to learn about and help Jews who were in danger. In the case of the Romanian Jews, Crémieux's renown as minister of justice in the Second Republic helped the Central Committee immensely in this regard. In 1866, Crémieux went to Bucharest where he met with Romanian nationalist leaders, urging them to stay faithful to the universalist principles of 1848. Crémieux's republican connections also made it possible for him to deliver a speech before the entire Romanian government, since many of them were ardent Francophiles happy to hear from a former leader of the French Second Republic.[18] Smaller acts on behalf of persecuted Jews by sympathetic Parisian Jews who had international connections were also common, even when the donors were not very active in the Alliance. To take but one example, in 1870, the Eastern Railroad Company announced that it would transport Polish Jewish orphans at half-fare.[19] Though a public company, the company was largely controlled by the Pereire brothers, who donated money to the Alliance without taking an active role in its direction.[20] Leaders seem to have stopped using their personal and professional contacts to help carry out the projects only when the Alliance had established a permanent international institutional network of its own, composed of local committees, project administrators, and schools.

While in practice, centers outside of France proved to be of the utmost importance in how Alliance projects were run, the organization itself always maintained a symbolic center in France, and French Jews controlled the production of its rhetoric. This is clear from the tensions that arose between the French Jewish leadership of the Alliance and the members of local committees in Great Britain, Germany, and Austria. As Zosa Szajkowski has shown, these tensions were centered over the organization's priorities and the fact that its leadership was dominated by the French. In response to these problems, a group of British Jews founded their own organization, the Anglo-Jewish Association (AJA), in 1870, and Austrian Jews founded the Israelitische Allianz in 1873. Both organizations always maintained cordial relations with the Alliance and cooperated with it in many circumstances. In addition, after a fierce and very public power struggle with the Parisian leadership, a group of German Jews founded the Hilfsverein der Deutschen Juden in 1901. There too, though, the Alliance's membership continued to grow, with many people belonging to more than one organization.[21]

These conflicts and tensions between the Central Committee and the local committees elsewhere in Western Europe reveal than the "universality" of the "Israelite Alliance" did not mean that nationality was unimportant in the organization. Furthermore, members of different nationalities never had truly equal access to positions of influence. Rather, French Jews maintained control over the direction of the organization as well as the production of its rhetoric. As a result, French Jews' cultural biases—including even their understanding of Judaism and Jewish identity—were clearly present in the Alliance's publications, school curricula, and political advocacy work.

The Republican Origins of the Language of Solidarity

Laced with Jewish religious phrases and imagery, the Alliance's rhetoric of Jewish international solidarity appears, at first glance, to be grounded in Jewish textual tradition. Yet here too, French Jews' particular perspective on Judaism is clearly visible. Indeed, a closer look at this rhetoric reveals that the roots of this language lay as much in the modern French liberal and republican tradition as they did in Judaism. By deploying decidedly Jewish language in a way that resonated clearly with contemporary republican ideals, Alliance leaders built on the strategies they had developed in the 1850s, in which they followed the example of Christian socialists by sanctifying their secular political ideals with religious language. In this way, Alliance leaders' use of this rhetoric formed an important part of their ongoing process of acculturation within liberal and republican circles in the 1860s and 1870s. By grounding republican concepts within Jewish tradition, Alliance leaders found a way to express their Jewish identity in terms meaningful in French political culture.

As Alliance leaders described it, Jewish solidarity represented the essence of Jewish social values, including a feeling of connectedness across great distances and an unwavering sense of justice rooted in Jewish tradition. Yet in their view, this solidarity did not set Jews apart from gentiles; it was an open solidarity, solidified in democratic institutions, intended to redeem the entire world. Furthermore, since it was not tied to any particular state, Alliance leaders depicted their organization as one that was free to operate in the arena in which citizens of different nations came together in the name of the liberal values they shared. As Lazard Isidor, the chief rabbi of France, told the Alliance's general assembly in 1873,

> The Alliance Israélite is the highest expression of Jewish solidarity, and Jewish solidarity, Messieurs, is what is greatest in the Jewish faith; it is inscribed in the Bible with the fires of Sinai; it is written in our history with the blood of our martyrs; it is written in our hearts with the milk of our mothers; it is what our forebears called *the glorification of God* [*kadosh ha-shem*], and they lived and died for it.

> The Alliance is not a French, German, or English alliance, it is Jewish, it is universal! This is why it works, this is why it succeeds![22]

Alliance leaders sacralized their work by using religious language to talk about modern ideals in much the way liberals and republicans had been doing since the July Monarchy era. The very fact that the French word *alliance* means "covenant" (in the religious sense) as well as "union" served to underscore the point that Alliance leaders made regularly at their annual meetings and in their publications: the Alliance was a moral institution doing sacred work by connecting Jews to each other and organizing them to lend each other aid in the name of "civilization." To motivate their members to lend a hand to the cause, they often made reference to the traditional Jewish concept of divine election, suggesting that the Jews had been chosen to advance the cause of civilization in the world. For example, in 1863, the Alliance's first president, Louis Koënigswarter, described the Jews as the *trait d'union* (hyphen) between East and West, and the Alliance as fostering "sentiments of fraternity" and respect for other religions.[23] In 1864, Alliance secretary Narcisse Leven described the organization as creating new ties between members of the "Great Family of Israel," in a common cause of "propagating those ideas of emancipation and progress which only certain countries are privileged to have."[24] In his first address as president in 1865, Adolphe Crémieux described the Alliance as a "veritable moral power, stronger than the sword," evoking a prophetic image of peace through shared values.[25] While certainly Jewish, this language was never meant to separate Jews out from the gentiles among whom they lived, and indeed, in using it, Alliance leaders were deeming basic liberal and republican ideals to be sacred.

To the same end, Crémieux also used Jewish mystical terminology in his fund-raising speeches. In an 1866 speech, he glorified the organization as a network of contributors in these terms: "Contribute, and let each contributor pledge to procure one more ember for society; let us thus form a chain whose first link is in Heaven."[26] Here Crémieux appears to have been making reference to two crucial concepts from Jewish mystical tradition: "gathering sparks" (*nitzotzot*); and the "chain of tradition" (*shalshelet ha-kabala*). Both ideas refer to ways in which humans can relate to God. The first is the human activity of gathering the "sparks" of divinity which have fallen dispersed throughout the world—in mystical tradition, this was the way people could "heal the world" (*tikkun olam*). Second, people could transmit the oral traditions that linked Jews to their ancient past, which was itself seen as holy, since that chain linked Jews to the prophets, and ultimately back to Moses and God. In this tradition as in the rhetoric of the Alliance, forming a "chain" was itself a way to "heal the world," for it created a bond among the enlightened which would cement the world into a single society.[27]

Alliance leaders further sanctified their organization by referring to it as a *faisceau*, a term that some listeners may have connected to Jewish mysticism as well. In nineteenth-century French, this term meant cluster, bundle, or in optics, a beam of light, and was particularly popular among republicans and Freemasons. Unlike a "network" (in French, *réseau*, referring to networks of people but also systems of highways, railroads, and canals), a *faisceau* is defined as a thing in itself rather than by what moves through it. When they used the term, Alliance leaders conveyed a sense of power through the united action of the membership. To take but one example, Crémieux, in one instance, referred to the Alliance as a "*faisceau* that maintains a sacred, indestructible tie."[28] For some listeners familiar with mystical traditions, this word—which also means "beam," as in a "beam of light"—may have had another resonance. The authors of the *Zohar*, a classic work of Jewish mysticism recently translated into French by the philosopher and consistory leader Adolphe Franck (1809–93), had described God using the metaphor of a light beam. As a beam of light, God contains all lights (which represent all beings), as you can see when you split a beam of white light into rays of different colors.[29] While most French Jews may not have been aware of this resonance, many of the Alliance leaders would have been, given their pride in Franck's scholarly success. In addition, for Crémieux, a thirty-third degree Freemason, using the metaphor of a light beam probably resonated with Masonic symbolism. For Freemasons, the *delta* (a luminous triangle with an eye in its center) symbolized "the presence of the Grand Architect of the Universe in the Temple."[30] In both traditions, the symbolism connoted the presence of the divine on earth through the sacred tie between members of the network of enlightenment.

The masthead of the Alliance's journal, the *Bulletin de l'Alliance Israélite Universelle*, conveyed this same message using the language of symbols (see Figure 5.1). It showed two hands shaking across a globe under two tablets, upon which the word *echad* (one) was written in Hebrew. Rays of light shine out from the word. The hands represent the international cooperation of Alliance members; the tablets with the word *echad* represent Judaism; and the light shining from it looks like the light shining forth from the Masonic *delta*, indicating the presence of the sacred. Readers were clearly meant to understand that Jewish international cooperation was a sacred endeavor.

The Alliance's motto—which was also part of the *Bulletin*'s masthead—reinforced this sense of divine purpose in common action. *Kol yisrael arevim zeh bazeh*, a Talmudic injunction, resonated powerfully with modern political ideas.[31] Alliance leaders translated this Hebrew phrase as "Tous les israélites sont solidaires les uns des autres [All Israelites are in solidarity with one another]," shortening it in 1887 to "Tous les israélites sont solidaires [All Israelites are in solidarity]," likely because they decided that the earlier translation could be misinterpreted as separatist. This phrase meant more than merely working

Figure 5.1. Masthead of the Bulletin de l'Alliance Israélite Universelle.

together. *Arevim*—like the French word *solidaires*—has a distinctly financial connotation, meaning guarantor, responsible, or liable, and is related to an Aramaic verb meaning to take over a debt or an obligation. The responsibility that Jews had for each other was to be understood as an obligation or a debt to or on behalf of one other.

Such explicitly Jewish religious language might obscure the decidedly French, secular, and republican origins of the terminology Jews were appropriating in constructing modern Jewish solidarity, but only if we were to forget that since the July Monarchy, the most ardent proponents of French state secularism had systematically used religious language in their struggle to limit the power of the Church, and the republicans of 1848 had done the same. Indeed, the term *solidarity* itself—a rather obscure term of jurisprudence until about 1840—played an important role in the French republican movement. Pierre Leroux was the first to define solidarity as a social and political ideal rather than a juridical fact. He first wrote about it in his 1839 *La Grève de Samarez* and in his 1840 book *De l'humanité*, he claimed that this ideal was an essential part of the "dogma" that he—like the Saint-Simonians with whom he had parted ways in 1831—remained intent on building to support a new, post-revolutionary world order. Distinct as it was from the traditional Catholic order, the new order was nonetheless religious, its dogma designed to support the work of replacing the remnants of feudalism with a new system which deemed as sacred the fundamental equality and unity of all people.

In *De l'humanité*, Leroux argued that the French Revolution had brought with it a new revelation of the "mutual solidarity of men." This new axiom was meant to express a greater sense of social obligation and interdependence than traditional Christian notions of charity. In the past, Leroux stated, "inequality" was the rule and people were divided into separate "castes." This had changed with the French Revolution; now, all people were finally able to come together in what he called a "universal caste." Knowing this new truth, he added, endowed the French with a "mission" to end all the different kinds of wars dividing the people of the world and to unite them as "humanity," and he wrote about this mission with a decidedly messianic and activist tone: "Whatever happens, may France contemplate the mission God gave her!"[32] Leroux defined the "new man" as understanding and acting upon his relatedness to all other people. The "*cité* of the future" was a universal city, in which all citizens were bound to each other with ties of "solidarity."

Using the term *solidarity* enabled Leroux to clarify his relationship to Catholicism. His "solidarity" was a Christian concept, derived from the idea that all people were *solidaires* in Adam's original sin and in their redemption through Christ. But this Christianity bore a closer resemblance to that of the eighteenth-century deists than to that of nineteenth-century Catholic *ultras*. Like other Romantic historians, Leroux believed that the same truth was revealed over and over again in history, but each time it was revealed, people came closer to understanding it and established structures and institutions in accordance with their understanding. This historical account of revelation made it possible to see an affinity between different religions. Like Saint-Simon, Leroux did not see Christianity, Judaism, and the religious spirit of the French Revolution as competing truths; they were different versions of the same truth, each depending upon on the preceding one.[33] For Leroux, the most recent revelation of "liberty, equality, fraternity" was a new, more perfect revelation of Christianity's "solidarity" in the sacrifice of Jesus and the Hebrew Bible's story of collective guilt for the sin of Adam.[34] While this revelation was to reach everyone, not just members of the same faith, it was religious: God was the ultimate basis of human solidarity, the source of creation and revelation.

Leroux's ideas had wide appeal among groups looking to reaffirm the legitimacy of certain aspects of the heritage of Old Regime, especially associational life and religion, without rejecting the ideology of the revolution. As André Gueslin and William H. Sewell, Jr., have explored in greater depth, utopian thinkers and members of the workers' associations in the 1840s saw voluntary associations as necessary building blocks of a new, noncompetitive order that they too described with a fervent, messianic tone.[35] "Solidarity" captured an idea that these groups were also trying to describe: that civic virtue was based in the fact of universal social interdependence and that society depended upon a sense of mutual obligation. "Solidarity" was also appealing because of its relationship to religion, especially for the socialists and romantic thinkers of the July Monarchy who shared Leroux's interest in Christianity or Christian morality while seeking to distance themselves from traditional Catholicism and the clergy. Leroux had found a word that meant nothing in Catholic tradition and could thus be used by anticlericals. At the same time, he made the term distinctly religious and explicitly identified its religiosity with the revolution of 1789. Among those who picked up the term were the Christian socialist Pierre-Joseph Proudhon and the Fourierist Alphonse Toussenel.[36] Michelet used it in his 1846 *Le Peuple* to urge legislators to take responsibility for social ills, and used it again in 1848 to explain the difference between Christian society and the society created by the revolution of 1789. "Instead of the fraternity of heritage that Christianity taught," he wrote, "the revolution taught fraternity in justice, with personal responsibility: each counting for himself, but wanting to count with the others, wanting to create fraternal solidarity."[37] The philosopher Auguste Comte—a former Polytechnicien who, like Léon Halévy and Augustin Thierry, had worked as a secretary for Saint-Simon as a young man but had abandoned the Saint-Simonian movement early on—theorized the concept in depth in his 1852 *Catéchisme positive*. Like Leroux, Comte put forth a new system of thought designed to teach its readers about "the solidarity . . . that should reign in the end between all the regions of the human planet, wherever they may be."[38] The Romantic writer George Sand, with whom Leroux had founded the leftist *Revue Indépendante* in 1841, also adopted the term. In her 1855 *Histoire de ma vie*, she wrote, "The most lively and religious source of progress of the human spirit is, to speak the language of my time, the notion of *solidarity*."[39]

In 1848, the republican left added the term *solidarity* to its ideological arsenal, alongside the related concepts of *fraternity*, *justice*, and *philanthropy*. During the Second Republic, *solidarity* was used by socialists, republicans, anticlericals, and religious reformers as a moral term distinct from Catholic tradition. As the historian Marcel David reports, in the revolution of 1848, *solidarity* was used interchangeably with *fraternity*, even among the most anticlerical of *montagnards* like Alexandre Ledru-Rollin. It was used by left-wing clubs in the spring of 1848, in official descriptions of the republican festivals of May 1848, and in the feminist newspaper *La Voix des Femmes*.[40] No longer tied as strictly to its juridical definition, *solidarity* became first a philosophical concept referring to the fact of human interdependence, and later a call for charitable, brotherly action on behalf of others. In David's estimation, the republicans of 1848 made "solidarity" a rallying cry for "reparative justice," based in the notion that the "social debt must be honored." Solidarity was at once a fact and a call to action, the product of a powerful fusion of traditional Christian notions and French revolutionary ideology.[41] As such, it became a term of the left and, like the "civilizing mission," disappeared from the ideological arsenal of conservatives in the middle of the nineteenth century.[42]

With the waning of the Second Republic, the term became more closely tied to the defense of the republic. Minister of the Interior Ledru-Rollin and the radical republican Charles Delescluze helped found an association called La Solidarité Républicaine in October 1848 to protect the republican government against the monarchist threat. The organization was decidedly activist; its early pamphlets were filled with appeals for unified action against the forces threatening the fragile democracy. The leaders of the Solidarité Républicaine also supported a new newspaper, called *La République Démocratique et Sociale*, which diffused republican propaganda. The association was declared illegal in early 1849, at which point it became a secret society, many of whose members (including Delescluze) would resurface in the Paris Commune.[43] La Solidarité Républicaine inspired those who would embrace the politics of "solidarity" in later years with its rhetoric, its commitment to republicanism, and its activism. The organization had a central office in Paris, headed by seventy members, and departmental offices to form what they called a national network of supporters who vowed to defend the republic.

Republicans often used the term *faisceau* to describe their network, and thereby gave their supporters an image to associate with the abstract concept of "solidarity" in a way that sheds additional light on the use of this term by Alliance leaders. The leaders of the Solidarité Républicaine, for example, referred to their group as a *faisceau* dedicated to protecting the republic against would-be despots. Using this term thus linked the Alliance to this contemporary republican tradition—and more specifically, the republican opposition to Napoleon III—and grounded it in an ancient republican heritage, since *fasces*, the word's Latin root, referred specifically to the bundle of rods and an ax given to consuls in republican Rome as a symbol of their power.

By the time Jewish leaders adopted the term in the 1850s, "solidarity" meant something quite different in political discourse than it had in the Napoleonic Code. As a republican term, *solidarity* designated a strong, activist notion of social responsibility. The term was the product of a mediation between socialist religious thought, liberalism, and the republicanisms of ancient Rome, 1789, and 1848. *Solidarity* implied order and religiosity; at the same time, it implied fraternity, equality, and connectedness between segments of society. More inclusive than conservative Catholic notions that excluded Jews from the social body, *solidarity* was a religious term without being exclusively Christian. In addition, the term was important to the *montagnards*, among whom Adolphe Crémieux sat in the Chamber during the Second Republic.[44]

Still, some Jews may have been wary about appropriating the term *solidarity* because of its historical association with a corporate past. This problem likely contributed to the reticence of Jewish writers to use the term in talking about the relationship among Jews in the 1830s and 1840s, although they were not necessarily ignorant of its new meaning. Gustave d'Eichthal, for example, did not use it in the 1830s or 1840s to talk about relations among Jews, but he did use it in other contexts. In his 1839 *Lettres sur la race noire et la race blanche*, he wrote, "Since the time of the Revolution of 1789, Jewish emancipation and black emancipation have always walked abreast, and have been, so to speak, *solidaires* with each other."[45] This was a metaphorical "solidarity" of fate, not an active, self-defined "solidarity" between members of a same religion. Jacques Altaras and Joseph Cohen used the term more like Leroux did in their 1842 report about the Algerian Jews. Citizenship, they explained, was about more than nationality; it was a *solidarité* of morality and civic obligation. They wrote:

> The *patrie* is not just the land where one is thrown and where one lives. It has more spiritual elements, moral elements. . . . It is most of all in the civil relations between man and the state, in the rights, in the duties of the citizen, in the political laws that give men their existence . . . in society, in a word, in this chain of principles which unites all the members of the nation to each other in a sort of solidarity.[46]

From a Jewish perspective, this national solidarity was integrationist rather than separatist, based on a morality that all citizens shared.

If Jews did not speak of *Jewish* solidarity in anything but its juridical sense before 1850, the ways in which they did describe Judaism and the bonds that tied Jews to one another set the stage for adopting the new terminology of "solidarity." As we have seen, since the 1820s, French Jewish writers portrayed Judaism as a revealed, dignified moral code and identified its tenets with elements of French state ideology, especially liberty, equality, and fraternity. Identifying Judaism with civic virtues was not the same, however, as calling Jews *solidaires*. Using the term *solidarity* in the new way emerged only with the formation of the political alliance that a new generation of acculturated Parisian Jews, born in the 1820s, forged with other republicans in the decades following 1848. As Philip Nord has argued, Jewish institutions and informal "networks of sociability" were important arenas of republican opposition during the Second Empire, in which "democratic experimentation and education" took place.[47] Using the term *solidarity* was one way in which Jewish leaders allied themselves with other republican opponents of Napoleon III. At the same time, they further redefined Judaism and Jewish identity in modern terms.

The first article in the Jewish press that called specifically for *Jewish* solidarity was written by Jules Carvallo and appeared in *L'Univers Is-raélite* in February 1851. Carvallo was a graduate of the Ecole Polytechnique and one of the first Jews employed by the Bridges and Highways Ministry. He was also active in Jewish administration and republican politics, despite the fact that his republican ties may have been the reason his professional superiors at the ministry came to despise and ultimately dismiss him in 1865. He was associated with the Pereire brothers and the newspaper magnate Jules Mirès, helped to found the newspaper *L'Opinion Nationale* in 1843, and served on the Paris Consistory as well. The aim of *L'Opinion Nationale*, "the defense of oppressed people everywhere," foreshadowed that of the Alliance Israélite Universelle.[48]

Carvallo's 1851 article was written in the political lexicon of the former Saint-Simonians and republicans whose ideas he shared. He described the nineteenth century as the time of the "emancipation of the suffering classes," and included the Jewish people among the suffering. Like other republicans of 1848, Carvallo argued that the remedy for oppression lay in the granting of political rights. Wherever Jews were included in the social order, he observed, they were successful in the arts, sciences, and administration; wherever they were excluded from the social order, they were at the lowest rungs of society. It was time, he argued, to bring an end to the "inequality" between the Jews of the different parts of the world. Carvallo called upon his readers to act on the "solidarity of the heart" that they felt with oppressed Jews everywhere. He suggested that representatives of all the synagogues of the world come to Paris to establish a permanent committee to which any Jew could turn in a time of persecution. Creating such a committee would end Jewish weakness, he argued, for dispersion and division were the source of powerlessness, and forming a Jewish *faisceau* would help Jews everywhere to "take a seat at the banquet of life."[49] Using the term *banquet* further linked Carvallo's suggestions to the republican movement, since it was in the "campaign of the banquets" of the last years of the July Monarchy that deputies associated with Odilon Barrot's dynastic left—Crémieux included—toured the country, circumventing restrictions on political assemblies by serving dinner to their audiences, and gave speeches that drew immense support for their ideas about electoral reform, political freedoms, and the problem of poverty. The campaign of the banquets was well known to Carvallo's readers, since it had served as a launching pad for the 1848 revolution and many of the democratic ideas expressed there came to shape the programs of the Second Republic.[50]

In using the term *Jewish solidarity*, Carvallo was mobilizing the same complicated and somewhat contradictory set of concepts that were current in republican political culture at the time. It was religious without being narrowly Jewish; it glorified charity and assistance without abandoning egalitarianism; it was addressed to a particular group but was explicitly not separatist; and it was aimed at the entire world without seeking to erase national sovereignty or specificity. Championing the rights of the oppressed in other countries in the name of universal values was explained as a natural extension of the French Revolution. This too made sense in the contemporary context: the French republicans of 1848, for example, had applauded and supported the revolutions of 1848 throughout Europe.

Similarly, a closer examination of the early work of the Alliance Israélite Universelle reveals its concerns to have been linked to those of contemporary French republicans, such as the right to work, the expansion of suffrage, and establishing a new relationship between religion and the state. Using republican rhetoric, Alliance leaders linked Judaism and the defense of the Jewish people to the ideals of the revolutions of 1789 and 1848. The organization's earliest projects were based in a republican sensibility as well: the defense of the persecuted Syrian Christians that we examined in Chapter 4, the establishment of schools for Jews in Muslim lands, and a campaign for citizenship rights for the Jews in southeastern Europe. In structure too, the Alliance resembled contemporary political organizations and voluntary associations like the Solidarité Républicaine and Masonic lodges, rather than the traditional Jewish *communauté* or French state agencies like the consistory. The administration was divided into three levels: "simple members, a committee, and an office." Simple members could join either by writing to the office or by being introduced by a current member, and the sixty members of the Central Committee were to be elected unanimously every three years by the outgoing committee. The Central Committee was led by six officers, who were elected by majority vote from their own ranks. Members were required to donate only six francs to the organization, and the only other requirement was that the candidate "enjoy a perfect honorability."[51]

In the early years, especially, the leaders of the Alliance were explicit that while their goal was to help "those who suffer on account of being Israelite," they hoped that non-Jews would join their organization. In the first issue of their *Bulletin*, one founder wrote:

> We will welcome with joy men of all faiths and all opinions convinced that the success of our principles is tied to that of all the true principles, so that our cause can join with the cause of progress all over the world. . . . Who would dare to say that we work in an exclusive sense?. . . . [W]hat we seek is, above all, moral progress, to which no creature could feel . . . indifferent.[52]

Although the Alliance never gained much of a non-Jewish membership, the theme of unity between Jews, Christians, and eventually Muslims was always important in Alliance rhetoric, linking their work to the universalist ideology of Leroux and the republicans he inspired. In his 1863 presidential address, Koënigswarter claimed that the Alliance's mission came from the Hebrew Bible, and emphasized that this text was the basis for all three monotheistic religions. As such, the Alliance's work would foster "sentiments of fraternity" and respect between the religions.[53] Upon his election as president in 1864, Crémieux too stated, "The Alliance is not addressed to our *culte* alone; it is addressed to all *cultes*; it seeks to penetrate all religions, just as it penetrates all countries." Later in the same speech he grew even bolder, claiming, "The Jewish religion is the mother of the religions that spread civilization."[54] The moral sensibility of the Alliance leaders was not intended as exclusive, but it was religious. This, they argued in the spirit of Leroux or Saint-Simon, was because religion in the contemporary era was meant to unite people in a common moral "solidarity."

Other republican concepts were central in Alliance rhetoric in its first decades as well, and these too were grounded in Jewish tradition. In his 1871 presidential address, Crémieux issued a call for reparative justice, describing the organization as creating a "total union, perfect equality in this alliance of brothers, sons of a same God, children of this ancient family . . . against those barbaric and stupid acts, we stand, in the name of the persecuted, we demand justice and reparation."[55] Crémieux also prioritized education and the right to work as essential for making Jews "useful" and integrated into the societies where they lived. This focus on "useful work" can in part be explained by the fact that since the revolution, reformers had insisted that work and vocational instruction were necessary for French Jews to be "regenerated," or made useful in society. But French Jews were also mobilizing a newer rhetoric current in the political culture of their own generation. By embracing the idea that manual labor was the basis of the social order, and that all workers were "children of the same God," Alliance leaders created an important link between their mission and the republican programs of 1848 and beyond.

Even Alliance leaders' use of religious terminology to sanctify their endeavor seems to have been inspired more by contemporary political messianism than by traditional Judaism alone. This seems evident in Alliance leaders' choice to consecrate their work by systematically using mystical concepts like *tikkun olam* ("to heal the world"), an idea developed initially by sixteenth-century students of kabbalah. This mystical concept, still relatively obscure at that time, was useful to Alliance leaders because it related to a global, even cosmic order, and thus reflected the Alliance's inclusive, universal aspirations. It could also be contrasted to the traditional Jewish concept of *tzedakah* (charity), which was ordinarily given to help the sick, the widowed, the orphaned, the poor, and so on, rather than transforming the social or political order. *Tikkun olam* was messianic in its universal, transformative, and ultimately redemptive potential. The use of such language consecrated the fundamentally republican goal of changing the entire social order through collective action.

A similar point can be made about the Alliance's use of the religious concept of divine election or chosenness. Unlike *tikkun olam*, this was a traditional religious concept well known in French Jewish circles. Yet even with this concept, Alliance leaders seem to have been inspired as much by republican ideals as by traditional Judaism alone. For example, Chief Rabbi Isidor invoked this concept to explain how connections among Jews could result in the redemption and unity of all people, and represented a fulfillment of biblical prophesy: "The *Alliance Universelle*! But the word is not new and the idea is not new. The Prophet said it before you; listen to the words of the Prophet: 'If you want to hasten the reign of justice, if you want to make truth triumph over error and make iniquity disappear, then form a *faisceau*, make an *alliance* for goodness.'"[56] Providing his own rather loose translation of what appear to be the words of Isaiah (42: 6–7), Isidor implied that uniting as a global network would fulfill the Jewish mission to bring the Messiah. The translation connects Isaiah's words with contemporary French political ideas, and also reverses the logic of the prophesy. One English (Jerusalem Bible) translation renders this passage as follows: "I the Lord have called thee in righteousness, and will hold thy hand, and will keep thee, and give thee as a covenant for the people, for a light to the nations; to open the blind eyes, to bring out the prisoners from the prison, and them that sit in darkness out of the prison house." The terms *alliance* and *faisceau* do not appear in the English translation, but in French, *alliance* is a good translation of *covenant*, and *faisceau* is an acceptable translation of *light*. In highlighting Isaiah's use of these words, Isidor was rooting important republican concepts in Jewish religious tradition. In addition, he was encouraging action by shifting the agency from the Lord to the Jewish people and thereby reversing the prophecy's logic. In Isidor's rendering, it is the Jewish people who will act, by coming together as a *faisceau* or *alliance*, to "make iniquity disappear," as opposed to the traditional notion that the Lord "makes iniquity disappear" by making a covenant with the Jewish people. While reminding Alliance members of their covenant with God, Isidor was at once reinterpreting the words of Isaiah as a call for unity and action and rooting republican concepts in Jewish tradition.

The Jewish tradition evoked by Alliance leaders was not just the textual tradition; the term *solidarity* itself harkened back to a hated aspect of the corporate past. Was this resonance intentional? Probably—but in the new context, the resonance was most likely intended to inspire voluntary contributions based in a sense of moral and religious obligation. Let us keep in mind that this new meaning for *solidarity* developed only after the juridical "solidarity" of French Jews, their collective responsibility for each others' debts and transgressions, had finally been eradicated from French law. Alliance leaders encouraged donations by using terms of "obligation" only when no actual legal obligations existed any longer. On the most basic level, the rhetoric was a strategy for fund-raising.

On another level, Alliance leaders were using the rhetoric of solidarity to talk about the place of Judaism and Jewish identity in the modern world in terms that made sense in contemporary republican political culture. Jewish leaders developed a discourse of international Jewish solidarity which was at once new *and* linked to their religious and historical traditions. William Sewell's words about the development of feelings of class solidarity among workers apply to the development of Jewish solidarity as well; it was "a generalization, a projection to a higher level, of feelings of corporate solidarity."[57] That is, in using the language of solidarity in the second half of the nineteenth century, Jewish leaders were translating the morality of obligation of traditional communal life to suit a radically different situation. Paradoxically, once translated, these feelings of obligation had an opposite function than the legal corporate obligations of the past. "Solidarity" was no longer a set of obligations that set Jews apart as semi-autonomous communities living isolated from each other amidst hostile nations. Jewish "solidarity" was now conceived as connective, creating bonds of obligation among Jews and their gentile neighbors, among dispersed Jews, and ultimately, among all the peoples of the world. By expressing solidarity with one another in the way that they did, Alliance leaders connected their Jewishness to their republican convictions. In so doing, they placed themselves firmly within the increasingly strong networks of opposition to Napoleon III in the 1860s, whose leaders and guiding ideals would shape the policies of the Third Republic.

The Campaign for the Romanian Jews

By using this decidedly republican rhetoric and infusing it with Jewish religiosity, Alliance leaders not only created a new language to express their Jewish identity; they also garnered support for their political advocacy programs. Jewish leaders found French republican diplomats to be good allies in their efforts on behalf of the beleaguered Jews of the new nation of Romania because they shared a commitment to advancing state secularism at home and abroad. Alliance leaders also sought to influence other European leaders because they, like the French, were in the process of making commercial treaties with the Romanians at the time of the campaign. Jewish leaders were more than aware that their solidarity depended on the new spirit of liberalism they saw growing in the realm of diplomacy. When the campaign began, many Western European states had already come to embrace a liberal agenda, and Jews sought to persuade them to make Jewish rights a central part of that agenda. As we shall see, their campaign's success was limited. Although Alliance leaders were able to persuade French republicans to champion Jewish rights in their diplomatic efforts, and were even able to persuade leaders of some other European nations to do the same, ultimately, they failed to find a way to compel the Romanian government to grant full citizenship rights to all Romanian Jews. Examining how the Alliance's advocacy efforts were received by diplomats in this international arena lends additional support to the finding that beyond Jewish circles, the Alliance's rhetoric resonated most strongly in the French republican context, and yet even there, its effectiveness proved surprisingly limited.

French Jews first became interested in Romania in the wake of the Crimean War. Moldavia and Wallachia, two principalities formerly under Ottoman rule, took their first step toward unity after the 1856 Congress of Paris. The 1856 treaty stipulated that the new Romanian constitution would have to receive the approval of the Great Powers. In 1858, another Paris conference laid out the basic outlines under which the new Romanian state would be run. This 1858 treaty, like the 1856 one before it, failed to guarantee equal rights to Jews. Furthermore, the treaty, also like its 1856 predecessor, did not allow for complete unification because both Austria and Turkey still hoped to gain sovereignty over the principalities themselves and thus rejected Romanian self-determination altogether. In 1859, however, Moldavia and Wallachia were effectively unified when they both elected Prince Alexandru Cuza to lead their nominally separate governments. While the liberal Cuza did not introduce systematic discrimination against the Jews, he still did not grant them equality. The issue had been deferred rather than closed, however, since Romanian nationalists still claimed that they would eventually grant religious freedoms. In the late 1850s, the Jewish problem in Romania was about more than just Romanian prejudice; it also stemmed from a strong disagreement between the Great Powers themselves about the status of religious minorities. While France supported freedom of conscience, Austria, Turkey, and Russia were not yet willing to cede Romania permanent independence, and Russia wanted Romania to be an explicitly Christian state.[58]

Like most French liberals and republicans, the leaders of the Alliance had hopes that the new Romanian state would be modeled on the French state, and as such, that Jews in Romania would have the same rights as Jews in France. The French emperor himself was committed to Romanian independence for both ideological and strategic reasons, in the context of his liberal policy to uphold the *principe de nationalité*. Helping to establish an independent Romania, modeled on France, would also situate a natural political ally for France right in between Russia and Turkey.[59] Due to the emperor's interest in the emerging nation, French Jews' advocacy for Romanian Jewish rights was a logical part of a broader political strategy. Here, as in Algeria and in the Damascus affair, they demanded that the French state make religious freedom a central part of any state policy regarding areas beyond French borders.

There were also more direct ties between Romanian nationalism and France. The Romanian nationalists who had fought for unification were led by the brothers Ion and Dmitrie Brătiano, Nicolae Balcescu, and C. A. Rosetti, all of whom received their political education in France and maintained close ties to French republicans. The Brătiano brothers and their allies had fought since 1848 not only to unify the principalities, but to achieve a number of French-inspired revolutionary goals. These included the abolition of all remnants of feudalism (in this case, Ottoman style), granting equal rights to all citizens, the establishment of civil liberties, the reform of the tax code, establishing universal suffrage in regular elections of a sovereign prince, public education, the abolition of the death penalty, and equal rights for Jews and gypsies.[60] The treaties following the Crimean War proved advantageous for these nationalists, for their agenda fit well with those of France and Great Britain, who sought to achieve a new balance of power in the Balkans by establishing independent states to sit between the hostile Russian and Ottoman Empires.[61]

From the start, French Jewish advocates followed Napoleon III's line of reasoning about Romania; but interested as they were in religious freedoms, they stressed that a secular model of state administration was central to the *principe de nationalité*. The first French Jew to write about Romanian nationalism was Armand Lévy (1827–91), who would later work with the Alliance.[62] In a work entitled *Napoléon III et les principautés roumaines*, he attempted to persuade the Great Powers to unify Romania under a single government when they convened in Paris in 1858. In Lévy's view, granting equal rights to the Jews was a necessary part of Romanian national unification. Both Jewish rights and Romanian nationalism, he argued, were in the best interest of Romania, France, and the world, for they would eventually help create a peaceful and ethical world system. Lévy's views were shaped by French internationalist politics as well as Romanian politics. He himself had befriended Rosetti and other Romanian nationalists when they were in Paris and had become quite committed to their cause.[63] In his book, he argued that advancing "civilization" in the Balkans would be good for all humanity, because this area sat poised between East and West. Whereas in his estimation Austria was failing to recognize this as in their best interest, Napoleon III had embraced it, and would do everything he could to "regenerate" the East. Doing this, in Lévy's mind, necessarily entailed establishing a secular state, for establishing a balance between East and West depended on creating states which themselves embraced the equality of all people regardless of their religion.[64]

While Lévy certainly rejoiced over the unification of the two principalities under Cuza, he failed to convince the Great Powers about the necessity of granting Jews equal rights, and the 1858 treaty had merely deferred the issue. Though Romanian Jews had asked Lévy to intervene on their behalf at the 1858 Convention of Paris, the treaty had guaranteed the freedom and equality of only Christian Moldavians and Wallachians, promising that this equality "may be extended to other religions by legislation."[65] Under Cuza, who ruled until 1866,

Romania's two hundred thousand Jews remained in a tenuous, though hopeful situation.[66] While Jews were not emancipated collectively under Cuza, a new legal category, "native Jews," was created, under which some Jews could obtain citizenship. "Native Jews" included only those who had completed army service as an officer; who had attended a Romanian university or had received a doctorate or *licentiate* from a foreign university; or who owned a factory that employed fifty or more people. Restricted as this was, it meant that some Jews at least could be considered Romanian. Furthermore, the new Civil Code of 1864 granted all residents of Romania the same civil rights, and granted Jews the right to apply for naturalization.[67] Still, nothing could be certain, and no Jew was actually granted citizenship under Cuza.

In 1866, Cuza was forced to abdicate, and soon afterward, a German Catholic prince, Carol Hohenzollern-Sigmaringen, was brought to power and a constituent assembly ratified the first national constitution. Prince Carol was more conservative than Cuza, but revolutionaries like Rosetti and Ion Brătiano occupied important positions in his government. Under his rule, Romanian Jews—both native and foreign—were systematically denied political and eventually civil rights. Article 7 of the 1866 Constitution stated that only Christian foreigners could be naturalized Romanian.[68] Beyond categorically excluding foreign Jews from citizenship, this effectively established a link between Christianity and Romanian citizenship in ways that worked against native Jews as well. In addition, from 1867 to 1871, Jews were the object of popular violence in a number of towns, most notably in Galatz, on the Russian border in Moldavia, and in Jassy, where Jews accounted for over half the total population.[69] At the same time, a number of restrictive laws were passed that effectively limited the civil rights of Jews. The Rural Laws of 1866, 1867, and 1869 denied Jews the right to reside permanently in the countryside, and forbade them to buy houses or farms there. The liquor laws of 1869–73 denied Jews the right to own cabarets, inns, taverns, or to sell liquor or tobacco. Vagrancy laws were specifically designed to be used against foreign Jews, in spite of the fact that the 1864 Civil Code had guaranteed all people, citizen or foreigner, the same rights. The vagrancy laws were upheld by the courts, which distinguished "useful" immigrants from vagabonds by specifying a sum of money an immigrant needed to have to gain rights. As most Jewish refugees from Russia were poor, they were effectively barred from taking up residence. If they were already present in the countryside and did not meet this require-ment, they could and would be expelled.[70] Expulsions of individual Jews—beginning with recent immigrants but eventually including others as well—began in the 1870s, and the numbers rose over the next two decades.[71]

The Alliance's Central Committee was aware of the situation in Romania from the time the organization was founded because the Bucharest Jews wrote directly to them about their plight as early as 1861. Local Alliance committees were founded in thirty-four Roman-ian towns before 1870 (with two separate committees in Bucharest, one Romanian and one Russian), and their connection to the Central Committee grew stronger as the persecutions increased. Regular let-ters from local committees in Bucharest, Galatz, and Jassy kept the Central Committee abreast of the rising tide of violence and new dis-criminatory legislation, and the news was duly reported in the *Bul-letin*.[72] In 1861, the Alliance's president Jules Carvallo promised pub-licly that the Alliance would help the Romanian Jews to become full citizens.[73] By 1862, the *Bulletin* contained a regular report on the Ro-manian situation, and the texts of discriminatory laws were reprinted in full. The Central Committee publicized the situation in other French liberal newspapers like *Le Siècle*, *Le Temps*, and *L'Opinion Na-tionale*, and Jewish advocates in London and Berlin similarly passed along the news to their national liberal newspapers. The Central Com-mittee wrote to the Romanian National Assembly on behalf of the Romanian Jews as well.[74] In January 1866, just a month before the new Romanian Constitution was promulgated, Brătiano met with the members of the Central Committee to assure them he was truly a champion of religious freedom, and Rosetti sent them a telegram promising that Jews would be guaranteed equal rights in the Consti-tution. The Central Committee wrote with the happy news to the Jews of Bucharest and Jassy.[75]

Yet Brătiano and Rosetti did not keep their promises, and condi-tions worsened for the Romanian Jews. At this point, the Alliance relied on fulfilling its role as what Crémieux had called a "moral power," generating arguments for Romanian Jewish emancipation and presenting them to Romanian nationalists, stressing their shared commitment to liberalism.[76] In 1868, after new discriminatory laws were passed, the Central Committee used these same moral arguments in writing to representatives of the Great Powers, including the Austrian ambassador to France, Metternich, the British ambassador Lord Lyons, and the Prussian ambassador.[77] In so doing, the Alliance was attempting to establish itself as a liberal interest group in the diplomatic arena whose objectives were moral rather than specifically "Jewish," and as such, allied with liberal nations and liberal factions in emerging nations. This role fit well with their more general aim to show the world that Jewish solidarity stemmed from values common to all "civilized" people. It was in this spirit that Crémieux spoke with Romanian leaders in Bucharest in 1866, and they assured him that they shared the Alliance's commitment to liberalism, and that Romanian Jews would eventually obtain equal rights. Having made his career by persuading liberals to make religious freedoms central in their political agendas, Crémieux was applying the same tactics in Romania.[78]

Soon after Crémieux's return from Bucharest, however, it became clear that the strategies that had worked in France and colonial Algeria were beginning to fail in Romania. In July 1867, Prince Carol's personal secretary, Emile Picot, met with the Central Committee of the Alliance in Paris to discuss how to help the Romanian Jews achieve equal rights. After providing details about the new liquor laws and reporting about the recent anti-Jewish riots in Moldavia, Picot explained Prince Carol's reservations about emancipating the Jews, arguing that Jews should not be emancipated because they were a foreign element whom the populace hated, and they could not be granted citizenship until they proved themselves to be "Romanian." He suggested that the Alliance should concentrate on helping Romanian Jews to "renounce everything that distinguishes their outward appearance from the other inhabitants of the country."[79] While Picot claimed to be sympathetic to his country's Jews, Alliance leaders rightly heard him as justifying their exclusion with arguments that were all too familiar. Crémieux responded by saying that the Romanian Jews, like all other Romanians who had lived under the yoke of foreign rule, owed their cultural backwardness to centuries of oppression. It was their pariah legal status that made Romanian Jews backward, he argued. Citing the experience of French Jews, Crémieux wrote that there was clear evidence that citizenship, not language or dress, was what regenerated people.[80] Clearly, the liberal rhetoric of "civilization" was not enough to overcome Romanian leaders' negative attitudes about the Jews in their country.

After this exchange, Alliance leaders recognized the need for a new strategy. While maintaining its role as a moral spokesman and publicist, the Central Committee began to rely more heavily on advocates better situated to influence politics in Romania. If their rhetoric was unpersuasive in the Romanian context, they thought, perhaps it would work in the context of the other Western European nations engaged in diplomatic negotiations with the Romanians. The Italian Jews were the first to act somewhat independently. In 1866, when Italy began to draw up a commercial treaty with Romania, they urged their government to pressure Romania to grant equal rights to Jews as part of the treaty. The Italian Jews argued that Italy should not trade with "uncivilized" nations, and since "civilization" necessarily entailed equality for Jews, the Italians should not trade with Romania. In fact, they argued, it was a legal necessity for the Italians to require that Jews in Romania receive equal rights as part of the commercial treaty. Since the Italian government offered its Jewish citizens equal protection, they were bound to require that Romania allow Jews basic rights, because the discriminatory laws in Romania forbade all Jews—even Italian Jews—from owning property. Reporting on their work to the Central Committee in Paris, the Italian Jews expressed their hope that Jews in France and Great Britain would appeal to their Ministries of Foreign Affairs with the same demand. "The Romanians say that if they give foreign Israelites equality, they will have to give equality to native Israelites," the Italians wrote to the Central Committee. "But if the Romanians do not want to change their public law in conformity with civilization, should we Italians change ours to be contrary to civilization?"[81]

The British Jews used a similar strategy to persuade their government to help the Romanian Jews. Like the Italians, they stressed the liberal idea of religious tolerance that all Western European nations shared, and suggested that it was the duty of the British to "civilize" the Romanians. In 1867, the Jewish politician Sir Francis Goldsmid went before the House of Commons to persuade its members to condemn Prince Carol and to have their ambassador to Romania, Mr. Green, meet with the prince. Alderman David Salomons and Lord Stanley both raised their voices in support of the Romanian Jews. Stanley suggested that the British state work with the French, since Emperor Napoleon III had already spoken out against the exclusion of Jews in Romania. Like the Italians, the British Jews convinced their government that Jewish emancipation was an important component of their own liberal ideology. Lord Stanley promised that Great Britain would work with the French to exert a "moral pressure from the civilized nations of Europe."[82]

In the wake of the Franco-Prussian War, new advocates took more prominent roles in the campaign as well. An American Jew, Benjamin Franklin Peixotto (1834–90), arrived in Bucharest as consul of the United States in Romania in January 1871. Peixotto was a former president of B'nai B'rith, and the State Department intended his (unpaid) consulship as a way to enable him to conduct "missionary work for the benefit of the people he represents."[83] Unlike the European states, the United States had little economic or political interest in Romania in the 1860s and 1870s, and it was likely for this reason that Peixotto was named to his position, which would probably not have existed otherwise. Soon after his appointment, Peixotto took over the role of coordinating the efforts of the Romanian Jews in pleading their case before Romanian authorities, and reported on his progress to the Alliance.[84]

Jewish advocates developed a nationally demarcated division of labor in their campaign. Yet even after Jews outside of France became the main actors, the Alliance maintained a symbolic role as the name unifying them in their struggle, and developed the rhetoric that placed their work above simply "Jewish" interests, making it in the interest of humanity in general. In October 1871, Peixotto wrote to the Central Committee that while all advocates had a common cause, "Israel and humanity," they nonetheless had different roles to play. He himself had "the best of relations with the Prince [Carol], his government, and the leaders and members of the different political parties" in Bucharest. But to succeed, Peixotto thought the Central Committee had to continue its work of encouraging Jews around the globe. "If Vienna, Berlin, and London were not but waiting for your initiative to act, I would not call upon your untiring and generous energies; but all these cities have their eyes turned to Paris. Paris is still France, and France is still the guiding light, human liberty and fraternity."[85] In Peixotto's mind, without a symbolic center in France, the campaign would fail because its ideological backbone would be lost.

By 1872, Peixotto was firmly established in Bucharest, and the European Jewish leaders with whom he communicated—Goldsmid in London, Leven in Paris, the eminent banker Gerson Bleichröder in Berlin—published the information in their national newspapers (including of course the *Bulletin de l'Alliance Israélite Universelle*). When it was no longer safe to publish under his own name in Romania, Peixotto began to publish under the pseudonym J. Egalité, and sent copies of his letters to France and Great Britain to shore up support when his own influence began to wane. Even if the Romanians would not listen to him, he wanted liberals in France and Great Britain to try to teach the Romanian leaders the "principles of justice and humanity."[86]

At the behest of Bleichröder, Alliance members from all over Europe met in Brussels in October 1872 to develop and coordinate new strategies to help the Romanian Jews. In keeping with their universalist rhetoric, they held that the legal discrimination and popular violence against the Romanian Jews "should not be examined from the special point of view of religion; more importantly, it is about the rights of people, moral laws, and the great laws of humanity," and that the "interests of general civilization . . . are at stake here."[87] By helping the Romanian Jews, they believed themselves to be educating all Romanians in modern political philosophy, based on the shared values of Judaism and Christianity. "Let us lead the Christian Romanians to place the sacred dogma of fraternity, which their sacred book proclaims as much as ours does, as the foundation of their morality; by doing so we will have conquered the practical philosophy of that nation . . . that anticipates occupying a place of distinction among the nations of Europe."[88] A commission, based in Vienna, was established to run primary and normal schools for the Romanian Jews, and to send money for immediate relief, if necessary. This decision further reflects the Alliance's ideological commitment to social integration through the acquisition of political rights and education.

Unfortunately, the newly coordinated efforts of the advocates had little effect on the rising tide of discrimination against the Romanian Jews. Even with the Berlin bankers agreeing—in theory at least, if not always in reality—not to lend money to the Romanians until they emancipated the Jews, the antisemitic legislation, violence, and expulsions continued.[89] By 1875, the advocates based in Vienna took new measures to force the Romanian government to stop their legal discrimination against Jews. When Austria began to negotiate a commercial treaty with Romania, the commission approached the Austrian diplomats to include a clause requiring equality for all before the law, regardless of religion. However, Romania staunchly resisted, and Austria, eager to sign the treaty and little committed to the cause, signed anyway. Under article 1, even Jewish Austrians would be forbidden to buy or sell rural properties in areas where such transactions were limited to Christians. Russia soon followed, signing a virtually identical commercial treaty with Romania in March 1876.[90] Romania then embarked upon efforts to make similar agreements with France, Germany, Great Britain, and Italy. With Romania unwilling to budge, the Alliance further focused its attention on appealing to the remaining European diplomats, hoping their moral arguments would sway them not to sign treaties with Romania unless the Romanian Jews were emancipated.

To this end, the Alliance held another special meeting in Paris in December 1876. Because the representatives of the Great Powers planned to meet in Constantinople in January to respond to a wave of uprisings in Bosnia-Herzegovina and throughout the Balkans (which had themselves resulted in renewed conflict between Russia and Turkey), the Jewish advocates thought it timely to prepare their arguments and to appoint delegates to send to the congress. At their meeting, they wrote a *Mémoire en faveur des israélites de l'Orient*, which they later sent to representatives of each of the Powers, urging them to take moral concerns into account in considering trade agreements or any other diplomatic treaty. They also sent a new collection of documents about the Balkan Jews that was painstakingly compiled by the Alliance's secretary, Isidore Loeb, entitled *La Situation des israélites en Turquie, en Serbie et en Roumanie*.[91]

The Great Powers held two major congresses to discuss the Balkan situation. The first was in Constantinople, planned as a response to the Bosnian uprising. The second was in Berlin in the summer of 1878, to repair the damage created by the April 1877 war between Russia and Turkey, which had destroyed the fragile arrangement created by the Constantinople congress. The Alliance sent delegates to both congresses, arming them with information about the mistreatment of Jews in the Balkans. These delegates were prepared to convince anyone who would listen that the "civilized" nations should neither recognize nor trade with nations that did not guarantee equal rights to their Jewish inhabitants. Gerson Bleichröder and the Berlin Alliance committee played crucial roles at the 1878 congress as well, working behind the scenes to convince Bismarck that being a friend to the Jews would serve his economic and political interests.[92]

Alliance leaders had understood quite well that these congresses would be crucial in determining the future of Jews in the Balkans. In Crémieux's mind, these congresses would have to resolve the issue of the status of religious groups if they were to create a durable peace, since the Balkan nations clamoring for recognition were multiethnic societies in which Jews, Muslims, Roman Catholics, and Eastern Orthodox Christians lived together.[93] He, Bleichröder, and the other advocates also understood that the Congress of Berlin offered a rare opportunity because the interests of "civilization" coincided with the political and economic interests that Austria, France, and Germany had in the Balkans. The "solidarity" between Jewish rights, political and economic self-interest, and abstract ideals provided excellent conditions for turning things around for the Romanian Jews.

In Berlin, the Alliance's wishes were finally fulfilled, and Crémieux had the pleasure of hearing that it was the moderate republican French foreign minister, William Henry Waddington, who proposed the clause requiring that citizens of all faiths be granted equal rights. The diplomats in Berlin voted unanimously to include Waddington's proposal as article 44 of the treaty:

> In Romania, the distinction of religious creed and confession cannot be used against anyone as a motive for exclusion or incapacity, as regards the enjoyment of civil and political rights, admission to public employment and honors, or exercise of different professions or industries in any locality whatsoever. The freedom and open practice of all religions shall be assured to all citizens of the Romanian state, and also to foreigners, and no hindrance shall be placed on the hierarchical organization of the different communions, and no one shall hinder their relations with their spiritual leaders. Citizens of all Powers, merchants or others, shall be treated in Romania, without distinction of religion, on a footing of perfect equality.[94]

Perhaps just as exciting for Crémieux were Waddington's words explaining the idea behind article 44. At the July 1 meeting of the congress, Waddington said, "Romania, asking to join the great European Family, ought to accept the obligations, and even the drawbacks of the position, the benefits of which she claimed . . . for a long time there would not be found again an opportunity so solemn and decisive to affirm anew the principles which constitute the honor and security of civilized nations."[95] Finally, it seemed, all Europe had joined in the same solidarity upon which the Alliance itself was built: a solidarity of moral interest based in toleration, freedom, equality, and brotherhood.

For Alliance leaders, the Congress of Berlin represented a real success for Jewish international solidarity, helping to secure rights for Jews in Romania, and simultaneously, to make religious freedom and equality key factors in the minds of the diplomats who had the power to determine membership in what Waddington had referred to as the "family" of nations. Crémieux, for example, wrote to Waddington to applaud him for bringing "the civilizing principle" of "liberty, equality, and fraternity" to the international arena in Berlin.[96] Jewish solidarity was not merely for Jews, Alliance leaders believed; its ultimate goal was universal, representing the triumph of "civilization"—a hallowed ideal that encompassed state secularism, the right to work and to vote, education, free trade, and national self-determination—over what they characterized as prejudice, feudalism, despotism, and narrow self-interest. Bringing "civilization" to the rest of the world was conceived in messianic terms, a special duty incumbent on Alliance leaders both as Jews and as Frenchmen that would have a redemptive effect for all humanity.

The reception of article 44 among French republicans reveals that the Alliance's rhetoric of solidarity was effective among French anticlericals, if only briefly. In the first, shaky years of the Third Republic, they found even greater support from a range of republican political leaders like Waddington, Jules Simon, and Léon Gambetta (a former protégé of Crémieux's), at a moment when the anticlerical movement was in the process of realizing some of its most important goals. As François Furet has noted, the religious question had been central in the republican effort to maintain power during the turbulent 1870s, giving the political struggles between democratic and aristocratic factions the "very French tone of civil war."[97] Firmly in power since the crisis of May 1877, these anticlerical republicans responded to the Congress of Berlin with the same joy and hope that Alliance members had, connecting Waddington's work abroad with their own political program at home. To take but one example, the journalist Charles Fauvety, a Protestant minister and former Saint-Simonian, wrote that the Congress of Berlin's resolutions were a perfect model for establishing full secularism in the French government. "This blessing of freedom which the Congress of Berlin has assured for all inhabitants of the Turkish Empire, will our Parliament make us wait for it? And cannot M. Waddington get his government to grant the French people, in France, what he got for the Christians in Turkey?"[98] Like Alliance leaders, Fauvety depicted the protection of religious freedoms as a "universal" concern that would simultaneously end divisions in France and in the world.[99] Like the Alliance, Fauvety and other advocates of secularism thus had goals on the international as well as the domestic front, even though the problems they addressed, the history from which their movement developed, and the set of concepts they mobilized were all particular to the French setting.

Yet ultimately, the realization of the Alliance's hopes at the Congress of Berlin depended upon something that proved much more fleeting: the willingness of the Great Powers, including France, to include religious tolerance clauses in commercial and political treaties, and then to enforce them. Reading article 44 as the inevitable triumph of "civilization," in which trade and diplomatic relations would be made dependent upon a nation's commitment to the spirit of the French Revolution, Alliance leaders and optimistic republicans saw their ideals as so universal that they appear to have been somewhat blind to the complicated motivations that led other actors—Bismarck in particular—to support it. As such, they were equally blind to the reasons why things would soon fall apart. Unlike Jews in France, Jews in Germany and Austria—not to mention Romania—had not built strong alliances with those in power over a shared political stake in the advancement of "civilization" and religious tolerance. Indeed, as Fritz Stern has shown, Bismarck's support for article 44 was based less on ideological commitment than on his imperial ambitions in eastern and southeastern Europe.[100] Thus, while the climate in France would remain relatively favorable for this politics of religious tolerance, things could and did change quickly in Germany. By early 1879, it was clear that Romania was not going to comply willingly with article 44, and indeed, the revised constitution of October 1879 did not make Jews citizens of Romania. Supporting the Jews in Romania was part of Bismarck's realpolitik only briefly; he was too much an opportunist to stay committed to this cause when it became unpopular in both Germany and Romania. In early 1880, Great Britain, upon Bismarck's urging, recognized Romania as well. Austria and Russia, devoted to the Jewish cause only briefly, had not needed such convincing to recognize Romania after it failed to emancipate its Jewish residents. The same year, also upon Bismarck's urging, France too recognized Romania, demonstrating that even in the context where it was designed to make the most sense, the rhetoric of solidarity was not sufficient to convince the republicans in power to put the issue of Romanian Jewish citizenship before other political needs. Although Alliance leaders continued to publicize the plight of the Romanian Jews, they could no longer convince the Great Powers that helping them was in the interest of all humanity.[101]

Without real international consensus that religious tolerance was central to "civilization" and that advancing "civilization" should be a central goal in all commercial and political treaties, the Alliance's cause suffered. Romanian Jews were the most immediate victims of the breakdown of consensus. The Great Powers' unwillingness to enforce article 44 of the Treaty of Berlin meant that the expulsions, violence, and discriminatory legislation continued unabated, and Romanian Jews received citizenship only in 1945.[102] Worse still, without the support of the Powers, the Alliance lost whatever prestige it had enjoyed in Bucharest in the 1860s and 1870s, and became a target of attack itself. While Romanian Jews continued to write to the Alliance for help, and Emmanuel Veneziani and Armand Lévy stayed in Bucharest as advocates, they pleaded with the Central Committee to stop writing to them on Alliance letterhead, and to stop using their names in articles in the European press.[103] The Alliance, no longer able to link the cause of Jewish emancipation to the interests of the Great Powers, and under vicious attack in Romania, found itself powerless to use its strategies of publicity and moral argumentation. The underlying reasons for this breakdown would perplex French Jewish leaders until the 1890s, and in certain respects, beyond. What was emerging in Romania—and in Germany, Austria, Algeria, and, with a short delay, in metropolitan France as well—was a new form of antisemitism that made Jewish international solidarity itself a target.

Conclusion

The Alliance Israélite Universelle's rhetoric of international Jewish solidarity was a universalist rhetoric that linked liberal values to Jewish tradition in a way that mobilized French Jews on behalf of Jews in other countries. Alliance members saw their work as grounded in Judaism as they had come to understand it, by bringing the ideals of liberty, equality, and fraternity to the world, uniting all peoples in a peaceful order. Jewish solidarity in the name of these ideals was not understood as a particularist endeavor. Rather, it was to be an example for the rest of humanity, showing them how people living far away from each other could share basic values. In this way, the Alliance was not seeking to separate Jews from the rest of humanity, but to foster a larger, global solidarity.

Borrowing language from French republicans was a powerful means for these acculturated French Jewish leaders to define their Jewish identity as relevant in the secular circles in which they moved. Framed in these universalist terms, their expressions of Jewishness were favorably received by non-Jewish republicans as well. As we saw in Chapter 4, expressions of Jewish religiosity in the public arena were welcomed in anticlerical circles as an antidote to Catholic religiosity. Similarly, during the early Third Republic, championing Jewish rights in the name of "civilization," in word if not always in deed, served as a way for anticlerical leaders to affirm their commitment to religious equality and freedom even as they pursued policies limiting Church influence in French life.

Yet the rhetoric of Jewish international solidarity was less persuasive in other contexts. As is clear from the failure of the Alliance's campaign to compel the Romanians to grant Jews citizenship, not all world leaders—not even all leaders committed to republicanism, as many Romanian officials were—agreed that granting Jews equal rights was necessary in a modern democracy. Indeed, in the late 1870s, a new form of anti-Jewish politics emerged in Romania that depicted the Alliance's efforts to help the Romanian Jews gain citizenship as a sinister effort to manipulate world leaders for their own selfish gain. As we shall see in Chapter 6, the politics of solidarity, which developed as a strategy of self-defense by linking Jewish rights to the advancement of liberal ideals in the world, came under attack by the emerging international antisemitic movement almost immediately after its initial success at the Congress of Berlin.

Six   The Myth of Jewish Power

By the time the Third Republic was firmly established in the 1870s, Jewish international solidarity had become a central feature of French Jewish life. This rhetoric emerged initially as part of French Jews' strategy to secure their own equality by making Jewish rights central to the liberal agenda and later, the republican agenda in all aspects of state policy. With this goal in mind, the creators of Jewish international solidarity never sought to create an exclusive form of Jewish nationalism. On the contrary, they believed Jewish rights to be most secure in integrated societies under secular institutions of governance, and therefore advocated the political, social, and economic integration of Jews in the places where they lived, including, of course, France. Like the other French republicans whose political rhetoric they shared, they worked at home and abroad for the practical realization of the French revolutionary ideals they deemed sacred, including most importantly, the protection of religious freedoms and the equal treatment of all citizens before the law. This agenda, in their minds, necessarily entailed the destruction of all separate Jewish communal institutions burdened with the political functions of taxation, representation, and governance. In this sense, Jewish international solidarity was as much an expression of its proponents' dedication to republicanism, anticlericalism, and integration to the surrounding society as it was an expression of their strong sense of Jewish identity and their feeling of connectedness to Jews in the rest of the world.

200   Yet in the 1880s, Jewish international solidarity, its architects, the institutions established in its name and their leaders were vilified in a

way that rightly horrified its proponents. In a new political movement emerging on the right, the very public expressions of Jewish international solidarity we have examined here served as evidence that French Jews saw themselves as a "tribe apart" in spite of their long-standing political rights and their apparent social assimilation, and worse, that they had organized a powerful conspiracy, working with Protestants and Freemasons through the corrupt republic to bring economic and moral ruin to France and all gentiles. These charges became central in the construction of the new right-wing political movement that distinguished itself from traditional Jew-hatred by calling itself "anti-semitic." The movement was inspired by rhetoric developed in the German antisemitic parties founded in the late 1870s, and took recent events in Romania and Algeria as key evidence. Yet while these foreign influences were certainly important, French antisemitism was largely a homegrown affair. Edouard Drumont's twelve-hundred-page treatise *La France juive*, first published in early 1886, played an especially important role in articulating French antisemites' litany of charges against the Jews. These included traditional Catholic claims about the Jewish religion (the charges of blood libel and deicide were included, as were attacks on Jewish mystical texts and the Talmud), as well as traditional populist claims about Jews' nefarious economic behavior, articulated in a way that resonated with contemporary socialism by attacking Jewish financiers, especially the Rothschilds, as capitalist exploiters. Yet the overarching point of *La France juive* represented a relatively new political position conceivable only in the context of the struggles over the role of the Church in state affairs. Pulling from some of the more vicious Catholic political writing of the 1860s and 1870s against the anticlerical republican movement and infusing it with traditional anti-Jewish prejudice, Drumont identified the revolution, the anticlerical tradition, and accordingly, the Third Republic as a modern manifestation of the eternal Jewish plot to destroy the Church and Christendom, beginning with France, with the help of the Protestants and the Freemasons.

Critical to the argument of *La France juive* was an extensive chapter, entitled "Crémieux and the Alliance Israélite Universelle," which pointed an accusatory finger at Jewish international solidarity itself. Here, Drumont outlined the supposed plot of Crémieux, the

> Jewish Prince, to confiscate the French Revolution for the profit of Jewry, to give a strictly Jewish character to an idealist movement built on hopes for a better world. At the end of his life, [Crémieux] prepared and proclaimed loudly the arrival of the messianic age, the long-awaited era in which all the nations of the world would be subordinate to Israel, in which all men would work for the race blessed by Jehovah.[1]

In laying out the details of this supposed plot for world domination, Drumont mentioned Crémieux's legal cases against the *more judaïco*, his support for secular education, his leadership in French Freemasonry, and his mentorship of the republican Léon Gambetta, whom Drumont falsely identified as Jewish and attacked throughout the book. Most importantly, Drumont focused at great length on Crémieux's authorship of the Government of the National Defense's decree of October 24, 1870, granting citizenship to the Jews of Algeria, as well as his work with the Alliance Israélite Universelle. For Drumont and his followers, these acts of solidarity proved that Jews were using the institutions of French government to destroy gentiles (especially Christians and the Catholic Church) for their own material benefit.[2]

The publication of *La France juive* represents an important marker in the history of Jewish international solidarity, for with it, the myth of Jewish power was born. As conceived by Drumont and the movement that developed under his leadership, this myth has three fundamental components: first, the persistence of Jewish separatism; second, the Jewish quest for world domination; and third, the republic itself (and liberalism more broadly) as a means for carrying out this plan. Here, I use the term *myth* as Pierre Birnbaum has, in both its lay sense and in the sense used by twentieth-century cultural theorists like Freud and Lévi-Strauss. On the one hand, the myth of Jewish power is untrue; and yet on the other hand, it is truer than true, a fiction that serves to organize reality for those who believe in it. As Birnbaum has explored more fully elsewhere, the myth of Jewish power itself—the myth that liberalism and the republic are, in some fundamental sense, part of a sadistic Jewish plot to dominate and destroy—became a force whose impact has had surprising reach.[3]

While it is beyond the scope of this study to examine the complex roots of modern French antisemitism, one cannot fully understand the history of Jewish international solidarity without contending with the myth of Jewish power. The appearance of the myth in the 1880s marked solidarity's coming of age, and in an important sense, it represented a turning point in the history of Jewish politics because of Jews' subsequent awareness and anxiety over how their actions might be cast by their enemies. Solidarity was no longer a mere rhetorical strategy; it was a mythic reality. As such, the advent of this myth represents not only the end of the story we have examined here; it also represents an important analytic obstacle to understanding the construction of Jewish international solidarity itself. Because the myth of Jewish power cast solidarity as a Jewish takeover of the republic, we now have difficulty understanding solidarity for what it was, even when we dismiss the myth as false. Far from a mere chimera, solidarity was a rhetorical strategy Jewish leaders used to participate in the anticlerical struggles of the nineteenth century in a way that neither erased their Jewishness nor represented the persistence of an old feeling of separatist Jewish corporatism. Thus, while leaving to others the task of explaining the rise of antisemitism as a mass political movement in the last decades of the nineteenth century, this chapter examines how the antisemitic movement in France and colonial Algeria cast Jewish international solidarity as a conspiracy operating through the republic, thereby marking the end of an important era in the history of Jewish self-defense.

The Emergence of the Myth

Antisemitic political parties, leagues, and newspapers emerged first in Algeria and central Europe in the 1870s and in metropolitan France in the mid-1880s. The myth of Jewish power is one key element that distinguishes this organized political antisemitic movement from the more traditional forms of Jew hating it replaced. Historians agree that this myth is as distinctive a marker of this new movement as its use of racial terminology, its economic critique of Jews as bankers and industrial capitalists (the socialist August Bebel famously called antisemitism the "socialism of fools"), and its strong, exclusive nationalist backbone, features from which it cannot fully be separated.[4] Like these other new elements, the myth transcended the boundaries separating the Romanian, German, Austrian, Hungarian, Algerian and French antisemitic movements, and would become especially important in Russia, where the *Protocols of the Elders of Zion*, a forgery meant to substantiate this myth, first surfaced in the early twentieth century, written, significantly, in French.[5] Building on a traditional prejudice that painted Jews as xenophobic and separatist, the myth of Jewish power added a distinctly new element designed to mobilize the Christian public by claiming that Jews were in the process of taking over the world for their own selfish ends.

The myth that Jews were carrying out their quest for world domination through the French republic in particular and other institutions of liberalism more generally played a particularly important role in rallying support for the movement because it served as a link between traditional prejudice and contemporary political issues. In France, Algeria, and central Europe, the antisemitic parties and newspapers singled out for special attack the Alliance Israélite Universelle and the 1870 Crémieux decree emancipating the Jews of Algeria, painting them as incontrovertible proof of the progress of the Jewish plot. The identification of liberalism and the French republic as elements of a Jewish conspiracy made for a potent brew, drawing a level of support for this political movement that surprised French Jewish newspaper editors, consistory leaders, and Alliance members. Far from disappearing with the increasing social and political integration of Jews, the hatred leveled against them appears to have increased, with detractors now attacking the very strategies of self-defense that Jewish leaders had only recently developed. By the end of the 1880s, these attacks were ubiquitous in the public area, taking center stage in the new political movement against liberalism and republicanism.

A hallmark of late-nineteenth-century French antisemitism was its use of direct citations, both real and invented, from Jews' own writings to prove that a conspiracy was in fact underway. The first French writer to take the liberal universalist language of contemporary Jewish international solidarity and depict it as proof of a sinister Jewish conspiracy was the Catholic legitimist Henri Gougenot des Mousseaux, in his *Le Juif, le judaïsme, et la judaïsation des peuples chrétiens*, published in 1869. Gougenot presented "proof," by way of directly citing an article in *L'Univers Israélite*, that after centuries of persecution, Jews in the nineteenth century had become "a flourishing society with access to the most powerful thrones."[6] This, he implied, meant that they were close to meeting their ultimate ambition for wealth and power. The Alliance Israélite Universelle was singled out as a key part of the plan. Gougenot presented much of the Alliance's own rhetoric, culled from the pages of its *Bulletin*, to prove that the organization used dogma from the Freemasons and the occult, and had sought to gain support from gentiles by allying themselves with secret societies as well as with their "distinguished service for the equality and moral progress of our [i.e., Christian] coreligionists."[7] Gougeonot argued that the press, too, was a crucial ingredient of the Jewish plot. Using its power, the Jews would foment revolutions everywhere, and would finally achieve world domination with the help of secret societies and philanthropic organizations that may appear innocuous or beneficial, but were in fact "each . . . a living stitch of the immense web [*réseau*] that is encircling the globe."[8] Economic power was crucial as well: "Gold is the master of the world," Gougenot wrote. "Gold owns us, and the Jew owns the gold."[9] Here too he supplied evidence of Jewish wealth from proud reports that had appeared in the Jewish press. A final part of the plot involved the recent persecutions of Jews in Romania, about which he also quoted directly from the Jewish press. This, Gougenot claimed, had provided an excuse for Jews in France and Germany to dictate the policy of their own leaders and through them, to oppress the innocent people of Romania.[10]

According to historian Léon Poliakov, charges of a Jewish-Masonic conspiracy against the entire human species, of the sort that Gougenot leveled against the Alliance in 1869, dated back to French Catholic legitimist writings from the First Empire, in which Jews replaced Protestants as the face of the Antichrist.[11] Similar charges had been made in the clerical press in the heated religious conflicts of the mid-nineteenth century. Louis Veuillot's *L'Univers*, for example, had spoken about the Alliance in these terms in numerous articles that blamed the Jews for the increasing liberalization of Napoleon III's stance vis-à-vis the Catholic Church. Pope Pius IX (in office until 1878) had not explicitly embraced these terms himself, but he was extremely supportive of Veuillot; his successor Leo XIII went so far as to bless Gougenot after *Le Juif* appeared.[12] What was new here was not the idea of a Jewish conspiracy, but rather, the strategy of assembling Jewish leaders' own messianic, universalist, and distinctly republican rhetoric, as found in their most public writings in the 1860s, to prove that the system for world domination was largely in place, operating through the liberal government. In this way, Gougenot treated the messianic, universalist, and self-congratulatory rhetoric he found in the French Jewish press in much the way that he and other anti-Jewish writers before him treated the Talmud and other exclusively Jewish writings. Meticulously citing Jewish sources in his long footnotes, Gougenot used Jews' own words as seemingly incontrovertible proof of their fundamental misanthropy and pride, and their growing power over Western leaders.

Gougenot des Mousseaux's book made little impact on the French reading public, despite some positive reviews in the Catholic press.[13] Indeed, although the offended editor of *L'Univers Israélite* petitioned the Central Consistory to take action against Gougenot, as they had, to great success, against Veuillot for his defamatory remarks during the 1858 Mortara affair, the Central Consistory declined, seeing the work as too unimportant, part of a fading prejudice.[14] As former Central Consistory president Max Cerfberr wrote of the matter,

> I make a big distinction between newspapers, pamphlets, and books; [books] are read little, and when they are, it is only by the educated, whose feelings are hard to influence. It's different with newspapers that penetrate into the little towns and the countryside, which can have a terrible effect on poor and ignorant souls. . . . I think that if we initiate judicial action against the author of this book . . . we would be doing him the same immense favor that the Catholic clergy did for Mr. Renan; thus, we should abstain.[15]

The other consistory leaders, including its new president, Alphonse de Rothschild, concurred. Joseph Cohen added that it would be particularly unwise to give unnecessary publicity to Gougenot at present, when freedom of the press was increasing. Cohen was now more experienced than when he had traveled to Algeria to prepare a report on the Jews for the War Ministry, but he remained just as committed to liberalism and was optimistic about the direction that the emperor's policy was taking. As such, he saw no point in giving Gougenot undue publicity. "All these attacks against Judaism will not prevail over the principles of freedom of conscience and religion that will soon be the law of modern society," he wrote. "Marching toward progress and happiness means stirring up the dust of these calumnies that can neither hurt nor stain us."[16]

The Crémieux Decree and Algerian *Anti-Judaïsme*

Cohen's optimism about what republicanism would mean for Jewish security was to be challenged in the next decade in Algeria, where the myth of Jewish power would become a powerful force in colonial politics. The Algerian *anti-juif* movement, as it was called, emerged soon after the interim Government of the National Defense had established civil rule in the colony. After the capture of Emperor Napoleon III in the Franco-Prussian War in early September 1870, and the ensuing collapse of the Second Empire, this interim government began to work from Tours. It was there that Crémieux, serving as minister of justice, penned the decrees that brought a formal end to military rule in the colony in the final months of 1870. The decrees gave settlers the same rights as metropolitan citizens by dividing the colony into *départements*, instituting jury trials, and granting citizens in the colony the right to elect representatives.[17] Alongside these, Crémieux issued the decree that came to bear his name, which granted French citizenship to all native Algerian Jews. For Crémieux, the emancipation decree was but a particularly important part of a larger issue of "civilizing" Algeria by placing it under civil control and creating a colonial

citizenry with the same rights, obligations, and entitlements as metropolitan citizens. This, he and the other members of the Government
of the National Defense believed, was crucial for restoring order in
the colony, since in September and October, republicans in Algiers
had risen up against the military government, demanding civil rule.[18]

Civil rule brought elections, and elections seem to have brought political *anti-judaïsme*. The first Algerian antisemitic league was founded
in July 1871 over the issue of voting in the town of Miliana; from then
on, elections would remain at the center of the *anti-juif* movement.
This was an important issue in Algeria, where the voting system as a
whole was notoriously corrupt. Votes were regularly traded in blocs,
and thus, metropolitan political labels like "Opportunist" and "Radical"—the moderate and left-wing republicans, respectively—could
take on very different meanings locally, having to do with how votes
were brokered. In this context, Jewish leaders were accused of selling
a "Jewish vote," usually to support Opportunists against their Radical
opponents. As a correspondent in the *Radical Algérien*, an *anti-juif*
newspaper in Algiers, wrote in 1885,

> Universal suffrage is incompatible with the Algerian Jewish elec-
> torate. . . . [I]n the hands of the greater part of native Jews, the
> ballot too often becomes a commercial commodity for trafficking.
> For a long time, and for a long time to come, the native Jewish vote
> will remain the element that corrupts French universal suffrage. . . .
> It is thus in the name of French public law . . . in the name of the
> freedom, independence, and morality of universal suffrage itself that
> we seek your patriotic support for the repeal of the political rights
> section of the imprudent naturalization decree of October 24, 1870,
> that now weighs on the three Algerian *départements*.[19]

How are we to understand the emergence of a political voice depicting native Jewish electors as both powerful and corrupt? First, it
is important to know that native Jews comprised a relatively large
percentage of the Algerian electorate in the early Third Republic,
bearing in mind that the vast majority of the colony's residents were
Arabs, who did not possess voting rights. With a population of about
thirty-three thousand in 1870 and rising to about fifty thousand by
the 1890s, Jews represented 15 percent of the electorate in the three

Algerian *départements*, and up to 50 percent in some towns, numbers significant enough to swing elections.[20] In addition, because of the comparatively high birthrate of the Algerian Jews and some immigration from Morocco, the percentage of Jews in the electorate was perceived to be growing rapidly. Historian Geneviève Dermenjian's statistics on Oran, for example, reveal that from 1891 to 1896, the period in which that city's major *anti-juif* crisis began, the Jewish population of the city went from 6,294 to 10,651, while the number of French (French-born and naturalized Europeans together) went from 21,202 to 27,523.[21] Compare this to the Jewish population in metropolitan France in 1889, who numbered 68,000 or a tiny 0.18 percent of a population of about 38 million, roughly the same percentage as in 1789.[22]

More important than these demographic statistics, however, is the likely reality of political corruption. Academic historians who have looked seriously into the matter concur that some degree of corruption must have been present, but that Jewish corruption was but one part of a larger corrupt milieu.[23] Even this, of course, is hard to substantiate, since at the same moment, many candidates either made *anti-judaïsme* central to their election platforms or found other ways of courting an *anti-juif* vote, so it is hard to imagine Jews voting for them. Blaming Simon Kanoui, an important Jewish leader in Oran, for election disappointment and political corruption became a mainstay of the *anti-juif* press in that city, which historian Charles-Robert Ageron has called "the hotbed of Algerian anti-Judaism." *Anti-juifs* in Algiers made similar claims, and in both places, these attacks did much to mobilize the multiethnic but very Catholic settler working class.[24] In the 1880s and 1890s, elections in Algeria were an occasion for intense anti-Jewish rhetoric focusing on particular Jewish leaders, often leading to mob violence in the streets that could rage for days before the police were able to restore order.[25] This kind of violence erupted in Tlemcen in 1881, in Algiers in 1884 and 1885, in Mostaganem and Oran in 1897, and in towns across Algeria in 1898, when the *anti-juif* leader Max Régis of Algiers went so far as to call for an autonomist, *anti-juif* revolution, announcing, "We will water the tree of our liberty with Jewish blood."[26]

Yet while Jews' participation in the corrupt Algerian voting system was crucial to the *anti-juif* movement's rhetoric and its remarkable success in mobilizing adherents, it cannot be explained simply as a reaction to the corruption of Jewish leaders or to Jewish voting patterns. Indeed, attempts to block native Jews from voting or to have them stripped of their citizenship rights predates the corruption of the system, traceable back to the reactions of colonial administrators to the Crémieux decree that had made Jews electors in the first place. Although colonial administrators were not part of any organized anti-Jewish movement at the time, their objections to the Jewish emancipation decree of 1870 became the cornerstone of much of the movement's language in the 1880s.

The emancipation decree of October 24, 1870, was issued at a moment of colonial as well as metropolitan chaos. It granted citizenship to native Algerian Jews collectively and forcibly, whether or not they had sought to be naturalized as French as individuals, as permitted by an 1865 *sénatus-consulte*, a measure that had proven necessary because few Algerian Jews had chosen to apply for citizenship. Initially, the decree did not provoke much of a response in the colony. It was first challenged in late July 1871 by Charles du Bouzet, prefect of Oran, with the support of Lucet, prefect of Constantine, and Walsin-Esterhazy, the commanding general in Algiers. The timing of du Bouzet's pamphlet says much about his reasoning. In the spring of 1871, Algerian Muslims had launched a revolt of their own, seeing in the chaos caused by the war and the settler uprising in Algiers an opportunity to rid Algeria of the French altogether.[27] In spite of strong evidence to the contrary, du Bouzet argued the Crémieux decree was responsible for the Muslim Arab revolt, the worst the colony had seen since the conquest had become secure, because the Muslim Arabs were jealous of the Jews' newly won status. As a commission supporting the decree's abrogation would later put it, "The Arabs most devoted to France were the most humiliated and irritated by the naturalization decree. They said bitterly that it was not the Jews who were becoming French, it was the French becoming Jewish."[28]

Statements like this one reflect the anti-Jewish attitudes of settlers rather than those of the Muslim Arabs, whose concern at the time was to throw off French rule, not to gain citizenship. Anti-Arab cultural bias was also important to du Bouzet's argument. He claimed that Jews could not be citizens because of their Arab dress, language, and culture. Like Muslim Arabs, he contended, they did not want citizenship; they would not make good soldiers and their votes would outweigh those of the French *colons* and distort elections. Du Bouzet also argued that Jewish jurors would provoke resentment, especially from Muslims, who held them in contempt. With the support of the other prefects, du Bouzet assembled these objections as a petition to the National Assembly, asking for the immediate abrogation of the decree.[29]

Crémieux read the prefect's objections not as the emergence of a new kind of politics—for that would come later—but rather, as an old and familiar prejudice against Jews. Stressing evidence of Jews' increasing acculturation through consistory education and their desire to become citizens (despite the fact that few had applied for it), Crémieux implied that du Bouzet was motivated primarily by prejudice.[30] Defending the decree before the National Assembly, Crémieux asserted that reform through a new legal organization represented the true spirit of French law, and that any opposition to this was an opposition to the values of tolerance and civilization. "They are saying, in all seriousness, the same things against the Algerian Jews that they said in 1790, 1807, and again in 1818 against the Jews of France," he wrote. "How much time is needed, even in the most civilized countries, to put an end to religious prejudice?"[31]

In fact, the situation was quite complex. In defending the decree, Crémieux was forced to acknowledge that in spite of the establishment of consistories in Algeria and the destruction of native systems of government, Algerian Jews, like Algerian Muslims, still seemed hesitant to give up their Jewish *statut personnel*, which allowed them to pass property and conduct civil affairs according to traditional Jewish law. Crémieux would later argue that this was because Jews would never choose to abandon what they believed was the "law of God," but that if a new legal system were imposed on them, they would be obligated to follow it, under the Jewish legal principle *dina d'malkhuta dina*.[32] The reality was more complex even than this, given the fact that certain important practices—divorce, for example—were illegal under French law but permitted under Jewish law. The power dynamic between French Jews and Algerian Jews, as well as the possibility of retaining communal status, as the Muslims had, may also have played a role in Algerian Jews' choices. Crémieux mentioned none of these factors, however, in explaining the rationale of the collective emancipation decree after it was challenged.

Moreover, Algerian Jews' reticence to become citizens was in fact only part of the problem that the decree of October 24, 1870, was meant to resolve. Without citizenship, Algerian Jews were in an extremely precarious legal situation. They were still governed by Jewish law in civil matters like the sale of property, marriage, and inheritance, and yet the institutions which had traditionally overseen these transactions were dismantled by the *ordonnance* of November 9, 1845. Matters were complicated even further by the 1851 decree that brought all marriage and property exchange contracts executed by Algerian Jews under the jurisdiction of French courts. French courts were thus expected to understand, interpret, and enforce Jewish law; but as members of the Algerian consistories complained, they were reticent to do so because of their limited knowledge of it.[33] Consistory rabbis would not administer Jewish law either, for their express role was purely religious. In addition, to be married under French law, a French birth certificate was required.[34] This left the Algerian Jews without the means to marry or pass property legally if they chose to retain their status as *israélites indigènes*, as most did, and it seems likely that the old institutions were still functioning illegally to take care of these problems. The partial assimilation of the Algerian Jews had caused quite a legal mess and was a very different situation than the Muslims faced, since Muslims had retained communal institutions, even though they too had been transformed radically by French rule.

In response to these problems, a number of French jurists working in the colony published works in the 1860s that argued, as the Central Consistory had argued since the 1840s, that the only way to rectify the legal problems caused by the 1845 *ordonnance* was to grant citizenship to the Algerian Jews and thereby bring them completely under French jurisdiction. Though most War Ministry officials opposed collective emancipation, an important alliance between a contingent of French lawyers in Algeria and the French Jewish establishment in Paris was formed over this issue, nurtured by Crémieux's trips to the colony, and all agreed about the nature of the problem and its solution.[35]

The 1865 *sénatus-consulte* permitting Algerian Jews, as well as Algerian Muslims, to apply for citizenship was meant as a partial solution to the problem. Yet this solution did not work, since only a handful of Jews, and even fewer Muslims, became French citizens under this law, and the vast majority of the Jews who did apply for citizenship were Moroccan born, having settled just across the Algerian border in the Oran area (this western border was established only in 1845).[36] The idea of granting citizenship forcibly and collectively to all Algerian Jews as an alternative means of rectifying Jews' legal problems preceded the collapse of the Second Empire, and was by no means Crémieux's alone. Based on a thorough examination of the archival record, Ageron found that after 1866, there was general agreement among colonial jurists and metropolitan policy makers that collective emancipation was necessary. The liberal Emile Ollivier, minister of justice and worship, had even penned a proposal for a decree in March 1870 to this effect, a plan that was not abandoned until the government fell. In June 1870, the War Ministry too conceded that collective emancipation was necessary, and it was Marshal Patrice MacMahon, then governor-general of Algeria, who demanded that the decree contain a clause stating that no exceptions or delays be allowed, a clause that du Bouzet would later find particularly objectionable. After the emperor was captured and Crémieux was appointed temporary minister of justice, he merely adapted the existing decree—whose final form was determined by MacMahon—to the new circumstances.[37]

Although he himself did not, by any means, bear sole responsibility for emancipation of the Jews of Algeria, Crémieux was clearly proud that it bore his name. His statements about the decree reflect the politics of solidarity he had long embraced, and reveal a remarkable unselfconsciousness that would have been unthinkable for a Jewish leader in the 1890s, when antisemitism was a true political force. Until his death in early 1880, he spoke of it as his greatest lifetime achievement and took full ownership of it as an act of sincere devotion to the Jewish people and to the French republic, whose fortunes, he believed, were fundamentally intertwined. His naïveté about how this might be interpreted in the colony is apparent from an exchange he had with the deputies representing Algeria in the Chamber in 1874. In explaining the need for making citizenship obligatory, he said:

> M. CRÉMIEUX: God thought of everything. . . . He gave a wise and admirable prescription. . . . "Wherever you live, you will follow the law of the land faithfully, if it is imposed upon you." Take note of those words, "If it is imposed upon you." . . . So if you say to a Jew, "If you want to be French, you will be French! If you don't want it, you won't be," then this Jew must say, "I cannot adopt doctrines that are not my own, I cannot accept a law that is not my own." And so, Messieurs, since I knew these things, I imposed the law upon them. (General hilarity—applause from several places.)

> M. LE COMTE OCTAVE DE BASTARD: So you consecrated yourself as the Eternal Father!

> M. CRÉMIEUX: Don't believe that any of these Jews have reproached me for making them French. Not one, do you hear me, has revolted against this decree; they have all accepted it happily, just as we accepted the benefits of France in 1791. And how! A persecuted race, seen as inferior and cursed, elevated immediately to the same level as their persecutors. . . . We are French, we want to live and die as Frenchmen! Call on us, we are ready![38]

Evidently, Crémieux saw the main charge against the Jews as one of a lack of patriotism and insufficient acculturation. From the joking and, retrospectively, naïve way in which this most savvy of nineteenth-century French Jewish leaders said, "I imposed the law upon them," it is apparent that the myth of Jewish power, so central to Algerian and French antisemitism by the 1890s, had not yet taken on importance in 1874, when Crémieux made these remarks. Lawyer to the core, Crémieux would never have missed an opportunity for rebuttal, as we see even here, where he confronts directly what he believes to be the underlying charge against the Jews. His boastful words about "imposing the law" on Algerian Jews were those of someone long used to portraying himself as a wily underdog, proud to be a sign of the revolution's universality and its ability to regenerate even the most oppressed and reviled. These words were intended for an audience that assumed Jewish powerlessness, not Jewish power.

After Crémieux's death in 1880, though, the idea that the emancipation decree had taken place because of Jewish domination of the republic in a moment of weakness became a cornerstone of the myth of Jewish power in Algeria. Although many of du Bouzet's arguments were taken up by the *anti-juifs*, they were dwarfed by new claims focused on the secret machinations of metropolitan Jews rather than solely on native Algerian Jews' lack of French national sentiment or Arab resentment. A seemingly left-wing economic critique of Jews as bankers exercising undue influence in metropolitan politics played an important role here. It was of little importance to *anti-juifs* that Crémieux himself was a lawyer and not a banker, and had long championed the rights of workers; the decree became a potent example, among others, of how Jewish bankers controlled the government. Although anti-Jewish writings that critiqued capitalism as "Jewish" and attacked Jewish bankers as having undue influence had appeared in France in the 1840s, none of the left-wing political movements in France had made demands that Jews be stripped of citizenship or expelled from the country central to their political platforms, nor had anti-Jewish attacks taken center stage in their writings in the way that they did in the work of right-wing Catholic political writers like Louis Veuillot.[39] Yet in Algeria in the 1880s, the concept that powerful, corrupt Jewish bankers had established a system that hurt ordinary *colons* became central to Algerian *anti-juifs'* repertoire of charges against what they referred to in Algiers as the "Jewish-Opportunist system," and in Oran, "Kanouisme," after Simon Kanoui, the president of the Oran Consistory and the main target of the city's local *anti-juif* movement.[40]

In speaking of Jewish power as a system or an –*ism*, the *anti-juifs* implied that local Jewish leaders, Parisian Jews, and deputies whose politics they disliked were all part of a same conspiracy of the strong against the weak. In this regard, the Alliance Israélite Universelle became a shorthand term to describe a Jewish financial cabal in league with Freemasons, seeking to dominate through corruption and cir-cumventing democratic processes through bribery and quid pro quo. As one radical newspaper put it in 1887:

> Jewish Freemasonry has understood that it can put its hand on the colony thanks to the weakness of the government of the republic. The directors of the tribes of Israel will follow the progress of the consistories' influence in Algerian politics very carefully. Like the Je-suits, they have a general in Paris who centralizes all the information and directs the forward march of the Semites. . . . The Jews are much more powerful than the Jesuits, because they possess the entire public fortune. No government in Europe is strong enough to resist it, knowing full well that the Jewish bankers will bring them to failure or bankruptcy just by closing their windows to them.[41]

By the 1890s, the *anti-juifs* were a powerful political voice with their own newspapers and candidates who blamed French and Algerian Jew-ish greed, misanthropy, and control over the republic for political cor-ruption and instability, as well as settler poverty. Many of their journals carried the title *Petit*—the *Petit Algérien*, the *Petit Colon*, the *Petit Fanal Oranais*, the *Petit Africain*, the *Petit Constantinois*, and so on. These ti-tles demonstrate the *anti-juifs*' self-perception as exploited "little guys," and further reflect how central this left-wing critique of Jews as finance capitalists controlling the republic was to the movement.

The rhetorical force of Algerian *anti-judaïsme* came from the way it combined this populism with a theory that a metropolitan, republican Jewish conspiracy was responsible for the failure of democracy and economic well-being in Algeria. Their best weapon was the press. Journalists in all the major cities of the colony wrote regularly of a Jewish political conspiracy influential in Paris and thus more power-ful than other political forces in the colony. In 1883, for example, the *Courrier d'Oran* wrote of "the Prussian barons of Parisian finance that belong to the Semitic world," as having "maneuvered around our gov-ernors to prevent them from ratifying the vote of the Oran City Coun-cil."[42] This newspaper was aimed to appeal to an audience of *petits* who shared a strong Catholic sensibility, as is apparent from how com-monly *anti-juif* journalists defined the conspiracy's target as "Christianity" or "Christians." One article, for example, referred to the Alliance Israélite Universelle as a "true anti-Christian league" whose goal was "[to glorify] the Golden Calf that would dominate everything, and whose colossal statue would rest on Christianity's ruins, sold to Mammon and paid for by the children of Israel."[43]

Anti-Arab cultural prejudice played an important role in *antijudaïsme* as well, although in a rather complicated way. On the one hand, most authors were concerned to stress that Arabs hated the Jews and had risen up in 1871 against the government because of the Crémieux decree. Yet this seeming sympathy for the Muslims was but thinly disguised self-interest. At the same time, Algerian Jews were attacked as fanatical and incapable of democracy in ways that drew from their supporters' negative views about all Arabs, including Muslims, adding to the sense that the Judeo-Masonic conspiracy involved a degree of black magic. For example, one radical *anti-juif* Algiers paper played off its readers' prejudices in this way:

> M. [Edouard] Millaud [minister of public works, then visiting Algiers] received the order from the General of the Alliance Israélite Universelle to get the Muslims of the southern desert to come and pay tribute to him, in order to confirm the submission of the Crescent to the Golden Calf. That is why a *fantasia* with two thousand indigenous riders was held in his honor. . . . M. [Eugène] Etienne [deputy from Oran] who is very Jewish, being from all the financial groups, was made master of ceremonies.[44]

The ceremony imagined by this author, with its images of idol worship and secrecy, shows how close Algerian *anti-judaïsme* was to Gougenot des Mousseaux's. Although it came from the political left rather than the political right, and was not part of the metropolitan Catholic establishment's struggle against the anticlericals, it nonetheless depended, in large part, on the Catholic position that Jews and Freemasons were connected to the occult, the Antichrist, or the devil. Ageron has argued that this shared prejudice worked particularly well in the Algerian context because of the large population of Mediterranean Catholic immigrants and especially Spaniards, for whom the shared hatred of the Jews as a "deicidal race" served as an opportunity for coalition building in an otherwise segregated colony.[45] By the 1890s, all these elements had combined to create a powerful settler political movement with wide support across the colony.

The Myth According to Drumont

By the time Edouard Drumont wrote *La France juive*, political antisemitism was already flourishing in colonial Algeria to such a degree that he could write, "It is perhaps by way of Algeria that the antisemitic campaign in France will begin."[46] In a certain sense, Drumont was right. Although political antisemitism had been flourishing in neighboring Germany since the late 1870s, metropolitan France remained relatively calm in the early 1880s, and it was only the Catholic press, increasingly embittered by the measures republicans had taken toward achieving their anticlerical goals, that attacked Jews and Judaism routinely. In 1881, Hippolyte Prague of *Les Archives Israélites* followed the founding and quick failure of the first French antisemitic newspaper, *L'Anti-Juif*, reporting with pride that this movement, whose "subversive doctrine" was "born in a neighboring country," was so weak in France. "None of this is worth a single moment of our attention, no more than the crocodile tears that this newspaper shed for . . . the emancipation of our fathers which, according to him, was the cause of all the bloody scenes of the French Revolution!!!"[47] The situation was no different the following year, when *Les Archives Israélites* reported that *l'antisémitisme* had spread from Romania, Russia, and Germany to Algeria, where it had taken hold only among "wild radicals" because of "misunderstandings" about Algerian Jewish voting, but was still not a force in France.[48] The quick failure of the second French antisemitic newspaper in 1883 and of a third in 1884 supports *Les Archives'* position: antisemitism in France was practically nonexistent in the early 1880s.[49]

By the end of the decade, however, things had changed. To explain antisemitism's emergence in France, historian Léon Poliakov has stressed the economic depression of 1882–90 as a factor that created the necessary conditions.[50] Historians also point to the importance of the spectacular, well-publicized failure of the Catholic bank, the legitimist Eugène Bontoux's Union Générale in February 1882, within a month of its founding. The bank had drawn a wide range of Catholic investors and been championed in the Catholic press, and its failure was widely—and erroneously—blamed on the Rothschilds and came to form an important part of the myth of Jewish power in France.[51] Other scandals, such as the Panama Canal financial scandal of the late 1880s, in which numerous deputies were implicated, were also portrayed as signs that "Jewish financiers" were corrupt, predatory, and politically powerful. Yet as with the Crémieux decree in Algeria, these were but the conditions and the elements from which a myth could be made.

As historian Robert Byrnes had argued convincingly, the catalytic force that turned antisemitism into a real political force in France was the publication of Drumont's *La France juive* itself.[52] Although a well-known journalist, Drumont initially had some trouble finding a publisher for the book. Marpon and Flammarion finally agreed to publish it, but only if Drumont would pay for the first print run of two thousand copies and assume the burden for any libel suits the book might provoke. Drumont agreed, and the book came out in mid-April 1886. In true Balzacian fashion, *La France juive* was noticed only when, thanks to the intervention of Drumont's friend Alphonse Daudet, it received some provocative, largely negative reviews in the press. In the beginning of May, Drumont won a much-publicized duel against Arthur Meyer, the editor of the newspaper *Le Gaulois*, whose reputation he had tarnished in the book. This appearance of controversy helped sales immensely. By mid-June, more than seventy thousand copies had been sold. *La France juive* became the most widely read book in France, putting antisemitism on the French political map for the first time.[53]

As in the Algerian *anti-juif* movement, Drumont's antisemitism was built on a firm foundation of traditional Catholic prejudice against the Jews. However, Drumont's connection to political Catholicism was much more direct, and this made for an antisemitic platform that differed noticeably from colonial *anti-judaïsme*. Drumont himself had become a fervent Catholic in the early 1880s, and claimed to have been motivated to denounce the Jewish takeover of the republic because of

the flood of anticlerical legislation that the Opportunists had produced since 1879. These included the Ferry laws, which made education secular, free, and obligatory; the expulsion of Catholic monks
from France; and the abolition of the Catholic theology faculties in
the universities.[54] These factors certainly influenced the warm reception that *La France juive* would receive in the Catholic press. Since the
1870s, Catholic newspapers like *L'Univers*, *Le Monde*, and *L'Assemblée
Nationale* had blamed Jews for the progress of the anticlericals. An article in the *L'Assemblée Nationale* in 1874 had argued that the Jews had
been "the instigators of the persecution directed against the Catholic
Church in Italy, Germany, and Switzerland," and, with their Protestant allies, they were now embarking upon "the most violent aggres-
sions against our parliamentary majority that defends conservative interests, values Catholic freedom [and] likes to pray."[55] Furthermore,
although Pope Leo XIII officially denounced Drumont's book, the
French Catholic press received it with great enthusiasm. Byrnes reports that at the end of its review of Drumont's book, *La Croix* urged
its readers that like Christ, the French nation should rise up from Jewish domination, and *Le Monde*, a paper closely associated with the
archbishop of Paris, had praised Drumont as a "good soldier of Jesus."[56] In denouncing the republic as a Jewish conspiracy, Drumont
thus participated in the decades-old Catholic battle against a republican movement that used Jewishness as a powerful emblem.

Although Drumont followed in Gougenot's footsteps in both his
base of support and in the accusation he leveled against the Jews, his
language was a bit different. Drawing on German antisemitic rhetoric,
Drumont began by using a watered-down version of contemporary
philological race theory to make an absolute distinction between the
Aryans, "from a Sanskrit word meaning *noble, illustrious, generous,*
which, as we know, designates the superior white family," and the
Jews, who, as members of the Semitic race, have provoked conflict
with the Aryans since "the first days of history."[57] Despite the racial
framework, Drumont's depictions of the Jews drew more from traditional religious conceptions of the difference between Jews and Christians than from the recent perspective of the philologists he cites in
the book. For example, citing Littré for these purposes, Drumont ar-

gues that although the Aryan race had come originally from Iran, to-day its direct descendants were the "Western Christians."[58] Drumont's use of racial categories was in fact but a thin veil for describing a conflict between Jews and Christians. Moreover, beyond drawing on traditional religious definitions to define races, Drumont's argument depends on the same long-entrenched negative stereotypes about the Jews that Algerian *anti-juifs* mobilized. He wrote that for the Jew, "against the Christian, the goy, all means are good means," and that the Talmud contains such commands as: "You can and you must kill the best of the goyim. The money of the goyim comes down from the Jew; thus it is permitted to steal from him and cheat him."[59] The Jews, as he described them, are foreign, physically repulsive, greedy, and rich, possessing "half the capital circulating in the world." With their money, they attract weak gentiles who "fall to their feet before the Golden Calf," eager to do their bidding.[60]

La France juive also details the history of what Drumont refers to as the Semitic "conquest" of France, with more than half the story unfolding in the nineteenth century and reaching its climax in the Third Republic, when the "Jews," under the leadership of the Opportunist Gambetta, took power and began to persecute the Church. It is here that Drumont most resembles the Algerian *anti-juifs*, whom he so admired. Like them, Drumont argued that the republic was a front for the Jews and that through it, Jews were carrying out their plan to dominate the world for their own profit. Throughout the century, Drumont argues, French leaders had been in the service of the Jewish bankers, and especially Rothschild, serving a foreign master for the sake of money rather than the good Catholic people of France. In his history, Drumont identified a whole set of political acts as the work of the "Jews"—the expulsion of the Jesuits, the Saint-Simonian movement, Napoleon's loss at Waterloo, the loss of the Franco-Prussian War, the brutal repression of the Paris Commune, the anticlerical measures taken since 1870, the crash of the Union Générale—in ways that played well with readers embattled against the republic.

Drumont was particularly harsh in his portraits of Gambetta, Jules Simon, Waddington, and other influential anticlericals, whom he insists on identifying as Jewish in spite of the fact that their actual non-Jewish backgrounds were well known. For instance, in describing a set of meetings he imagined having taken place between Simon and Gambetta in 1870, as they prepared to exploit France's weakness to pursue their own ends for "Jewry" as part of the Government of the National Defense, Drumont writes:

> Note that in these meetings, where the fate of France was being decided, there was no voice representing native Frenchmen, men of French origin, sons of Frenchmen, the ones who worked the land and who created the Fatherland. The dialogue was conducted just between two foreign Jews; one Italian, whose family came from Germany where they were called Gamberlé, the other Swiss, whose name was originally Schweizer, then Suisse on his birth certificate, and now Simon as his pen name. Neither one of them had received any mandate to govern.
>
> It doesn't hurt to imagine that the true representatives of this country, the ones who pay, who fight and who die, are just waiting in an antechamber somewhere for these Israelites to be done with their conversation.[61]

Like the Algerian *anti-juifs*, Drumont's book was aimed at making as powerful as case as possible that the French government was not truly representative of its people, but was rather a "politico-financial dictatorship" of the Jews, defined as a foreign race long bent on destroying the Aryan race and Christendom.[62] Ultimately, the kind of provocative rhetoric that we see in this passage was a call to "native-born Frenchmen" to rise up against the republic, finally exposed as a cabal of foreign Jewish financiers and those who serve them. Such rhetoric combined a pseudosocialist economic critique with the concerns of the clerical party in a particularly powerful way.

Drumont also provided examples of Jewish domination outside of France, using the writings of the antisemitic leaders in other countries to make his case. In so doing, Drumont was at once able to generate additional evidence to support his claims of a Jewish conspiracy, and made common cause with much more powerful antisemitic parties in Germany, Hungary, Austria, and Algeria. The German case was particularly crucial. According to Drumont, German Jews had already achieved economic dominance and had even corrupted Bismarck and were responsible for his anti-Catholic position in the *Kulturkampf*. To support these claims, Drumont was able to cite German antisemites themselves, who had built quite an arsenal of charges like this one, from an antisemitic newspaper in Posen in 1876, "[The local committee of the Alliance] is an international association, as much as the Jesuits are. . . . The illness from which all the states of Europe are suffering, is less the persecution of the Jews than the universal supremacy of the Jews through money."[63] Building on these German antisemites' claims, Drumont added these German Jews were now waging the same war against religion through the republican movement in France.[64]

Claims generated by antisemites in Romania also served as an important source of information for Drumont. In a certain sense, this was easily accomplished, because Romanian antisemites had reached out to the French people in the 1870s, seeking their sympathy in their effort to restrict citizenship in the new nation to Christians only. A group of antisemitic students in Bucharest published a manifesto in French that was widely reprinted in the French press in 1875. The manifesto claimed that the French, of all people, should understand why Romanians would want to keep the Jews living in their midst from obtaining equal rights, since French Jews had not proved worthy of the citizenship they had obtained in 1791, and in recent years, had proved to be traitors, responsible for France's loss in the Franco-Prussian War. Worse, they argued, French Jews had used the war for their own selfish ends: "At the moment when the Fatherland was in the most extreme peril, when a third of France was smoking with blood and fire, Mr. Crémieux saw nothing more urgent than to bestow citizenship rights on the Jews of Algeria; he thus ignited a sort of civil war in the great and rich French possession, just as the Fatherland was ripped apart by the worst and most cruel invasion."[65]

Drumont proved to be as interested in the Jews of Romania as the Romanian antisemites had been in the Jews of France. In Drumont's eyes, the Congress of Berlin, at which the Great Powers put conditions on their recognition of Romania, represented yet another example of how powerful the Jews had become. Waddington, he argued, had devoted all his efforts at the conference to serve the Jews by seeking emancipation for the Romanian Jews, a loathsome people responsible for all of the struggling nation's ills. All Jewry, Drumont reported, had celebrated in their co-optation of Waddington. As proof that the Congress of Berlin was the result of a successful Jewish plot, Drumont reprinted a passage from the *Bulletin de L'Alliance Israélite Universelle*:

> Crémieux, in a meeting of the Alliance Israélite, exclaimed . . . "My faith in our beautiful situation today is great! Ah! Let me give all due credit to the noble, loyal and pure behavior of our minister of foreign affairs, *our* Mr. Waddington."
>
> This word *our* seems to indicate that Waddington is of Jewish origin; unless Crémieux meant that the minister of foreign affairs was theirs because they had paid him.
>
> Jew, or paid by the Jews, Waddington didn't hold back from defending his race or earning his pay. He worked hard for the Treaty of Berlin, which meant death for Romania, with typically Jewish ferocity. France, thanks to him, generous France, played the role of the policeman clutching the wrists of a poor nation so that the Jew could pour his wrath into the mouth of the dying man.[66]

The Congress of Berlin proved to be a powerful example for Drumont's argument about Jewish power through the republic, and his contacts with antisemites in other countries provided a long-lasting base of support. These contacts were further solidified in late 1886, when Drumont attended the Romano-European Antisemitic Congress, where he met with Hungarian Gyozo Istoczy, the German Adolph Stoecker, and other central European antisemitic luminaries with whom he traded ideas and information.[67]

By the end of the 1880s, Drumont's particular kind of antisemitism was developing into a significant political force whose depth and breadth would become frighteningly apparent in the Dreyfus affair, particularly in the wave of violence and political contestation that swept across both France and Algeria in 1898.[68] By 1892, when Drumont founded his newspaper, *La Libre Parole*, antisemitism had clearly arrived; the paper was the first daily devoted solely to the antisemitic political cause and had a circulation of two hundred thousand within months of its founding.[69] Drumont's popularity continued to grow, and in 1898, with the support of Max Régis, he was elected by a landslide to represent Algiers in the Chamber of Deputies.[70]

Fanned by the political and economic crises of the end of the century, the antisemitic movement Drumont inspired and led had its origins in the French Catholic establishment's reactions to the Opportunists' anticlerical measures, but as it developed, its rhetoric came to resemble that of the Algerian *anti-juifs* by depicting the republic itself as a massive conspiracy of Jewish bankers.[71] Antisemites across Europe and Algeria depicted French Jews' expressions of "solidarity" with Jews in other countries, their strategy of building alliances with republicans, and their rhetoric linking Jewish emancipation to the progress of civilization in the world as evidence that the Jews were successfully co-opting liberalism and republicanism for their own sinister ends. For these antisemites, Jewish solidarity was an especially heinous kind of corporatism, in which Jews worked together to dominate others.

The End of an Era?

The antisemitic movement fundamentally recast the meaning of Jewish international solidarity, which as we have seen, was itself a relatively recent invention conceived in part as a means to achieve and to secure Jews' full equality before the law. Jews themselves used this rhetoric to demonstrate their commitment to liberal ideals and to forge alliances by minimizing issues of religious disagreement and emphasizing the universalism of their goals. And yet, although Jews' rhetoric of solidarity had been an expression of commitment to the republic and the universalist values upon which it had been built, antisemites used Jews' very words to prove that the French government had pledged itself to defend narrowly "Jewish" interests, interests perceived as at odds with the well-being of the French nation. In this way, antisemites twisted Jews' own words in such a way that their meaning was fundamentally altered.

In one particularly illustrative example, Drumont reprinted a passage from an 1882 *Archives Israélites* article on Gambetta, in which Elie-Aristide Astruc, chief rabbi of Brussels, had written that with his anticlerical measures, Gambetta had "pledged the Fatherland against antisemitism, teaching us forevermore that the regeneration of men, inside or outside, can only take place through freedom, a common law, and brotherhood." To this, Drumont added his own observations: "freedom of education, a common law for the clerical orders, human regeneration through financial fiddling; you can see it all here. What nerve!"[72] Astruc's gratitude and optimism was typical of the Jewish leadership's view of the power of the alliance it had formed with non-Jewish republicans like Gambetta over a shared commitment to state secularism. But in Drumont's treatise, of course, these very words took on a sinister quality, proof that Gambetta, a "Jew," in Drumont's eyes, was using the state for narrowly Jewish ends. For this reason, the rise of the antisemitic voice in French politics in the 1890s marked the end of an era in Jewish self-defense in France, forcing Jewish leaders to use caution in deploying the rhetoric of solidarity and to develop other means of self-defense.

The myth of Jewish power proved long-lasting. As Pierre Birnbaum has shown, the myth that Jews controlled the republic remained the hallmark of French antisemitism well into the twentieth century. These attacks centered on individual Jews in prominent positions. Just as nineteenth-century Algerian *anti-juifs* had focused their attacks on Kanoui, and just as Drumont had pointed his finger at particular leaders he identified as "Jews" (Gambetta, Crémieux, Simon), so too did twentieth-century antisemites continue to focus their accusations about the republic's corruption on particular Jews in political life, such as Léon Blum and Pierre Mendès France. To a certain degree, these attacks follow a logic that we can easily understand. As Birnbaum points out, the French republic was indeed built on a firm foundation of secularism, separating itself from the Church and wresting control over education from it.[73] Moreover, as we have seen, as part of the heated conflict between anticlericals and the supporters of the Church, Jews had been used at times as potent symbols of what each side represented. Antisemitism would take this old battle of signs to a new level.

Although the particular accusation that Jews had, in the words of Drumont, "confiscated the French Revolution for Jewry" was a distinctly French political accusation, its impact was as global as the French Revolution's.[74] The *Protocols of the Elders of Zion*, a forgery "found" in Russia following the failed revolution of 1905 that went through four editions in 1906 and 1907 alone, represents a similar claim by purporting to be a record of a powerful group of French-speaking Jews seeking to dominate the world by making liberal governments their puppets.[75] Similarly, Hitler saw liberalism as a front for Jewish exploitation, citing the *Protocols* as incontrovertible evidence to this effect. Even today, groups seeking to denounce Western liberal governments for expanding their economic and political influence beyond their borders in the name of liberal values often depict these states as a front for "Jewish" interests. Here too, the global reach of the myth of Jewish power follows a certain logic. Just as some liberals in the West had made securing equal rights for Jews an important symbolic (if not always real) part of their "civilizing mission," so too would liberalism's detractors point to this element as a powerful sign that liberalism was not an ideology that served the best interest of the greater community.

The remarkable strength of the myth of Jewish power made it quite difficult for Jewish public figures in the 1890s to continue with the same rhetorical strategies of self-defense that Crémieux had employed, since the words of well-known Jewish leaders were so easily and regularly twisted. In this sense, the publication of *La France juive* represents the end of an era in the history of Jewish international solidarity. This, of course, does not mean that French Jews in the 1890s abandoned their struggle against prejudice, discrimination, or defamation, as previous generations of scholars assumed erroneously.[76] On the contrary, as Pierre Birnbaum has recently documented in a detailed study, even in 1898, at the height of the Dreyfus affair, when French Jews experienced the most widespread anti-Jewish defamation and violence they had ever seen, they responded actively, both as individuals and through institutions, speaking as proud French citizens and as proud Jews, just as previous generations had. Yet some of the most important Jewish leaders, including, most importantly, Zadoc Kahn, chief rabbi of France, Alphonse de Rothschild, the president of the Central Consistory, and Narcisse Leven, the president of the Alliance Israélite Universelle, used caution in how they responded to the antisemitic fervor provoked by the Dreyfus affair, and were more reserved in public than their counterparts in previous generations had been. Given that their actions would most certainly have been used as further evidence of a Jewish conspiracy, their public stance makes a great deal of sense. Such caution should not be confused with passivity, of course; these leaders worked to help Alfred Dreyfus and, after some prodding from the Jewish press, which remained vocal throughout the 1890s, also spoke out publicly against antisemitism at the height of the events of 1898.[77] Although Dreyfus was pardoned and the republic held firm against the challenges posed by antisemites, the myth of Jewish power had clearly arrived by the end of the century, and its existence would force Jewish leaders to rethink their strategies of self-defense.

Even so, rethinking strategies of self-defense never meant abandoning Jewish international solidarity altogether. Although a new generation coming of age during the Dreyfus affair would criticize previous generations of French Jews as too assimilated, sacrificing their Jewishness to appear more French, they too would embrace certain elements of the politics of solidarity in their firm belief that the progress of "civilization" was the best way to secure Jewish rights. Even Zionism, as Michael Graetz has suggested, retained a notion that bringing religious tolerance and equality to the entire world was a necessary part of the advancement of civilization. Even when adopting what was, fundamentally, a radically different political strategy, Zionists remained committed to the progress of "civilization" and sought to extend the values they associated with it to the entire world.[78] Thus, while the rise of antisemitism marked the end of an era in the history of Jewish politics, it did not bring an end to solidarity altogether. The hope that religious tolerance, freedom, and equality, increased wealth, feelings of brotherhood between nations, and national sovereignty would bring an end to the persecution of Jews and to all forms of oppression lived on into the twentieth century.

Conclusion

By distorting the relationship between Jews and the French state, and by painting Jewish expressions of concern for Jews elsewhere as evidence of a separatist, malevolent conspiracy, antisemites created a powerful myth. Awareness of this myth can make it difficult to understand nineteenth-century Jewish international solidarity for what it was: a political rhetoric that aimed to secure Jewish rights in France by embracing the French revolutionary heritage and attempting to bring its fruits to the rest of the world. Too often, even when we dismiss this myth as false, we nonetheless misapprehend the rhetoric of solidarity that it twisted, dismissing it as foolishness based in self-hatred or bad faith. In this sense we follow in the footsteps of early Zionists who saw themselves as making a fundamental break with the political strategies of the past by denigrating them as inauthentic and weak. Yet when we do this, we unwittingly underestimate the degree to which in the century following emancipation, the leaders of French Jewry truly did see their Frenchness and their Jewishness as fundamentally intertwined, and we underestimate the power of this political strategy and its impact on modern Jewish life. We also miss an opportunity to develop a more nuanced understanding of a set of important historical issues, including the modernization of Jewish life, the construction of secularism, and the ideals that shaped modern imperialism, diplomacy, and human rights discourse.

As we have seen here, the French Jews who developed the rhetoric of Jewish international solidarity sought to defend their own rights by linking them to the progress of the revolutionary tradition in the world, as they understood it. In this sense, Jewish expressions of commitment to French republican values were not signs of the abandonment of Jewish identity for a French one, nor were the Jewish expressions of commitment to Jews elsewhere signs of the persistence of ancient tribal feelings. Instead, each of these dual commitments appears to have reinforced the other. By placing the rhetoric and practices that made up Jewish international solidarity in the historical context in which it arose, it is clear that far from leading to an erasure of Jewish identity, as scholars previously believed, Jews' integration into French political culture provided new ways of affirming their commitment to Jews all over the world, and new reasons for doing so.[1] This did not represent a co-optation of the republic by Jews working for purely unpatriotic, misanthropic ends, as antisemites would claim; but it did represent an expression of an enduring, powerful identity rooted in a rhetoric developed initially for self-defense. Only when this strategy faced new, unforeseen challenges from antisemites did new political strategies, such as Zionism and Jewish socialism, develop among a younger generation.

Looking at the history of the rise of Jewish international solidarity makes it possible to achieve a more nuanced understanding of the transformations in Jewish life in nineteenth-century France. While dispersed Jews have always felt connected to each other in some way, "solidarity" is a particularly modern articulation of this feeling, and it is, in crucial ways, the product of assimilation to secular European political culture. This is clear from what we have seen in the transformation of the meaning of the term *solidarity* itself in Jewish discourse. In the century following the revolution, French Jews replaced an old form of "solidarity" with a new one. In 1789, French Jews were organized as locally defined *communautés* that were treated by French law as *in solidum*—a Roman law status that the Napoleonic Code would translate as "solidarity"—in which individual members were held legally accountable for one another's debts or transgressions. In 1889, they were citizens of France whose "solidarity" was of a more sentimental variety, linking them both to their fellow citizens and to Jews elsewhere in the world. "Solidarity" in this later form entailed a shared commitment to the progress of "civilization," identified with democratic institutions, a liberal ideology, and especially, equal rights for people of all faiths. This new solidarity did not aim to exclude non-Jews, and indeed, in certain instances, it helped French Jews to secure a place for themselves within the secular agencies of French policy making. Yet at the same time, it created new ties and a renewed sense of kinship between dispersed Jews, uniting them in a shared "mission" to bring the entire world together in a liberal world order.

In making this enormous transformation, French Jews redefined old terms from their corporate organization and applied them first to their understanding of their own citizenship in France, and then, to the new world order. Whereas Jews in eighteenth-century corporations were *solidaires* in that they had fiscal and legal responsibilities to each other mediated through their communal institutions, after they became citizens, they eventually came to use this same term in the way that Pierre Leroux and the socialists and republicans he inspired did— to describe the sentimental, brotherly bonds of mutual obligation that held citizens together. This transformation could never have taken place if, as part of their experience in revolutionary and Napoleonic France, Jews had not identified their religion with French civic virtues, and had their communal institutions dissolved and replaced with state agencies. In this context, French Jewish leaders came to see Judaism as a proper pedagogy for citizenship, and it became possible to conceive of Judaism itself as a means for teaching a new kind of "solidarity" linking citizens to one another.

French Jews extended these bonds of solidarity to Jews in the rest of the world when France itself sought to extend its institutions and its ideology beyond its territorial borders in the middle of the nineteenth century. Questions of foreign and colonial policy became important to Jewish leaders because these areas, like education, were battlegrounds for anticlericals seeking to limit the influence of sectarian Catholic concerns in politics. In a more direct way than other anticlericals, Jews were particularly worried, fearing that if France pursued Catholic aims abroad or French agents were permitted to act on their prejudices against foreign Jews, the fragile rights they themselves had so recently won could be challenged as well. Accordingly, French Jews argued that France needed to see its mission in foreign and colonial policy as a "civilizing mission," rather than a Catholic mission. In so doing, they cemented their alliances with other anticlericals who shared their view that the revolutionary dream would only be realized with the broadest possible application of the principle of equality before the law, and with religious freedom in all areas of French policy.

French Jews' expressions of "solidarity" with Jews in other countries were an outgrowth of this commitment to making all areas of French state policy secular. By the late nineteenth century, French Jews described themselves as having responsibilities toward Jews in other countries, and indeed, toward the entire world, because they were committed to the extension of the French model of secular ideology and institutions to every national context. In their work for Jews elsewhere, French Jews thus perceived themselves as working in the name of French values, which they, like other Frenchmen, saw as universal. French Jewish leaders sought to extend these values to Jews under French jurisdiction in the colonies, and to make them part of the agenda in French diplomacy as well. In so doing, they contributed to the republican agenda and helped make religious equality a central part of that agenda.

Yet French Jews' expressions of solidarity were, at the same time, an articulation of a commitment to the Jewish people. Through the consistories, the press, and the Alliance Israélite Universelle, French Jews expressed feelings of obligation and connection to all Jews everywhere. These feelings were indeed a new form of what Jews had called "solidarity" in the early part of the century, albeit with a quite different connotation. Jewish leaders had objected to juridical "solidarity" because they saw it as separatist, obligatory, and communal, as well as oppressive. While the new kind of "Jewish solidarity" that emerged after 1850 was not by any means oppressive, the Jewish leaders who developed this rhetoric described solidarity as an obligation (although it was in fact voluntary), and their work was meant to bind Jews together as a kind of international "community" (although they went to great lengths to explain why this new community was connected to the gentiles among whom Jews lived). Different as the old solidarity was from the new, the latter was clearly an heir of the former.

Yet, Jewish solidarity should not be seen as purely a new application of an old set of concepts. Rather, it emerged from the long and complicated process of emancipation and integration in nineteenth-century France. This notion adds to our understanding of the development of Jewish internationalism in important ways. Historians Michel Abitbol, Jay Berkovitz, Michael Graetz, and Aron Rodrigue have convincingly argued that Western Jewish international advocacy and educational programs were profoundly marked by the emancipationist ideology of "regeneration" developed by French Jews in the revolution and its aftermath.[2] This study has shown that in addition, the very feeling of connectedness that French Jews felt to Jews elsewhere, as well as the reasons they provided for reaching out to them, were themselves reshaped by the experience of integration. Conceived as expressions of reparative justice, social obligation, universalist religiosity, charity, and brotherhood, these feelings and their articulations were profoundly shaped by the discourses of French liberalism, socialism, and republicanism.

As such, our examination of the rise of Jewish international solidarity also sheds light on the construction of a secular republic over the course of the century following the French Revolution. The ideology of the modern French state was universalist not only in that it based its legitimacy on an affirmation of human freedom, equality, and brotherhood, but also in that its goal was to extend its values to all humanity. While some scholars have read in this universalism an erasure of minority identities, this was certainly not the case for the Jews, as the story of the rise of modern Jewish solidarity makes clear. While the doctrine of the Sanhedrin and the institutional form of the consistory changed Judaism in important ways, they did not erase Jewish identity. The Napoleonic vision of French society was to rationalize and incorporate all former corporate bodies within a single state apparatus, subordinating them to secular state authority. Making Jews part of that apparatus did not exclude Judaism, nor did it make Jewish identity a solely "private" matter. French universalism, as French Jews understood it, allowed Jews to reaffirm their commitment to their religion as well as their connections to Jews throughout the Diaspora.

Furthermore, this study also adds to our understanding of the history of the relationship between religions and the French state during the succession of nineteenth-century regimes that scholars often group together as a "regime of concordats." From the First Empire to the

Third Republic, Catholicism and a revolutionary model of secularism competed bitterly for supremacy, and numerous solutions were attempted until a lasting compromise between Catholicism and the state was reached under the Third Republic. This study has considered the history of this long and multifaceted battle from the perspective of Jews who saw their rights best guaranteed by the liberal ideals of religious freedom and equality, and a liberal state that claimed universality because it governed people of different faiths as equals. From this vantage point, the path to secularism looks a bit different than it does when considered from a purely Catholic or purely anticlerical perspective. From the revolutionary Civil Constitution of the Clergy to the anticlerical measures of early Third Republic, it is clear that when anticlerical measures were devised, the most important objective was to transform the social and political role of the Catholic Church in French life. Even so, in attempting to limit the Church's political and social role, anticlericals often appropriated language that resembled clerical language to consecrate their own secular endeavor. In this sense, state secularization represented a redeployment of Christian concepts even though its proponents aimed to bar the Church from its traditional role in French life.

In the process of implementing their measures, anticlerical policy makers faced strong resistance from the Church. Because of the heated and protracted nature of the struggles that ensued, a space was created as well for a fundamental transformation of French Jewish life. In different ways over the course of the century, French Jews were able to use the measures created by anticlericals to simultaneously guarantee Judaism's continued existence in France and to cement their position as allies in the battle for secularism. In this way, the revolutionaries, liberals, socialists, and republicans who contributed to the shaping of French secularism also provided a framework within which new kinds of Jewish institutions, new understandings of Judaism, and new forms of Jewish identity would be built and would flourish.

Looking at the movement to limit the role of the Church in public life from a Jewish perspective also nuances our view of the anticlerical movement's perspective on religion. From the time of the revolution to the Third Republic, those who sought to limit the place of the Church in public affairs were interested in developing a kind of religiosity with which to consecrate the new state, giving it a firm foundation and using religion to educate its citizens. As part of this effort, anticlericals increasingly supported Jewish leaders' identification of Judaism with the French revolutionary tradition and with the French "civilizing mission" in foreign and colonial policy. Although in the 1830s and 1840s, a wide range of liberal Catholics and Christian socialists used the Christian tradition to imagine a new relationship between Church and state that would support a democratic system, by the 1850s and 1860s, most anticlericals had come to see Christianity (especially Catholicism) and the revolutionary tradition as diametrically opposed. Yet liberals and republicans appreciated Jewish expressions of religiosity in the political arena. Building on the images of Jews that were used as symbols in the art and literature of the Romantic period, liberals used Jews and Judaism as symbols for their political agenda. For those who used this symbolism, Judaism represented an authentic religiosity in a way that highlighted their tolerance and gave an air of holiness to their political agenda. Acceptance of Jewish expressions of religiosity served to grant a degree of credibility to their efforts to replace Catholicism with an obviously different kind of religiosity. This did not, of course, mean the state was becoming "Jewish" (as Algerian and French antisemites would later claim), but rather, that some anticlericals used Jews as a symbol for the moral superiority and greater universality of liberalism or republicanism, as compared to its arch foe, *ultramontane* Catholicism.

Because it operated in the sphere where national interests and international negotiations and ambitions overlapped, the history of the rise of Jewish international solidarity also sheds light on why the international arena was so important to republicans. Like the revolutionaries, Saint-Simonians, and liberals upon whose ideas their movement was built, republicans saw the French Revolution's scope as global; extending it to people elsewhere through what appeared to them as purely philanthropic "solidarity" was an unquestioned sign of its greatness. Looking at this story from the perspective of French Jews, the centrality of religious issues in shaping French imperialism, diplomacy, and the nascent language of international human rights is strikingly apparent. Establishing secularism meant creating a new "mission" for France in the world, on a par with the Catholicism it replaced. Participating in these struggles in an effort to secure their own position, French Jews too supported the extension of French revolutionary ideology through imperialism and the establishment of informal influence in areas beyond France's borders, as "liberating" or "regenerating" the people who were affected.

For the French Jewish leaders who created modern international solidarity, this universalist mission was also the fulfillment of the Jewish theological doctrine of divine election. They utilized messianic language to motivate Jews all over the world to participate in the construction of a new global "civilization," thereby becoming conduits through which new ideas and institutional forms would be spread. As Zadoc Kahn, the eminent French rabbi who would later serve as chief rabbi of France, said at the twenty-fifth anniversary meeting of the Alliance Israélite Universelle:

> We hope that our Alliance Israélite Universelle will obtain the sympathies of all men of heart, whatever their faiths or their nationalities may be, or rather, we hope that one day the Alliance Israélite Universelle will be able to disappear to make room for the Universal Alliance. Once all countries are conquered definitively by the idea of justice and respect for the sacred rights of humanity, as soon as the Earth is no longer home to hatred or divisions or violence, and once the peoples become, following the words of the Prophets, like a single family, enlightened by the light of truth, directed by the same spirit of tolerance and charity, and that, far from ripping itself apart with its own hands . . . applies itself to fighting human evil with equitable and reparative laws, with instruction . . . and with work . . . , oh! Then we will no longer need the Alliance, all men will be united by an alliance of concord and fraternity. Amen![3]

This new understanding that Jews had a mission to unite the world with their own solidarity fundamentally reshaped Jewish identity, linking it more closely to the ideology and even the apparatus of the secular state. Jewish identity itself became tied to the process of global integration, and the divinely ordained mission of the Jews was redefined to facilitate the construction of the liberal world system. Even after the late-nineteenth-century antisemitic movements portrayed expressions of Jewish international solidarity as proof that Jews were not truly integrated into the nations where they lived, French Jews continued to assert that their work on behalf of Jews elsewhere was a truly patriotic endeavor. In their minds, their work did not set them apart from their fellow citizens; it bound them to the rest of the nation in a common purpose. As Pierre Birnbaum has explored more fully, Jews in the Third Republic were firmly committed to republican government and participated in state administration on a level never before seen. This commitment stemmed not only from the new opportunities afforded to them, but also from their identification with French state ideology.[4]

The fact that Jewish international solidarity had its origins in contemporary liberal and republican discourse does not mean that the logic upon which it rested was internally consistent. Nor, for that matter, did it mean that its proponents were able to succeed in their goal of assuring Jewish security in the "civilized" West, or in areas under its influence, in a lasting way. Indeed, as we have seen, the logic upon which Jewish international solidarity was built was full of contradictions, and the Jewish leaders who worked in its name—particularly those associated with the Alliance Israélite Universelle—became prime targets for antisemites in ways that no one could have predicted. While Alliance leaders explained tirelessly that Jewish unity and progress were meant to better the world as a whole, they were never in fact able to stem the tide of the antisemitic movement, nor were they able to reconcile the contradictory notions of integrationism and separatism inherent in their rhetoric. Such contradictions are inherent in all kinds of universalist ideologies, albeit in very different ways. *Solidarity* was a term that could and did apply to different, overlapping, and sometimes even conflicting groups, especially ones that saw themselves as oppressed: nations, races, religions, the working class, women, and myriad other configurations of people. What all these forms of "solidarity" share is the activist, stirring tone in which it is invoked, and the sense that ultimately, the sacred bonds of solidarity will bring about universal redemption.

Notes

Abbreviations Used in the Notes

AAIU   Archives of the Alliance Israélite Universelle
AIF   *Les Archives Israélites de France*
AN   Archives Nationales
ARS   Archives de la Bibliothèque de l'Arsenal
BAIU   *Bulletin de l'Alliance Israélite Universelle*
BUAC   Brandeis University Archives, Consistoire Collection
CAHJP   Central Archives for the History of the Jewish People
UI   *L'Univers Israélite*

Introduction

1. "Discours prononcé par M. le Rabbin Emile Lévy of Verdun," in *La Révolution française et le rabbinat français*, ed. Benjamin Mossé (Avignon: La Caravane, 1890), 137. All translations are mine unless otherwise stated.

2. Arthur Hertzberg, *The French Enlightenment and the Jews: The Origins of Modern Anti-Semitism* (New York: Schocken, 1967); Hannah Arendt, *The Origins of Totalitarianism* (New York: Harcourt Brace Jovanovich, 1951).

3. Phyllis Cohen Albert, "Ethnicity and Jewish Solidarity in Nineteenth-Century France," in *Mystics, Philosophers, and Politicians: Essays in Jewish Intellectual History in Honor of Alexander Altmann*, ed. Jehuda Reinharz and Daniel Swetschinski (Durham, N.C.: Duke University Press, 1982), 249–74; Jay Berkovitz, *The Shaping of Jewish Identity in Nineteenth-Century France* (Detroit: Wayne State University Press, 1989), and *Rites and Passages: The Beginnings of Modern Jewish Culture in France, 1650–1860* (Philadelphia: University of Pennsylvania Press, 2004); Michael Graetz, *The Jews in Nineteenth-Century France: From the French Revolution to the Alliance Israélite Universelle*, trans. Jane Marie Todd (Stanford, CA: Stanford University Press, 1996); Paula E. Hyman, *The Emancipation of the Jews of Alsace: Acculturation and Tradition in the Nineteenth Century* (New Haven, CT: Yale University

Press, 1991); and Ronald S. Schechter, *Obstinate Hebrews: Representations of Jews in France, 1715–1815* (Berkeley and Los Angeles: University of California Press, 2003).

4. My reference here is to Eugen Weber's classic history *Peasants into Frenchmen: The Modernization of Rural France, 1870–1914* (Stanford, CA: Stanford University Press, 1976).

5. William H. Sewell, Jr., *Work and Revolution in France: The Language of Labor from the Old Regime to 1848* (New York: Cambridge University Press, 1980); Caroline Ford, *Creating the Nation in Provincial France: Religion and Political Identity in Brittany* (Princeton, NJ: Princeton University Press, 1993), 5. Other examples of this type of work include Schechter, *Obstinate Hebrews*; Weber, *Peasants into Frenchmen*; James R. Lehning, *Peasant and French: Cultural Contact in Rural France During the Nineteenth Century* (New York: Cambridge University Press, 1995). For an excellent collection which brings together studies of a large number of groups as well as theoretical perspectives, see Dominique Colas, Claude Emeri, and Jacques Zylberberg, eds., *Citoyenneté et nationalité: Perspectives en France et au Québec* (Paris: Presses Universitaires de France, 1991).

6. Berkovitz, *Shaping of Jewish Identity*, and Graetz, *Jews in Nineteenth-Century France*.

7. On France, see Berkovitz, *Shaping of Jewish Identity*, and *Rites and Passages*; Pierre Birnbaum, *The Jews of the Republic: A Political History of State Jews in France from Gambetta to Vichy*, trans. Jane Marie Todd (Stanford, CA: Stanford University Press, 1996); David Cohen, "La Promotion des juifs à l'époque du Second Empire, 1852–1870," 2 vols. (doctoral diss., Université de Provence, 1980); Graetz, *The Jews in Nineteenth-Century France*; Hyman, *The Emancipation of the Jews*; Frances Malino, *The Sephardic Jews of Bordeaux: Assimilation and Emancipation in Revolutionary and Napoleonic France* (Tuscaloosa: University of Alabama Press, 1978); Christine Piette, *Les Juifs de Paris, 1808–1840: La Marche vers l'assimilation* (Quebec: Université de Laval, 1983); Simon Schwarzfuchs, *Du Juif à l'israélite: Histoire d'une mutation, 1779–1870* (Paris: Fayard, 1989); Perrine Simon-Nahum, *La Cité investie: La "Science du judaïsme" français et la République* (Paris: Cerf, 1991). Some excellent examples from other national contexts include David Sorkin, *The Transformation of German Jewry, 1780–1840* (Oxford: Oxford University Press, 1987); Marion Kaplan, *The Making of the Jewish Middle Class: Women, Family and Identity in Imperial Germany* (Oxford: Oxford University Press, 1991); Hillel Kieval, *The Making of Czech Jewry: National Conflict and Jewish Society in Bohemia, 1870–1918* (New York: Oxford University Press, 1988); and David Cesarani, ed., *The Making of Modern Anglo-Jewry* (Oxford: Blackwell, 1990). There are also several excellent edited volumes that bring together work on different national experiences in ways that make it easy to compare them. See especially Pierre Birnbaum and Ira Katznelson, eds., *Paths of Emancipation: Jews, States, Citizenship* (Princeton, NJ: Princeton University Press, 1995); Frances Malino and David Sorkin, eds., *From East and West: Jews in a Changing Europe, 1750–1870* (London: Black-

well, 1990); and Jonathan Frankel and Steven J. Zipperstein, eds., *Assimilation and Community: The Jews in Nineteenth-Century Europe* (Cambridge: Cambridge University Press, 1992).

8. Aron Rodrigue, *French Jews, Turkish Jews: The Alliance Israélite Universelle and the Politics of Jewish Schooling in Turkey, 1860–1925* (Bloomington: Indiana University Press, 1990), 18–19.

9. Recent scholarship that examines the "religiosity" of secularism as it evolved in France includes Dale K. Van Kley, *The Religious Origins of the French Revolution: From Calvin to the Civil Constitution of the Clergy, 1560–1791* (New Haven, CT: Yale University Press, 1996); Pierre Manent, "Quelques remarques sur la notion de 'sécularisation,'" in *The French Revolution and the Creation of Modern Political Culture*, ed. François Furet and Mona Ozouf, vol. 3, *The Transformation of Political Culture, 1789–1848* (Oxford: Pergamon, 1989), 351–57; and Mona Ozouf, *Festivals and the French Revolution*, trans. Alan Sheridan (Cambridge, MA: Harvard University Press, 1988). On the nineteenth century, see Edward Berenson, "A New Religion of the Left: Christianity and Social Radicalism in France, 1815–1848," in *French Revolution and the Creation of Modern Political Culture*, ed. Furet and Ozouf, 3: 543–60; Jacques-Olivier Boudon, *Napoléon et les cultes: Les Religions en Europe à l'aube du XIXe siècle* (Paris: Fayard, 2002); and Pierre Rosanvallon, *Le Sacre du citoyen: Histoire du suffrage universel en France* (Paris: Gallimard, 1992). Classic nineteenth-century approaches to this issue include Edgar Quinet, *Le Christianisme et la Révolution française* (Paris: Imprimeurs-Unis, 1845), and Philippe-Joseph-Benjamin Buchez and Pierre Célestin Roux-Lavergne, *Histoire parlementaire de la Révolution française*, 40 vols. (Paris: Paulin, 1834–38).

10. Schechter, *Obstinate Hebrews*.

11. Alice Conklin, *A Mission to Civilize: The Republican Idea of Empire in France and West Africa, 1895–1930* (Stanford, CA: Stanford University Press, 1997).

12. For two notable examples in the scholarly literature, see Michael Marrus, *The Politics of Assimilation: The French Jewish Community at the Time of the Dreyfus Affair* (Oxford: Clarendon, 1971), 196–242, and Arendt, *Origins of Totalitarianism*, 117–19.

13. Pierre Birnbaum, *The Anti-Semitic Moment: A Tour of France in 1898*, trans. Jane Marie Todd (New York: Hill and Wang, 2003), 309–31.

Chapter 1. The Jewish Citizen

1. Phyllis Cohen Albert, *The Modernization of French Jewry: Consistory and Community in the Nineteenth Century* (Hanover, NH: Brandeis University Press, 1977); Jay Berkovitz, *The Shaping of Jewish Identity in Nineteenth-Century France* (Detroit: Wayne State University Press, 1989), 84; Michael Graetz, *The Jews in Nineteenth-Century France: From the French Revolution to the Alliance Israélite Universelle*, trans. Jane Marie Todd (Stanford, CA: Stanford University Press, 1996), 17–40.

2. For the story of emancipation in all its rich detail, see Robert Badinter, *Libres et égaux: L'Emancipation des juifs, 1789–1791* (Paris: Fayard, 1989); David Feuerwerker, *L'Emancipation des juifs en France, de l'ancien régime à la fin du Second Empire* (Paris: Albin Michel, 1976); Paula E. Hyman, *The Jews of Modern France* (Berkeley and Los Angeles: University of California Press, 1998); Frances Malino, *A Jew in the French Revolution: The Life of Zalkind Hourwitz* (Oxford: Blackwell, 1996); Ronald Schechter, *Obstinate Hebrews: Representations of Jews in France, 1715–1815* (Berkeley and Los Angeles: University of California Press, 2003); Simon Schwarzfuchs, *Du Juif à l'israélite: Histoire d'une mutation, 1779–1870* (Paris: Fayard, 1989); Zosa Szajkowski, *Jews and the French Revolutions of 1789, 1830, and 1848* (New York: Ktav, 1970).

3. Berkovitz, *Shaping of Jewish Identity*, 14; Aron Rodrigue, *French Jews, Turkish Jews: The Alliance Israélite Universelle and the Politics of Jewish Schooling in Turkey, 1860–1925* (Bloomington: Indiana University Press, 1990), 4–8. On "regeneration," see also Alyssa Goldstein Sepinwall, *The Abbé Grégoire and the French Revolution: The Making of Modern Universalism* (Berkeley and Los Angeles: University of California Press, 2005).

4. Gary Kates, "Jews into Frenchmen: Nationality and Representation in Revolutionary France," in *The French Revolution and the Birth of Modernity*, ed. Ferenc Fehér (Berkeley and Los Angeles: University of California Press, 1990), 109; Schechter, *Obstinate Hebrews*, 155–63.

5. Schechter, *Obstinate Hebrews*, 155–63.

6. Hyman, *The Jews of Modern France*, 30–34; Szajkowski, *Jews and the French Revolutions*.

7. All population numbers for Jews before the Revolution are estimates. This one is from Patrick Girard, *Les Juifs de France de 1789 à 1860: De l'émancipation à l'égalité* (Paris: Calmann-Lévy, 1976), 22.

8. All three essays were later published: Grégoire, *Essai sur la régénération physique, morale et politique des Juifs* (Metz: Claude Lamort, 1789); Hourwitz, *Apologie des Juifs en réponse à la question; Est-il des moyens de rendre les Juifs plus heureux et plus utiles en France?* (Paris: Gattey, 1789); and Thiéry, *Dissertation sur cette question: Est-il des moyens de rendre les Juifs plus heureux et plus utiles en France?* (Paris: Knapen, 1788). For the history of the essay contest itself, see Feuerwerker, *L'Emancipation des juifs en France*, 49–142; and Malino, *Jew in the French Revolution*, 15–59.

9. Thiéry, *Est-il des moyens de rendre les Juifs?* 84–94.

10. Grégoire, *Essai sur la régénération*, chap. 19.

11. Hourwitz, *Apologie des Juifs*, 36–39.

12. Ibid., 77. This translation by Frances Malino appears in *Jew in the French Revolution*, 49.

13. *Archives parlementaires*, 1st ser., 10: 756. This translation by J. Rubin from Paul R. Mendes-Flohr and Jehuda Reinharz, eds., *The Jew in the Modern World: A*

Documentary History (New York: Oxford University Press, 1980), 104. The text of these debates is also reprinted in abridged form in Richard Ayoun, ed., *Les Juifs de France: De l'émancipation à l'intégration, 1787–1812* (Paris: L'Harmattan, 1997).

14. *Archives parlementaires*, 10: 754–56.

15. Ibid., 10: 758. The decision to table the issue was made on December 24; see ibid., 10: 782. For a nuanced reading of the debates of that week, see Malino, *Jew in the French Revolution*, 80–81.

16. Jean Cavignac, *Les Israélites bordelais de 1780 à 1850: autour de l'émancipation* (Paris: Publisud, 1991), 15.

17. Malino, *Jew in the French Revolution*, 222, n. 39. The population was concentrated in the suburb of Saint-Esprit.

18. Arthur Hertzberg, *The French Enlightenment and the Jews: The Origins of Modern Anti-Semitism* (New York: Schocken, 1967), 63.

19. David Silveyra, agent et député, Furtado jeune, Louis Nounez, and Silveire, *Adresse présentée à l'Assemblée nationale par le Député des Juifs Espagnols et Portugais, établis au Bourg Saint-Esprit-lès-Bayonne* (Paris: Houry et Debure, 1790).

20. *Archives parlementaires*, 10: 365. On the emancipation of the southwestern Jews, see Frances Malino, *The Sephardic Jews of Bordeaux: Assimilation and Emancipation in Revolutionary and Napoleonic France* (Tuscaloosa: University of Alabama Press, 1978), 40–64.

21. Godard's number estimating the Jewish population of revolutionary Paris at 500 is low; historians today estimate it at no lower than 750. "Discours prononcé, le 28 janvier 1790, par M. Godard, avocat au Parlement, l'un des représentants de la commune, en présentant à l'Assemblée générale de la commune une députation de Juifs de Paris," in Ayoun, *Les Juifs de France*, 114–16. Hourwitz, interpreter of languages at the Bibliothèque du Roi, probably aided Godard in constructing the demand; see Malino, *Jew in the French Revolution*, 92–96.

22. "Discours prononcé, le 28 janvier 1790, par M. Godard," 117–18.

23. Feuerwerker, *L'Emancipation des juifs en France*, 360.

24. "Nouveau mémoire pour les Juifs de Lunéville et de Sareguemines [*sic*]; présenté à l'Assemblée Nationale, le 26 février 1790," in Ayoun, *Les Juifs de France*, 119–21. For more on these communities, see Françoise Job, *Les Juifs de Lunéville au XVIIIe et XIXe siècles* (Nancy: Presses Universitaires de Nancy, 1989).

25. Schechter, *Obstinate Hebrews*, 173.

26. See Keith Baker, "Sovereignty," in *A Critical Dictionary of the French Revolution*, ed. François Furet and Mona Ozouf (Cambridge, MA: Belknap, 1989), 844–59; and J. K. Wright, "National Sovereignty and the General Will: The Political Program of the Declaration of Rights," in *The French Idea of Freedom: The Old Regime and the Declaration of Rights of 1789*, ed. Dale K. Van Kley (Stanford, CA: Stanford University Press, 1994), 199–233.

27. *Archives parlementaires*, 10: 755.

28. See, for example, Hannah Arendt, *The Origins of Totalitarianism* (New York: Harcourt Brace Jovanovich, 1951); Hertzberg, *The French Enlightenment and the Jews*, 360–61, 367; Shmuel Trigano, "From Individual to Collectivity: The Rebirth of the 'Jewish Nation' in France," in *The Jews of Modern France*, ed. Frances Malino and Bernard Wasserstein (Hanover, NH: Brandeis University Press, 1985), 247–49; Trigano, *La République et les juifs après Copernic* (Paris: Les Presses d'aujourd'hui, 1982).

29. On how revolutionaries sought to remake the relationship between religions and the state in this era, see Nigel Aston, *Religion and Revolution in France, 1780–1804* (Washington, DC: Catholic University of America Press, 2000); John McManners, *The French Revolution and the Church* (New York: Harper and Row, 1970); Timothy Tackett, *Religion, Revolution, and Regional Culture in Eighteenth-Century France: The Ecclesiastical Oath of 1791* (Princeton, NJ: Princeton University Press, 1986); and Dale K. Van Kley, *The Religious Origins of the French Revolution: From Calvin to the Civil Constitution of the Clergy, 1560–1791* (New Haven, CT: Yale University Press, 1996).

30. Aston, *Religion and Revolution*, 146–47, 162.

31. As reprinted in Ayoun, *Les Juifs de France*, 127. For an insightful analysis of this September debate, see Malino, *Jew in the French Revolution*, 112–13.

32. Ayoun, *Les Juifs de France*, 127–29.

33. Berr Isaac Berr, *Lettre d'un Citoyen, membre de la ci-devant communauté des Juifs de Lorraine, à ses confrères, à l'occasion du droit de citoyen actif, rendu aux Juifs par le décret du 28 [sic] septembre 1791* (Nancy: Haener, 1791), 12–17.

34. On the debts of the former Jewish *communautés*, see Chapter 2. For a sense of some of the chaos in Jewish life during the Revolutionary era, see Szajkowski, "Synagogues During the French Revolution of 1789–1800," in *Jews and the French Revolutions*, 809–25, and Simon Schwarzfuchs, *Napoleon, the Jews and the Sanhedrin* (London: Routledge, Kegan and Paul, 1979), 11–21.

35. On Napoleon's religious policy, see Jacques-Olivier Boudon, *Napoléon et les cultes: Les Religions en Europe à l'aube du XIXe siècle* (Paris: Fayard, 2002).

36. Berr Isaac Berr made such a request, as did community leaders in Metz. See Robert Anchel, *Napoléon et les juifs* (Paris: Presses Universitaires de France, 1928), 66–67, and Schwarzfuchs, *Napoleon, the Jews and the Sanhedrin*, 37–41. A very detailed but anonymous plan for Jewish organization on the Protestant consistory model was submitted to the Ministry of Worship in early 1806; see AN F19 10014.

37. On these attacks and the extent of Jewish usury in Alsace in the early empire, see Schwarzfuchs, *Napoleon, the Jews and the Sanhedrin*, 28–54. Statistics on Jewish money lending in Eastern France were compiled by the government in 1806; see AN F19 11004. The publications complaining about Jewish usury greatly exaggerated its extent, and Alsatian courts ruled in favor of the Jews in court proceedings. The lawyer Poujol suggested to the minister of cults, Jean Portalis, that

Jews be stripped of their citizenship rights, at least until they stopped lending money and integrated more fully through intermarriage. His ideas were published though eventually censored.

38. Molé advised against a Saturday meeting, but Champagny, the minister of the interior, went ahead with the original plan, in Schwarzfuchs's estimation, "to show that the French state did business on the Sabbath, and that all citizens were to take cognizance of the fact." See *Napoleon, the Jews and the Sanhedrin*, 54.

39. Hyman, *The Jews of Modern France*, 41.

40. Diogène Tama, *Transactions of the Paris Sanhedrin or Acts of the Assembly of Israelitish Deputies of France and Italy Convoked at Paris by Imperial and Royal Decree Dated May 30, 1806*, trans. F. D. Kirwan, ed. Ellis Rivkin (Cincinnati: Hebrew Union College–Jewish Institute of Religion, 1956). The original handwritten minutes can be found in AN F19 11005.

41. Tama, *Transactions of the Paris Sanhedrin*, 10–12, 30–31.

42. Ibid., 22–24.

43. Ibid., 24.

44. Ibid.

45. Ibid., 23. Cf. Jesus' Golden Rule, which is traditionally formulated as "Do unto others as you would have them do unto you"—see Matt. 7:12 or Luke 6:31.

46. Tama, *Transactions of the Paris Sanhedrin*, 22–23. The original wording of "settled and independent nation" is "corps de nation," which could be interpreted to refer to the recent past as well as an ancient one. Original wording from AN F19 11005.

47. In their answer to the fifth question, they made this allusion to the deliverance from Egypt more explicit by stating that they considered their "incorporation into the Great Nation" as "political redemption." See Tama, *Transactions of the Paris Sanhedrin*, 23.

48. In this, they built on arguments from the revolutionary era as well, including one made by Clermont-Tonnerre in the debates of December 1789. See ibid., 32–33, 35.

49. Ibid., 33.

50. Ibid., 34–36.

51. Abraham Furtado, *Mémoire sur les projets de décrets présentés au conseil d'état concernant les israélites* (Paris: Plassan, n.d.), esp. 10–15.

52. Napoleon's attitude was documented by Commissioner Pasquier in his memoirs. See Schwarzfuchs, *Napoleon, the Jews and the Sanhedrin*, 80–81.

53. Napoleon wrote this in a letter to Champagny, as cited in ibid., 82.

54. The organization of the consistories was laid out in the proceedings of the Sanhedrin; it was made official by the decree of March 17, 1808. For the Sanhedrin proceedings, see Diogène Tama, *Collection des actes de l'assemblée des notables israélites de France et du royaume d'Italie, convoquée à Paris par décret de Sa Majesté impériale et royale, du 30 mai 1806* (Paris: Chez l'editeur, 1807). This section is not

reprinted in Rivkin's 1956 edition of Kirwan's translation. For the text of the 1808 decree on the organization of the consistories, see Albert, *The Modernization of French Jewry*, 348–49.

55. From the draft of this letter read at the meeting of September 24, 1806, in Tama, *Transactions of the Paris Sanhedrin*, 66.

56. Abraham de Cologna, "Discours prononcé à la grande synagogue de Paris, à l'occasion de l'ouverture du Grand Sanhedrin," in AN F19 11005.

57. "Déclarations des rabbins," 1809, in Archives du Consistoire Central, Paris 1A2. Also reprinted in Ayoun, *Les Juifs de France*, 188–97.

58. The phrase is Robespierre's, *Archives parlementaires*, 10: 757.

59. "Extrait d'un note de l'Empereur au sujet de la réunion de l'Assemblé des notables et du Sanhedrin," n.d., in CAHJP FCC 2.

Chapter 2. Alliances with Restoration Liberals

1. For an institutional history of the consistory, see Phyllis Cohen Albert, *The Modernization of French Jewry: Consistory and Community in the Nineteenth Century* (Hanover, NH: Brandeis University Press, 1977).

2. Christine Piette, *Les Juifs de Paris, 1808–1840: La Marche vers l'assimilation* (Quebec: Université de Laval, 1983).

3. Jack Bakunin, *Pierre Leroux and the Birth of Democratic Socialism, 1797–1848* (New York: Revisionist Press, 1976); Edward Berenson, "A New Religion of the Left: Christianity and Social Radicalism in France, 1815–1848," in *The French Revolution and the Creation of Modern Political Culture*, ed. François Furet and Mona Ozouf, vol. 3, *The Transformation of Political Culture, 1789–1848* (Oxford: Pergamon, 1989), 543–60; Sébastien Charléty, *Histoire du saint-simonisme (1825–1864)*, 2nd ed. (Paris: Paul Hartmann, 1931); Alan B. Spitzer, *The French Generation of 1820* (Princeton, NJ: Princeton University Press, 1987); Laurent Theis, "Guizot et le problème religieux," in *François Guizot et la culture politique de son temps*, ed. Marina Valensise (Paris: Gallimard, 1991), 251–63; Georges Weill, *L'Ecole saint-simonienne: Son Histoire, son influence jusqu'à nos jours* (Paris: Félix Alcan, 1896).

4. Adolphe Crémieux, *Plaidoyer sur cette question: Le Juif français doit-il être soumis à prêter le serment more judaïco?* (Nîmes: Gaude, 1827), 7.

5. Zosa Szajkowski, "Autonomy and Communal Jewish Debts," in *Jews and the French Revolutions of 1789, 1830, and 1848* (New York: Ktav, 1970), 643–44.

6. *Code civil des français* (Paris: Imprimerie de la République, 1804), "Obligations" section, articles 1197 to 1216.

7. Leroux wrote: "J'ai le premier introduit le terme de solidarité, pour l'introduire dans la philosophie, c'est à dire, suivant moi dans la religion de l'avenir. J'ai voulu remplacer la charité du christianisme par la solidarité humaine [I was the first to introduce the term solidarity into philosophy, that is, into the religion of the future. I wanted to replace Christian charity with human solidarity]." Cited in

Charles Gide, *La Solidarité: Cours au Collège de France 1927–28* (Paris: Presses Universitaires de France, 1932), 32.

8. Henri Mazeaud, Léon Mazeaud, Jean Mazeaud, and François Chabas, *Leçons de droit civil*, vol. 2, *Obligations: Théorie générale* (Paris: Montchrestien, 1985), 1092–97.

9. *Code civil des français*, articles 395–96, 1033, 1197–1216, 1442, 1887, and 2002.

10. Gide, *La Solidarité*, and J. E. S. Hayward, "Solidarity: The Social History of a Concept in Nineteenth-Century France," *International Review of Social History* 4, no. 2 (1959): 261–84.

11. Szajkowski, "Autonomy and Communal Jewish Debts," 628–30.

12. Ibid., 631–34.

13. Ibid., 700–724.

14. Decree of September 5, 1810, in AN F19 11000.

15. Szajkowski, "Autonomy and Communal Jewish Debts," 694.

16. This was especially true in the former Papal States, where a high rate of emigration left only poor Jews behind to pay the debts. For example, Jassé-Haïm Crémieu, son of the former *syndic* David Crémieu, was held individually responsible for the Carpentras debt in a court ruling in Year VII. See ibid., 646.

17. Aaron Ravel, Aaron Vidal, and [Jean-Baptiste] Milhaud, *Observations pour des juifs d'Avignon à la Convention nationale*, 3 vendémiaire an III (1794), in *La Révolution française et l'émancipation des juifs* (Paris: D'Histoire sociale, 1968), vol. 5, no. 17, 16.

18. Szajkowski, "Autonomy and Communal Jewish Debts," 635–40.

19. Report on the Italian communal debts, 1807, in AN F19 1847. Though the debts were ruled to have been incurred illegally, the communities were still held responsible for paying them.

20. Statements of the General Council of Metz of January 11, 1792, as cited in Szajkowski, "Autonomy and Communal Jewish Debts," 639.

21. Jean-Baptiste-Michel Saladin, *Rapport fait par Saladin, au nom d'une commission spéciale, composée des représentans Grégoire, Chappuy, Louvot et Saladin, sur les pétitions des Juifs de Metz et d'Avignon* (Paris: Imprimerie nationale, 7 fructidor an V [1797]).

22. François-Marie-Joseph Riou de Kersalaun, *Rapport fait par Riou sur les pétitions des Juifs de Metz et d'Avignon, au nom d'une commission spéciale* (Paris: Imprimerie Nationale, 4 frimaire an VI [1797]).

23. See the March 30, 1801, ruling by the Moselle prefecture as excerpted in Szajkowski, "Autonomy and Communal Jewish Debts," 644–45, n. 119.

24. This position found its best elaboration in the discussion by council member Darracq of the nationalization of Jewish communal property in Bordeaux. See *Opinion de Darracq dans l'affaire des Juifs de Bordeaux* (Paris: Imprimerie nationale, an VII [1799]).

25. Szajkowski, "Autonomy and Communal Jewish Debts," 654, 671–72, 684–91.

26. *Observations de MM. Les Syndics des Créanciers des anciennes carrières ou communautés juives, d'Avignon, de Carpentras, et de l'Isle, au département de Vaucluse, avec les pièces justificatives à l'appui de leur pétition à la Chambre de MM. les Députés, pour obtenir la révocation du rejet de l'amendement prononcé dans la séance du 6 juillet 1820,* AN F19 11013, 10–11. (Also in AN F19 11030.)

27. *Rapport de M. le Marquis Forbin des Issarts, député de Vaucluse, au nom de la Commission des Pétitions, présenté à la Chambre des Députés, dans la séance du 5 avril 1821,* AN F19 11013. (Also in AN F19 11030.)

28. Constant to Crémieux, July 8, 1821, in AN 369/AP/1, no. 182.

29. Szajkowski, "Autonomy and Communal Jewish Debts," 600.

30. *Copie du jugement du Tribunal de la Seine: Dreyfuss v. Posac, receveur-precepteur du 24e arrondissement de perception de la ville de Paris, 1845.* In BUAC III-1-d.

31. These decrees are reprinted in full in Richard Ayoun, ed., *Les Juifs de France: De l'émancipation à l'intégration, 1787–1812* (Paris: L'Harmattan, 1997), 203–11.

32. Paula E. Hyman, *The Emancipation of the Jews of Alsace: Emancipation and Tradition in the Nineteenth Century* (New Haven, CT: Yale University Press, 1991), 17–18. The decision of Alsatian courts to reintroduce the *more judaico* as a strategy meant to intimidate Jewish witnesses in Infamous Decree cases seems to support Hyman's contention that the decree was not enforced by other authorities (see the discussion of the matter of the oath below). The Central Consistory's views about the effects of the Infamous Decree are evident in their discussions from 1820, when its renewal was proposed in the Chamber of Deputies; see the entry dated March 4, 1820, in "Procès-verbaux des déliberations du Consistoire central," Archives du Consistoire Central, IB2. On poverty in eastern France, see Zosa Szajkowski, "Poverty and Social Welfare Among French Jews (1800–1880)," in *Jews and the French Revolutions,* 1133–61.

33. Abraham Furtado, *Mémoire sur les projets de décrets présentés au conseil d'état concernant les israélites* (Paris: Plassan, n.d.), 4. This phrase was used in his discussion of the part of the decree which required Jews to serve for each other in the army rather than being allowed to find replacements of any religion, as other citizens were.

34. Ibid., 10, 15.

35. The petition and other documents from this struggle are reprinted and analyzed in Rina Neher-Bernheim, ed., *Documents inédits sur l'entrée des juifs dans la société française (1750–1850),* 2 vols. (Tel Aviv: Diaspora Research Institute, 1977), 2: 29–97.

36. Central Consistory to the minister of the interior, September 7, 1820, in CAHJP HM1055.

37. Letter from Minister of Justice Marguerite-Louis François Du Port-Dutertre to all royal tribunals and commissariats, January 10, 1792, as cited in David Feuerwerker, *L'Emancipation des juifs en France, de l'ancien régime à la fin du Second Empire* (Paris: Albin Michel, 1976), 565–67.

38. Ibid., 587.

39. Ibid., 566, 70.

40. Letter from the Upper Rhine Consistory to the Central Consistory, August 9, 1809, as cited in ibid., 575.

41. The defendant in the case was Emmanuel Dreyfus of Mulhouse, the appeals court in Colmar. As cited in ibid., 578–79.

42. From the *Journal de jurisprudence civile, commerciale et notarial et de la cour d'Appel séant à Colmar* 4, no. 8 (February 1809), article 64e, as cited in ibid., 575.

43. Feuerwerker, *L'Emancipation des Juifs*, 568.

44. These are Feuerwerker's words, summarizing the holding of the Mainz court in November 1808; see ibid., 572.

45. Ibid., 576–87.

46. Adolphe Crémieux, *Second plaidoyer sur cette question: Le Juif français doit-il être soumis à prêter le serment more judaïco?* (Nîmes: Gaude, 1827), 4–5.

47. Ibid., 23–27; Crémieux, *Plaidoyer sur cette question*, 3.

48. Crémieux, *Plaidoyer sur cette question*, 3, 6, 18–19.

49. Ibid., 32.

50. Paris Consistory to Crémieux, February 1, 1827 (letter signed Baruch Weil, fils aîné, sec., Seligman Michel, Baruch Weil, J. Javal, Président, J. Hatzfeld), in Archives of the Jewish Theological Seminary of America, New York, Archive 36, 23/7. On the fate of the oath in Eastern France up to 1846, see Feuerwerker, *L'Emancipation des Juifs*, 628–24.

51. Solomon Posener, *Adolphe Crémieux, 1796–1880*, 2 vols. (Paris: Félix Alcan, 1934), 1: 44–54.

52. Ibid., 51–52, 61–62, 83.

53. On the *doctrinaires*, see Pierre Rosanvallon, *L'Etat en France de 1789 à nos jours* (Paris: Seuil, 1990), esp. 116–17, and *Le Moment Guizot* (Paris: Gallimard, 1985); Pierre Manent, *Histoire intellectuelle du libéralisme: Dix leçons* (Paris: Calmann-Lévy, 1987), 199–219; Aurelian Craiutu, *Liberalism Under Siege: The Political Thought of the French Doctrinaires* (Lanham, MD: Lexington, 2003).

54. For the full text of these decrees, see Albert, *The Modernization of French Jewry*, 345–49.

55. Protestantism in France included several different denominations; one can hardly speak of it as a single entity. On its history in this period, see Daniel Robert, *Les Eglises réformées en France (1800–1830)* (Paris: Presses Universitaires de France, 1961). On the importance of centralization to the process of controlling Jewish belief and practice, see Jay Berkovitz, *The Shaping of Jewish Identity in*

Nineteenth-Century France (Detroit: Wayne State University Press, 1989); Michael Graetz, *The Jews in Nineteenth-Century France: From the French Revolution to the Alliance Israélite Universelle*, trans. Jane Marie Todd (Stanford, CA: Stanford University Press, 1996); Albert, *The Modernization of French Jewry*.

56. On all of these important changes, see Albert, *The Modernization of French Jewry*, 352.

57. Ibid.

58. Piette, *Les Juifs de Paris*, 60–61, 85–88. Piette shows that as more Jews moved to the capital, the Saint-Avoye neighborhood became poorer and the wealthier Jews moved closer to the area around the Bourse, which was still a reasonable walk from the synagogues of the older neighborhood.

59. Of the first twenty-five men listed on an 1825 report prepared by the Paris Consistory of the Jews in Paris paying the highest taxes, ten were bankers and eight were wholesalers (*négociants*, which involved banking as well), and the others were in related professions. See "Liste des cinquante israélites les plus imposés de la circonscription de Paris," 1825? CAHJP FCPa40. A slightly different list (with the same names in the same order but providing more information) appears in Léon Kahn, *Le Comité de bienfaisance: L'Hôpital, l'orphélinat, les cimetières*, Histoire de la communauté israélite de Paris, vol. 3 (Paris: A. Durlacher, 1886), 204–12.

60. On the second generation of the Restoration Parisian Jewish elite, see Piette, *Les Juifs de Paris*, esp. 71–81; Berkovitz, *Shaping of Jewish Identity*, 111–26; Léon Kahn, *Les Juifs à Paris depuis le VIe siècle* (Paris: A. Durlacher, 1889). On the level of integration of Crémieux, Achille Fould, Léon Halévy, and Olinde Rodrigues in liberal circles, see Spitzer, *French Generation of 1820*.

61. Albert, *The Modernization of French Jewry*.

62. See, for example, the Central Consistory to the minister of the interior, September 23, 1810; December 28, 1815; April 7, 1816; and February 17, 1818, in CAHJP HM 1053–54.

63. Peter N. Stearns, *Priest and Revolutionary: Lamennais and the Dilemma of French Catholicism* (New York: Harper and Row, 1967), 29–30.

64. Many of these *rôles de répartition* are preserved in the CAHJP archives.

65. For Bordeaux *rôles de répartition*, 1818–30, see CAHJP FCB01–18 and Klau Library, Hebrew Union College Archives, Sephardic Jews Collection; for Strasbourg, see CAHJP FCBR26 (1809 *rôle de repartition*).

66. For this, see especially the Bordeaux *rôles de répartition* (CAHJP FCB01–18; Klau Library, Hebrew Union College Archives, Sephardic Jews Collection); and "Liste des cinquante israélites les plus imposés de la circonscription de Paris."

67. Crémieux to Monteux, May 16, 1821, in AN 369/AP/1, no. 162. In the letter, Crémieux goes on to say that he plans to write to a number of liberal deputies (Constant, Kératy, Lafayette, Chabaud-Latour, Saint-Aulaire, and Chauvelain) and encourages Monteux to contact Manuel. Given the weakness of the liberal

camp at the time, however, change came from within the consistory rather than from the Chamber.

68. Central Consistory to the Amsterdam Consistory, November 6, 1812, in CAHJP HM1053. By "North" and "South," the Central Consistory is referring to Ashkenazim and Sephardim, respectively.

69. Central Consistory to the minister of the interior, October 7, 1819, in CAHJP HM1055.

70. Albert, *The Modernization of French Jewry*, 352.

71. Central Consistory to the Amsterdam Consistory, August 23, 1813, in CAHJP HM1055.

72. Central Consistory to the Strasbourg Consistory, December 31, 1810, in CAHJP HM1053.

73. Central Consistory to the Amsterdam Consistory, August 23, 1813, in CAHJP HM1055. See also Albert, *The Modernization of French Jewry*, 199–202, on the evolution of the term *synagogue* in consistory discourse.

74. Central Consistory to the consistories of the empire, 1810, in BUAC, I-1-a.

75. Central Consistory to the minister of the interior, April 7, 1816, in CAHJP HM1054.

76. As described in the "Procès-verbaux du Consistoire central," July 2, 1819, Archives du Consistoire Central, IB2.

77. Documents regarding the steps taken by Central Consistory leaders in 1830 and 1831 are reprinted in Neher-Bernheim, *Documents inédits sur l'entrée des juifs*, 2: 267–76.

78. For information on the ownership of synagogues in some representative eighteenth-century Jewish *communautés* (Metz, Bordeaux, Bayonne, Marseilles), consult Szajkowski, *Jews and the French Revolutions*, 151–219, 67–88, 809–25.

79. Napoleon established this as the legal rate of interest as early as 1799 when he first reestablished public credit. Louis Bergeron, *France Under Napoleon* (Princeton, NJ: Princeton University Press, 1981), 53–54.

80. "Projet d'édification d'une synagogue," Bordeaux, August 27, 1809, from Hebrew Union College, Sephardic Jews Collection, as seen on microfilm at CAHJP HM4942.

81. Ibid.

82. Florin Aftalion, *L'Economie de la Révolution française* (Paris: Hachette, 1987), 29–31.

83. Alain Beltran and Pascal Griset, *La Croissance économique de la France, 1815–1914* (Paris: Armand Colin, 1988), 76–143.

84. The *ordonnance royale* was dated June 29, 1819, as cited in the Central Consistory's letter to the minister of the interior, January 10, 1825, in CAHJP HM1056. Albert reports that the building was completed in 1822: *The Modernization of French Jewry*, 180.

85. Central Consistory to the minister of worship, December 7, 1830, in CAHJP HM1056.

86. Central Consistory to the minister of worship of February 6, 1831, in CAHJP HM1056. The request was made again on January 10, 1832; December 9, 1832; and May 25, 1837.

87. Central Consistory to the minister of worship, May 25, 1837, in CAHJP HM1057. In 1837, Colonel Max Cerfberr, then president of the Central Consistory, proposed that the debt be liquidated by the creation on non–interest bearing bonds, amortized over twenty years and reimbursed by lottery. Evidently, the proposal was not accepted. See his 1837 letter to his "Coreligionnaires," in BUAC I-1-a.

88. Central Consistory to the minister of worship, January 20, 1839, in CAHJP HM1058.

89. Central Consistory to the minister of worship, August 28, 1840, in CAHJP HM1058; Central Consistory to the Paris Consistory, February 10, 1841; January 25, 1844; and January 11, 1849, in CAHJP HM1059.

90. Central Consistory to the Paris Consistory, January 11, 1849, in CAHJP HM1059.

91. Central Consistory to the minister of the interior, November 20, 1831, in CAHJP HM1057.

92. For this particular observation, see Rosanvallon, *L'Etat en France*, 116–17. On the *doctrinaires*, see also Craiutu, *Liberalism Under Siege*; Rosanvallon, *Le Moment Guizot*; Louis Girard, *Les Libéraux français, 1814–1875* (Paris: Aubier, 1985), 69–79.

93. William Gibson, *The Abbé de Lamennais and the Liberal Catholic Movement in France* (London: Longmans, Green, 1896), 44–75, and Nora E. Hudson, *Ultra-Royalism and the French Restoration* (Cambridge: Cambridge University Press, 1936), 119–20.

94. Bakunin, *Pierre Leroux*, 10–12; Girard, *Les Libéraux français*, 106–10.

95. For biographical information on this family, see Henri Loyette, ed., *Entre le théâtre et l'histoire: La Famille Halévy, 1760–1960* (Paris: Fayard, 1996); Diana Hallman, *Opera, Liberalism and Antisemitism in Nineteenth-Century France: The Politics of Halévy's "La Juive,"* Cambridge Studies in Opera (Cambridge: Cambridge University Press, 2002).

96. Berkovitz, *Shaping of Jewish Identity*, 61.

97. Elie Halévy, "Réponse à quelques objections relatives à *l'Institution israélite*," *L'Israélite Français* 1 (1817): 249–52.

98. Elie Halévy, "La Piété filiale," *L'Israélite Français* 1 (1817): 293–300.

99. Elie Halévy, *Instruction religieuse et morale à l'usage de la jeunesse israélite* (Paris: Chez l'auteur et Gerson-Lévy, 1820).

100. A., "Sur la Tolérence réligieuse," in *L'Israélite Français* 1 (1817): 225–37.

101. François Guizot, "Des moyens du gouvernement de l'opposition dans l'état actuel de la France," in *Oeuvres Choisies* (Brussels: Meline, Cans, 1848), 223.

102. Theis, "Guizot et le problème religieux," esp. 255.

103. Gabriel Salvador, *J. Salvador: Sa vie, ses oeuvres et ses critiques* (Paris: Cal-mann-Lévy, 1881), 22. On Salvador's life, see also Graetz, *The Jews in Nineteenth-Century France*, chap. 6.

104. Joseph Salvador, *Histoire des institutions de Moïse et du peuple hébreu*, 3 vols. (Paris: Ponthieu, 1828). For insightful analyses of these works, see especially James Darmesteter, "Joseph Salvador," *Annuaire de la Société des Etudes Juives* 1 (1881); Graetz, *The Jews in Nineteenth-Century France*, chap. 6; and Paula E. Hy-man, "Joseph Salvador: Proto-Zionist or Apologist for Assimilation?" *Jewish Social Studies* 34 (1972): 1–22.

105. Salvador, *Histoire des institutions de Moïse*, 1: 103, 111.

106. Review dated February 10, 1823, as cited in Darmesteter, "Joseph Salvador," 19.

107. *Le Globe*, April 19, 1829, as cited in Salvador, *J. Salvador*, 57–68. On Ré-musat in this period, see Spitzer, *French Generation of 1820*, 97–128; Bakunin, *Pierre Leroux*, 29–31.

108. Edward Berenson, *Populist Religion and Left-Wing Politics in France, 1830–1852* (Princeton, NJ: Princeton University Press, 1984); Bakunin, *Pierre Leroux*; Berenson, "A New Religion of the Left."

109. The best histories of this movement remain Charléty, *Histoire*; Frank E. Manuel, *The Prophets of Paris: Turgot, Condorcet, Saint-Simon, Fourier, and Comte* (New York: Harper and Row, 1962), 149–93; Weill, *L'Ecole saint-simonienne*.

110. Central Consistory to Isaac Rodrigues, Berr Leon Fould, and Worms de Romilly (all three had major banking houses and were close friends and collabo-rators), March 27, 1818, in CAHJP HM1054.

111. Emile and Isaac Pereire were Olinde Rodrigues' cousins, who initially es-tablished themselves working for the Fould and Isaac Rodrigues banks; Emile later married Olinde's sister Rachel-Herminie. Edouard and Henry Rodrigues were the sons of Benjamin Rodrigues, who served first on the Paris Consistory and then on the Central Consistory; this family was unrelated to Olinde and Eu-gène's. Gustave d'Eichthal was the grand-nephew of Berr Isaac Berr on his ma-ternal side; his father Louis, an immigrant from Germany, had trained with Isaac Rodrigues (Olinde's father) as a young man in the Fould bank. Gustave later mar-ried Cécile Rodrigues (b. 1823), daughter of Edouard Rodrigues. There is still one other Rodrigues family who came to Paris from Bordeaux a bit later than the other two Rodrigues families; Isaac Rodrigues (b. 1765), who served on the Cen-tral Consistory, was sometimes called "Is. Rodrigues aîné" in consistory docu-ments. He was the husband of Esther Gradis and father of Eugénie Foa (b. 1796), Hippolyte Rodrigues (b. 1812), and Léonie Rodrigues Halévy (b. 1820; married Fromental Halévy in 1842). All three elder Rodrigues—Benjamin, "banquier"; Isaac, "fils, professeur de tenue de livres"; and Isaac, "négociant"—participated in the Napoleonic Assembly of Notables in 1806, and both Isaacs were members of

the 1807 Sanhedrin. To make matters even more confusing, according to Leon Halévy's biographical sketch of his brother, all of these families—the Halévys, the Benjamin Rodrigues, the Pereire brothers, and both sets of Isaac Rodrigues supposedly lived in the same apartment building on the rue Monthalon in overlapping periods. This information was compiled primarily from Gustave d'Eichthal, "Notes sur ma vie," in ARS MS 14408, and from Jean Cavignac, *Dictionnaire du judaïsme bordelais aux XVIIIe et XIXe siècles: Biographies, généologies, professions, institutions* (Bordeaux: Archives départementales de la Gironde, 1987).

On Jews in the Saint-Simonian movement, see Barrie M. Ratcliffe, "Crisis and Identity: Gustave d'Eichthal and Judaism in the Emancipation Period," *Jewish Social Studies* 37 (1975): 122–40; Michael Graetz, "Une Initiative saint-simonienne pour l'émancipation des juifs: Lettres de Gustave d'Eichthal sur son voyage en Autriche," *Revue des Etudes Juives* 129, no. 1 (1970): 67–84; Graetz, *Jews in Nineteenth-Century France*, 110–42; Barrie M. Ratcliffe, "Les Pereire et le saint-simonisme," *Economies et sociétés: Cahiers de l'ISEA* 5, no. 6 (1971): 1215–55; Zosa Szajkowski, "The Jewish Saint-Simonians and Socialist Antisemites in France," *Jewish Social Studies* 9 (1947): 33–60.

112. Henri de Saint-Simon and Eugène Rodrigues, *Nouveau Christianisme: Lettres d'Eugène Rodrigues sur la religion et la politique; L'Education du genre humain, de Lessing, traduit, pour la première fois, de l'allemand par Eugène Rodrigues* (Paris: Le Globe, 1832), 11. On the New Christianity, see ibid., and Olinde Rodrigues, *Religion saint-simonienne: Appel* (Paris: Le Globe, 1831).

113. Spitzer, *French Generation of 1820*, 153.

Chapter 3. Jewish Identities in the Age of Romanticism

1. Adolphe Crémieux, *Plaidoyer sur cette question: Le Juif français doit-il être soumis à prêter le serment more judaïco?* (Nîmes: Gaude, 1827), 31.

2. Eugénie Foa, *La Juive: Histoire du temps de la Régence*, 2 vols. (Paris: Arthus Bertrand, 1835), 1: 309.

3. The fact that Restoration Jewish leaders supported their children in their endeavors in the greater French world is not entirely surprising; as we have seen, the elder generation was liberal in outlook and did not believe that positions of leadership in the institution should be inherited, but rather, chosen freely and earned through merit. Adolphe Crémieux is a case in point; his father, David, was a merchant, but he sent young Adolphe to the Lycée Impérial in Paris and supported him fully in his desire to become a lawyer. As we have seen, Crémieux was highly assimilated into liberal circles and also became a major leader of French Jewry. The Halévy brothers' case is also telling; Elie sent Léon to the Lycée Charlemagne and Fromenthal to the Conservatoire, and the family continued to live together for the rest of the brothers' lives. Fromenthal became a highly successful composer and served on the Paris Consistory; Léon became a prolific writer, never assumed a position of leadership in Jewish institutions, participated

in the Saint-Simonian movement, and married a Protestant woman, Alexandrine (Nanine) LeBas.

Thus, while I concur with Michael Graetz on the long-term significance as well as the basic structure of the identity forged by members of this generation, I disagree with his contention that these changes to Jewish identity took place on the "periphery" of French Jewish institutional life (by which he means, far from the center of consistorial power) and only later made their way to its institutional "center." On the contrary, most of the Jewish members of the Generation of 1820 were born in the heart of the consistorial elite, and many of their parents had themselves abandoned traditional practice, or in the case of some of the Sephardi members, had never known it in their lives. For his "periphery to center" argument, see Michael Graetz, *The Jews in Nineteenth-Century France: From the French Revolution to the Alliance Israélite Universelle*, trans. Jane Marie Todd (Stanford, CA: Stanford University Press, 1996), 6–16.

4. Ibid.

5. On the so-called "Jewish element" within Saint-Simonianism, see Zosa Szajkowski, "The Jewish Saint-Simonians and Socialist Antisemites in France," *Jewish Social Studies* 9 (1947): 33–60; Graetz, *Jews in Nineteenth-Century France*, chaps. 4 and 5; Georges Weill, "Les Juifs et le saint-simonisme," *Revue des Etudes Juives* 31, no. 62 (1895): 261–73; Barrie M. Ratcliffe, "Les Pereire et le saint-simonisme," *Economies et sociétés: Cahiers de l'ISEA* 5, no. 6 (1971): 1215–55; and Ratcliffe, "Crisis and Identity: Gustave d'Eichthal and Judaism in the Emancipation Period," *Jewish Social Studies* 37 (1975): 122–40.

6. With the possible exception of Léon Halévy; yet even he claimed to know no Hebrew. See his *Résumé de l'histoire des juifs modernes* (Paris: Lecointe, 1828), vii–viii. Interestingly, none of the Jewish Saint-Simonians broke with their families when they began to participate in the movement. Even their rejection of Jewish observance cannot be seen as a break from their parents, since most of their parents—even the ones who were consistory leaders—were not observant themselves. Furthermore, it was these parents who happily paved the way, in a certain sense, for their children's integration into the social networks in which Saint-Simonianism emerged, sending them to *lycées* and to the Ecole Polytechnique. On the religious indifference of Benjamin Rodrigues, Isaac Rodrigues, Berr Léon Fould, and Olry Worms de Romilly, see Christine Piette, *Les Juifs de Paris, 1808–1840: La Marche vers l'assimilation* (Quebec: Université de Laval, 1983), 136.

7. Olinde Rodrigues, *Religion saint-simonienne: Appel* (Paris: Le Globe, 1831), 4.

8. Piette, *Les Juifs de Paris*, 183. As Piette shows, Myrtil Maas (a graduate of the Ecole Polytechnique as well, who later became a consistory leader and a giant in the world of insurance) and Léon Halévy faced the same barrier to their own academic aspirations.

9. Louis Bergeron, *Banquiers, négociants et manufacturiers parisiens du directoire à l'Empire* (Paris: Ecole des hautes études en sciences sociales, 1978), 56.

10. D'Eichthal, "Notes sur ma vie," in ARS MS 14408/10.

11. D'Eichthal, "La Juive" (first version), in ARS MS 14390/4.

12. *Le Globe*, January 16, 1832, as cited in Sébastien Charléty, *Histoire du saint-simonisme (1825–1864)*, 2nd ed. (Paris: Paul Hartmann, 1931), 148.

13. Henri de Saint-Simon and Eugène Rodrigues, *Nouveau Christianisme: Lettres d'Eugène Rodrigues sur la religion et la politique; L'Education du genre humain, de Lessing, traduit, pour la première fois, de l'allemand par Eugène Rodrigues* (Paris: Le Globe, 1832), 11.

14. Frank Paul Bowman, *French Romanticism: Intertextual and Interdisciplinary Readings* (Baltimore: Johns Hopkins University Press, 1990), 14–33; Jack Bakunin, *Pierre Leroux and the Birth of Democratic Socialism, 1797–1848* (New York: Revisionist Press, 1976), 1–19; Edward Berenson, "A New Religion of the Left: Christianity and Social Radicalism in France, 1815–1848," in *The French Revolution and the Creation of Modern Political Culture*, ed. François Furet and Mona Ozouf, vol. 3, *The Transformation of Political Culture, 1789–1848* (Oxford: Pergamon, 1989), 543–60; Edward Berenson, *Populist Religion and Left-Wing Politics in France, 1830–1852* (Princeton, NJ: Princeton University Press, 1984).

15. Saint-Simon and Rodrigues, *Nouveau Christianisme*; Eugène Rodrigues, *Lettres d'Eugène Rodrigues sur la religion et la politique* (Paris: Le Globe, 1832), 133–46.

16. Isaac Pereire, *La Question religieuse* (Paris: C. Motteroz, 1878), 55, 86.

17. Rodrigues, *Lettres*, 286.

18. Edgar Quinet, *Les Tablettes du Juif errant*, vol. 11 of *Oeuvres complètes*, 30 vols., 5th ed. (Paris: Hachette, 1899).

19. Joseph Jacobs, "The Wandering Jew," in *The Jewish Encyclopedia*, ed. Cyrus Adler, Isidore Singer, et al. (New York: Funk and Wagnalls, 1901–6).

20. Charléty, *Histoire*, 153.

21. Saint-Simon and Rodrigues, *Nouveau Christianisme*, 17. Cited by d'Eichthal in "La Juive" (2nd version), in ARS MS 14390/5.

22. "La Juive" (2nd version), in ARS MS 14390/5.

23. Léon Halévy, *Résumé de l'histoire des juifs anciens* (Paris: Lecointe et Durey, 1825), 67, 383–84.

24. Joseph Salvador, *Histoire des institutions de Moïse et du peuple hébreu* 3 vols. (Paris: Ponthieu, 1828), 1: 337.

25. Rodrigues, *Religion saint-simonienne*, 4.

26. "La Juive" (1st version).

27. Rodrigues, *Lettres*, 270. See also Henri Fournel, *Articles sur l'hérédité de la propriété* (Paris: Le Globe, 1831).

28. "The Successive Transformation of Man's Exploitation by Man and the Rights of Property," 6th session, February 25, 1829; "The Constitution of Property and the Organization of the Banks," 7th session, March 11, 1829: both in Georg G. Iggers, trans., *The Doctrine of Saint-Simon: An Exposition; First Year, 1828–1829*

(New York: Schocken, 1972); this second article is likely the work of Gustave d'Eichthal.

29. "Lettre à un banquier," in *L'Organisateur: Journal de la doctrine saint-simonienne* (October 23, 1830): 74–80.

30. Gustave d'Eichthal to Adolphe d'Eichthal, August 4, 1829, in ARS MS 14407/11.

31. D'Eichthal, "Lettre à M. Freslon, avocat à Angers, en réponse à cette question: Qu'est devenu le saint-simonisme? Et à cette autre—que peut être le dogme nouveau?" Undated MS in ARS MS 14389.

32. For a sense of their promotion of these goals later in life, see Olinde Rodrigues, *Théorie des banques* (Paris: Napoleon Chaix, 1848); Isaac Pereire, *Politique industrielle et commerciale: Budget des réformes* (Paris: C. Motteroz, 1877); Isaac Pereire, *Politique financière: La Conversion et l'amortissement* (Paris: C. Motteroz, 1879); and Pereire, *La Question religieuse.*

33. Derek Jonathan Penslar, *Shylock's Children: Economics and Jewish Identity in Modern Europe* (Berkeley and Los Angeles: University of California Press, 2001); Mitchell Hart, *Social Science and the Politics of Modern Jewish Identity* (Stanford, CA: Stanford University Press, 2000).

34. Bertrand Gille, *La Banque en France au XIXe siècle: Recherches historiques* (Geneva: Droz, 1970), 105–24; Gille, *Histoire de la maison Rothschild*, 2 vols. (Geneva: Droz, 1965–67), 1: 52, 64.

35. Moses Debré, *The Image of the Jew in French Literature from 1800 to 1908*, trans. Gertrude Hirschler (New York: Ktav, 1970), 21–28.

36. His observations have been collected and translated in Barrie Ratcliffe and W. H. Chaloner, eds., *A French Sociologist Looks at Britain: Gustave d'Eichthal and British Society in 1828* (Manchester: University of Manchester Press, 1977), 18–19 and passim.

37. Diana Hallman, *Opera, Liberalism and Antisemitism in Nineteenth-Century France: The Politics of Halévy's "La Juive,"* Cambridge Studies in Opera (Cambridge: Cambridge University Press, 2002), 210–12.

38. "La Juive" (2nd version; emphasis in original).

39. In a diary entry dated May 10, 1837, d'Eichthal remarked, "I am a Jew by nature because I can eat neither pig nor oysters" (ARS MS 14717). In a frustrated letter dated March 29, 1838, he wrote to his brother Adolphe, "You are a Jew, by birth, you carry on your flesh the undeniable sign of all members of his chosen people; you owe your position to your Jewish origin and your current association with other Jews, and yet you remain nonetheless unaware of all these facts" (ARS MS 14396/50).

40. Martin Seliger, "Race-Thinking During the Restoration," *Journal of the History of Ideas* 19, no. 2 (1958): 273–82; Ceri Crossley, *French Historians and Romanticism: Thierry, Guizot, the Saint-Simonians, Quinet, Michelet* (London: Routledge, 1993); Krystof Pomain, "Franks and Gauls," in *Realms of Memory:*

Rethinking the French Past, ed. Pierre Nora (New York: Columbia University Press, 1996), 56–62.

41. Seliger, "Race-Thinking," 273–82.

42. François Guizot, *Memoirs to Illustrate the History of My Time*, trans. J. W. Cole, 8 vols. (London: Richard Bentley, 1858–67; reprint, New York: AMS, 1974), 1: 284–87.

43. Halévy, *Résumé de l'histoire des juifs anciens*, 383.

44. Ibid., 381–86.

45. Keith Taylor, ed., *Henri Saint-Simon (1760–1825): Selected Writings on Science, Industry, and Social Organisation* (New York: Holmes and Meier, 1975), 111–23, 244–49.

46. "Le Chant d'Ahasvérus," in ARS MS 14393/2.

47. Gustave d'Eichthal and Ismayl Urbain, *Lettres sur la race noire et la race blanche* (Paris: Paulin, 1839); Gustave d'Eichthal, *Les Deux Mondes, servant d'introduction à l'ouvrage de M. Urquart, "La Turquie et ses ressources,"* (Paris: Bertrand, 1836); d'Eichthal, *De l'unité européenne* (Paris: Truchy, 1840).

48. The friendship between d'Eichthal and Michelet seems to have begun in 1837 and continued until Michelet's death. See their correspondence in ARS MS 14397; Jules Michelet's record of the friendship in his *Journal*, 2 vols. (Paris: Gallimard, 1958), passim; and Paul Viallaneix, *Michelet, les travaux et les jours: 1798–1874* (Paris: Gallimard, 1998), 124, 90.

49. *Introduction à l'histoire universelle*, in *Oeuvres complètes*, vol. 35 (Paris: Flammarion, 1897), and *Histoire romaine* (Paris: Hachette, 1831). On Michelet's view of race and history, see François Furet, "Michelet," in *Critical Dictionary of the French Revolution*, ed. François Furet and Mona Ozouf (Cambridge, MA: Belknap, 1989), 980–89, and Crossley, *French Historians and Romanticism*.

50. Jules Michelet, *Le Peuple* (Paris: Hachette, 1846), 330–31.

51. Edgar Quinet, *Le Christianisme et la Révolution française* (Paris: Imprimeurs-Unis, 1845), 210, 222.

52. The phrase "holy alliance of peoples" is from an anonymous voice interrupting d'Eichthal's speech about the new "holy alliance" made possible by the establishment of republics in 1848, which he made at the Congrès de la Paix of June 1849. See ARS MS 14720. For more on the emergence of the concept of a "Jewish race" in this particular historical context, see Lisa Moses Leff, "Self-Definition and Self-Defense: Jewish Racial Identity in Nineteenth-Century France," *Jewish History* 19, no. 1 (January 2005): 7–28.

53. This issue of Jewish self-construction in literature and the arts is treated in interesting ways in Rachel M. Brownstein, *Tragic Muse: Rachel of the Comédie-Française* (New York: Knopf, 1993); Hallman, *Opera, Liberalism and Antisemitism*; Magy Hamache, "Les Juifs dans les arts dramatiques au XIXe siècle: Regards croisés sur la tragédienne Rachel (1821–1858)," *Revue Historique* 293, no. 1 (1995): 119–33; Albert Joseph George, *The Development of French Romanticism: The Impact*

of the Industrial Revolution on Literature (Syracuse, NY: Syracuse University Press, 1955).

54. A slightly different, but complementary view of why Crémieux built his career in this way is presented in Alan B. Spitzer, *The French Generation of 1820* (Princeton, NJ: Princeton University Press, 1987), 243.

55. On Foa, see Leyla Ezdinli, "Altérite juive, altérité romanesque," *Romantisme* 81 (1993): 29–40; and Elisabeth-Christine Muelsch, "Eugénie Foa and the *Institut des Femmes*," in *Women Seeking Expression, 1789–1914*, ed. Rosemary Lloyd and Brian Nelson, 86–100 (Melbourne: Monash Romance Studies, 2000).

56. Elisabeth-Christine Muelsch, "Creativity, Childhood, and Children's Literature; or, How to Become a Woman Writer: The Case of Eugénie Foa," *Romance Languages Annual* 8 (1997): 69. Muelsch reports that Foa was later disinherited by her mother.

57. It appears that the two Isaac Rodrigues were not related, or at least, not closely. Upon the death of Isaac Rodrigues (1771–1846), Gustave d'Eichthal referred to him in his diary as the "père d'Olinde, d'Eugène, de Mme Emile Pereire . . . l'ami de Mme Nancy Rodrigue, mère de M. Edouard [father of Olinde, Eugène, and Mrs. Emile Pereire, friend of Mrs. Nancy Rodrigue, mother of Edouard]" (ARS MS 14721). D'Eichthal's reference to the relationship between Nancy Rodrigues and Isaac Rodrigues as one of *amitié* (friendship), rather than blood or marriage, thus suggests that there was no close blood tie between the two Isaacs. This interpretation is further borne out by a number of other facts presented in the d'Eichthal papers. In another diary entry, d'Eichthal writes that the following men were members of the meeting of Jewish leaders under Napoleon: "Isaac Rodrigues, et Rodrigue aîné, père et oncle de M. Edouard, Rodrigue fils (le père d'Olinde) [Isaac Rodrigues, and Rodrigue the elder, father and uncle of Edouard, Rodrigue junior (father of Olinde)]" (in ARS MS 14722). Indeed, the records of the 1806 Assembly of Jewish Notables verify the presence of three different Rodrigues, two representing the Gironde department, one representing the Seine department. Logically, we must conclude that there were two Isaac Rodrigues, and that they could not have been closely related to one another. On these families, see Jean Cavignac, *Dictionnaire du judaïsme bordelais aux XVIIIe et XIXe siècles: Biographies, généalogies, professions, institutions* (Bordeaux: Archives départementales de la Gironde, 1987), 110–12.

58. Chantal Bischoff, *Geneviève Straus, 1849–1926: Trilogie d'une égérie* (Paris: Balland, 1992), 15–18.

59. Foa, *La Juive*, 2: 250.

60. Hugo, preface to *Hernani* (1830), as cited in Peter Brooks, "An Oedipal Crisis," in *A New History of French Literature*, ed. Denis Hollier (Cambridge, MA: Harvard University Press, 1989), 651.

61. Hallman, *Opera, Liberalism and Antisemitism*, 128–36.

62. Edward Said, *Orientalism* (New York: Vintage, 1978).

63. Foa, *La Juive*, 1: 129–30.

64. William Vaughan, "The Visual Arts," in *The French Romantics*, ed. D. G. Charlton, vol. 2 of 2 (Cambridge: Cambridge University Press, 1984).

65. Hallman, *Opera, Liberalism and Antisemitism*, 218–20.

66. *La Juive*, 1: 334–35.

67. Ibid., 150.

68. Foa describes Jewish engagement in *Kiddoushim; ou, L'Anneau nuptial des hébreux*, 4 vols. (Paris: n.p., 1830), the redemption of the first-born and divorce in stories in Foa, *Rachel; ou, L'Héritage* (Paris: Henri Dupuy, 1833).

69. Hallman, *Opera, Liberalism and Antisemitism*, 210–12.

70. Foa, *La Juive*, 1: 247.

71. Ibid., 52–57.

72. D. G. Charlton, "Religious and Political Thought," in Charlton, *The French Romantics*, 1: 33–75.

73. Foa, *La Juive*, 1: 309.

Chapter 4. Secularism and the Civilizing Mission

1. Alice Conklin, *A Mission to Civilize: The Republican Idea of Empire in France and West Africa, 1895–1930* (Stanford, CA: Stanford University Press, 1997), 5–8.

2. Lucien Febvre, "*Civilisation*: Evolution of a Word and a Group of Ideas," in *A New Kind of History and Other Essays*, ed. Peter Burke (New York: Harper, 1973), 219–57; and R. A. Lochore, *History of the Idea of Civilization in France (1830–1870)* (Bonn: Ludwig Rohrscheid, 1935).

3. Adolphe Crémieux, "Journal de voyage en Egypte 1840 (accompli pour la défense d'israélites accusés du meurtre d'un prêtre catholique)," in AN 369/AP/1, Papiers Crémieux, MS pp. 53–56.

4. Jonathan Frankel, *The Damascus Affair: "Ritual Murder," Politics, and the Jews in 1840* (New York: Cambridge University Press, 1997).

5. Ibid., 19–20.

6. See, for example, Comte de Ratti-Menton, "Feuilleton de *l'Univers*: Assassinat du Père Thomas; Documents officiels," *L'Univers*, May 3, 1840.

7. Frankel, *The Damascus Affair*, 185–86.

8. *Montieur universel*, June 3, 1840, 1258, as cited in and translated by Frankel, *The Damascus Affair*, 189.

9. Central Consistory to the minister of foreign affairs, July 20, 1840, in CAHJP HM1058.

10. His claim is based on a thorough examination of such liberal newspapers as *Le Temps*, the *Quotidienne*, the *Journal des Débats*, and *Le Siècle*, throughout the spring and summer of 1840. Frankel, *The Damascus Affair*, 109–231.

11. Michel Berr, "Sur la liberté des cultes," *Mercure de France*, September 1814, 2, 10. An earlier publication reveals Berr to have been concerned with foreign policy as early as 1801. See his *Appel à la justice des nations et des rois, ou adresse d'un*

citoyen français au Congrès qui devait avoir lieu à Lunéville, au nom de tous les habitans de l'Europe qui professent la religion juive (Strasbourg: Levrault, 1801).

12. As excerpted in Eugène Roch, "Persécutions contre les juifs de Damas, à la suite de la disparition du R. P. Thomas, religieux de l'ordre des Capucins, et de son domestique: Recueil des documents," *L'Observateur des Tribunaux: Journal des Documents Judiciaires*, n.s., 1 (1840): 92.

13. "Nouvelles Accusations contre les juifs de Damas," *AIF* 4 (1843): 736–41; "Affaire des israélites de Marmara," *AIF* 5 (1844): 180–82; "Nouvelle Persécution à Damas," *AIF* 8 (1847): 625–28. On the publication of documents from the Damascus affair in the anti-Jewish press, see Frankel, *Damascus Affair*, 415.

14. "Nouvelle Accusation contre les Juifs en Orient," 737.

15. "Affaire des israélites de Marmara," 181.

16. André Kaspi, "Note sur Isidore Cahen," *Revue des Etudes Juives* 121 (1962): 417–25.

17. On Fould's hesitancy, see Roch, "Persécutions contre les juifs de Damas," 83.

18. Crémieux was one of the founders of the Comité Polonais in 1831, along with other distinguished liberals such as Béranger, Odilon Barrot, Armand Carrel, Dupont de l'Eure, Victor Hugo, and Lafayette. See Solomon Posener, *Adolphe Crémieux, 1796–1880*, 2 vols. (Paris: Félix Alcan, 1934), 1: 117.

19. For an account of the entire incident with Bloch's commentary, see "Nouvelles divers," *UI* 3 (1845–46): 22.

20. On Bugeaud, see Antony Thrall Sullivan, *Thomas-Robert Bugeaud: France and Algeria, 1784–1849; Politics, Power, and the Good Society* (Hamden, CT: Archon, 1983).

21. Determining population figures for Algeria is difficult because the conquest was gradual. Simon Schwarzfuchs reports that on the 1851 census, there were 21,048 Jews in all Algeria. See Simon Schwarzfuchs, *Les Juifs d'Algérie et la France (1830–1855)* (Jerusalem: Insistut Ben-Zvi, 1981), 21–29, for a discussion of the various estimates before and including that census.

22. Thomas-Robert Bugeaud, "Note sur notre établissement dans la province d'Oran par suite de la pait" (1837), in *Par l'épée et par la charrue: écrits et discours de Bugeaud*, ed. Paul Azan (Paris: Presses Universitaires de France, 1948), 47. He voiced a similar complaint about the Jews of Mostaganem in a letter to the Bureau of Algerian Affairs dated May 13, 1842, in Archives Nationales, Centre des Archives d'Outre Mer, Aix-en-Provence, Archives du gouverneur général de l'Algérie, 2EE2. On "regeneration," see Bugeaud to the minister of war, November 18, 1843, in 2EE5.

23. Schwarzfuchs, *Les Juifs d'Algérie*, 30–35.

24. C. E. Guyot, "Rapport au Conseil d'administration," April 2, 1844, in Centre des Archives d'Outre Mer, Algérie, fonds ministeriels, F80 1631.

25. "M. Altaras," in *UI* 2 (1845–46): 374–77; emphasis in original.

26. Pierre Guiral, *Marseille et l'Algérie, 1830–1841*, in *Annales de la Faculté des lettres d'Aix-en-Provence*, n.s., no. 15 (Gap: Ophrys, 1956), 156–80.

27. Central Consistory to the minister of worship, December 12, 1836, in CAHJP HM1057, and Central Consistory to the Marseilles Consistory, January 15, 1838, in CAHJP HM1058.

28. Schwarzfuchs, *Les Juifs d'Algérie et la France*, 42–43.

29. Isaac-Jacques Altaras and Joseph Cohen, "Rapport sur l'état moral et politique des israélites de l'Algérie et des moyens de l'améliorer," in Schwarzfuchs, *Les Juifs d'Algérie et la France*, 115–18, 119, 153–57, 160–70.

30. On the use of analogies to the French Revolution in Third Republican imperial policy, see Conklin, *A Mission to Civilize*, esp. chap. 3.

31. Altaras and Cohen, "Rapport," 190.

32. Ibid., 68.

33. Ibid., 114–19, 132–47.

34. Ibid., 119–31, 170–77 (this phrase appears on page 172).

35. For how this would secure French rule, see ibid., 184.

36. Minister of war to Janvier, March 3, 1843, in CAHJP AL 2357(2).

37. Meeting of March 29, 1843, *Procès-verbaux de la commission des israélites d'Algérie*, CAHJP AL 2357(4).

38. On French colonial policy vis-à-vis Muslim Algerians, see Charles-Robert Ageron, *Les Algériens musulmans et la France, 1871–1919*, 2 vols. (Paris: Presses Universitaires de France, 1968); on how French views of Islam informed these policies, see esp. 1: 293–96.

39. Meeting of March 31, 1843, *Procès-verbaux*, in CAHJP AL 2357(4).

40. Meeting of April 3, 1843, in ibid.

41. On the establishment of consistories in Algeria, see Richard Ayoun, "Les Efforts d'assimilation intellectuelle et l'émancipation législative des juifs d'Algérie" (paper presented at the Cultures juives méditerranéennes et orientales, Paris, 1982), 173–88; and Morton Rosenstock, "The Establishment of the Consistorial System in Algeria," *Jewish Social Studies* 18 (1956): 41–54.

42. Lazare Cahen, "Rapport sur la situation des israélites de la province d'Oran" (1850), in Schwarzfuchs, *Les Juifs d'Algérie et la France*, 221–23.

43. Michel Weill, "Situation des israélites en Algérie, rapport général, Alger," in Schwarzfuchs, *Les Juifs d'Algérie*, 284–86.

44. Michel Weill, *La Morale du Judaïsme*, 2 vols. (Paris: A. Franck, 1875).

45. Weill, "Situation des israélites," 294–95.

46. Ibid., 275, 302–3, 343–44.

47. Cf. Phyllis Cohen Albert, *The Modernization of French Jewry: Consistory and Community in the Nineteenth Century* (Hanover, NH: Brandeis University Press, 1977).

48. Lee Shai Weissbach, "The Nature of Philanthropy in Nineteenth-Century France and the *mentalité* of the Jewish Elite," *Jewish History* 8, nos. 1–2 (1994): 191–204. These terms appear on page 201.

49. "Menées fanatiques des rabbins indigènes d'Alger," *AIF* 11 (1850): 592.

50. On French Jewish work in the Ottoman Empire (especially schooling), see Aron Rodrigue, *French Jews, Turkish Jews: The Alliance Israélite Universelle and the Politics of Jewish Schooling in Turkey, 1860–1925* (Bloomington: Indiana University Press, 1990). The Central Consistory's petition can be found in "Intervention par le Consistoire central en faveur des israélites de la Turquie," *AIF* 15 (1854): 228–30. A similar appeal to the minister of foreign affairs can be found in "Lettre adressée par le Consistoire central au ministre des affaires etrangères," *AIF* 16 (1855): 217–18. On Albert Cohn's work in this period, see Isidore Loeb, *Biographie d'Albert Cohn* (Paris: A. Durlacher, 1878), 46–56.

51. Winfried Baumgart, *The Crimean War, 1853–1856* (London: Arnold, 1999), 3–4; and David Wetzel, *The Crimean War: A Diplomatic History* (Boulder, CO: East European Monographs, 1985), 39–48. On the Eastern Question, see J. A. R. Marriott, *The Eastern Question: An Historical Study in European Diplomacy*, 4th ed. (Oxford: Clarendon, 1940), esp. 225–84.

52. On the road to war, see William Miller, *The Ottoman Empire and Its Successors, 1801–1927* (London: Frank Cass, 1966), 199–222.

53. Baumgart, *The Crimean War*, 10.

54. See René Albrecht-Carrié, *A Diplomatic History of Europe Since the Congress of Vienna* (New York: Harper, 1958), 86–87; and Wetzel, *The Crimean War*, 41.

55. The Jewish press reported on these efforts continually, urging Jews to act in kind, especially since Catholic and Protestant activity in the East so often involved attempts to convert Jews as well as Muslims. See for example, "Revue de l'année 1847," *UI* 5 (1849–50): 20; "Les Sympathies des israélites de l'Occident pour leurs coreligionnaires de l'Orient," *AIF* 15 (1854): 367–68; "Chronique du mois," *AIF* 15 (1854): 453; and "Chronique du mois," *AIF* 16 (1855): 107–8.

56. César Famin, *Histoire de la rivalité et du protectorat des églises chrétiennes en Orient* (Paris: Firmin-Didot, 1853), esp. 1–6, 8, 14–18, 162–63, 459–61.

57. Ibid., 52–55.

58. On Sibour's liberal Catholicism, see Philip Spencer, *The Politics of Belief in Nineteenth-Century France: Lacordaire, Michon, Veuillot* (London: Faber and Faber, 1953), 148.

59. "Chronique," *UI* 9 (1853–54): 382. See also "Chronique du mois," *AIF* 15 (1854): 284. For a fuller account of the spectrum of Catholic responses to the war, see Spencer, *Politics of Belief*, 155–68.

60. Emile de Girardin, *Solutions de la Question d'Orient* (Paris: Librairie nouvelle, 1852), 25–41.

61. Edgar Quinet, *Le Christianisme et la Révolution française* (Paris: Imprimeurs-Unis, 1845). This quotation from page 209.

62. Edgar Quinet, *La Croisade autrichienne, française, napolitaine, et espagnole contre la république romaine* (Paris: Chamerot, 1849), 30. On the Rome Campaign

more broadly, see Emile Bourgeois and E. Clermont, *Rome et Napoléon III (1849–1870): Etude sur les origines et la chute du Second Empire* (Paris: Armand Colin, 1907), 3–196.

63. Quinet, *La Croisade*, 3–16, 21.

64. On this movement, see Philip A. Bertocci, *Jules Simon: Republican Anti-clericalism and Cultural Politics in France, 1848–1886* (Columbia: University of Missouri Press, 1978), 48–71. Two Jewish students at the Ecole Normale Supérieure (Eugène Manuel and Isidore Cahen, the son of the editor of *Les Archives Israélites de France*) were involved in the movement. See Michael Graetz, *The Jews in Nineteenth-Century France: From the French Revolution to the Alliance Israélite Universelle*, trans. Jane Marie Todd (Stanford, CA: Stanford University Press, 1996), 201–2; and on their reticence to become as fully involved as they might have liked, see Eugène Manuel, *Lettres de jeunesse* (Paris: Hachette, 1909), 15–16.

65. Laurent de l'Ardèche, in *Le Globe*, December 22, 1830, as cited in Lochore, *History of the Idea of Civilization*, 72.

66. Gustave d'Eichthal, *De l'unité européenne* (Paris: Truchy, 1840), 11.

67. Ibid., 32–33.

68. Girardin, *Solutions*, 60–62.

69. Ibid., 62–75.

70. Ibid., 86. For similar arguments, see the anonymous *Histoire diplomatique de la crise orientale de 1853 à 1856 d'après des documents inédits: Suivie d'un mémoire sur la question des lieux saints* (Brussels: Emile Flatau, 1858); M. Destrilhes, *Confidences sur la Turquie*, 2nd ed. (Paris: Dentu, 1855); and Barthélemy Prosper Enfantin, *Correspondance politique, 1835–1840* (Paris: Le Crédit, 1849), esp. 160–78. Enfantin, of course, is the former "Father" of the Saint-Simonians.

71. "Chronique," *UI* 9 (1853–54): 382.

72. Kaspi, "Note sur Isidore Cahen."

73. "Chronique du mois," *AIF* 15 (1854): 284–85.

74. "Les Israélites en Orient," *AIF* 15 (1854): 317.

75. Letter of the Central Consistory to the emperor, dated March 24, 1854, as published in "Intervention du Consistoire central des israélites de France en faveur des israélites de la Turquie," *AIF* 15 (1854): 228–29.

76. On *hatti Humayun* as well as the delicate diplomacy over its inclusion in the treaty signed at the Congress of Paris, see Winfried Baumgart, *The Peace of Paris 1856: Studies in War, Diplomacy, and Peacemaking*, trans. Ann Pottinger Saab (Santa Barbara, CA: ABC-Clio, 1981), esp. 128–30, 162–64.

77. "Les Rayas de la Turquie . . . et la Suisse," *AIF* 17 (1856): 188–90.

78. "Les Conséquences religieuses de la paix," *AIF* 17 (1856): 252–53.

79. On the evolution of the emperor's foreign policy, see William E. Echard, *Napoleon III and the Concert of Europe* (Baton Rouge: Louisiana State University Press, 1983); and Jean Tulard, "Nationalités (politique des)," in *Dictionnaire du Second Empire*, ed. Jean Tulard (Paris: Fayard, 1995), 904.

80. On the Mortara affair, see David I. Kertzer, *The Kidnapping of Edgaro Mortara* (New York: Vintage, 1997). For Catholic responses, see Spencer, *Politics of Belief*, 168–72.

81. On the academic uses of the term *civilization* from the 1820s to the 1840s, see Lochore, *History of the Idea of Civilization*, 9–33 and passim, and Febvre, "*Civilisation*," 240–44.

82. Febvre, "*Civilisation*," 244–48 and passim.

83. "Les Rayas de la Turquie," 184, 190.

84. "De la liberté de conscience en Europe," *AIF* 18 (1857): 693–95.

85. Isidore Cahen, "Simple voeu d'un honnête homme," *AIF* 20 (1859): 681–97.

86. Ibid., 693.

87. *Le Siècle*, November 11, 1859, as cited in ibid., 696.

88. Jules Simon, *La Libérté de conscience*, 4th ed. (Paris: Hachette, 1867), 8, 302–18.

89. Léon Hollanderski, *Dix-huit siècles de préjugés chrétiens* (Paris: Michel Lévy, 1869), 74.

90. For a full account of this conflict, see Leila Tarazi Fawaz, *An Occasion for War: Civil Conflict in Lebanon and Damascus in 1860* (Berkeley and Los Angeles: University of California Press, 1994); and, specifically on European intervention, Caesar E. Farah, *The Politics of Interventionism in Ottoman Lebanon, 1831–1860* (London: Tauris, 2000), 554–701.

91. Initially appearing in *Le Siècle* of July 12, 1860, the letter was reprinted widely in the Jewish press.

92. Some of these donations were publicized in the Jewish press during the summer of 1860; this list from the records kept by the Alliance Israélite Universelle, which managed the donations. See AAIU France XXXV B 309, "Souscriptions en faveur des chrétiens du Liban." Simon Bloch reported that by the beginning of August, the Alliance had collected over fifty thousand francs for the cause. See "La Persécution des chrétiens en Syrie," *UI* 14 (1859–60): 19.

93. On the foundation of the Alliance, see André Chouraqui, *Cent ans d'histoire: L'Alliance israélite universelle et la renaissance juive contemporaine; 1860–1960* (Paris: Presses Universitaires de France, 1965), 25–39, and Narcisse Leven, *Cinquante ans d'histoire: L'Alliance israélite universelle (1860–1910)*, 2 vols. (Paris: Félix Alcan, 1911), 1: 63–77. For a sociological profile of the founders of the Alliance, see Graetz, *The Jews in Nineteenth-Century France*, 194–288.

94. Isidore Cahen, "La Souscription pour les victimes de la Syrie," *AIF* 21 (1860): 433.

95. Both Crémieux's letter and Plée's response can be found in "Chrétiens du Liban," *Le Siècle*, July 12, 1860. Guéroult's response can be found in *L'Opinion Nationale* of July 15, 1860, and was reprinted in its entirety in the *UI* 14 (1859–60): 659–63.

96. As reprinted in *UI* 14 (1859–60): 662.

97. *La Cochinchine française en 1864* (Paris: Dentu, 1864), 44–45, as cited in Raoul Girardet, *L'Idée coloniale en France de 1871 à 1962* (Paris: La Table Ronde, 1972), 23.

98. "Six mille hommes et six mois," first published in the *Journal des Débats*, as excerpted in "Chronique du mois," *AIF* 21 (1860): 579.

99. Bloch, for example, claimed the term *crusade* for liberalism in "Chronique," *UI* 9 (1853–54): 382 (as cited above, n. 59). Similarly, G. Ben-Lévi wrote of a "new Holy Alliance of the people, a new crusade from free and enlightened circles . . . "; *AIF* 10 (1849): 671. This translation of Ben-Lévi's words from Graetz, *The Jews in Nineteenth-Century France*, 205.

100. Moses Hess, *The Revival of Israel: Rome and Jerusalem, the Last Nationalist Question*, trans. Meyer Waxman (Lincoln: University of Nebraska Press, 1995), 146–49.

101. On liberal anti-Catholicism, John McManners, *Church and State in France, 1870–1914* (London: Society for Promoting Christian Knowledge, 1972), 16–44, and Ceri Crossley, *French Historians and Romanticism: Thierry, Guizot, the Saint-Simonians, Quinet, Michelet* (London: Routledge, 1993); on Quinet's philo-Protestantism, see François Furet, "Quinet," in *Critical Dictionary of the French Revolution*, ed. François Furet and Mona Ozouf (Cambridge, MA: Belknap, 1989), 991–1002.

102. On the effect of Pope Pius IX's rejection of liberalism on French politics in the Second Empire, see Adrien Dansette, *Histoire religieuse de la France contemporaine: L'Église catholique dans la mêlée politique et sociale* (Paris: Flammarion, 1965), 263–324; Spencer, *Politics of Belief*, 122–75; and Hugh McLeod, *Secularization in Western Europe, 1848–1914* (New York: St. Martin's Press, 2000), 31–48.

Chapter 5. The Making of Modern Jewish Solidarity

1. Philip Nord, *The Republican Moment: Struggles for Democracy in Nineteenth-Century France* (Cambridge, MA: Harvard University Press, 1995).

2. On the Alliance's educational programs, see Michael Laskier, *The Alliance Israélite Universelle and the Jewish Communities of Morocco, 1862–1962* (Albany: State University of New York Press, 1983); and Aron Rodrigue, *French Jews, Turkish Jews: the Alliance Israélite Universelle and the Politics of Jewish Schooling in Turkey, 1860–1925* (Bloomington: Indiana University Press, 1990).

3. On the founding of the Alliance, see Narcisse Leven, *Cinquante ans d'histoire: L'Alliance israélite universelle (1860–1910)*, 2 vols. (Paris: Félix Alcan, 1911–20), vol. 1; André Chouraqui, *Cent ans d'histoire: L'Alliance israélite universelle et la renaissance juive contemporaine; 1860–1960* (Paris: Presses Universitaires de France, 1965); and Michael Graetz, *The Jews in Nineteenth-Century France: From the French Revolution to the Alliance Israélite Universelle*, trans. Jane Marie Todd (Stanford, CA: Stanford University Press, 1996), 249–88.

4. "Statuts de L'Alliance israélite universelle," *BAIU* (1860).

5. "Appel à tous les israélites," *BAIU* (1860), as translated in Paula Hyman, *The Jews of Modern France* (Berkeley and Los Angeles: University of California Press, 1998), 77–78.

6. *BAIU* (Second Semester 1866): 37.

7. Rodrigue, *French Jews, Turkish Jews*, 71–80.

8. On the Ecole Normale Israélite Orientale, see ibid., 73–74.

9. Numbers from Chouraqui, *Cent ans d'histoire*, 45. Zosa Szajkowski provides membership numbers of 11,364 for 1869 and 13,370 for 1871 that corroborate Chouraqui's numbers. See Zosa Szajkowski, "Conflicts in the Alliance Israélite Universelle and the Founding of the Anglo-Jewish Association, Viennese Allianz, and the Hilfsverein," *Jewish Social Studies* 19 (1957): 30.

10. Chouraqui, *Cent ans d'histoire*, 429–32.

11. *BAIU* (January 1862): 7–11; *BAIU* (January 1865): 6; *BAIU* (Second Semester 1867): 41.

12. These numbers are from Chouraqui, *Cent ans d'histoire*, 416–28. Among the forty-seven Parisians, I have included those who sat on the provisional committee of 1860, not all of whom were elected in the first election of 1862. The elections were held every three years at first and later, every four years. The first five—those that I have tabulated here—took place in 1862, 1865, 1868, 1872, and 1876.

13. Most Jewish immigrants in this period were from central Europe, as had been the case since the revolution. See Doris Bensimon-Donath, *Socio-démographie des juifs de France et d'Algérie* (Paris: ALC, 1976), 94.

14. Carvallo died and was buried in Tortosa, Spain, where many of his descendants lived. See AAIU France I A 3, and his Ponts et Chaussées file, in AN F14 2187.

15. Netter to Carvallo, n.d., in archives of the Jewish Theological Seminary of America, Archive 36, 25/Netter.

16. Chouraqui, *Cent ans d'histoire*, 40–41.

17. Ibid.

18. Leven, *Cinquante ans d'histoire*, 1: 115; *BAIU* (Second Semester 1866): 1–3; and Carol Iancu, "Adolphe Crémieux, l'Alliance israélite universelle et les juifs de Roumanie," *Revue des Etudes Juives* 133, nos. 3–4 (1974): 485–87.

19. *BAIU* (Second Semester 1870/First Semester 1871): 2.

20. On the company, see Rondo Cameron, *France and the Economic Development of Europe, 1800–1914: Conquest of Peace and Seeds of War*, 2nd ed. (Chicago: Rand McNally, 1961), 105, 146, 156, 172. On the Pereires' participation in the Alliance, see Issac Pereire's letter to Adolphe Crémieux, dated December 16, 1879, donating ten thousand francs to the Alliance, in AAIU France IV A 19.

21. Szajkowski, "Conflicts in the Alliance."

22. *BAIU* (First Semester 1873): 35.   23. *BAIU* (July 1863): 1–5.

24. *BAIU* (July 1864): 2.   25. *BAIU* (July 1865): 27.

26. *BAIU* (Second Semester 1866): 36.

27. On kabbalah, see Moshe Idel, *Kabbalah: New Perspectives* (New Haven, CT: Yale University Press, 1988). Idel reports that Adolphe Franck and Salomon Munk (also a member of the Central Consistory and the Alliance) popularized kabbalah among nineteenth-century Western European Jews.

28. *BAIU* (Second Semester 1871): 57.

29. Adolphe Franck, *La Kabbale; ou, La Philosophie religieuse des Hébreux* (Paris: Hachette, 1843), 178–98.

30. Robert Ambelain, *La Franc-maçonnerie oubliée (1352–1688–1720)* (Paris: Robert Laffont, 1985), 25. On Crémieux's involvement in Freemasonry, see Michel Gaudart de Soulages and Hubert Lamant, *Dictionnaire des franc-maçons français* (Paris: Albatros, 1995), 289.

31. Babylonian Talmud, *Shavout* 39a.

32. Pierre Leroux, *De l'humanité, de son principe, et de son avenir, où se trouve exposée la vraie définition de la religion et où l'on explique le sens, la suite et l'enchaînement du mosaïsme et du christianisme* (Paris: Fayard, 1985), 13–20.

33. Henri de Saint-Simon and Eugène Rodrigues, *Nouveau Christianisme: Lettres d'Eugène Rodrigues sur la religion et la politique; L'Education du genre humain, de Lessing, traduit, pour la première fois, de l'allemand par Eugène Rodrigues* (Paris: Le Globe, 1832).

34. Leroux, *De l'humanité*, 23.

35. André Gueslin, *L'Invention de l'économie sociale: Le XIXe siècle française* (Paris: Economica, 1987); and William H. Sewell, Jr., *Work and Revolution in France: The Language of Labor from the Old Regime to 1848* (Cambridge: Cambridge University Press, 1980), 162–218.

36. As cited in Pierre Larousse, *Grand Dictionnaire universel du XIXe siècle*, vol. 14, pt. 2 (Paris: Larousse, 1982), 840.

37. Jules Michelet, *Le Peuple* (Paris: Hachette, 1846), 189; and *Journal*, vol. 1 of 2, *1828–1848* (Paris: Gallimard, 1959), 667.

38. Auguste Comte, *Catéchisme positive* (Paris: Garnier, 1909), 150.

39. George Sand, *L'Histoire de ma vie*, in *Oeuvres complètes*, 110 vols. (Paris: Michel Lévy, 1879), 40: 6.

40. Marcel David, *Le Printemps de la fraternité: Genèse et vicissitudes, 1830–1851* (Paris: Aubier, 1992), 186, 188, 198, 249.

41. Ibid., 20.

42. I base my claim on a search for the word *solidarité* and its cognates on the ARTFL *Trésor de la langue française* database for the years prior to 1889 (see www.lib.uchicago.edu/efts/ARTFL/databases/TLF/).

43. See Alvin R. Calman, *Ledru-Rollin and the Second French Republic* (New York: Columbia University Press, 1922).

44. On Crémieux in the Second Republic, see Béatrice Philippe, "Les Juifs français et la seconde république de février à juin 1848," 2 vols. (doctoral diss., Université de Paris X-Nanterre, 1980), 1: 105–56; Daniel Amson, *Adolphe Crémieux,*

l'oublié de la gloire (Paris: Seuil, 1988); and Solomon Posener, *Adolphe Crémieux, 1796–1880*, 2 vols. (Paris: Félix Alcan, 1934).

45. Gustave d'Eichthal and Ismayl Urbain, *Lettres sur la race noire et la race blanche* (Paris: Paulin, 1839), 20.

46. Jacques Altaras and Joseph Cohen, "Rapport sur l'état moral et politique des israélites de l'Algérie et des moyens de l'améliorer," in *Les Juifs d'Algérie et la France (1830–1855)*, ed. Simon Schwarzfuchs (Jerusalem: Institut Ben-Zvi, 1981), 68.

47. Nord, *The Republican Moment*, 8, 64–89.

48. The scandal over which Carvallo was fired involved the financing of the Chemin de Fer du Midi. On this, see AN F7 2187. Carvallo compared this scandal to the Inquisition in several of his complaints to the minister, suggesting that he believed anti-Jewish prejudice as well as the more obvious antirepublicanism was involved. More documents on Carvallo that give a greater sense of his politics can be found in AAIU France I A 3; and Jewish Theological Seminary, Archive 77/Carvallo.

49. Jules Carvallo, "De la nécessité de former un congrès israélite," *UI* 6 (1851): 253–57.

50. François Furet, *Revolutionary France, 1770–1880*, trans. Antonia Nevill (Oxford: Blackwell, 1992), 381–83; Solomon Posener, *Adolphe Crémieux: A Biography*, trans. Eugene Golub (Philadelphia: Jewish Publication Society, 1940), 133–43.

51. Statuts de l'Alliance israélite universelle, *BAIU* (1860).

52. "Exposé," *BAIU* (1860): 16–17.

53. *BAIU* (July 1863): 1–5.

54. *BAIU* (July 1864): 17, 21.

55. *BAIU* (Second Semester 1871/First Semester 1872): 58–59.

56. *BAIU* (Second Semester 1867): 70.

57. Sewell, *Work and Revolution*, 212.

58. Iancu, "Adolphe Crémieux," 483–85.

59. On Napoleon III's interest in Romania after the Crimean War, see Paul Henry, "Napoleon III and the Balkans," in *Napoleon III and Europe*, ed. International Commission for the Teaching of History (Oxford: Pergamon, 1965), 41–65; William E. Echard, *Napoleon III and the Concert of Europe* (Baton Rouge: Louisiana State University Press, 1983), 58–91; and Pierre de la Gorce, *Histoire du Second Empire*, 5 vols. (New York: AMS, 1969), 1: 443–81.

60. Robert William Seton-Watson, *A History of the Roumanians: From Roman Times to the Completion of Unity* (Cambridge: Cambridge University Press, 1934), 220–68.

61. On the settlement of the Crimean War, see David Wetzel, *The Crimean War: A Diplomatic History* (Boulder, CO: East European Monographs, 1985).

62. In 1868, the Alliance sent Lévy to Bucharest as their correspondent. See his letter to Crémieux dated April 20, 1868, AAIU France IV A 19.

63. Carol Iancu, *Les Juifs de Roumanie (1866–1919): De l'exclusion à l'émancipation* (Aix-en-Provence: Editions de l'université de Provence, 1978), 57.

64. Armand Lévy, *Napoléon III et les principautés roumaines* (Paris: Dentu, 1858), 9–14.

65. Carol Iancu, *Jews in Romania, 1866–1919: From Exclusion to Emancipation*, trans. Carvel de Bussy (Boulder, CO: East European Monographs, 1996), 32–33.

66. This population statistic from 1860 is estimated by Leven, in *Cinquante ans d'histoire*, 1: 112; Leven himself notes that such statistics were notoriously inaccurate. Iancu, in contrast, cites a population figure (from the census) of under 130,000 for the same year. See *Jews in Romania*, 26.

67. On the definition of *native*, see Isidore Loeb, *La Situation des israélites en Turquie, en Serbie et en Roumanie* (Paris: Joseph Baer, 1877), 201–8.

68. Ibid., 208.

69. *BAIU* (Second Semester 1867): 9–13; *BAIU* (First Semester 1870): 11; *BAIU* (Second Semester 1870/First Semester 1871): 2.

70. These laws are reprinted in Loeb, *La Situation des israélites*, 111, 212–23.

71. Iancu, *The Jews in Romania*, 124–26.

72. AAIU Roumanie I C 1–3, and Roumanie II C 4–14; the earliest letter in this file is from 1861. On the Romanian committees, see Chouraqui, *Cent ans d'histoire*, 431.

73. *BAIU* (1861): 14.

74. *BAIU* (January 1862): 5, and *BAIU* (First Trimester 1864): 10–11.

75. *BAIU* (January 1866): 17.

76. See Leven, *Cinquante ans d'histoire*, 1: 172.

77. All of these letters were dated between April and August 1868. AAIU France V D 19.

78. And in keeping with his lifelong commitment to publicity, Crémieux reported on the situation in a letter to the readers of *Le Siècle* on July 28, 1866. See Leven, *Cinquante ans d'histoire*, 1: 116–17.

79. *BAIU* (Second Semester 1867): 5.

80. Crémieux to Picot, August 20, 1867, in AAIU Roumanie I C 1. The exchange is reprinted in large part in Iancu, "Adolphe Crémieux," 481–502.

81. The Italian Jews reported their argument to the Central Committee in their "Memorandum sur la traité de commerce de l'Italie avec la Roumanie" (1866), in AAIU I C 1.

82. *Discussion sur l'état des juifs en Roumanie à la Chambre des Lords et à la Chambre des Communes* (Paris: A. Chaix, 1867). See also *Correspondence Respecting the Condition and Treatment of the Jews of Servia and Roumania: 1867–76; Presented to the House of Commons by Command of Her Majesty, in Pursuance of Their Address Dated February 15, 1877* (London: Harrison and Sons, 1877).

83. Peixotto's appointment had been suggested by the wealthy American Jewish banker Joseph Seligman, a close friend of President Grant. This citation from Iancu, *The Jews in Romania*, 61–62. Fritz Stern claims that Peixotto's position as consul was unpaid; he does not mention how Peixotto supported himself. Fritz

Stern, *Gold and Iron: Bismarck, Bleichröder, and the Building of the German Empire*, 2nd ed. (New York: Vintage, 1979), 369.

84. On the role of Peixotto and other American Jews in the campaign, see Max J. Kohler and Simon Wolf, *Jewish Disabilities in the Balkan States: American Contributions Toward Their Removal, with Particular Reference to the Congress of Berlin* (New York: American Jewish Committee, 1916).

85. Peixotto to Crémieux, October 31, 1871, AAIU Roumanie I D 2. See also *BAIU* (Second Semester 1871/First Semester 1872): 76–77; the subfolder "Peixotto, 1872–1877," in AAIU Roumanie I C 2; and the letters in AAIU Roumanie I D 2.

86. Peixotto to the Central Committee, February 23, 1872, in AAIU Roumanie I D 2.

87. "Compte-rendu," *BAIU* (Second Semester 1872): 56.

88. "Procès-Verbal de la Conférence en faveur des israélites de Roumanie," in Jewish Theological Seminary of America, Archive 36/2/32.

89. Neumann, a member of the Berlin committee, made reference to this general boycott in a telegram to the Central Committee dated May 11, 1875, in AAIU Roumanie I D 1, and indicated that some were not observing it faithfully. In addition, Stern reports that Bleichröder himself continued to work on building railroads in Romania through the 1870s. See *Gold and Iron*, 360–69.

For a detailed description of the rising tide of antisemitism, and the local causes behind it, see Iancu, *The Jews in Romania*, 68–76. Loeb reprints much of the legislation and court rulings against the Jews in *Situation des israélites*, 228–54.

90. *BAIU* (Second Semester 1875): 6–9; see also *Les Conventions commerciales de la Roumanie devant le droit public européen* (Paris: Napoleon Chaix, 1878), 22; and Loeb, *Situation des israélites*, 186–87. On how Jewish Austro-Hungarian subjects were treated under the agreement, see *BAIU* (Second Semester 1876): 7–9.

91. Leven, *Cinquante ans d'histoire*, 1: 200–201.

92. The *mémoire* that the Central Committee sent to Berlin in 1878 included information and arguments similar to that included in the *mémoire* they sent to Constantinople in 1877. See *BAIU* (June 1878): 84–89. Both *mémoires* are reprinted in Carol Iancu, *Bleichröder et Crémieux: Le Combat pour l'émancipation des juifs de Roumanie devant le Congrès de Berlin; Correspondance inédite, 1878–1880* (Montpellier: Centre de recherches judaïques et hebraïques, Université Paul Valéry, 1987), 235–44. On Bleichröder's role, see Stern, *Gold and Iron*, 377–80.

93. *BAIU* (Second Semester 1876): 22.

94. Lucien Wolf, *Notes on the Diplomatic History of the Jewish Question, with Texts of Protocols, Treaty Stipulations and Other Public Acts and Official Documents* (London: Jewish Historical Society of England, 1919), 25–34.

95. Kohler and Wolf, *Jewish Disabilities in the Balkan States*, 66.

96. AIU Central Committee to Waddington, July 22, 1878, AN 369AP/2.

97. François Furet, *Revolutionary France, 1770–1880*, trans. Antonia Nevill (Oxford: Blackwell, 1992), 535.

98. "La Liberté des cultes en Turquie," *La Religion Laïque* 2, no. 24 (August 1878): 380. On Fauvety, see André Combes, *Histoire de la franc-maçonnerie au XIXe siècle* (Paris: Rocher, 1998), 405–6.

99. "La Solidarité sociale," *La Religion Laïque* 3, no. 27 (December 1878): 74.

100. Stern, *Gold and Iron*, 392.

101. A compelling examination of Bismarck's motivations as they evolved can be found in Stern, *Gold and Iron*, 377–93; on the demise of the campaign more broadly, see also Iancu, *The Jews in Romania*, 105–9, and *BAIU* (February 1879): 30–46.

102. Iancu, *The Jews in Romania*, 110–57.

103. Ascher to Loeb, in AAIU Roumanie II C 13; Veneziani folder in AAIU France VIII A 63.

Chapter 6. The Myth of Jewish Power

1. Edouard Drumont, *La France juive: Essai d'histoire contemporaine*, 2 vols. (Paris: Marpon and Flammarion, 1886), 2: 5.

2. Ibid., 2: 1–67; Stephen Wilson, *Ideology and Experience: Antisemitism in France at the Time of the Dreyfus Affair* (Rutherford, NJ: Fairleigh Dickinson University Press, 1982), 169–96; Frederick Busi, *The Pope of Antisemitism: The Career and Legacy of Edouard-Adolphe Drumont* (Lanham, MD: University Press of America, 1986); Robert F. Byrnes, *Anti-Semitism in Modern France*, 3 vols. (New Brunswick, NJ: Rutgers University Press, 1950), 1: 137–55.

3. On this myth in France, see especially Pierre Birnbaum, *Un Mythe politique: La "République juive" de Léon Blum à Pierre Mendès-France* (Paris: Gallimard, 1988).

4. On antisemitism, particularly in France, see Léon Poliakov, *Histoire de l'antisémitisme*, 2 vols. (Paris: Calmann-Lévy, 1981); Byrnes, *Anti-Semitism in Modern France*; Jacob Katz, *From Prejudice to Destruction: Anti-Semitism, 1700–1933* (Cambridge, MA: Harvard University Press, 1980); Wilson, *Ideology and Experience*; Michel Winock, *Nationalism, Anti-Semitism, and Fascism in Modern France*, trans. Jane Marie Todd (Stanford, CA: Stanford University Press, 1998); Zeev Sternhell, "The Roots of Popular Anti-Semitism in the Third Republic," in *The Jews in Modern France*, ed. Frances Malino and Bernard Wasserstein (Hanover, NH: University Press of New England, 1985), 103–34.

5. On the *Protocols*, see Norman Cohn, *Warrant for Genocide: The Myth of the Jewish World-Conspiracy and the Protocols of the Elders of Zion* (London: Eyre and Spottiswode, 1967); Stephen Eric Bronner, *A Rumor About the Jews: Antisemitism, Conspiracy, and the Protocols of Zion* (New York: Oxford, 2000).

6. Henri Gougenot des Mousseaux, *Le Juif, le judaïsme, et la judaïsation des peuples chrétiens* (Paris: Henri Plon, 1869), 268.

7. Ibid., 265–68.   8. Ibid., 333.

9. Ibid., 349.   10. Ibid., 417–53.

11. Poliakov, *Histoire de l'antisémitisme*, 2: 285.

12. Ibid., 2: 286–87. For more on the views of Pope Pius IX and Pope Leo XIII regarding the Freemasons and the Jews, see also Byrnes, *Anti-Semitism in Modern France*, 126–27.

13. Natalie Isser, *Antisemitism During the French Second Empire* (New York: Peter Lang, 1991), 118.

14. On Veuillot's anti-Jewish crusade and the consistory's response, see ibid., 27–47.

15. Letter from Colonel Max Cerfberr to Central Consistory, December 10, 1869, in BUAC I-11-a.

16. Undated notes by Joseph Cohen [December 1869], in ibid.

17. For his own account of these acts, see Adolphe Crémieux, *Gouvernement de la Défense nationale: Actes de la Délégation à Tours et à Bordeaux* (Tours: Ernest Mazereau, 1871). For more on how Jewish emancipation was part of a larger reorganization of Algeria, see Miriam Hoexter, "Les Juifs français et l'assimilation politique et institutionnelle de la communauté juive en Algérie (1830–1870)" (paper presented at the conference Les Relations intercommunautaires juives en méditerranée occidentale, XIIIe–XXe siècles, Abbaye de Sénaque, 1982), 154–61.

18. Claude Martin, *La Commune d'Alger (1870–1871)* (Paris: Héraklès, 1936).

19. *Le Radical algérien*, December 7, 1885, as cited in "Affaires algériennes," *AIF* 46 (1885): 406.

20. These statistics from Claude Martin, *Les Israélites algériens de 1830 à 1902* (Paris: Héraklès, 1936), 193; Charles-Robert Ageron, *Les Algériens musulmans et la France (1871–1919)*, 2 vols. (Paris: Presses Universitaires de France, 1968), 1: 585; Wilson, *Ideology and Experience*, 231. For statistics on population by ethnicity, see Michel Ansky, *Les Juifs d'Algérie du décret Crémieux à la libération* (Paris: Editions du Centre, 1950), 46–47.

21. Geneviève Dermenjian, *La Crise anti-juive oranaise (1895–1905): L'Antisémitisme dans l'Algérie coloniale* (Paris: L'Harmattan, 1986), 21.

22. This statistic based on the figure provided in Paula Hyman, *The Jews of Modern France* (Berkeley and Los Angeles: University of California Press, 1998), 92.

23. Dermenjian, *La Crise anti-juive*, 33–38; Elizabeth Friedman, *Colonialism and After: An Algerian Jewish Community*, Critical Studies in Work and Community (South Hadley, MA: Bergin and Garvey, 1988), 17–18; Martin, *Les Israélites algériens*, 193.

24. Ageron, *Les Algériens musulmans*, 1: 585.

25. On elections and the *anti-juif* movement, see Martin, *Les Israélites algériens*, passim; Zosa Szajkowski, "Socialists and Radicals in the Development of Antisemitism in Algeria (1884–1900)," *Jewish Social Studies* 10 (1948): 257–80; Ageron, *Les Algériens musulmans*, 1: 583–94; Dermenjian, *La Crise anti-juive*, 33–38.

26. This citation from Charles-Robert Ageron, *Modern Algeria: A History from 1830 to the Present*, trans. Michael Brett (London: Hurst, 1991), 63.

27. Ageron, *Les Algériens musulmans*, 1: 3–36.

28. The commission, called the Commission d'enquête sue les actes du Gouvernement de la Défense nationale en Algérie, presented its report in 1874. The report's author was Léon de la Sicotière. This section from the parts of the report reprinted in "Questions algériennes," *AIF* 35 (1874): 459.

29. Charles du Bouzet, *Les Israélites indigènes de l'Algérie: Pétition à l'Assemblée nationale contre le décret du 24 octobre 1870* (Paris: Schiller, 1871). On the question of whether the decree caused the Arab revolt, see Louis Forest, *La Naturalisation des juifs algériens et l'insurrection de 1871: Etude historique* (Paris: Société française d'imprimerie et de librairie [1897]).

30. Adolphe Crémieux, *Réfutation de l'exposé des motifs du projet de loi déposé le 21 juillet 1871 et portant abrogation du décret de la Délégation de Tours, en date du 24 octobre 1870* (Paris: Schiller, 1871); Adolphe Crémieux, *Réfutation de la pétition de M. du Bouzet* (Paris: Schiller, 1871); Solomon Posener, *Adolphe Crémieux, 1796–1880*, 2 vols. (Paris: Félix Alcan, 1934), 1: 235–40.

31. Crémieux, *Gouvernement de la Défense nationale*, pt. 1, 78.

32. "Questions algériennes," AIF 35 (1874): 339–40. He made the same argument in *Gouvernement de la Défense nationale*, pt. 1, 70.

33. "Annexe à la séance du 16 août 1871: Note sur le projet de loi relatif à la naturalisation des israélites indigènes de l'Algérie," *Procès-verbaux du Consistoire central*, Archives du Consistoire Central, IE6.

34. Richard Ayoun, *Typologie d'une carrière rabbinique: L'Exemple de Mahir Charleville*, 2 vols. (Nancy: Presses Universitaires de Nancy, 1993), 1: 239.

35. The works include J.C.F. [J. Casimir Frégier], *La Question juive en Algérie; ou, De la naturalisation des juifs algériens par un algérien progressiste, membre de la société historique algérienne* (Algiers: Bouyer, 1860); Jules Delsieux, *Essai sur la naturalisation collective des israélites indigènes* (Alger: Duclaux, 1860); E. Darbon, *De la situation des israélites indigènes quant à leur état civil* (Alger: Bastide, 1862); and J. E. Sartor, *De la condition juridique des étrangers, des musulmans et des israélites en Algérie: Suivie d'une traité sur la naturalisation en France et en Algérie* (Oran: Alessi, 1869). For an analysis of these works and their effect, see Jacques Cohen, *Les Israélites d'Algérie et le décret Crémieux* (Paris: Arthur Rousseau, 1900), 87–112.

36. Richard Ayoun has published a list of their names and birthplaces, and reports that most authors have counted only 152 naturalizations in this period. Among these, the vast majority were born in Morocco. See Ayoun, *Typologie d'une carrière rabbinique*, 2: 755–60. This number is far less than the 247 naturalizations that Charleville, as chief rabbi of Oran, reported at the time. Of these 247, Charleville reported 135 "indigènes" (who may well have been Moroccan-born—Charleville does not report their birth places) and 112 "étrangers." See Charleville to the Central Consistory, November 16, 1869, Archives du Consistoire de Paris, Icc 37, liasse 2, Consistoire d'Alger, 1865–69.

37. Ageron, *Les Algériens musulmans*, 1: 14–15. See also the deliberations of the Conseil du Gouvernement on this effects of the *sénatus-consulte* the late 1860s in Archives Nationales, Centre des Archives d'Outre-Mer, F80 1722.

38. "Questions algériennes," *AIF* 35 (1874): 338.

39. On left-wing anti-Judaism in France in the 1840s, see Katz, *Prejudice to Destruction*, 119–38; Byrnes, *Anti-Semitism in Modern France*, 115–25. Socialist writers who attacked Jewish banking as a form of "financial feudalism" include Leroux, Proudhon, Marx, and the Fourierist Alphonse Toussenel. The Jewish leadership, however, was far more concerned with the politically potent anti-Judaism of Veuillot. For a discussion anticapitalism and anti-Judaism in a later period, see Pierre Birnbaum, *Le Peuple et le gros: Histoire d'un mythe* (Paris: Grasset, 1979); Birnbaum, "Antisemitism and Anticapitalism in Modern France," in *The Jews of Modern France*, ed. Frances Malino and Bernard Wasserstein (Hanover, NH: Brandeis University Press, 1985), 214–23.

40. Friedman, *Colonialism and After*, 17; Dermenjian, *La Crise anti-juive*, 45–51 and passim.

41. From *Nouvelle Algérie* (May 12, 1887), as cited in "Liberté illimitée de la presse," *AIF* 48 (1887): 155.

42. As cited in "Affaires algériennes," *AIF* 44 (1883): 83.

43. *Courrier d'Oran*, January 22, 1881, as cited in "Affaires algériennes," *AIF* 42 (1881): 38.

44. From *Nouvelle Algérie* (May 12, 1887), as cited in "Liberté illimitée de la presse." For other interesting examples of this, see Georges Meynié, *Les Juifs en Algérie*, 2nd ed. (Paris: Nouvelle librairie parisienne, 1888); Emile Roger, *Nécessité de reviser le décret Crémieux* (Oran: n.p., 1882). Incidentally, Etienne, an Opportunist deputy representing Oran, was not Jewish.

45. Ageron, *Les Algériens musulmans*, 1: 585.

46. Drumont, *La France Juive*, 2: 47.

47. Hippolyte Prague, "Polémique: Un Nouveau Journal: L'Anti-Juif," *AIF* 42 (1881): 427.

48. "Chronique de la semaine," *AIF* 47 (1882): 387–88.

49. Byrnes, *Anti-Semitism in Modern France*, 135.

50. Poliakov, *Histoire de l'antisémitisme*, 2: 295.

51. Byrnes, *Anti-Semitism in Modern France*, 130–36.

52. Ibid., 137.

53. Ibid., 149–55; Busi, *Pope of Antisemitism*, 55–60.

54. Busi, *Pope of Antisemitism*, 56; Byrnes, *Anti-Semitism in Modern France*, 146–47.

55. "Politique et religion," *AIF* 34 (1873): 394–95.

56. Byrnes, *Anti-Semitism in Modern France*, 182.

57. Drumont, *La France juive*, 1: 5, 7.   58. Ibid., 5.

59. Ibid., 20.

60. Ibid., 520, 4.

61. Ibid., 389.

62. Ibid., 399.

63. As cited in "Chronique," *AIF* 37 (1876): 69.

64. Drumont, *La France juive*, 1: 420–25, 33.

65. "Le Manifeste des étudiants à Bucharest," *AIF* 36 (1875): 589.

66. Drumont, *La France juive*, 1: 454–55. The emphasis is Drumont's.

67. *AIF* 47 (1886): 269.

68. Pierre Birnbaum, *The Anti-Semitic Moment: A Tour of France in 1898*, trans. Jane Marie Todd (New York: Hill and Wang, 2003).

69. Byrnes, *Anti-Semitism in Modern France*, 332.

70. Busi, *Pope of Antisemitism*, 145.

71. Sternhell, "Roots of Popular Anti-Semitism."

72. Drumont, *La France juive*, 1: 563.

73. Birnbaum, *Un Mythe politique*, 31 and passim.

74. Drumont, *La France juive*, 2: 5.

75. Cohn, *Warrant for Genocide*, 111.

76. Including Byrnes, *Anti-Semitism in Modern France*, 140; Hannah Arendt, *The Origins of Totalitarianism* (New York: Harcourt Brace Jovanovich, 1951), 118; Michael Marrus, *The Politics of Assimilation: The French Jewish Community at the Time of the Dreyfus Affair* (Oxford: Clarendon, 1971), 196–242.

77. Birnbaum, *Anti-Semitic Moment*, 315–31; Hyman, *The Jews of Modern France*, 108–10.

78. Michael Graetz, *The Jews in Nineteenth-Century France: From the French Revolution to the Alliance Israélite Universelle*, trans. Jane Marie Todd (Stanford, CA: Stanford University Press, 1996), 287–88.

Conclusion

1. For one example of this perspective see Michael Marrus, *The Politics of Assimilation: The French Jewish Community at the Time of the Dreyfus Affair* (Oxford: Clarendon, 1971), 115. Marrus refers to Franco-Jewish identity as an "unstable doctrine," because "in seeking the identity of the Jewish spirit with the spirit of France, it seemed to be seeking the effacement of Judaism itself."

2. Michel Abitbol, "The Encounter Between French Jewry and the Jews of North Africa: Analysis of a Discourse, 1830–1914," in *The Jews of Modern France*, ed. Frances Malino and Bernard Wasserstein (Hanover, NH: Brandeis University Press, 1985), 31–53; Jay Berkovitz, *The Shaping of Jewish Identity in Nineteenth-Century France* (Detroit: Wayne State University Press, 1989), 230–46; Michael Graetz, *The Jews in Nineteenth-Century France: From the French Revolution to the Alliance Israélite Universelle*, trans. Jane Marie Todd (Stanford, CA: Stanford University Press, 1996), 249–88; Aron Rodrigue, *French Jews, Turkish Jews: The Alliance Israélite Uni-*

verselle and the Politics of Jewish Schooling in Turkey, 1860–1925 (Bloomington: Indiana University Press, 1990).

3. Zadoc Kahn, "L'Alliance israélite, Pourim 5645, le premier mars 1885," in *Sermons et allocutions*, 2nd ed., 1st ser. (Paris: A. Durlacher, 1893), 222–23.

4. Pierre Birnbaum, *The Jews of the Republic: A Political History of State Jews in France from Gambetta to Vichy*, trans. Jane Marie Todd (Stanford, CA: Stanford University Press, 1996).

Bibliography

Archival Collections

ARCHIVES OF THE ALLIANCE ISRAÉLITE UNIVERSELLE, PARIS

France A series	Dossiers des fondateurs
France B series	Comités locaux
France D series	Politique extérieure
Roumanie C series	Situation intérieure des juifs de Roumanie

ARCHIVES DE LA BIBLIOTHÈQUE DE L'ARSENAL, PARIS

Fonds d'Eichthal, correspondence and journal

ARCHIVES DU CONSISTOIRE CENTRAL, PARIS

A series	Actes constitutifs
B series	Procès-Verbaux
C series	Administration générale
E series	Consistoires départementaux
2E series	Algérie
3E series	Consistoire central: Affaires politiques et procédure
M series	Affaires étrangères

ARCHIVES NATIONALES, PARIS

F14 2187	Ponts et Chausées, Jules Carvallo
F19 11000–11060	Culte israélite
369/AP	Papiers Crémieux

ARCHIVES NATIONALES, CENTRE DES ARCHIVES D'OUTRE MER,
AIX-EN-PROVENCE

| F80 1615, F80 1631, F80 1675, F80 1722, F80 1748 | Algérie, fonds ministériels |

Oran prefecture, series 3U   Culte israélite, Oran
E and EE series   Archives du gouverneur général
                                    de l'Algérie, Correspondance politique

BRANDEIS UNIVERSITY ARCHIVES, WALTHAM, MASSACHUSETTS
Consistoire Collection

CENTRAL ARCHIVES FOR THE HISTORY
OF THE JEWISH PEOPLE, JERUSALEM

AL2357   Algeria
F series   miscellaneous records of French Jewry
FCAv, FCBo, FCBR,   records of consistories of Avignon, Bordeaux,
FCMar, FCMe, FCPa series   Bas-Rhin, Marseilles, Metz, and Paris
FCC series   letters received by Central Consistory
HM1053–62   Microfilm copy of the correspondence of the
                                    Central Consistory, 1810–70

CONSISTOIRE DE PARIS, PARIS

Icc 37–42   Consistoires, Algérie

FONDATION THIERS, PARIS

Fonds d'Eichthal, correspondence and clippings

HOUGHTON LIBRARY, HARVARD UNIVERSITY,
CAMBRIDGE, MASSACHUSETTS

Harvard bMs Judaica 40   Correspondence of Isaac-Jacques Altaras
                                    and Joseph Cohen

JEWISH THEOLOGICAL SEMINARY OF AMERICA, NEW YORK

Archive 36   French Jewish Communities Record Group
Archive 8   Algerian Consistory Records
Archive 27   Central Consistory Correspondence
Archive 77   Eugène Manuel Papers

KLAU LIBRARY, HEBREW UNION COLLEGE, CINCINNATI, OHIO

French Miscellany Collection
Sephardic Jews of Bordeaux Collection
Consistoire central des israélites de France Collection

Journals

Les Archives Israélites de France
Bulletin de l'Alliance Israélite Universelle
La Famille de Jacob
L'Israélite Français
Le Lien d'Israël
La Régénération
La Religion Laïque
La Revue Israélite
L'Univers Israélite

Other Works

Abitbol, Michel. "The Encounter Between French Jewry and the Jews of North Africa: Analysis of a Discourse, 1830–1914." In *The Jews of Modern France*, ed. Frances Malino and Bernard Wasserstein, 31–53. Hanover, NH: Brandeis University Press, 1985.

Aftalion, Florin. *L'Economie de la Révolution française*. Paris: Hachette, 1987.

Ageron, Charles-Robert. *Les Algériens musulmans et la France (1871–1919)*. 2 vols. Paris: Presses Universitaires de France, 1968.

———. *Modern Algeria: A History from 1830 to the Present*. Trans. Michael Brett. London: Hurst, 1991.

Agulhon, Maurice. *The Republican Experiment, 1848–1852*. Trans. Janet Lloyd. Cambridge: Cambridge University Press, 1983.

Albert, Phyllis Cohen. "Ethnicity and Jewish Solidarity in Nineteenth-Century France." In *Mystics, Philosophers, and Politicians: Essays in Jewish Intellectual History in Honor of Alexander Altmann*, ed. Jehuda Reinharz and Daniel Swetschinski, 249–74. Durham, NC: Duke University Press, 1982.

———. *The Jewish Oath in Nineteenth-Century France*. Spiegel Lectures in Modern Jewish History. Tel Aviv: Tel Aviv University Press, 1982.

———. *The Modernization of French Jewry: Consistory and Community in the Nineteenth Century*. Hanover, NH: Brandeis University Press, 1977.

———. "Nonorthodox Attitudes in Nineteenth-Century Judaism." In *Essays in Modern Jewish History*, ed. Frances Malino and Phyllis Cohen Albert, 121–41. New York: Herzl Press, 1982.

Albrecht-Carrié, René. *A Diplomatic History of Europe Since the Congress of Vienna*. New York: Harper, 1958.

Altaras, Isaac-Jacques, and Joseph Cohen. "Rapport sur l'état moral et politique des israélites de l'Algérie et des moyens de l'améliorer." In *Les Juifs d'Algérie et la France (1830–1855)*, by Simon Schwarzfuchs, 67–201. Jerusalem: Institut Ben Zvi, 1981.

Ambelain, Robert. *La Franc-maçonnerie oubliée (1352–1688–1720)*. Paris: Robert Laffont, 1985.

Amson, Daniel. *Adolphe Crémieux, l'oublié de la gloire*. Paris: Seuil, 1988.

Anchel, Robert. *Napoléon et les juifs*. Paris: Presses Universitaires de France, 1928.

Ansky, Michel. *Les Juifs d'Algérie du décret Crémieux à la libération*. Paris: Editions du Centre, 1950.

Archives parlementaires de 1787 à 1860, recueil complet des débats législatifs et politques des chambres françaises. Première série (1787–99). Ed. Jérôme Mavidal. Paris: P. Dupont, 1867–1913.

Arendt, Hannah. *The Origins of Totalitarianism*. New York: Harcourt Brace Jovanovich, 1951.

Aston, Nigel. *Religion and Revolution in France, 1780–1804*. Washington, DC: Catholic University of America Press, 2000.

Attal, Robert. "Le Consistoire de France et les juifs d'Algérie: Lettre pastorale du Rabbin Isidor (1873)." *Michael* 5 (1978): 9–16.

Aycard, M. *Histoire du Crédit Mobilier, 1852–1867*. Paris: Librairie internationale, 1867.

Ayoun, Richard. "Les Efforts d'assimilation intellectuelle et l'émancipation législative des juifs d'Algérie." Paper presented at the conference Cultures juives méditerranéennes et orientales, Paris, 1982.

———. "La Naturalisation individuelle des juifs d'Algérie." *Hamevasser—Le Messager: Bulletin d'information de l'union libérale israélite de France*, no. 70 (1984): 10–11.

———. *Typologie d'une carrière rabbinique: L'Exemple de Mahir Charleville*. 2 vols. Nancy: Presses Universitaires de Nancy, 1993.

———, ed. *Les Juifs de France: De l'émancipation à l'intégration, 1787–1812*. Paris: L'Harmattan, 1997.

Ayoun, Richard, and Bernard Cohen. *Les Juifs d'Algérie: Deux mille ans d'histoire*. Paris: Lattès, 1982.

Azan, Paul, ed. *Par l'épée et par la charrue: écrits et discours de Bugeaud*. Paris: Presses Universitaires de France, 1948.

Badinter, Robert. *Libres et égaux: L'Emancipation des juifs, 1789–1791*. Paris: Fayard, 1989.

Bail, Charles-Joseph. *Des juifs au dix-neuvième siècle; ou, Considérations sur leur état civil et politique en Europe, suivies de la notice biographique des juifs anciens et modernes, qui se sont illustrés dans les sciences et les arts*. Paris: Treuttel et Wurtz, 1816.

Bakunin, Jack. *Pierre Leroux and the Birth of Democratic Socialism, 1797–1848*. New York: Revisionist Press, 1976.

Balibar, Etienne. *Les Frontières de la démocratie*. Paris: Découverte, 1992.

Balzac, Honoré de. *César Birotteau*. Trans. Robin Buss. New York: Penguin, 1994.

———. *The Firm of Nucingen*. Trans. James Waring: Gutenberg e-book, 1998.

——. *Gobseck*. Paris: Flammarion, 1984.

——. *A Harlot High and Low*. Trans. Rayner Heppenstall. New York: Penguin, 1970.

——. *Lost Illusions*. Trans. Kathleen Raine. New York: Modern Library, 1997.

Barrot, Odilon. *Mémoires posthumes d'Odilon Barrot*. 2nd ed. Paris: Charpentier, 1875.

Barzun, Jacques. *The French Race: Theories of Its Origins and Their Social and Political Implications Prior to the Revolution*. 2nd ed. Port Washington, NY: Kennikat, 1962.

Baumgart, Winfried. *The Crimean War, 1853–1856*. London: Arnold, 1999.

——. *The Peace of Paris 1856: Studies in War, Diplomacy, and Peacemaking*. Trans. Ann Pottinger Saab. Santa Barbara, CA: ABC-Clio, 1981.

Beltran, Alain, and Pascal Griset. *La Croissance économique de la France, 1815–1914*. Paris: Armand Colin, 1988.

Benbassa, Esther. *Histoire des juifs de France*. Paris: Seuil, 1997.

Bénéton, Philippe. *Histoire des mots: Culture et civilisation*. Paris: Presses de la Fondation nationale des sciences politiques, 1975.

Bensimon-Donath, Doris. *Socio-démographie des juifs de France et d'Algérie*. Paris: ALC, 1976.

Berenson, Edward. "A New Religion of the Left: Christianity and Social Radicalism in France, 1815–1848." In *The French Revolution and the Creation of Modern Political Culture*, ed. François Furet and Mona Ozouf, vol. 3, *The Transformation of Political Culture, 1789–1848*, 543–60. Oxford: Pergamon, 1989.

——. *Populist Religion and Left-Wing Politics in France, 1830–1852*. Princeton, NJ: Princeton University Press, 1984.

Bergeron, Louis. *Banquiers, négociants et manufacturiers parisiens du directoire à l'Empire*. Paris: Ecole des hautes études en sciences sociales, 1978.

——. *France Under Napoleon*. Princeton, NJ: Princeton University Press, 1981.

Berkovitz, Jay. *Rites and Passages: The Beginnings of Modern Jewish Culture in France*. Philadelphia: University of Pennsylvania Press, 2004.

——. *The Shaping of Jewish Identity in Nineteenth-Century France*. Detroit: Wayne State University Press, 1989.

Berr, Berr Isaac. *Lettre d'un Citoyen, membre de la ci-devant communauté des Juifs de Lorraine, à ses confrères, à l'occasion du droit de citoyen actif, rendu aux Juifs par le décret du 28 [sic] septembre 1791*. Nancy: Haener, 1791.

——. *Lettre du Sieur Berr-Isaac-Berr, Négociant à Nancy, Juif, naturalisé en vertu des Lettres-patentes du Roi, enregistrées au Parlement de Nancy, Député des juifs de la Lorraine; à Monseigneur l'Evêque de Nancy, Député à l'Assemblée nationale*. N.p., 1790.

——. *Réflexions sur la régénération complète des Juifs en France*. Paris: Giguet and Michaud, 1806.

Berr, Michel. *Appel à la justice des nations et des rois, ou adresse d'un citoyen français au Congrès qui devait avoir lieu à Lunéville, au nom de tous les habitans de l'Europe qui professent la religion juive*. Strasbourg: Levrault, 1801.

———. *Lettre sur divers intérêts moraux et philosophiques, au rédacteur du journal de la Meurthe*. Nancy: Grimblot, 1834.

———. *Lettre sur les israélites et le judaïsme au directeur du Panorama des nouveautés parisiennes*. Paris: n.p., 1825.

———. *Lettre au rédacteur du progresseur sur la loi d'élection municipale en rapport avec le culte israélite, avec des notes sur les Pays-Bas, la peine de mort, le duel, etc.* Paris: Delaforest, 1829.

———. "Sur la liberté des cultes." *Mercure de France*, September 1814.

Berr-Bing, Isaiah. *Lettre du sieur I.B.B. Juif de Metz à l'auteur anonyme d'un écrit intitulé: Le cri d'un citoyen contre les juifs*. Metz: Collignon, 1787.

Berr-Bing, Isaiah, Mayer-Cahen Goudchau[x], and Louis Wolff. *Mémoire particulier pour la communauté des Juifs établis à Metz*. N.d.

Bertocci, Philip A. *Jules Simon: Republican Anticlericalism and Cultural Politics in France, 1848–1886*. Columbia: University of Missouri Press, 1978.

Betts, Raymond. *Assimilation and Association in French Colonial Theory, 1890–1914*. New York: Columbia University Press, 1961.

Birnbaum, Pierre. *The Anti-Semitic Moment: A Tour of France in 1898*. Trans. Jane Marie Todd. New York: Hill and Wang, 2003.

———. "Anti-Semitism and Anticapitalism in Modern France." In *The Jews of Modern France*, ed. Frances Malino and Bernard Wasserstein, 214–23. Hanover, NH: Brandeis University Press, 1985.

———. *The Jews of the Republic: A Political History of State Jews in France from Gambetta to Vichy*. Trans. Jane Marie Todd. Stanford, CA: Stanford University Press, 1996.

———. *Un Mythe politique: La "République juive" de Léon Blum à Pierre Mendès-France*. Paris: Gallimard, 1988.

———. *Le Peuple et le gros: Histoire d'un mythe*. Paris: Grasset, 1979.

———, ed. *Histoire politique des juifs en France: Entre universalisme et particularisme*. Paris: Presses de la Fondation nationale des sciences politiques, 1990.

Birnbaum, Pierre, and Ira Katznelson, eds. *Paths of Emancipation: Jews, States, Citizenship*. Princeton, NJ: Princeton University Press, 1995.

Bischoff, Chantal. *Geneviève Straus, 1849–1926: Trilogie d'une égérie*. Paris: Balland, 1992.

Bloch, Isaac. *Centenaire de la Révolution française: Service commémoratif célébré à la grande synagogue d'Alger*. Algiers: Imprimerie de l'association ouvrière, 1889.

———. *L'Isolement d'Israël: Sermon prononcé à la grande synagogue le samedi 12 septembre 1885*. Algiers: Michel Ruff, 1885.

Bloch, Simon. *La Foi d'Israël: Ses Dogmes, son culte, ses cérémonies et pratiques religieuses, sa loi morale et sociale, sa mission et son avenir*. Paris: n.p., 1859.

———. *Le Judaïsme et le socialisme*. Paris: n.p., 1850.

Bobango, Gerald J. *The Emergence of the Romanian National State*. Boulder, CO: East European Monographs, 1979.

Bois, Jean-Pierre. *Bugeaud*. Paris: Fayard, 1997.

Bouche, Denise. *Histoire de la colonisation française*. 2 vols. Paris: Fayard, 1991.

Boudon, Jacques-Olivier. *Napoléon et les cultes: Les Religions en Europe à l'aube du XIXe siècle*. Paris: Fayard, 2002.

Bourgeois, Emile, and E. Clermont. *Rome et Napoléon III (1849–1870): Etude sur les origines et la chute du Second Empire*. Paris: Armand Colin, 1907.

Bouzet, Charles du. *Les Israélites indigènes de l'Algérie: Pétition à l'Assemblée nationale contre le décret du 24 octobre 1870*. Paris: Schiller, 1871.

Bowman, Frank Paul. *French Romanticism: Intertextual and Interdisciplinary Readings*. Baltimore: Johns Hopkins University Press, 1990.

Boyarin, Daniel, and Jonathan Boyarin. "Diaspora: Generation and the Ground of Jewish Identity." *Critical Inquiry* 19, no. 4 (1993): 693–725.

Broers, Michael. "The First Napoleonic Regime, 1799–1815: The Origins of the Patriotic Right or the Zenith of Jacobinism?" In *The Right in France, 1789–1997*, ed. Nicholas Atkin and Frank Tallet, 19–34. London: Tauris, 1998.

Broglie, Albert de. "De la politique étrangère de la France depuis la Révolution de Février." *Revue des Deux Mondes* 23, no. 3 (1848): 293–321.

Bronner, Stephen Eric. *A Rumor About the Jews: Antisemitism, Conspiracy, and the Protocols of Zion*. New York: Oxford University Press, 2000.

Brooks, Peter. "An Oedipal Crisis." In *A New History of French Literature*, ed. Denis Hollier, 649–56. Cambridge, MA: Harvard University Press, 1989.

Brownstein, Rachel M. *Tragic Muse: Rachel of the Comédie-Française*. New York: Knopf, 1993.

Brubaker, Rogers. *Citizenship and Nationhood in France and Germany*. Cambridge, MA: Harvard University Press, 1992.

Brunschwig, Henri. *French Colonialism, 1871–1914: Myths and Realities*. New York: Praeger, 1964.

Buchez, Philippe-Joseph-Benjamin, and Pierre Célestin Roux-Lavergne. *Histoire parlementaire de la Révolution française*. 40 vols. Paris: Paulin, 1834–38.

Bugeaud, Thomas-Robert. "Note sur notre établissement dans la province d'Oran par suite de la paix" (1837). In *Par l'épée et par la charrue: écrits et discours de Bugeaud*, ed. Paul Azan. Paris: Presses Universitaires de France, 1948.

Bury, J. P. T., and R. P. Tombs. *Thiers, 1797–1877: A Political Life*. London: Allen and Unwin, 1986.

Busi, Frederick. *The Pope of Antisemitism: The Career and Legacy of Edouard-Adolphe Drumont*. Lanham, MD: University Press of America, 1986.

Byrnes, Robert F. *Anti-Semitism in Modern France*. Vol. 1 of 3. New Brunswick, NJ: Rutgers University Press, 1950.

Cahen, Abraham. *Consistoire israélite de Constantine: Lettre pastorale adressée aux fidèles de la circonscription.* Constantine: Arnolet, 1870.

Cahen, Lazare. "Rapport sur la situation des israélites de la province d'Oran" (1850). In *Les Juifs d'Algérie et la France (1830–1855)*, by Simon Schwarzfuchs, 203–41. Jerusalem: Institut Ben Zvi, 1981.

Calman, Alvin R. *Ledru-Rollin and the Second French Republic.* New York: Columbia University Press, 1922.

Cameron, Rondo. *France and the Economic Development of Europe, 1800–1914: Conquest of Peace and Seeds of War.* 2nd ed. Chicago: Rand McNally, 1961.

Carlisle, Robert B. *The Proffered Crown: Saint-Simonianism and the Doctrine of Hope.* Baltimore: Johns Hopkins University Press, 1987.

Carrithers, David W. "Montesquieu and the Spirit of French Finance: An Analysis of His *Mémoire sur les dettes de l'état* (1715)." In *Montesquieu and the Spirit of Modernity*, ed. David W. Carrithers and Patrick Coleman, 159–90. Oxford: Voltaire Foundation, 2002.

Castille, Hyppolite. *Les Frères Pereire.* Paris: n.p., 1861.

Cavignac, Jean. *Dictionnaire du judaïsme bordelais aux XVIIIe et XIXe siècles: Biographies, généalogies, professions, institutions.* Bordeaux: Archives départementales de la Gironde, 1987.

——. *Les Israélites bordelais de 1780 à 1850: Autour de l'émancipation.* Paris: Publisud, 1991.

Cesarani, David, ed. *The Making of Modern Anglo-Jewry.* Oxford: Blackwell, 1990.

Charléty, Sébastien. *Histoire du saint-simonisme (1825–1864).* 2nd ed. Paris: Paul Hartmann, 1931.

Charlton, D. G. *The French Romantics.* Vol. 1 of 2. Cambridge: Cambridge University Press, 1984.

Chevalier, Michel. "Système de la Méditerranée." *Le Globe*, January 20, 1832.

Chouraqui, André. *Between East and West: A History of Jews of North Africa.* Philadelphia: Jewish Publication Society, 1968.

——. *Cent ans d'histoire: L'Alliance Israélite Universelle et la renaissance juive contemporaine; 1860–1960.* Paris: Presses Universitaires de France, 1965.

Churchill, Colonel Charles Henry. *The Druzes and the Maronites Under the Turkish Rule, from 1840 to 1860.* London: Bernard Quaritch, 1862. Reprint, Reading, UK: Garnet, 1994.

Code civil des français. Paris: Imprimerie de la République, 1804.

Cohen, David. "La Promotion des juifs à l'époque du Second Empire, 1852–1870." 2 vols. Doctoral diss., Université de Provence, 1980.

Cohen, Jacques. *Les Israélites d'Algérie et le décret Crémieux.* Paris: Arthur Rousseau, 1900.

Cohn, Norman. *Warrant for Genocide: The Myth of the Jewish World-Conspiracy and the Protocols of the Elders of Zion.* London: Eyre and Spottiswode, 1967.

Collingham, H. A. C., and R. S. Alexander. *The July Monarchy: A Political History of France, 1830–1848*. London: Longman, 1988.

Cologna, Abraham de. *Lettre pastorale adressée par le Consistoire central des israélites de France dans la circonscription desquels il se trouve un ou plusieurs des départemens qui viennent d'être affranchis du décret du 17 mars 1808*. Paris: Sétier, 1818.

Combes, André. *Histoire de la franc-maçonnerie au XIXe siècle*. Paris: Rocher, 1998.

Comte, Auguste. *Catéchisme positive*. Paris: Garnier, 1909.

Conklin, Alice. *A Mission to Civilize: The Republican Idea of Empire in France and West Africa, 1895–1930*. Stanford, CA: Stanford University Press, 1997.

Les Conventions commerciales de la Roumanie devant le droit public européen. Paris: Napoleon Chaix, 1878.

Correspondence Respecting the Condition and Treatment of the Jews of Servia and Roumania: 1867–76; Presented to the House of Commons by Command of Her Majesty, in Pursuance of Their Address Dated February 15, 1877. London: Harrison and Sons, 1877.

Craiutu, Aurelian. *Liberalism Under Siege: The Political Thought of the French Doctrinaires*. Lanham, MD: Lexington, 2003.

Crémieux, Adolphe. *En 1848: Discours et lettres*. Paris: Calmann-Lévy, 1883.

———. *Gouvernement de la Défense nationale: Actes de la Délégation à Tours et à Bordeaux*. Tours: Ernest Mazereau, 1871.

———. *Liberté! Plaidoyers et discours politiques*. Paris: Pichon-Lamy et Dewez, 1869.

———. *Plaidoyer sur cette question: Le Juif français doit-il être soumis à prêter le serment more judaïco?* Nîmes: Gaude, 1827.

———. *Réfutation de l'exposé des motifs du projet de loi déposé le 21 juillet 1871 et portant abrogation du décret de la Délégation de Tours, en date du 24 octobre 1870*. Paris: Schiller, 1871.

———. *Réfutation de la pétition de M. du Bouzet*. Paris: Schiller, 1871.

———. *Second plaidoyer sur cette question: Le Juif français doit-il être soumis à prêter le serment more judaïco?* Nîmes: Gaude, 1827.

Crossley, Ceri. *French Historians and Romanticism: Thierry, Guizot, the Saint-Simonians, Quinet, Michelet*. London: Routledge, 1993.

Dainwaell, Georges. *Histoire édifiante et curieuse de Rothschild Ier, roi des juifs*. Paris, 1846.

Dansette, Adrien. *Histoire religieuse de la France contemporaine: L'Eglise catholique dans la mêlée politique et sociale*. Paris: Flammarion, 1965.

Darbon, E. *De la situation des israélites indigènes quant à leur état civil*. Alger: Bastide, 1862.

Darmesteter, James. "Joseph Salvador." *Annuaire de la Société des Etudes Juives* I (1881).

———. *Les Prophètes d'Israël*. Paris: Calmann-Lévy, 1892.

Darracq, François Balthazar, Corps Législatif, Conseil des Cinq-Cents, Séance du 18 floréal an VII. *Opinion de Darracq dans l'affaire des juifs de Bordeaux*. Paris: Imprimerie nationale, an VII (1799).

David, Marcel. *Le Printemps de la fraternité: Genèse et vicissitudes, 1830–1851*. Paris: Aubier, 1992.

Debré, Moses. *The Image of the Jew in French Literature from 1800 to 1908*. Trans. Gertrude Hirschler. New York: Ktav, 1970.

Deloye, Yves. "Citoyenneté et sens civique dans l'Algérie coloniale: L'Emancipation politique de la minorité juive au XIXème siècle." DEA, Université de Paris 1, 1987.

———. *Ecole et citoyenneté: L'Individualisme républicaine de Jules Ferry à Vichy, controverses*. Paris: Presses de la Fondation nationale des sciences politiques, 1994.

Delsieux, Jules. *Essai sur la naturalisation collective des israélites indigènes*. Algiers: Duclaux, 1860.

Dermenjian, Geneviève. *La Crise anti-juive oranaise (1895–1905): L'Antisémitisme dans l'Algérie coloniale*. Paris: L'Harmattan, 1986.

Dermenjian, Geneviève, and Benjamin Stora. "Les Juifs d'Algérie dans le regard des militaires et des juifs de France à l'époque de la conquête (1830–1855)." *Revue Historique* 284, no. 2 (1990): 333–39.

Derré, Jean-René. *Le Renouvellent de la pensée religieuse en France de 1824 à 1834: Essai sur les origines et la signification du mennaisisme*. Paris: Klincksieck, 1962.

Deslandres, Maurice. *Histoire constitutionnelle de la France de 1789 à 1870*. 2 vols. Paris: Armand Colin, 1932.

Destrilhes, M. *Confidences sur la Turquie*. 2nd ed. Paris: Dentu, 1855.

Discussion sur l'état des juifs en Roumanie à la Chambre des Lords et à la Chambre des Communes. Paris: A. Chaix, 1867.

Doyle, William. *The Oxford History of the French Revolution*. New York: Oxford University Press, 1989.

Drumont, Edouard. *La France juive: Essai d'histoire contemporaine*. 2 vols. Paris: Marpon and Flammarion, 1886.

Durkheim, Emile. *Le Socialisme, sa définition, ses débuts, la doctrine saint-simonienne*. Paris: Félix Alcan, 1928.

Echard, William E. *Napoleon III and the Concert of Europe*. Baton Rouge: Louisiana State University Press, 1983.

Eichthal, Gustave d'. *Les Deux Mondes, servant d'introduction à l'ouvrage de M. Urquart, "La Turquie et ses ressources."* Paris: Arthus Bertrand, 1836.

———. *Les Evangiles*. 2 vols. Paris: Hachette, 1863.

———. "Lettre à un banquier." *L'Organisateur: Journal de la doctrine saint-simonienne* (October 23, 1830): 74–80.

———. *La Sortie d'Egypte, d'après les récits combinés du Pentateuque et de Manethon: Son caractère et ses conséquences historiques*. 2nd ed. Paris: E. de Soye et Fils, 1872.

———. *Les Trois grands peuples méditerranéens et le christianisme*. Paris: Hachette, 1865.

———. *De l'unité européenne*. Paris: Truchy, 1840.

Eichthal, Gustave d', and Ismayl Urbain. *Lettres sur la race noire et la race blanche*. Paris: Paulin, 1839.

Elias, Norbert. *The Civilizing Process: Sociogenetic and Psychogenetic Investigations*. Trans. Edmund Jephcott. Revised ed. London: Blackwell, 2000.

Encrevé, André. *Les Protestants en France de 1800 à nos jours: Histoire d'une réintégration*. Paris: Stock, 1985.

Enfantin, Barthélemy Prosper. *Correspondance politique, 1835–1840*. Paris: Le Crédit, 1849.

———. *La Prophétie: Articles extraits du "Globe" du 19 février au 20 avril 1832*. Paris: Le Globe, 1832.

Ezdinli, Leyla. "Altérité juive, altérité romanesque." *Romantisme* 81 (1993): 29–40.

Famin, César. *Histoire de la rivalité et du protectorat des églises chrétiennes en Orient*. Paris: Firmin-Didot, 1853.

Farah, Caesar E. *The Politics of Interventionism in Ottoman Lebanon, 1831–1860*. London: Tauris, 2000.

Fawaz, Tarazi. *An Occasion for War: Civil Conflict in Lebanon and Damascus in 1860*. Berkeley and Los Angeles: University of California Press, 1994.

Febvre, Lucien. "*Civilisation*: Evolution of a Word and a Group of Ideas." In *A New Kind of History and Other Essays*, ed. Peter Burke, 219–57. New York: Harper, 1973.

Feuerwerker, David. *L'Emancipation des juifs en France, de l'ancien régime à la fin du Second Empire*. Paris: Albin Michel, 1976.

Foa, Eugénie. *La Juive: Histoire du temps de la Régence*. 2 vols. Paris: Arthus Bertrand, 1835.

———. *Rachel; ou, L'Héritage*. Paris: Henri Dupuy, 1833.

Ford, Caroline. *Creating the Nation in Provincial France: Religion and Political Identity in Brittany*. Princeton, NJ: Princeton University Press, 1993.

Forest, Louis. *La Naturalisation des juifs algériens et l'insurrection de 1871: Etude historique*. Paris: Société française d'imprimerie et de librairie [1897].

Fortescue, William. *Alphonse de Lamartine: A Political Biography*. London: Croom Helm, 1983.

Fourier, Charles. *Le Nouveau Monde industriel et sociétaire*. Paris: Anthropos, 1971.

Fournel, Henri. *Articles sur l'hérédité de la propriété*. Paris: Le Globe, 1831.

Franck, Adolphe. *La Kabbale; ou, La Philosophie religieuse des Hébreux*. Paris: Hachette, 1843.

Frankel, Jonathan. *The Damascus Affair: "Ritual Murder," Politics, and the Jews in 1840*. New York: Cambridge University Press, 1997.

Frankel, Jonathan, and Steven J. Zipperstein, eds. *Assimilation and Community: The Jews in Nineteenth-Century Europe*. Cambridge: Cambridge University Press, 1992.

Friedman, Elizabeth. *Colonialism and After: An Algerian Jewish Community*. Critical Studies in Work and Community. South Hadley, MA: Bergin and Garvey, 1988.

Furet, François. *Revolutionary France, 1770–1880*. Trans. Antonia Nevill. Oxford: Blackwell, 1992.

Furet, François, and Mona Ozouf, eds. *A Critical Dictionary of the French Revolution*. Cambridge, MA: Belknap, 1989.

Furtado, Abraham. *Mémoire sur les projets de décrets présentés au conseil d'état concernant les israélites*. Paris: Plassan, n.d.

George, Albert Joseph. *The Development of French Romanticism: The Impact of the Industrial Revolution on Literature*. Syracuse, NY: Syracuse University Press, 1955.

Gibson, William. *The Abbé de Lamennais and the Liberal Catholic Movement in France*. London: Longmans, Green, 1896.

Gide, Charles. *La Solidarité: Cours au Collège de France 1927–28*. Paris: Presses Universitaires de France, 1932.

Gille, Bertrand. *La Banque en France au XIXe siècle: Recherches historiques*. Geneva: Droz, 1970.

———. *Histoire de la maison Rothschild*. 2 vols. Geneva: Droz, 1965–67.

Girard, Louis. *Les Libéraux français, 1814–1875*. Paris: Aubier, 1985.

Girard, Patrick. *Les Juifs de France de 1789 à 1860: De l'émancipation à l'égalité*. Paris: Calmann-Lévy, 1976.

Girardet, Raoul. *L'Idée coloniale en France de 1871 à 1962*. Paris: La Table Ronde, 1972.

Girardin, Emile de. *Solutions de la Question d'Orient*. Paris: Librairie nouvelle, 1852.

Girardin, Saint-Marc. "Les Voyageurs en Orient." *Revue des Deux Mondes* 31, no. 4 (1861): 915–37.

Gorce, Pierre de la. *Histoire du Second Empire*. 5 vols. New York: AMS, 1969.

Gougenot des Mousseaux, Henri. *Le Juif, le judaïsme, et la judaïsation des peuples chrétiens*. Paris: Henri Plon, 1869.

Gouhier, Henri. *La Jeunesse d'Auguste Comte et la formation du positivisme*. 3 vols. Paris: Vrin, 1933.

Graetz, Michael. "Une Initiative saint-simonienne pour l'émancipation des juifs: Lettres de Gustave d'Eichthal sur son voyage en Autriche." *Revue des Etudes Juives* 129, no. 1 (1970): 67–84.

———. *The Jews in Nineteenth-Century France: From the French Revolution to the Alliance Israélite Universelle*. Trans. Jane Marie Todd. Stanford, CA: Stanford University Press, 1996.

Grégoire, Henri. *Essai sur la régénération physique, morale et politique des Juifs*. Metz: Claude Lamort, 1789.

Gueslin, André. *L'Invention de l'économie sociale: Le XIXe siècle française*. Paris: Economica, 1987.

Gugenheim, Marx. "Rapport sur la situation des israélites de la province de Constantine." In *Les Juifs d'Algérie et la France (1830–1855)*, by Simon Schwarzfuchs, 243–60. Jerusalem: Institut Ben Zvi, 1981.

Guiral, Pierre. *Adolphe Thiers; ou, De la nécessité en politique*. Paris: Fayard, 1986.

———. *Marseille et l'Algérie, 1830–1841. Annales de la Faculté des lettres d'Aix-en-Provence*, n.s., no. 15. Gap: Ophrys, 1956.

———. *Prévost-Paradol, 1829–1870: Pensée et action d'un libéral sous le Second Empire*. Paris: Presses Universitaires de France, 1955.

Guizot, François. *Histoire de la civilisation en France depuis la chute de l'empire romain*. Vol. 4. Rev. ed. Paris: Didier, 1859.

———. *Memoirs to Illustrate the History of My Time*. Trans. J. W. Cole. 8 vols. London: Richard Bentley, 1858–67. Reprint, New York: AMS, 1974.

———. "Des moyens du gouvernement de l'opposition dans l'état actuel de la France." In *Oeuvres Choisies*, 277–354. Brussels: Meline, Cans, 1848.

Halévy, Elie. *Instruction religieuse et morale à l'usage de la jeunesse israélite*. Paris: Chez l'auteur et Gerson-Lévy, 1820.

Halévy, Léon. *Résumé de l'histoire des juifs anciens*. Paris: Lecointe et Durey, 1825.

———. *Résumé de l'histoire des juifs modernes*. Paris: Lecointe, 1828.

Halévy, Léon, Adolphe de Leuven, and Ernest Jaime. *Grillo; ou, Le Prince et le banquier: Comédie-Vaudeville en 2 actes*. Paris: Variétés, 1832.

Halévy, Léon, Charles-Henri de Saint-Simon, Olinde Rodrigues, et al. *Opinions littéraires, philosophiques et industrielles*. Paris: Bossange, 1825.

Hall, John Richard. *The Bourbon Restoration*. London: Alston Rivers, 1909.

Hallman, Diana. *Opera, Liberalism and Antisemitism in Nineteenth-Century France: The Politics of Halévy's "La Juive."* Cambridge Studies in Opera. Cambridge: Cambridge University Press, 2002.

Hamache, Magy. "Les Juifs dans les arts dramatiques au XIXe siècle: Regards croisés sur la tragédienne Rachel (1821–1858)." *Revue Historique* 293, no. 1 (1995): 119–33.

Hart, Mitchell. *Social Science and the Politics of Modern Jewish Identity*. Stanford, CA: Stanford University Press, 2000.

Hayward, J. E. S. "Solidarity: The Social History of a Concept in Nineteenth-Century France." *International Review of Social History* 4, no. 2 (1959): 261–84.

Hazareesingh, Sudhir. *From Subject to Citizen: The Second Empire and the Emergence of Modern French Democracy*. Princeton, NJ: Princeton University Press, 1998.

Heffernan, Michael. "The French Right and the Overseas Empire." In *The Right in France, 1789–1997*, ed. Nicholas Atkin and Frank Tallet, 89–113. London: Tauris, 1998.

Helfand, Jonathan I. "Passports and Piety: Apostasy in Nineteenth-Century France." *Jewish History* 3, no. 2 (1988): 59–83.

Henry, Paul. "Napoleon III and the Balkans." In *Napoleon III and Europe*, ed. International Commission for the Teaching of History, 41–65. Oxford: Pergamon, 1965.

Hertzberg, Arthur. *The French Enlightenment and the Jews: The Origins of Modern Anti-Semitism*. New York: Schocken, 1967.

Hess, Jonathan M. *Germans, Jews, and the Claims of Modernity*. New Haven, CT: Yale University Press, 2002.

Hess, Moses. *The Revival of Israel: Rome and Jerusalem, the Last Nationalist Question*. Trans. Meyer Waxman. Lincoln: University of Nebraska Press, 1995.

Histoire diplomatique de la crise orientale de 1853 à 1856 d'après des documents inédits: Suivie d'un mémoire sur la question des lieux saints. Brussels: Emile Flatau, 1858.

Hoexter, Miriam. "Les Juifs français et l'assimilation politique et institutionnelle de la communauté juive en Algérie (1830–1870)." Paper presented at the conference Les Relations intercommunautaires juives en méditerranée occidentale, XIIIe–XXe siècles, Abbaye de Sénaque, 1982.

Hollanderski, Léon. *Dix-huit siècles de préjugés chrétiens*. Paris: Michel Lévy, 1869.

Hollier, Denis, ed. *A New History of French Literature*. Cambridge, MA: Harvard University Press, 1989.

Hourani, Albert. *Europe and the Middle East*. Berkeley and Los Angeles: University of California Press, 1980.

Hourwitz, Zalkind. *Apologie des Juifs en réponse à la question: Est-il des moyens de rendre les Juifs plus heureux et plus utiles en France?* Paris: Gattey, 1789.

Hudson, Nora E. *Ultra-Royalism and the French Restoration*. Cambridge: Cambridge University Press, 1936.

Hyman, Paula E. *The Emancipation of the Jews of Alsace: Acculturation and Tradition in the Nineteenth Century*. New Haven, CT: Yale University Press, 1991.

———. *The Jews of Modern France*. Berkeley and Los Angeles: University of California Press, 1998.

———. "Joseph Salvador: Proto-Zionist or Apologist for Assimilation?" *Jewish Social Studies* 34 (1972): 1–22.

Iancu, Carol. "Adolphe Crémieux, l'Alliance Israélite Universelle et les juifs de Roumanie." *Revue des Etudes Juives* 133, nos. 3–4 (1974): 481–502.

———. *Bleichröder et Crémieux: Le Combat pour l'émancipation des juifs de Roumanie devant le Congrès de Berlin; Correspondance inédite, 1878–1880*. Montpellier: Centre de recherches judaïques et hebraïques, Université Paul Valéry, 1987.

———. "L'Emigration des juifs roumains dans la correspondance diplomatique française (1900–1902)." Paper presented at the Proceedings of the Seventh World Congress of Jewish Studies, History of the Jews in Europe, Jerusalem, 1977.

———. *Les Juifs de Roumanie (1866–1919): De l'exclusion à l'émancipation*. Aix-en-Provence: Editions de l'université de Provence, 1978. Trans. by Carvel de Bussy as *Jews in Romania, 1866–1919: From Exclusion to Emancipation*. Boulder, CO: East European Monographs, 1996.

Idel, Moshe. *Kabbalah: New Perspectives*. New Haven, CT: Yale University Press, 1988.

Ideville, Henry-Amédée, comte d'. *Le Maréchal Bugeaud, d'après sa correspondance intime et des documents inédits, 1784–1849*. 3 vols. Paris: Firmin-Didot, 1882.

Iggers, Georg G., ed. and trans. *The Doctrine of Saint-Simon: An Exposition; First Year, 1828–1829*. New York: Schocken, 1972.

Isser, Natalie. *Antisemitism During the French Second Empire*. New York: Peter Lang, 1991.

Jacobs, Joseph. "The Wandering Jew." In *The Jewish Encyclopedia*, ed. Cyrus Adler, Isidore Singer, et al. New York: Funk and Wagnalls, 1901–6.

Jardin, André, and André-Jean Tudesq. *Restoration and Reaction, 1815–1849*. Trans. Elborg Forster. Cambridge: Cambridge University Press, 1983.

J.C.F. [J. Casimir Frégier]. *La Question juive en Algérie; ou, De la naturalisation des juifs algériens par un algérien progressiste, membre de la société historique algérienne*. Algiers: Bouyer, 1860.

Jennings, Lawrence. *France and Europe in 1848: A Study of French Foreign Affairs in Time of Crisis*. Oxford: Clarendon, 1973.

Job, Françoise. *Les Juifs de Lunéville au XVIIIe et XIXe siècles*. Nancy: Presses Universitaires de Nancy, 1989.

Johnson, Douglas. *Guizot: Aspects of French History, 1787–1874*. London: Routledge and Kegan Paul, 1963.

Julien, Charles-André. *Histoire de l'Algérie contemporaine: La Conquête et les débuts de la colonisation (1827–1871)*. Paris: Presses Universitaires de France, 1964.

Kahn, Léon. *Le Comité de bienfaisance: L'Hôpital, l'orphelinat, les cimetières*. Histoire de la communauté israélite de Paris, vol. 3. Paris: A. Durlacher, 1886.

———. *Histoire des écoles communales et consistoriales israélites de Paris (1809–1884)*. Histoire de la communauté israélite de Paris, vol. 1. Paris: A. Durlacher, 1884.

———. *Les Juifs à Paris depuis le VIe siècle*. Histoire de la communauté israélite de Paris, vol. 5. Paris: A. Durlacher, 1889.

Kahn, Zadoc. *Sermons et allocutions*. 2nd ed. 1st ser. Paris: A. Durlacher, 1893.

Kaplan, Marion. *The Making of the Jewish Middle Class: Women, Family and Identity in Imperial Germany*. Oxford: Oxford University Press, 1991.

Kaspi, André. "Note sur Isidore Cahen." *Revue des Etudes Juives* 121 (1962): 417–25.

Kates, Gary. "Jews into Frenchmen: Nationality and Representation in Revolutionary France." In *The French Revolution and the Birth of Modernity*, ed. Ferenc Fehér, 103–16. Berkeley and Los Angeles: University of California Press, 1990.

Katz, Jacob. *Emancipation and Assimilation: Studies in Modern Jewish History*. Gregg International, 1972.

———. *From Prejudice to Destruction: Anti-Semitism, 1700–1933.* Cambridge, MA: Harvard University Press, 1980.

———. *Tradition and Crisis: Jewish Society at the End of the Middle Ages.* Trans. Bernard Dov Cooperman. New York: Schocken, 1993.

Kellogg, Fredrick. *The Road to Romanian Independence.* West Lafayette, IN: Purdue University Press, 1995.

Kertzer, David I. *The Kidnapping of Edgaro Mortara.* New York: Vintage, 1997.

Kieval, Hillel. *The Making of Czech Jewry: National Conflict and Jewish Society in Bohemia, 1870–1918.* New York: Oxford University Press, 1988.

Kley, Dale K. Van. *The Religious Origins of the French Revolution: From Calvin to the Civil Constitution of the Clergy, 1560–1791.* New Haven, CT: Yale University Press, 1996.

Kohler, Max J., and Simon Wolf. *Jewish Disabilities in the Balkan States: American Contributions Toward Their Removal, with Particular Reference to the Congress of Berlin.* New York: American Jewish Committee, 1916.

Kriegel, Annie. *Les Juifs et le monde moderne: Essai sur les logiques de l'émancipation.* Paris: Seuil, 1977.

La Sicotière, Léon de, ed. *Assemblée nationale—enquête parlementaire. Actes du Gouvernement de la Défense nationale: Rapports de la commission et des sous-commissions; télégrammes; pièces diverses, dépositions des témoins; pièces justificatives; table analytique générale et nominative.* 3 vols. Paris: Librairie des publications législatives, 1876.

Lamennais, Félicité de. *Des progrès de la Révolution et de la guerre contre l'église.* 2nd ed. Paris: Belin-Mandar et Devaux, 1829.

———. *Les Paroles d'un croyant de Lamennais, texte publié sur le manuscrit autographe avec des variantes: Une Introduction et un commentaire.* Ed. Yves le Hir. Paris: Armand Colin, 1949.

Landes, David. "The Old Bank and the New: The Financial Revolution of the Nineteenth Century." In *Essays in European Economic History, 1789–1914,* ed. F. Crouzet, W. H. Chaloner, and W. M. Stern, 112–27. London: Edward Arnold, 1969.

Laskier, Michael. *The Alliance Israélite Universelle and the Jewish Communities of Morocco, 1862–1962.* Albany: State University of New York Press, 1983.

Lazare, Bernard. "Juifs de Roumanie." *Cahiers de la Quinzaine* 4, no. 13 (1903): 81–84.

Leca, Jean. "La Citoyenneté entre la nation et la société civile." In *Citoyenneté et nationalité: Perspectives en France et au Québec,* ed. Dominique Colas, Claude Emeri, and Jacques Zylberberg, 479–505. Paris: Presses Universitaires de France, 1991.

Leff, Lisa Moses. "'Jewish Solidarity' in Nineteenth-Century France: The Evolution of a Concept." *Journal of Modern History* 74 (March 2002): 33–61.

———. "Self-Definition and Self-Defense: Jewish Racial Identity in Nineteenth-Century France." *Jewish History* 19, no. 1 (January 2005): 7–28.

Lehning, James R. *Peasant and French: Cultural Contact in Rural France During the Nineteenth Century.* New York: Cambridge University Press, 1995.

Leroux, Pierre. *De l'humanité, de son principe, et de son avenir, où se trouve exposée la vraie définition de la religion et où l'on explique le sens, la suite et l'enchaînement du mosaïsme et du christianisme.* Paris: Fayard, 1985.

Leven, Narcisse. *Adolphe Crémieux: Conférence faite à la société des études juives, le 21 janvier 1888.* Paris: A. Durlacher, 1905.

———. *Cinquante ans d'histoire: L'Alliance Israélite Universelle (1860–1910).* 2 vols. Paris: Félix Alcan, 1911–20.

Lévy, Armand. *Napoléon III et les principautés roumaines.* Paris: Dentu, 1858.

Lochore, R. A. *History of the Idea of Civilization in France (1830–1870).* Bonn: Ludwig Röhrscheid, 1935.

Loeb, Isidore. *Biographie d'Albert Cohn.* Paris: A. Durlacher, 1878.

———. *La Situation des israélites en Turquie, en Serbie et en Roumanie.* Paris: Joseph Baer, 1877.

Loewe, Louis, ed. *The Diaries of Sir Moses and Lady Montefiore, Comprising Their Life and Work as Recorded in Their Diaries from 1812 to 1883.* 2 vols. London: Griffith, Farran, Okeden, and Welsh, 1890.

Loyette, Henri, ed. *Entre le théâtre et l'histoire: La Famille Halévy, 1760–1960.* Paris: Fayard, 1996.

Lynch, Katherine A. *Family, Class, and Ideology in Early Industrial France: Social Policy and the Working-Class Family, 1825–1848.* Madison: University of Wisconsin Press, 1988.

Maistre, Joseph de. *Les Soirées de Saint-Pétersbourg; ou, Entretiens sur le gouvernement temporel de la providence.* Paris: Vieux Colombier, 1960.

Malino, Frances. *A Jew in the French Revolution: The Life of Zalkind Hourwitz.* Oxford: Blackwell, 1996.

———. "From Patriot to Israélite: Abraham Furtado in Revolutionary France." In *Mystics, Philosophers, and Politicians: Essays in Jewish Intellectual History in Honor of Alexander Altmann,* ed. Jehuda Reinharz and Daniel Swetschinski, 213–48. Durham, NC: Duke University Press, 1982.

———. *The Sephardic Jews of Bordeaux: Assimilation and Emancipation in Revolutionary and Napoleonic France.* Tuscaloosa: University of Alabama Press, 1978.

Malino, Frances, and David Sorkin, eds. *From East and West: Jews in a Changing Europe, 1750–1870.* London: Blackwell, 1990.

Manent, Pierre. *Histoire intellectuelle du libéralisme: Dix leçons.* Paris: Calmann-Lévy, 1987.

———. "Quelques remarques sur la notion de 'sécularisation.'" In *The French Revolution and the Creation of Modern Political Culture,* ed. François Furet and

Mona Ozouf, vol. 3, *The Transformation of Political Culture, 1789–1848*, 351–57. Oxford: Pergamon, 1989.

Manuel, Albert. "Les Consistoires israélites de France: Les Consistoires de Paris (1806–1905)." *Revue des Etudes Juives* 82 (1926): 521–32.

Manuel, Eugène. *Lettres de jeunesse*. Paris: Hachette, 1909.

Manuel, Frank E. *The Prophets of Paris: Turgot, Condorcet, Saint-Simon, Fourier, and Comte*. New York: Harper and Row, 1962.

Marriott, J. A. R. *The Eastern Question: An Historical Study in European Diplomacy*. 4th ed. Oxford: Clarendon, 1940.

Marrus, Michael. *The Politics of Assimilation: The French Jewish Community at the Time of the Dreyfus Affair*. Oxford: Clarendon, 1971.

Martin, Claude. *La Commune d'Alger (1870–1871)*. Paris: Héraklès, 1936.

———. *Les Israélites algériens de 1830 à 1902*. Paris: Héraklès, 1936.

Mayeur, Jean-Marie, and Madeleine Rebérioux. *The Third Republic from Its Origins to the Great War, 1871–1914*. Trans. J. R. Foster. Cambridge: Cambridge University Press, 1984.

Mazeaud, Henri, Léon Mazeaud, Jean Mazeaud, and François Chabas. *Leçons de droit civil*. Vol. 2, *Obligations: Théorie générale*. Paris: Montchrestien, 1985.

McLeod, Hugh. *Secularization in Western Europe, 1848–1914*. New York: St. Martin's Press, 2000.

McManners, John. *Church and State in France, 1870–1914*. London: Society for Promoting Christian Knowledge, 1972.

———. *The French Revolution and the Church*. New York: Harper and Row, 1970.

Meknis, Richard. "Patriarchs and Patricians: The Gradis Family of Eighteenth-Century Bordeaux." In *From East and West: Jews in a Changing Europe, 1750–1850*, ed. Frances Malino and David Sorkin, 11–45. London: Blackwell, 1990.

Mendelssohn, Moses. *Jerusalem*. Trans. Allan Arkush. Hanover, NH: Brandeis University Press, 1983.

Ménerville, Pinson de. *Dictionnaire de législation algérienne, code annoté et manuel raisonné des lois, ordonnances, décrets, décisions et arrêtés, publiés au bulletin officiel des actes du gouvernement; suivi d'une table alphabétique des matières et d'une table chronologique des lois, décrets, etc. Première volume, 1830–1860*. Vol. 1 of 2. Paris: Bastide, 1867.

Meyer, Pierre-André. *La Communauté juive de Metz au XVIII siècle*. Nancy: Presses Universitaires de Nancy, 1993.

Meynié, Georges. *Les Juifs en Algérie*. 2nd ed. Paris: Nouvelle librairie parisienne, 1888.

Michelet, Jules. *Histoire romaine*. Paris: Hachette, 1831.

———. *Introduction à l'histoire universelle*. Vol. 35 of *Oeuvres complètes*. Paris: Flammarion, 1897.

———. *Journal*. 2 vols. Paris: Gallimard, 1958.

——. *Le Peuple*. Paris: Hachette, 1846.

Miège, Jean-Louis, ed. *Les Relations intercommunautaires juives en Méditerranée occidentale, XIIIe–XXe siècles*. Paris: Centre national de la recherche scientifique, 1982.

Miller, William. *The Ottoman Empire and Its Successors, 1801–1927*. London: Frank Cass, 1966.

Morsy, Magali, ed. *Les Saint-simoniens et l'Orient: Vers la modernité*. Aix-en-Provence: Edisud, 1989.

Mossé, Benjamin, ed. *La Révolution française et le rabbinat français*. Avignon: La Caravane, 1890.

Mosse, George L. *Toward the Final Solution: A History of European Racism*. New York: Fertig, 1978.

Muelsch, Elisabeth-Christine. "Creativity, Childhood, and Children's Literature; or, How to Become a Woman Writer: The Case of Eugénie Foa." *Romance Languages Annual* 8 (1997): 66–73.

——. "Eugénie Foa and the *Institut des Femmes*." In *Women Seeking Expression, 1789–1914*, ed. Rosemary Lloyd and Brian Nelson, 86–100. Melbourne: Monash Romance Studies, 2000.

Munk, Salomon. *Mélanges de philosophie juive et arabe*. Paris: A. Franck, 1859.

——. *Palestine: Description historique, géographique et archéologique*. Paris: Firmin-Didot, 1845.

——. *La Philosophie chez les juifs*. Paris: Wittersheim, 1848.

Neher-Bernheim, Rina, ed., *Documents inédits sur l'entrée des juifs dans la société française (1750–1850)*. 2 vols. Tel Aviv: Diaspora Research Institute, 1977.

Netter, Moïse. *La Révolution française et le Judaïsme: Discours prononcé à la cérémonie du 11 mai 1889*. Saint-Etienne: Imprimerie du Stéphanois, 1889.

Nicaise, E. *L'Antisémitisme en Algérie*. Algiers: Casabianca, 1898.

Nicolet, Claude. *L'Idée république en France: Essai d'histoire critique*. Paris: Gallimard, 1982.

Nord, Philip. *The Republican Moment: Struggles for Democracy in Nineteenth-Century France*. Cambridge, MA: Harvard University Press, 1995.

Note sur la situation des israélites en Roumanie au point de vue des relations internationales. Paris: Maréchal, 1875.

Ozouf, Mona. *Festivals and the French Revolution*. Trans. Alan Sheridan. Cambridge, MA: Harvard University Press, 1988.

Pascal, Georges de. *La Juiverie*. Paris: Henri Gauthier, 1887.

Penel-Beaufin, Arthur-Louis. *Législation générale du culte israélite en France, en Algérie et dans les colonies, à la portée de tous (organisation, fonctionnement et régime financier): Lois, ordonnances, décrets, arrêtés, circulaires, avis, décisions, avant et après 1789 jusqu'à nos jours, avec des notes explicatives, une table chronologique, et une table analytique très complète*. Paris: V. Giard et E. Brière, 1894.

Penslar, Derek Jonathan. "The Origins of Jewish Political Economy." *Jewish Social Studies* 3 (1997): 26–60.

———. *Shylock's Children: Economics and Jewish Identity in Modern Europe.* Berkeley and Los Angeles: University of California Press, 2001.

Pereire, Isaac. *La Banque de France et l'organisation du crédit en France.* Paris: Paul Dupont, 1864.

———. *Politique financière: La Conversion et l'amortissement.* Paris: C. Motteroz, 1879.

———. *Politique industrielle et commerciale: Budget des réformes.* Paris: C. Motteroz, 1877.

———. *La Question religieuse.* Paris: C. Motteroz, 1878.

Pétition adressée au Sénat et à la Chambre des Députés de Roumanie par un nombre d'israélites de Jassy en date du 20 avril 1868. Jassy: Goldner, 1868.

Peyre, Henri. *What Is Romanticism?* Trans. Roda Roberts. Tuscaloosa: University of Alabama Press, 1978.

Philippe, Béatrice. *Etre juif dans la société française du moyen âge à nos jours.* Paris: Montalba, 1979.

———. "Les Juifs français et la seconde république de février à juin 1848." 2 vols. Doctoral diss., Université de Paris X-Nanterre, 1980.

Piette, Christine. "Citoyenneté et judaïsme: Le Cas du juif parisien après la Révolution." In *Citoyenneté et nationalité: Perspectives en France et au Québec,* ed. Dominique Colas, Claude Emeri, and Jacques Zylberberg, 149–60. Paris: Presses Universitaires de France, 1991.

———. *Les Juifs de Paris, 1808–1840: La Marche vers l'assimilation.* Quebec: Université de Laval, 1983.

Pinet, Gaston. "L'Ecole polytechnique et les saint-simoniens." *Revue de Paris* 3 (1894): 73–96.

Pinto, Isaac de. *Apologie pour la nation juive ou reflexions critiques sur le premier chapitre du VII. tome des oeuvres de monsieur de Voltaire, au sujet des juifs.* Amsterdam: J. Joubert, 1762.

———. *Traité de la circulation et du crédit: Contenant une analyse des fonds d'Angleterre, et de ce qu'on appelle Commerce ou Jeu d'Actions; un Examen critique de plusieurs Traités sur les Impôts, les Finances, l'Agriculture, la Population, le Commerce, et d'autres objets politiques.* Amsterdam: Marc Michel Rey, 1771.

Poliakov, Léon. *Histoire de l'antisémitisme.* 2 vols. Paris: Calmann-Lévy, 1981.

Pomain, Krystof. "Franks and Gauls." In *Realms of Memory: Rethinking the French Past,* ed. Pierre Nora, 1: 27–76. New York: Columbia University Press, 1996.

Posener, Solomon. *Adolphe Crémieux, 1796–1880.* 2 vols. Paris: Félix Alcan, 1934. Trans. by Eugene Golub as *Adolphe Crémieux: A Biography.* Philadelphia: Jewish Publication Society, 1940.

Poujade, Eugène. *Chrétiens et Turcs: Scènes et souvenirs de la vie politique, militaire et religieuse en Orient.* 3rd ed. Paris: Didier, 1867.

Price, Roger. *The French Second Empire: An Anatomy of Political Power*. Cambridge: Cambridge University Press, 2001.

Procacci, Giovanna. *Gouverner la misère: La Question sociale en France, 1789–1848*. Paris: Seuil, 1993.

Proudhon, Pierre-Joseph. *What Is Property?* Trans. Donald R. Kelley and Bonnie G. Smith. Cambridge: Cambridge University Press, 1993.

La Question des israélites de Roumanie. Paris: A. Franck, 1869.

La Question juive dans les Chambres Roumaines: Compte-rendu des séances de la Chambre des Députés et du Sénat du mois de mars 1879. 2nd ed. Paris: Alliance Israélite Universelle, 1879.

Quinet, Edgar. *Ahasvérus*. Vol. 11 of *Oeuvres complètes*. 30 vols. 5th ed. Paris: Hachette, 1899.

———. *Le Christianisme et la Révolution française*. Paris: Imprimeurs-Unis, 1845.

———. *La Croisade autrichienne, française, napolitaine, et espagnole contre la république romaine*. Paris: Chamerot, 1849.

———. *Le Génie des religions*. Vol. 1 of *Oeuvres complètes*. 30 vols. 5th ed. Paris: Hachette, 1899.

———. *Les Tablettes du Juif errant*. Vol. 11 of *Oeuvres complètes*. 30 vols. 5th ed. Paris: Hachette, 1899.

Rabi, Wladimir. *Anatomie du judaïsme français*. Paris: De Minuit, 1960.

Rapport, Michael. *Nationality and Citizenship in Revolutionary France: The Treatment of Foreigners, 1789–1799*. Oxford: Clarendon, 2000.

Ratcliffe, Barrie M. "Crisis and Identity: Gustave d'Eichthal and Judaism in the Emancipation Period." *Jewish Social Studies* 37 (1975): 122–40.

———. "Les Pereire et le saint-simonisme." *Economies et sociétés: Cahiers de l'ISEA* 5, no. 6 (1971): 1215–55.

———. "Some Jewish Problems in the Early Careers of Emile and Isaac Pereire." *Jewish Social Studies* 34 (1972): 189–206.

Ratcliffe, Barrie, and W. H. Chaloner, eds. *A French Sociologist Looks at Britain: Gustave d'Eichthal and British Society in 1828*. Manchester: University of Manchester Press, 1977.

Ratti-Menton, Comte de. "Feuilleton de *l'Univers*: Assassinat du Père Thomas; Documents officiels." *L'Univers*, May 3, 1840.

Ravel, Aaron, Aaron Vidal, and [Jean-Baptiste] Milhaud. *Observations pour des juifs d'Avignon à la Convention nationale*. 3 vendémiaire an III (1794). Paris: Editions d'histoire sociale, 1968.

Raymond, Xavier. "La Syrie et la question d'Orient." *Revue des Deux Mondes* 29, no. 2 (1860): 399–425.

Reardon, Bernard. *Liberalism and Tradition: Aspects of Catholic Thought in Nineteenth-Century France*. Cambridge: Cambridge University Press, 1975.

Rémusat, Charles de. *Mémoires de ma vie*. 5 vols. Paris: Plon, 1959.

———. "L'Opinion publique et la politique extérieure de la France." *Revue des Deux Mondes* 28, no. 1 (1860): 5–31.

Renan, Ernest. "De l'avenir religieux des sociétés modernes." *Revue des Deux Mondes* 29, no. 4 (1860): 761–97.

Riou de Kersalaun, François-Marie-Joseph. *Rapport fait par Riou sur les pétitions des Juifs de Metz et d'Avignon, au nom d'une commission spéciale.* Paris: Imprimerie Nationale, 4 frimaire an VI (1797).

Robert, Daniel. *Les Eglises réformées en France (1800–1830).* Paris: Presses Universitaires de France, 1961.

Roch, Eugène. "Persécutions contre les juifs de Damas, à la suite de la disparition du R. P. Thomas, religieux de l'ordre des Capucins, et de son domestique: Recueil des documents." *L'Observateur des Tribunaux: Journal des Documents Judiciaires,* n.s., 1 (1840): 1–92.

Rodrigue, Aron. *French Jews, Turkish Jews: The Alliance Israélite Universelle and the Politics of Jewish Schooling in Turkey, 1860–1925.* Bloomington: Indiana University Press, 1990.

———. "Rearticulations of French Jewish Identities After the Dreyfus Affair." *Jewish Social Studies* 2 (1996): 1–24.

Rodrigues, Eugène. *Lettres d'Eugène Rodrigues sur la religion et la politique.* Paris: Le Globe, 1832.

Rodrigues, Hippolyte. *Les Trois Filles de la Bible.* 2 vols. Paris: Michel Lévy, 1866.

Rodrigues, Olinde. *Préface des oeuvres de Saint-Simon: Le Disciple de Saint-Simon au public.* Paris, 1832.

———. *Religion saint-simonienne: Appel.* Paris: Le Globe, 1831.

———. *Théorie des banques.* Paris: Napoleon Chaix, 1848.

Roger, Emile. *Nécessité de reviser le décret Crémieux.* Oran: n.p., 1882.

Rosanvallon, Pierre. *L'Etat en France de 1789 à nos jours.* Paris: Seuil, 1990.

———. *Le Moment Guizot.* Paris: Gallimard, 1985.

———. *La Monarchie impossible: Les Chartes de 1814 et de 1830.* Paris: Fayard, 1994.

———. *Le Sacre du citoyen: Histoire du suffrage universel en France.* Paris: Gallimard, 1992.

Rosenstock, Morton. "The Establishment of the Consistorial System in Algeria." *Jewish Social Studies* 18 (1956): 41–54.

Rouard de Card, Edgard. *Etude sur la naturalisation en Algérie.* Paris: Berger-Levrault, 1881.

Said, Edward. *Orientalism.* New York: Vintage, 1978.

Saint-Simon, Henri de, and Eugène Rodrigues. *Nouveau Christianisme: Lettres d'Eugène Rodrigues sur la religion et la politique; L'Education du genre humain, de Lessing, traduit, pour la première fois, de l'allemand par Eugène Rodrigues.* Paris: Le Globe, 1832.

Saladin, Jean-Baptiste-Michel. *Rapport fait par Saladin, au nom d'une commission spéciale, composée des représentans Grégoire, Chappuy, Louvot et Saladin, sur les pétitions des Juifs de Metz et d'Avignon*. Paris: Imprimerie nationale, 7 fructidor an V (1797).

Salvador, Gabriel. *J. Salvador: Sa vie, ses oeuvres et ses critiques*. Paris: Calmann-Lévy, 1881.

Salvador, Joseph. *Histoire des institutions de Moïse et du peuple hébreu*. 3 vols. Paris: Ponthieu, 1828.

———. *Jésus-Christ et sa doctrine: Histoire de la naissance de l'église, de son organisation et de ses progrès pendant le premier siècle*. 2 vols. Paris: Guyot et Scribe, 1838.

———. *Loi de Moïse ou système religieux et politique des Hébreux*. Paris: Ridan, 1822.

———. *Paris, Rome, Jérusalem, ou la question religieuse au XIXe siècle*. 2 vols. Paris: Michel Lévy, 1860.

Sand, George. *L'Histoire de ma vie*. Vol. 40 of *Oeuvres complètes*. 110 vols. Paris: Michel Lévy, 1879.

Sartor, J. E. *De la condition juridique des étrangers, des musulmans et des israélites en Algérie: Suivie d'une traité sur la naturalisation en France et en Algérie*. Oran: Alessi, 1869.

Schalit, A. "Rapport sur la situation des juifs algériens." Paris: Alliance Israélite Universelle, 1900.

Schechter, Ronald S. *Obstinate Hebrews: Representations of Jews in France, 1715–1815*. Berkeley and Los Angeles: University of California Press, 2003.

Schwarzfuchs, Simon. *Du Juif à l'israélite: Histoire d'une mutation, 1779–1870*. Paris: Fayard, 1989.

———. *Les Juifs d'Algérie et la France (1830–1855)*. Jerusalem: Institut Ben-Zvi, 1981.

———. *Napoleon, the Jews and the Sanhedrin*. London: Routledge, Kegan and Paul, 1979.

Scott, John A. *Republican Ideas and the Liberal Tradition in France, 1870–1914*. New York: Columbia University Press, 1951.

Scott, Sir Walter. *Ivanhoe*. New York: Penguin, 1982.

Seliger, Martin. "Race-Thinking During the Restoration." *Journal of the History of Ideas* 19, no. 2 (1958): 273–82.

Senger, M. *L'Esprit des loix mosaïques*. Bordeaux: Labottiere, 1775.

Sepinwall, Alyssa Goldstein. *The Abbé Grégoire and the French Revolution: The Making of Modern Universalism*. Berkeley and Los Angeles: University of California Press, 2005.

Seton-Watson, Robert William. *A History of the Roumanians: From Roman Times to the Completion of Unity*. Cambridge: Cambridge University Press, 1934.

Sewell, William H., Jr. *Work and Revolution in France: The Language of Labor from the Old Regime to 1848*. Cambridge: Cambridge University Press, 1980.

Silveyra, David, agent et député, Furtado jeune, Louis Nounez, and Silveire. *Adresse présentée à l'Assemblée nationale par le Député des Juifs Espagnols et Portugais, établis au Bourg Saint-Esprit-lès-Bayonne*. Paris: Houry et Debure, 1790.

Simon, Jules. *La Liberté de conscience*. 4th ed. Paris: Hachette, 1867.

Simon-Nahum, Perrine. *La Cité investie: La "Science du judaïsme" français et la République*. Paris: Cerf, 1991.

———. "Le Judaïsme émancipé face à la loi dans la France du XIXe siècle." *Pardès* 22 (1996): 91–102.

Sorkin, David. *The Transformation of German Jewry, 1780–1840*. Oxford: Oxford University Press, 1987.

Soulages, Gaudart de, and Hubert Lamant. *Dictionnaire des franc-maçons français*. Paris: Albatros, 1995.

Spencer, Philip. *Politics of Belief in Nineteenth-Century France: Lacordaire, Michon, Veuillot*. London: Faber and Faber, 1953.

Spitzer, Alan B. *The French Generation of 1820*. Princeton, NJ: Princeton University Press, 1987.

Staum, Martin S. "Paris Ethnology and the Perfectibility of 'Races.'" *Canadian Journal of History* 35 (2000): 435–72.

Stearns, Peter N. *Priest and Revolutionary: Lamennais and the Dilemma of French Catholicism*. New York: Harper and Row, 1967.

Stern, Fritz. *Gold and Iron: Bismarck, Bleichröder, and the Building of the German Empire*. 2nd ed. New York: Vintage, 1979.

———, ed. *The Varieties of History: From Voltaire to the Present*. New York: Meridian, 1956.

Sternhell, Zeev. *Neither Right nor Left: Fascist Ideology in France*. Trans. David Maisel. Princeton, NJ: Princeton University Press, 1986.

———. "The Roots of Popular Anti-Semitism in the Third Republic." In *The Jews in Modern France*, ed. Frances Malino and Bernard Wasserstein, 103–34. Hanover, NH: University Press of New England, 1985.

Sullivan, Antony Thrall. *Thomas-Robert Bugeaud: France and Algeria, 1784–1849; Politics, Power, and the Good Society*. Hamden, CT: Archon, 1983.

Szajkowski, Zosa. "Conflicts in the Alliance Israélite Universelle and the Founding of the Anglo-Jewish Association, the Viennese Allianz, and the Hilfsverein." *Jewish Social Studies* 19 (1957): 29–50.

———. "The Jewish Saint-Simonians and Socialist Antisemites in France." *Jewish Social Studies* 9 (1947): 33–60.

———. *Jews and the French Revolutions of 1789, 1830, and 1848*. New York: Ktav, 1970.

———. "Socialists and Radicals in the Development of Antisemitism in Algeria (1884–1900)." *Jewish Social Studies* 10 (1948): 257–80.

Tackett, Timothy. *Religion, Revolution, and Regional Culture in Eighteenth-Century France: The Ecclesiastical Oath of 1791*. Princeton, NJ: Princeton University Press, 1986.

Talmon, J. L. *Political Messianism: The Romantic Phase*. London: Secker and Warburg, 1960.

Tama, Diogène. *Collection des actes de l'assemblée des notables israélites de France et du royaume d'Italie, convoquée à Paris par décret de Sa Majesté impériale et royale, du 30 mai 1806.* Paris: Chez l'editeur, 1807.

———. *Transactions of the Paris Sanhedrin or Acts of the Assembly of Israelitish Deputies of France and Italy Convoked at Paris by Imperial and Royal Decree Dated May 30, 1806.* Trans. F. D. Kirwan. Ed. Ellis Rivkin. Cincinnati: Hebrew Union College–Jewish Institute of Religion, 1956.

Taylor, Keith, ed. *Henri Saint-Simon (1760–1825): Selected Writings on Science, Industry, and Social Organisation.* New York: Holmes and Meier, 1975.

Tchernoff, Iouda. *Le Parti républicain sous la monarchie de juillet: Formation et évolution de la doctrine républicaine.* Paris: Pedone, 1901.

Terquem, Olry [Tsarphati, pseud.]. *Lettres tsarphatiques.* Paris: 1824–37.

Tezcano, D. Rosetti. *La Roumanie et le juif devant l'Europe.* Bacau: L'Indépendance, 1877.

Theis, Laurent. "Guizot et le problème religieux." In *François Guizot et la culture politique de son temps,* ed. Marina Valensise, 251–63. Paris: Gallimard, 1991.

Thiéry, Claude-Antoine. *Dissertation sur cette question: Est-il des moyens de rendre les Juifs plus heureux et plus utiles en France?* Paris: Knapen, 1788.

Trenard, Louis. *Salvandy en son temps.* Lille: Publications de la Faculté de lettres et sciences humaines de l'Université de Lille, 1968.

Trigano, Shmuel. "From Individual to Collectivity: The Rebirth of the 'Jewish Nation' in France." In *The Jews of Modern France,* ed. Frances Malino and Bernard Wasserstein, 245–81. Hanover, NH: Brandeis University Press, 1985.

———. "The Notion of a 'Jewish Community' in France: A Special Case of Jewish Identity." In *Jewish Identities in the New Europe,* ed. Jonathan Webber, 179–88. London: Littman Library of Jewish Civilization, 1992.

———. *La République et les juifs après Copernic.* Paris: Les Presses d'aujourd'hui, 1982.

Tulard, Jean. "Nationalités (politique des)." In *Dictionnaire du Second Empire,* ed. Jean Tulard, 904. Paris: Fayard, 1995.

Uhry, Isaac. *Recueil des lois, décrets, ordonnances, avis du conseil d'état, arrêtés et règlements concernant les israélites depuis 1850, suivi d'un appendice contenant: 1. Une notice historique sur les israélites de l'Algérie, par Ab. Cahen, Grand Rabbin d'Alger; 2. Diverses notes relatives a l'émancipation des israélites algériens; Ce recueil fait suite à celui publié en 1851, par M. Achille-Edmond Halphen.* Bordeaux: Imprimerie générale d'Emile Crugy, 1878.

Van Kley, Dale K. *The Religious Origins of the French Revolution: From Calvin to the Civil Constitution of the Clergy, 1560–1791.* New Haven, CT: Yale University Press, 1996.

———, ed. *The French Idea of Freedom: The Old Regime and the Declaration of Rights of 1789.* Stanford, CA: Stanford University Press, 1994.

Vaughan, William. "The Visual Arts." In *The French Romantics,* ed. D. G. Charlton, 2 vols., 2: 308–32. Cambridge: Cambridge University Press, 1984.

Viallaneix, Paul. *Michelet, les travaux et les jours: 1798–1874*. Paris: Gallimard, 1998.

Vieillard, Philippe. *Dissertation sur la Demande des Juifs de Paris; tendant à être admis au rang de Citoyens actifs: Lue à l'Assemblée de la Commune de Paris*. Paris: n.p., n.d.

Vincent, K. Steven. *Pierre-Joseph Proudhon and the Rise of French Republican Socialism*. New York: Oxford University Press, 1984.

Vital, David. *A People Apart: The Jews in Europe, 1789–1939*. Oxford: Oxford University Press, 1999.

Vogelin, Eric. "The Growth of the Race Idea." *Review of Politics* 2, no. 3 (1940): 283–317.

Wahnich, Sophie. *L'Impossible citoyen: L'Etranger dans le discours de la Révolution française*. Paris: Albin Michel, 1997.

Weber, Eugen. "Gauls Versus Franks: Conflict and Nationalism." In *Nationhood and Nationalism in France: From Boulangism to the Great War, 1889-1918*, ed. Robert Tombs, 8–21. New York: HarperCollins, 1991.

———. *Peasants into Frenchmen: The Modernization of Rural France, 1870–1914*. Stanford, CA: Stanford University Press, 1976.

Weil, Moïse. *Le Centenaire de la Révolution: Discours prononcé, le samedi matin 11 mai 1889*. Oran: Consistoire d'Oran, 1889.

Weill, Georges. *L'Ecole saint-simonienne: Son Histoire, son influence jusqu'à nos jours*. Paris: Félix Alcan, 1896.

———. "Emancipation et humanisme: Le Discours idéologique de l'Alliance Israélite Universelle au XIXe siècle." *Nouveaux Cahiers* 52 (1978): 1–20.

———. *L'Europe du XIXe siècle et l'idée de nationalité*. Paris: Albin Michel, 1938.

———. *La France sous la Monarchie Constitutionnelle (1814–1848)*. 2nd ed. Paris: Félix Alcan, 1912.

———. *Histoire du parti républicain en France, 1814–1870*. Paris: Félix Alcan, 1900.

———. "Les Juifs et le saint-simonisme." *Revue des Etudes Juives* 31, no. 62 (1895): 261–73.

Weill, Michel. *Le Judaïsme: Ses Dogmes et sa mission*. 4 vols. Paris: A. Franck, 1868.

———. *La Morale du Judaïsme*. 2 vols. Paris: A. Franck, 1875.

———. "Situation des israélites en Algérie, rapport général, Alger." In *Les Juifs d'Algérie et la France (1830–1855)*, by Simon Schwarzfuchs, 279–372. Jerusalem: Institut Ben Zvi, 1981.

Weissbach, Lee Shai. "The Nature of Philanthropy in Nineteenth-Century France and the *mentalité* of the Jewish Elite." *Jewish History* 8, nos. 1–2 (1994): 191–204.

Wetzel, David. *The Crimean War: A Diplomatic History*. Boulder, CO: East European Monographs, 1985.

Wieworka, Michel. *The Arena of Racism*. Trans. Chris Turner. London: Sage, 1995.

Wilson, Stephen. *Ideology and Experience: Antisemitism in France at the Time of the Dreyfus Affair*. Rutherford, NJ: Fairleigh Dickinson University Press, 1982.

Winock, Michel. *Nationalism, Anti-Semitism, and Fascism in Modern France*. Trans. Jane Marie Todd. Stanford, CA: Stanford University Press, 1998.

———. *Les Voix de la liberté: Les Ecrivains engagés au XIXe siècle*. Paris: Seuil, 2001.

Wolf, Lucien. *Notes on the Diplomatic History of the Jewish Question, with Texts of Protocols, Treaty Stipulations and Other Public Acts and Official Documents*. London: Jewish Historical Society of England, 1919.

Wright, J. K. "National Sovereignty and the General Will: The Political Program of the Declaration of Rights." In *The French Idea of Freedom: The Old Regime and the Declaration of Rights of 1789*, ed. Dale K. Van Kley, 199–233. Stanford, CA: Stanford University Press, 1994.

Index

Abitbol, Michel, 233
Abyssinia (Ethiopia), 2, 165
actions. *See* bond selling
Adam (biblical figure), 173
Ageron, Charles-Robert, 209, 213, 217
Ahasverus (the wandering Jew), 89–90,
    99. *See also* Jews: as wanderers and
    internationalists
Ahasvérus (Quinet), 89
AJA (Anglo-Jewish Association), 164, 167
Albert, Phyllis Cohen, 4, 17, 58
Alexandre (Bordeaux notable), 66
Algeria: and Alliance Israélite Universelle,
    164, 166, 185; antisemitism in, 198, 203,
    204, 207–19, 221, 222, 225, 226; art de-
    picting women of, 107–8; citizenship for
    Jews in, 133, 137, 202, 204, 210, 212–13;
    Jews under French colonial rule in, 13,
    118, 120–22, 127–38, 147, 156, 157, 177, 189,
    201, 207, 210–11, 231–32; number of Jews
    in, 127, 208–9, 261n21
Algiers (Algeria), 133, 134, 208, 209, 224
Ali, Mohammed, 120, 124
Allgemeine Zeitung des Judentums (newspa-
    per), 123
Alliance Israélite Universelle, 8; achieve-
    ments of, 158, 159; antisemitic attacks
    against, 198, 201–2, 204–6, 215–16, 223,
    237; establishment of, 2, 3, 151–52, 157,
    159, 160–61, 166; goals of, 2, 3, 152, 159,
    161, 162, 178, 180, 195–96, 198–99, 232,
    236; ideology of, 157, 160, 165; member-

ship growth of, 164, 179, 267n9; rhetoric
    and practices of, 13–14, 154, 157–99,
    227–28; and Romanian Jewish citizen-
    ship campaign, 184, 188–99; Syrian
    Christians' aid from, 151–53, 179, 265n92
Alphandéry (creditor), 54
Alsace, 58; anti-Jewish sentiments in, 6,
    30, 31, 52–53; Ashkenazi Jews in, 20–21,
    28–29; Jewish citizenship granted in, 27;
    Jewish legal disabilities in, 31, 43, 46,
    49–53, 55, 248n33. *See also* Lorraine; Up-
    per Rhine Department
Altaras, Isaac-Jacques, 128, 129–32, 134,
    176–77
American Jewish Joint Distribution Com-
    mittee, 2
Amsterdam Consistory, 62
Anglo-Jewish Association (Great Britain),
    164, 167
Anspach, Philippe, 131, 133
Antichrist, 205, 217
anticlericalism. *See* Catholic Church;
    secularism
L'Anti-Juif (newspaper), 218
anti-juif movement (Algeria), 198, 203,
    204, 207–19, 221, 222, 225, 226
antisemitism: in Algeria, 198, 203, 204,
    207–19, 221, 222, 225, 226; vs. anti-Jewish
    prejudice, 201, 203–4, 211; Catholic
    Church's association with, 148, 152, 201,
    204–6, 209, 215, 216–22, 225, 234; Jewish
    international solidarity attacked by, 4,

198, 200–230, 236–37; rise of, 2, 14, 199, 203–7, 218–19; in Romania, 187–89, 192–93, 198, 199. *See also* prejudice; violence
"Appel aux israélites" (Alliance Israélite Universelle), 160, 161–62
Arabic language, 129
Arabs (in Algeria), 127–28, 208, 215, 217. *See also* Muslims
Les Archives Israélites de France (newspaper), 123, 125, 134, 137, 145, 146, 160, 218, 225
Ardoin family, 94
Arendt, Hannah, 4
Artaud, Nicolas, 132
article 44 of Congress of Berlin treaty, 195–98
artisans, 5
Aryans, 220–22
Ashkenazi Jews, 17, 20–23, 28–29, 58, 62–63
L'Assemblée Nationale (newspaper), 220
Assembly of Jewish Notables (Napoleonic), 30–39, 50, 104, 253*n*111, 259*n*57
assignats, 93
assimilation. *See* integration
Aston, Nigel, 26–27
Astruc (Bordeaux notable), 66
Astruc, Elie-Aristide, 160, 225–26
Austria, 2, 139; Alliance Israélite Universelle in, 164, 167, 192–93; antisemitism in, 198, 204, 222; and Romania, 184–86, 189, 192, 194, 197
Avignon (France), 17, 46, 47, 60
avignonnais Jews, 17

Babylon, 33
Bailly, Etienne, 76
Balcescu, Nicolae, 185
Balkan countries, 2, 186, 193, 194. *See also* Ottoman Empire; *specific Balkan countries*
Balzac, Henri de, 95–96
bankers, businessmen, and financiers, 93, 192, 193; antisemitic characterizations of, 14, 95, 201, 204, 205, 215–16, 219, 221, 222, 225; Catholic, 219; children of, as integrated into French society, 82, 85–87,

94, 95–96, 104; as consistory leaders, 58–59, 76; as essential to civilized society, 144, 145; Jews as restricted to becoming, 23; Jews depicted as being racially equipped to be, 98, 101–2; literary depictions of, 105, 106, 108, 110–11; right to earn a living as, 36; socialist views of, 275*n*39. *See also* bond selling; credit; money lending
Bank of France, 93, 94
"banquet," 178
Barante, Prosper, 69
Barrault, Emile, 76, 87, 91, 96
Barrot, Odilon, 178
Bayonne area (France), 23, 49, 58. *See also* St. Esprit
Bazard, Saint-Amand, 76, 90
Bebel, August, 204
Ben-Lévi, G., 266*n*99
Berkovitz, Jay, 4, 7, 17, 18, 233
Berlin (Germany), 194–99, 223–24
Berr, Berr Isaac, 28–29, 34, 72, 86, 123, 244*n*36, 253*n*111
Berr, Michael, 123, 124
Berry, Duchesse de, 105
Bible: as basis of morality, 29, 34, 153, 192; Jewish solidarity inscribed in, 168, 181–82; oaths sworn on, 51, 53; three major religions based on, 144, 180. *See also* Talmud
Birnbaum, Pierre, 202–3, 226, 227, 237
Bismarck, Otto von, 194, 197, 222
Blanc family, 94
Bleichröder, Gerson, 192, 194, 271*n*89
Bloch, Simon, 126, 145–46, 153, 265*n*92
"blood libel" accusations, 120, 121, 125, 201
Blum, Léon, 226
B'nai B'rith, 191
Bonald, Louis de, 71
bond selling (*actions*), 65–68, 79, 86, 94
Bontoux, Eugène, 219
Bordeaux Consistory, 61, 65–67
Bordeaux region (France), 23, 49, 58, 86, 104–5, 247*n*24
Bosnia-Herzegovina, 193, 194

Bourbon monarchy. *See* Restoration France

Bourse neighborhood (Paris), 58, 250*n*58

Brancas tax, 46

Bratiano, Dmitrie, 185

Bratiano, Ion, 185, 187, 188

Brazil, 164

Bretons, 5

Britain. *See* Great Britain

Brittany, 146

Bucharest (Romania), 166, 188, 189, 191–92, 198, 223

Buchez, Philippe-Joseph-Benjamin, 76, 88

Bugeaud, Thomas-Robert, 127–28

Bulgaria, 164

Bulletin de l'Alliance Israélite Universelle, 161, 164–65, 171, 180, 188, 192, 205, 224

Byrnes, Robert, 219, 220

Cahen, Isidore, 125, 146–50, 264*n*64; and Alliance Israélite Universelle, 152, 153, 160, 161, 166

Cahen, Lazare, 134, 135

Cahen, Samuel, 91, 125, 137, 146, 160

canals, 66, 145

capitalism, 145, 146, 149; Jews depicted as exploiters of, 201, 204, 215, 227. *See also* bankers, businessmen, and financiers

Capuchins, 120, 121

Carmelites district (Paris), 24

Carol Hohenzollern-Sigmaringen (prince), 187, 189, 191

Carpentras (France), 46, 60, 247*n*16

Carvallo, Jules, 152, 160–61, 166, 177–79, 188, 269*n*48

Catéchisme des industriels (Saint-Simon), 99

Catéchisme positive (Comte), 174

Catholic Church, 101; in Alsace, 52; antisemitism associated with, 148, 152, 201, 204–6, 209, 215, 216–22, 225, 234; attempts to displace, from its central role in French politics, 6, 7, 9–11, 13, 26–28, 31, 34, 39, 84, 85, 89, 96, 102, 118–20, 125, 137–39, 142–43, 145–56, 172, 199, 222, 226, 231–34; in the Balkans, 194; corporatist debts of, 44, 46; and education, 40, 140,

142, 143; French bank associated with, 219, 221; and French Revolution, 27, 38, 235; Jewish converts to, 23, 47, 87, 89, 91, 95–97, 104, 105, 148; and Muslims' conversion, 129, 263*n*55; no longer official state religion after Revolution of 1830, 106; as official state religion during Old Regime, 76, 88; as official state religion during Restoration period, 41, 43, 44, 60, 71, 73, 77; vs. Protestants, 73, 145, 149, 205; Roman vs. Orthodox disputes in, 139, 141, 145, 194; Saint-Simonianism designed to replace, 76, 79; special payments to, required of Jews, 46; state financial support for, 26, 31, 60; in Sweden, 149; tradition of resistance to, 5; *ultramontane* wing of, 13, 70, 71, 73, 75, 89, 119–21, 127, 138, 140, 141, 146, 148, 155, 235. *See also* Capuchins; Christianity; Crusades; Inquisition; Jesuits; Papal states; religion(s); Rome Campaign; secularism; settlers; theocracy; *specific popes*

cattle trade, 20

Cavaillon (France), 46

Central Asia, 165

Central Consistory (Paris): on communal debts, 49, 50–51; composition and organization of, 37, 57–59, 61–65, 86, 120, 227; and French antisemitism, 206–7; on French colonial policy, 122–24, 129, 131–33, 136, 138, 147, 212; on Judaism as set of beliefs rather than community, 79; on *more judaïco*, 52, 53; and new Paris synagogue, 68, 69; on state support for Jewish schools, 64, 70, 73–74

Cerfberr, Alphonse, 59

Cerfberr, Max, 59, 82, 132, 133, 206

"chain of tradition," 169–70

Chamber of Deputies, 48, 49, 64, 121–22, 126, 133, 137, 176, 224, 251*n*67

"Le Chant d'Ahasvérus" (d'Eichthal), 99

charity (philanthropy), 63, 151, 152, 165, 166–67, 179; Christian notions of, 172; credit as form of, 92; Judaism as requiring, 109–15, 131, 181, 182–83; lack of,

111–13; vs. money lending, 35, 36; secular forms of, 135–37, 156; synagogue-building as, 65–68, 79. *See also* solidarity

Charleville (Oran rabbi), 274*n*36

Charte (of 1814), 12, 40, 43–44, 55, 64, 71. *See also* Charte (of 1830); Constitution

Charte (of 1830), 106, 136

Chateaubriand, François-René de, 88, 103, 107

Chemin de Fer du Midi, 269*n*48

Chevalier, Michel, 143

China, 165

Christian Holy Alliance, 101. *See also* Catholic Church

Le Christianisme et la Révolution française (Quinet), 142

Christianity: Alliance Israélite Universelle on, 180; Jewish converts to, 23, 47, 87, 89, 91, 95–97, 104, 105, 148; Judaism's similarities to, 34, 72, 73, 78, 87, 90, 96, 99, 122, 173, 174, 192; Michelet's rejection of, 154; new forms of, 42; persecution of adherents of, 55, 140, 147, 151–52; religious liberty as fostered by true spirit of, 73; rhetoric of, used to advance liberal interests, 88, 131, 152–55, 168–76, 179, 181, 234; in Romania, 185, 187, 192, 223; Saint-Simonians' view of a new, 10, 42, 75–78, 87–91, 95, 112, 115, 144, 172. *See also* Catholic Church; Protestant religions

Church of the Holy Sepulcher (Jerusalem), 139

cities: churches owned by, 60, 68; as *communautés*, 45, 47; synagogues owned by, 68, 79. *See also specific cities*

citizenship (emancipation), 5, 168; for Algerian Jews, 133, 137, 202, 204, 210, 212–13; as Alliance Israélite Universelle goal, 165; campaign for Jewish, in Romania, 158, 159, 166, 179, 183–98; as not erasing Jewish identity, 4–5, 14, 17, 81–82, 84–85, 158, 203, 230, 233, 236; for French Jews during French Revolution, 6, 17, 18–36, 40, 218; integration associated with, in France, 4, 5, 12, 33, 233; Jews

depicted as not proving worthy of French, 223; Judaism's association with, 10, 12, 19, 29–38, 40, 41, 72–74, 131–33, 135, 137, 179, 231, 235; national and international manifestations of, 8, 9, 15, 18, 118, 130–31, 225, 230; rights of, listed, 21; threats to Jews', in eastern France, 244*n*37. *See also* equality; integration; national identities; secularism; solidarity

Civil Code of 1804 (France), 45–46, 53

Civil Code of 1864 (Romania), 187

Civil Constitution of the Clergy (1790), 26–27, 34, 234

civilization: bringing of to colonies as French imperialist mission, 2, 3, 11, 13, 117–56, 232; and "civilizing mission" as a term, 148–49, 154, 159, 175, 227, 235; France portrayed as champion of, 122–26, 129–30, 137, 147–48, 152–53, 192, 195–96; Jews as leaders in mission for, 150–57, 207–8, 227, 230–31, 236–37; measuring progress toward, 150–51, 199; secularism as part of the mission for, 11–13, 118–20, 123–56, 160, 195–96, 231–32, 235–37; solidarity as part of progress toward, 2, 14, 117–19, 157, 160, 169, 192, 225, 230–31; underpinnings of, 161–62; and Zionism, 228. *See also* equality; fraternity; messianism; morality; regeneration; religious freedom

"civilizing mission." *See* civilization

clerical party. See *ultramontane* wing (of Catholic Church)

Clermont (France), 61

Clermont-Tonnerre, Stanislas de, 22, 25–28, 50, 245*n*48

clothing trade, 20

Cohen, Joseph, 129, 132, 134, 176–77, 207

Cohn, Albert, 138

collèges, 42

Colmar Appeals Court, 52

Cologna, Abraham de, 37

Colombia, 164

colonies. *See* imperialism; *specific colonies*

Comédie-Française, 102

Commission d'enquête sur les actes du Gouvernement de la Défense nationale en Algérie, 210, 274n28

communautés (traditional Jewish communal bodies), 179; in Algeria, 128–34, 137, 212; arguments for dissolving of, 22; consistories as replacing, 40, 41, 79; consistories' early similarities to, 59–61; debts of, passed on to individuals during Restoration era, 43–50, 56, 61, 78, 182–83, 230, 231, 247n16; dissolving of, 4, 12, 17, 19, 30, 38, 47, 156, 200, 231; synagogue-financing by, 65–67. *See also* corporatism; *kehilla*

Comte, Auguste, 83, 87, 174

Concordat (of 1801), 31

Congress of Berlin, 194–99, 223–24

Congress of Paris, 147, 148, 184

Congress of Vienna, 123

Conklin, Alice, 11, 119

Conservatoire de Paris, 254n3

Considerations sur la France (Maistre), 71

consistories: colonial, 39, 129, 130–31, 133, 134, 137, 163, 211, 216; creation of, 30, 37, 38, 40, 41; defined, 17; Jewish, 37, 41, 50–51, 53, 56–70, 77–79, 179, 232, 233; Jews' efforts to obtain, 32; Protestant, 31, 37, 41, 57; regeneration as a systematic program of, 18; responsibilities of, 59–60, 63–64, 69–70, 212; and Saint-Simonians, 77; secularism as undergirding, 39, 40; swearing-in oaths for service in, 51; and tax collection, 41, 48, 59–61, 63–64, 67, 78–79. *See also* Central Consistory; religion(s); *specific local consistories*

Constant, Benjamin, 49, 56, 71

Constantine (Algeria), 133–35

Constantinople, 193–94

Constituent Assembly (France), 24, 26, 30

Constitution (French), 20, 27–29, 72–74, 123. *See also* Charte (of 1814); Charte (of 1830); Civil Constitution of the Clergy

Le Constitutionnel (newspaper), 75

Constitutions (Romanian), 187, 188, 197

Convention of Paris (1858), 186

conversos, 23

corporatism, 52–53; abolition of formal institutions of, 28, 44, 45, 133–34, 156; in Algeria, 128–34, 137, 212; antisemitic characterizations of Jewish solidarity as, 225; arguments used by Jewish leaders to free themselves from remnants of, 12, 18, 41–80; as collective oppression, 50, 51, 61, 78, 157, 176–77, 231, 232; debts associated with, 43, 44–50, 56, 61, 78, 182–83, 230, 247n16; examples of, 45; as feudal institution, 43, 130, 134; French Jewish life transformed to citizenship from, 40, 56–70; as separatist, 21–22, 84, 203. *See also* Catholic Church; *communautés*; feudalism; individual freedoms; *solidarité*

Council of Constance, 106

Council of Five Hundred, 48, 247n24

coup d'état (Louis Napoleon's), 138, 142

Cour de Cassation, 55

Courrier de Marseille (newspaper), 129

Courrier d'Oran (newspaper), 216

"Course on the History of Civilization in France" (Guizot), 98

"court Jews," 94

Cousin, Victor, 83

credit: French views of, 93; myth of Jews as having invented, 94–95; and property rights, 36, 93; Saint-Simonians on, 91–96. *See also* money lending

Crédit Mobilier bank, 83, 94

Crémieux, Adolphe, 161, 196; on Algerian commission, 132, 133; and Algerian Jews' citizenship, 202, 204, 207–18, 223; and Alliance Israélite Universelle, 161–62, 169, 170, 180–81; antisemites on, 201–2, 204, 223, 226; in Chamber of Deputies, 126, 137, 176; and communal debts, 46–47, 49, 56, 79; and Damascus Jews, 1, 121–26, 158; education of, 59, 83, 254n3; on French citizenship and religion, 43, 155; on Jewish consistories, 61; on *more judaïco*, 54–56, 79, 202; as proud of his Jewish identity, 81, 83, 103, 124–26, 213–15, 227; and Romanian Jews, 166,

189–90, 194, 195, 224, 270*n*78; on Syrian
    Christians, 151, 152
Crémieux, David, 247*n*16, 254*n*3
Crémieux, Jassé-Haïm, 247*n*16
"Crémieux decree," 202, 204, 207–8,
    210–15, 217
Crete, 164
Crimean War, 11, 119, 138–49, 184, 185–86
*La Croisade autrichienne, française, napoli-
    taine, et espagnole contre la république ro-
    maine* (Quinet), 142
La Croix (newspaper), 220
Crusades, 140–44, 146, 148, 153, 266*n*99
Cuvier, Charles-Frédéric, 132
Cuza, Alexandru, 184, 186–87
Cyrus the Great, 33

Dacosta (Bordeaux notable), 66
Damascus, 129, 151; defense of Jews in, 1–2,
    13, 120–27, 138, 157, 158, 185
Daudet, Alphonse, 219
David, Félicien, 91
David, Marcel, 174–75
debts (communal), 43, 44–50, 56, 61, 78,
    182–83, 230, 247*n*16
Declaration of the Rights of Man and Citi-
    zen, 22, 25, 27
Delacroix, Eugène, 107–8
Delescluze, Charles, 175
De l'humanité (Leroux), 172–73
De l'unité européenne (d'Eichthal), 144
democracy, 142, 150, 159, 160, 168, 177, 178,
    231; Catholic Church as opposed to, 235;
    Jews as circumventing, 216. *See also*
    divine right vs. constitutional govern-
    ment; elections; French Revolution;
    republicans
Dermenjian, Geneviève, 209
dina d'malkhuta dina, 33, 211
divine election (of Jews), 169, 181–82, 236,
    257*n*39
divine right vs. constitutional government,
    73–75
divorce, 33, 110, 128, 211–12
doctrinaires, 42, 57, 69–70, 78
The Doctrine of Saint-Simon, First Year, 93

Dreyfus, Alfred, 228. *See also* Dreyfus affair
Dreyfus, Emmanuel (of Mulhouse),
    249*n*41
Dreyfus affair, 13, 224, 227–28
Dreyfuss (Metz resident), 49
Drumont, Edouard, 201–3, 218–26
Druses, 151
du Bouzet, Charles, 210–11, 213, 215
Dupin, André, 55–56
Duvergier, J. B., 76
Duveyrier, Charles, 143

Eastern Crisis (1840), 118
Eastern Orthodox Church, 139, 141, 145,
    194
"Eastern Question," 139, 141
Eastern Railroad Company, 166–67
Ecole Normale Israélite Orientale, 163
Ecole Normale Supérieure, 86, 161, 264*n*64
Ecole Polytechnique, 76, 86, 87, 99, 174,
    177, 255*nn*6,8
Edgeworth, Maria, 110
education: Alliance Israélite Universelle's,
    159, 163, 165, 179; Berr's proposals regard-
    ing, 29; Catholic Church's role in, 40,
    140, 142, 143; consistories' rules for Jew-
    ish, 57–58, 60, 63, 64; of elite French
    Jewish children, 42, 59, 82–87, 161, 255*n*6;
    French king on, 69; Jewish, as instilling
    civic values, 72–74, 211; in the Ottoman
    Empire, 138, 146; primary school, 64; for
    Romania, 193; secular, 132–37, 220, 226;
    state support for Jewish, 64, 70, 73–74.
    See also *lycées*; morality; secularism
Egalité, J., 192. *See also* Peixotto
Egypt, 34, 120, 125, 164
Eichthal, Adolphe d', 87, 94, 257*n*39
Eichthal, Annette d', 87
Eichthal, Gustave d', 76, 105, 176, 253*n*111;
    as convert to Christianity, 87, 105; as
    proud of his Jewish identity, 81, 96–97;
    as Saint-Simonian, 85, 86–87, 90–94,
    96–97, 99–100, 103, 144
Eichthal, Louis d', 85, 94, 253*n*111
elections (Algerian), 208–10, 218
emancipation. *See* citizenship

Encyclopédie catholique, 140
Enfantin, Barthélemy-Prosper, 76, 83, 87, 90, 91
England. *See* Great Britain
Enlightenment. *See* liberalism; regeneration
Ennery, Marchand, 91
equality (legal): Charte of 1814 as guaranteeing, 12, 40, 43–44, 55, 64; Declaration of the Rights of Man and Citizens on, 22, 25; as French state ideology, 177; Jews' campaigns for, in France, 6, 12, 40–80, 122–26, 156, 157, 181, 200, 226, 229; lack of, for Jews, 30; as liberal idea, 2, 55, 78, 139, 172, 178, 179, 200, 234; *more judaïco* as attack on, 54–55; religious basis for, 29, 32; for religious minorities in other countries, 9, 117–56, 160, 162, 185–200. *See also* citizenship; corporatism
Essai sur l'indifférence en matière de religion (Lamennais), 71, 73
Esther (Biblical figure), 81, 114
Ethiopia (Abyssinia), 2, 165
Etienne, Eugène, 217

faisceau, 170–71, 175–76, 178, 182
Famin, César, 140
Fauvety, Charles, 196
Febvre, Lucien, 119
Félix, Elisa-Rachel, 102
Fellman (War Ministry official), 132
Femmes d'Alger (Delacroix), 107–8
Ferry laws, 220
Festival of the Federation, 26–27
feudalism: corporatism as part of, 43, 130, 134; end of, in France, 43, 172; property as backbone of, 93; resistance to, in foreign policy, 119, 130, 137, 147, 185, 196; Saint-Simonians on, 87; socialists on "financial," 275n39. *See also* Catholic Church; corporatism; inheritance; Old Regime
Feuerwerker, David, 52
First Empire, 205, 233. *See also* Napoleon Bonaparte
Foa, Eugénie, 81–83, 102–16, 125, 253n111, 259n56

Foa, Hippolyte, 104
Foa, Joseph, 104
Fonsèque (Bordeaux notable), 66
Forbin des Issarts (marquis), 49
Ford, Caroline, 5
foreign policy (French): Catholic Church's influence on, 9, 11, 119–21, 125, 137–56; French Jews' preferences for secularism in, 7, 12, 13, 15, 80, 117–56, 184–98, 219–20, 231–32, 235–36. *See also* civilization; imperialism; secularism; *specific countries and wars*
Fould, Achille, 59, 82, 85
Fould, Benoît, 59, 85, 121, 126
Fould, Berr Léon, 59, 85, 94–95
Fourier, Charles, 88, 112, 174
France: Alliance Israélite Universelle based in, 160–65, 167; alliances forged between Jews and liberal groups in, 6–7, 9, 12–14, 81–102, 118–19, 139, 142, 157, 159, 184, 189, 194–96, 198–202, 220, 225–26, 228–30, 232, 235–37, 255n3; antisemitism in, 11, 14, 198, 201–4, 214, 218–29; attempts to displace Catholic Church from its central role in politics of, 6, 7, 9–11, 13, 26–28, 31, 34, 39, 84, 85, 89, 96, 102, 118–20, 138–39, 142–43, 145–56, 172, 199, 222, 226, 231–34; as champion of civilization, 122–26, 129–30, 137, 147–48, 152–53, 192, 195–96; Jewish integration in, 3–8, 12–14, 38–39, 42, 65–67, 81–82, 84–87, 101, 116, 158, 168, 177, 230, 233, 236, 254n3, 255nn3,6; Jews' corporate disabilities in, 7, 12, 15, 18, 20–21, 40, 43; Jews depicted as foreigners in, 21–22, 48–50, 52–53, 56, 222, 237; number of Jews in, 19, 209; race in history of, 97–99; as responsible for prerevolutionary debts, 44, 48; revolutionary ideals in, 3, 6, 7, 9, 13, 14, 17–18, 25–26, 32, 37, 40, 42, 43, 50, 56–57, 88, 117, 122–23, 126, 136–37, 143, 147, 153, 154, 175, 179, 192, 198, 200, 229; and Romania, 184–86, 192–94, 197. *See also* Algeria; Catholic Church; Chamber of Deputies; Charte; consistories; Constitution; Crimean War; First Empire; French

Revolution; imperialism; Jews; July Monarchy; liberalism; National Assembly; national identities; Old Regime; Paris; patriotism; religion(s); religious freedom; Restoration France; Revolution of 1830; Second Empire; secularism; solidarity; Third Republic; university system; *specific rulers of*

La France juive (Drumont), 201–3, 218–25, 227

Franck, Adolphe, 170, 268*n*27

Franco-Prussian War, 191, 207, 221, 223

Frankel, Jonathan, 121, 123

Frankfurt (Germany), 95

Franks, 99

fraternity, 33; as Alliance Israélite Universelle goal, 169, 180, 195, 236; as French state ideology, 3, 173–77, 192, 195, 198; as Jewish concept, 72, 131, 135

freedom of religion. *See* religious freedom

Freemasons, 170–71, 179, 201, 202, 205–6, 216, 217

free trade, 118

The French Enlightenment and the Jews (Hertzberg), 4

French language, 29, 72, 74, 87, 163, 204, 223, 226–27

French Revolution: antisemites on, 201–2, 218, 226; Catholic Church's resistance to, 27, 38, 235; as ending corporatism, 44, 45; as granting citizenship to Jews, 6, 17, 18–23, 28, 40, 218; ideals of, 2, 3, 7, 9, 13, 14, 17–18, 25–26, 32, 37, 40, 42, 43, 50, 56–57, 88, 117, 122–23, 126, 136–37, 143, 147, 153, 154, 175, 192, 200; ideology of, as having universal application, 118, 148, 155, 158, 161–62, 172–73, 175, 179, 198, 215, 232, 233, 235–36; Jewish emigration following, 48; Jewish patriotism during, 23–24, 32, 33–34; justice linked to, 82, 115, 161, 174; as liberating Jews from oppression, 82, 84; Michelet's work on, 154; roots of Jewish international solidarity in, 12, 17–18, 117–19, 154, 172–76, 197, 231; secularism as a legacy of Napoleon and, 18,

25–27, 38–40, 97, 231, 236; as uniting diverse people of France, 97–98, 101, 103; as ushering in a new age in need of a new religion, 76, 77, 114, 142, 144, 152, 235. *See also* citizenship; civilization; corporatism; Declaration of the Rights of Man and Citizen; equality; feudalism; fraternity; individual freedoms; Napoleon Bonaparte; regeneration; religious freedom; republicans; Revolution of 1830

Freud, Sigmund, 202

Furet, François, 196

Furtado (Bordeaux notable), 66

Furtado, Abraham, 36, 37, 50–51

Fürth (Bavaria), 71, 72, 86

Galatz (Moldavia), 187, 188

Galicia, 165

Gambetta, Léon, 196, 202, 221–22, 225–26

Garnier, Francis, 153

"gathering sparks," 169–70

Le Gaulois (newspaper), 219

Gauls, 98, 99

Gazette des Tribunaux, 55

"Generation of 1820," 59, 81–116, 255*n*3; defined, 83

Gérando, Joseph-Marie, baron de, 136

German language, 73, 123

Germany (including Bavaria, Rhineland): Alliance Israélite Universelle in, 164, 167, 188, 192, 194; antisemitism in, 2, 198, 201, 204, 218, 220, 222–24; congresses in, 194–99, 223–24; French Jews from, 71, 72, 86, 95, 253*n*11; Jewish citizenship under French occupation of, 39, 44, 53, 123; Jewish international solidarity in, 2, 3, 205, 220; Jews in, 52, 197; questions in, about Judaism's morality, 121

Gibraltar, 164

Gille, Bertrand, 94

Girardin, Emile de, 141–46

Gironde Department (France), 104

Le Globe (newspaper), 75, 76

Godard, Jacques, 24

Golden Rule, 34

Goldsmid, Francis, 191, 192

Goudchaux, Michel, 59, 83

Gougenot des Mousseaux, Henri, 205–7, 217, 220

Government of the National Defense, 222; Crémieux decree by, 202, 204, 207–8, 210–15, 217

Gradis, David, 66, 104

Gradis, Esther (Eugènie Foa's mother), 104, 253n111, 259n56

Graetz, Michael, 4, 7, 8, 17, 83, 228, 233, 255n3

grandes écoles, 59

Grant, Ulysses S., 270n83

Great Britain, 149; and Alliance Israélite Universelle, 164, 166, 167; credit innovations in, 95; and Crimean War, 139, 140, 186; Jews in, 1, 2, 33, 122; questions in, about Judaism's morality, 121; race in history of, 97–98; and Romania, 188, 190–92, 197

Great Powers (and Romania), 158, 184–86, 189, 193–95, 197–98, 223. *See also specific countries*

Greece, 141

Green, Mr. (British ambassador to Romania), 191

Grégoire, Henry, 21

La Grève de Samarez (Leroux), 172

Guéroult, Adolphe, 143, 152–53

Gueslin, André, 173

Gugenheim, Marx, 134

Guizot, François, 42, 69, 73, 97, 98, 144, 148, 149

Guyot, C. E., 128

gypsies, 185

Halévy, Elie, 42, 71–74, 254n3

Halévy, Esther-Zélie, 72

Halévy, Flore, 72

Halévy, Fromenthal, 59, 71, 81, 82, 102, 105, 253n111, 254n3

Halévy, Léon, 59, 71, 76, 79, 82, 102, 174, 255n8; on clerical intolerance, 106, 110;

education of, 254n3; on Jewish identity, 81, 98, 99, 109; on Judaism as a universal moral code, 42; religious rhetoric of, 153; as Saint-Simonian, 85, 91–92, 96

Halévy, Mélanie, 72

Halévy Bizet Strauss, Geneviève, 105

Hallman, Diana, 106

Halphen, Salomon, 59

Harrington (Edgeworth), 110

Hart, Mitchell, 94

hatti Humayun, 147, 149

Hebrew language, 29, 72, 74, 163, 255n6

Heine, Heinrich, 102, 106

Hep! Hep! riots, 44

Hertzberg, Arthur, 4

Herz, Henri, 102

Herz, Jacques, 102

Hess, Moses, 153

Hilfsverein der Deutschen Juden (Germany), 167

Hillel, 34

Histoire de ma vie (Sand), 174

Histoire des institutions de Moïse et du peuple hébreux (Salvador), 74, 92

Histoire romaine (Michelet), 100

Hitler, Adolf, 227

Hollanderski, Léon, 151

Hourwitz, Zalkind, 21–22, 24

Hugo, Victor, 83, 113

Huguenots. *See* Protestant religions

Les Huguenots (Scribe), 106

human rights discourse, 11, 150, 152–53, 228, 229, 235–36

Hungary, 204, 222, 224

Hus, Jan, 106

Hyman, Paula, 4, 32

Iancu, Carol, 270n66

Idel, Moshe, 268n27

immigrants: consistories as controlling Jewish, 60; Parisian Jews as, 21, 58, 71–72, 165–66

imperialism (French): citizenship extended to colonial Jews through, 39; "civilizing mission" of, 2, 3, 11, 13, 117–56, 160,

195–96, 231–32, 235; colonial protection
for Catholics under, 121, 125; French
Jews' work for equal rights for religious
minorities under, 9–11, 13, 80, 117–58,
235–36; treatment of colonial Jews under,
13, 39, 118, 127–38, 147, 156, 157, 177, 189,
201, 207, 210–11, 231–32. See also civilization; foreign policy; specific emperors,
colonies, and periods of
individual freedoms: extreme, 111–13, 115; as
French Revolution legacy, 118; law's application to, rather than to communal
groups, 22, 25, 26, 41, 43, 46, 50–51, 56, 79
Indochina, 153
industrialism, 118, 145
"Infamous Decree" (of 1808), 43, 49–51, 72,
76, 248n33
inheritance, 93–94; of communal debts, 47,
78; as immoral way of transferring
wealth, 93; and Jewish law, 128, 212;
merit vs., 62, 76–77, 94, 254n3
Inquisition, 54, 55, 125, 143, 269n48. See
also conversos; torture
Instruction religieuse et morale à l'usage de la
jeunesse israélite (Halévy), 72–73
integration (assimilation): Christians as advocating intermarriage to increase Jewish, 245n37; as not erasing Jewish identity, 4–5, 14, 17, 81–82, 84–85, 158, 203,
230, 233, 236; French citizenship associated with, 4, 5, 12, 33, 233; as increasing
antisemitism, 204; Jews as having a long
history of, 33; of Jews in France, 3–8,
12–14, 38–39, 42, 65–67, 81–82, 84–87, 101,
116, 158, 168, 177, 233, 236, 254n3, 255nn3,
6; solidarity as growing out of Jewish, in
modern nations, 1, 4–8, 12–15, 84, 101–2,
116, 158, 168, 177, 200, 230, 233, 236
intermarriage, 33, 74, 255n3; Christians as
advocating Jewish assimilation through,
245n37; in La Juive, 105–6, 108, 113–15;
partial, of Algerian Jews, 212
internationalism. See Jews: as wanderers
and internationalists; solidarity
Introduction à l'histoire universelle
(Michelet), 100

Iran, 221
Iraq, 164, 165
Ireland, 152
Isaiah (biblical figure), 182
Isambert, François, 121
Isidor, Lazard, 168–69, 181–82
Islam, 99, 132, 143, 145. See also Muslims;
Ottoman Empire
L'Isle-sur-Sorgue (France), 46, 60
Israel, 2, 36, 153. See also Jerusalem; Pales-
tine; Sanhedrin; Zionist movement
L'Israélite Français (newspaper), 72
Israelitische Allianz, 167
Istoczy, Gyozo, 224
Italy, 220; Alliance Israélite Universelle in,
164, 190; as part of French empire, 39,
47; republicanism in, 142–43
Ivanhoe (Scott), 108, 110

Jacques, Amadée, 143
Janvier, Eugène, 131, 133
Jassy (Moldavia), 187, 188
Javal, Jacques, 59
Javal, Léopold, 59, 82
Jerusalem, 104, 139
Jesuits, 75, 142, 216, 221, 223
Jesus Christ, 88–90, 173, 220; Jews depicted
as having killed, 87, 95–96, 99, 201,
217–18
"Jewish conspiracy," 14, 201–28
Jewish identity: integration as not erasing,
4–5, 14, 17, 81–82, 84–85, 158, 203, 230,
233, 236; and Jewish international solidarity, 200, 230, 233, 236; national identity as compatible with, 4–7, 12, 17, 18,
21–24, 29, 32, 38–39, 72, 168, 229–30,
255n3; national identity as incompatible
with, 4, 14, 52, 276n1; pride in, 81–85,
96–97, 102–3, 109–11, 113–14, 124–26,
213–15, 227; as racial, 96–102, 115; Saint-
Simonians' view of, 84–102
Jews: Alliance Israélite Universelle as
based on traditions of, 158, 160, 161,
168, 169–71, 180–83; in the Balkans, 194;
bankers and businessmen among, 14,
58–59, 76, 82, 85–87, 94, 95–96, 98, 101–2,

104, 108, 110–11, 201, 204, 205, 275n39; "blood libel" against, 120, 121, 125, 201; as "chosen," 169, 181–82, 236, 257n39; Christian-born, 110; "conspiracy" of, 14, 122, 200–228; as converts to Catholicism, 23, 47, 87, 89, 91, 95–97, 104, 105, 148; as deicidal, 87, 95–96, 99, 201, 217–18; "Eastern," 117–56; emigration of, 2, 48; legal disabilities of, 6, 20–22, 40, 43, 44–45, 47, 49–53, 55, 248n33; measuring civilization's progress by rights of, 150–51, 199; nineteenth-century prejudice against, 6, 19–21, 30, 31, 36, 50, 51–53, 58, 82, 118, 120–21, 125, 127–29, 137, 146, 149, 152, 155, 156, 161, 178, 180, 189–90, 201, 211, 248n33, 255n8, 269n48; number of, in Alsace and Lorraine, 20; number of Algerian, 127, 208–9, 261n21; number of French, 19, 209; number of Romanian, 187, 270n66; as oriental and exotic, 13, 82, 103–4, 107–8, 114, 115–16; papal authorities' kidnapping of children of, 148, 152, 206; as purported foreigners in France, 21–22, 48–50, 52–53, 56, 222, 237; as purported foreigners in Romania, 189; among Saint-Simonians, 13, 81–82, 84–102, 255n3; self-defense strategies of, 10, 13, 41, 43, 117–18, 121, 137, 147, 156–58, 199, 203, 204, 226–30; as a separate nation, 21–22, 48, 50, 75, 133, 201, 202, 204, 229; as symbol for France's left-wing, 10–13, 20, 79, 84, 85, 87–103, 115–17, 220, 226–27, 234–35; violence against, 6, 44, 165, 187–89, 192–93, 198, 209, 224, 227; as wanderers and internationalists, 14, 84, 89–92, 95, 99–101, 104, 116, 165–66. *See also* antisemitism; Ashkenazi Jews; *communautés*; integration; Jewish identity; Judaism; liberalism; money lending; race theory; Sephardi Jews; solidarity; violence; *specific countries and persons*

Jews in Nineteenth-Century France (Graetz), 8
Journal des Débats (newspaper), 128, 141
Judah (Kingdom of), 162–63
Judaism: association of, with French citizenship, 10, 12, 19, 29–38, 40, 41, 72–74, 131–33, 135, 137, 179, 231, 235; charity required by, 109–15, 131, 181, 182–83; Christianity's similarities to, 34, 72, 73, 78, 87, 90, 96, 99, 122, 173, 174, 192; consistory system's impact on, 17, 58, 62–63, 233; defamation of, in nineteenth-century French press, 6, 8, 118, 120, 121, 125, 128–29, 137, 158, 205; elite Jews' lack of familiarity with basic, 85–86, 91, 97, 101; Foa's portrayal of a "new," 113–14; in French left-wing political symbolism, 10–13, 20, 84, 85, 87–103, 115–17, 220, 226–27, 234–35; justice's association with, 24, 100, 115, 160, 168; law in, 33, 74, 92, 100, 128, 161, 211–12; mysticism associated with, 169–71, 181, 201; as only non-Christian religion recognized, administered, and supported by French state, 9, 30, 31, 37; not relegated to the private realm in France, 10, 12, 17, 25–26, 28, 29, 38, 40, 233; religion of, vs. corporations associated with, 28; as requiring obedience to national laws, 32, 33; as separatist, 21, 84, 201, 203, 211; as set of beliefs rather than community, 79, 115; traditional practice of, 103, 109–10, 113–14, 255nn3,6; as universal moral code, 10, 13, 24, 29, 30, 40–42, 70–75, 84, 92, 99, 102, 103–4, 108–16, 124–25, 135, 137, 177, 189, 235; usury charges linked to, 17. *See also* charity; Jewish identity; Jews; solidarity
Judith (biblical figure), 81, 114
Le Juif, le judaïsme, et la judaïsation des peuples chrétiens (Gougenot des Mousseaux), 205–7
Le Juif Errant (Merville and Maillau), 89
Le Juif Errant (Sue), 90
La Juive (Foa), 102–16, 125
La Juive (Halévy and Scribe), 106, 108–10
July Monarchy, 9, 59, 155; colonial rule under, 118–26; Jewish expenses incorporated into state budget by, 69–70; Jewish legal disabilities removed during, 40, 65; left-wing rhetoric during, 88, 100, 122–26, 169, 172, 174, 178; public-works financing during, 66

justice: as Alliance Israélite Universelle
  goal, 182, 192, 236; French Revolution
  linked to, 82, 115, 161, 174; as goal of humanity, 123, 182; as goal of secularist
  "civilizing mission," 38, 145–46, 148, 150;
  Judaism's association with, 24, 100, 115,
  160, 168; reparative, 175, 180, 233. *See also*
  equality; law

kabbalah, 181, 268*n*27
Kahn, Zadoc, 227, 236
Kanoui, Simon, 209, 215, 226
Kates, Gary, 19–20
kehilla, 61, 63. See also *communautés*
Le kidouschim (Foa), 103
Koënigswarter, Louis, 169, 180

Laffitte, Jacques, 93, 94
Lamartine, Alphonse de, 83, 103, 107, 113
Lambert, Charles, 91
Lamennais, Félicité de, 71, 73, 88
Landau, Ezekiel, 53
Laskier, Michael, 159
Latin language, 74
Laurent de l'Ardèche, P. M., 76
law: application of French, to individuals
  rather than to groups, 22, 25, 26, 41,
  43, 50–51, 56, 79; Civil Code of 1804
  (France), 45–46, 53; French liberals'
  hopes for, 92–93, 145, 147, 149; Jewish,
  33, 74, 92, 100, 128, 161, 211–12; Jews' discriminatory treatment built into French,
  6, 20–22, 40, 43, 44–45, 47, 49–53, 55,
  248*n*33; Napoleonic, 51, 52, 176, 230;
  post-revolutionary, as forbidden to distinguish between religions, 12, 25–26, 40,
  43, 44, 51, 54, 56, 64, 69; ramifications of
  prejudice against French Jews in, 6,
  47–53, 58, 82, 248*n*33, 255*n*8; Roman, 45;
  in Romania, 187. *See also* equality; individual freedoms; justice; *more judaïco*;
  taxation
Law, John, 93, 105
Lebanon, 152
LeBas, Alexandrine, 254*n*3

Le Chapelier, Isaac-René-Guy, 23
Ledru-Rollin, Alexandre, 175
Législation primitive (Bonald), 71
Lemoinne, John, 141
Leo XIII (pope), 206, 220
Leroux, Pierre, 75, 76, 83, 88, 90, 113, 132,
  180, 275*n*39; on *solidarité*, 45, 172–74, 177,
  231
Lesseps, Fernand de, 143
Lessing, Gotthold Ephraim, 110, 114
lettres patentes, 23, 52
Lettres sur la race noire et la race blanche
  (d'Eichthal), 100, 176
Leven, Narcisse, 152, 161, 166, 169, 192, 227,
  270*n*66
Lévi-Strauss, Claude, 202
Lévy, Armand, 186, 198
Lévy, Emile, 3
Lévy, Fleurette, 86
liberalism (enlightenment): attempts to
  extend, to French colonies, 117–56; attempts to extend, to world, 157–99, 205,
  235–36; of French Jews, 6–7, 9, 12, 42–80,
  83, 84–102, 108–10, 114–16, 118–19, 168,
  198–200, 225–27; goals of, 144, 231, 234;
  influence of, on Jews, 70–78; as not irreligious, 10–12, 38, 77, 84, 154–56, 172, 174,
  180, 234–35; Jews as symbol for, 10–13,
  20, 84, 85, 87, 88–103, 115–17, 220, 226–27,
  234–35; as part of "Jewish conspiracy," 14,
  201–28; rhetoric of, 12, 18, 42, 96–104,
  122–26, 131, 148–58, 168–76, 179, 181, 233,
  237; Romantic literature as expressing,
  106; among Western European countries, 1–3. *See also* civilization; equality;
  religious freedom; republicans; secularism; socialists (utopian)
La Liberté de conscience (Simon), 150
Liberté de Penser movement, 143, 264*n*64
liberty. *See* religious freedom
La Libre Parole (newspaper), 224
Libya, 164
light imagery, 170–71, 182
liquor laws (Romania), 187–89
Littré, Emile, 220

loans. *See* money lending
Lochore, R. A., 119
Loi de Moïse (Salvador), 74, 75, 92
Lopès-Dubec (president of Bordeaux Consistory), 66
Lorraine, 58; Ashkenazi Jews in, 20–21, 24, 28–29; Jewish citizenship granted in, 27; Jewish legal disabilities in, 31, 43, 49–50. *See also* Alsace
lotteries, 65–67
Louis Napoleon, 138, 140, 142
Louis-Philippe (Duc d'Orléans, later king of France), 105, 106, 133
Louis XIV (king of France), 105
Louis XVI (king of France), 23, 27
Louis XVIII (king of France), 44, 64–65, 69, 73
"loving the stranger" doctrine, 34–35
Lower Rhine Consistory, 53
Lucet (prefect of Constantine), 210
Lunéville (Lorraine region), 24, 33
Luther, Martin, 106
Luxembourg, 164
Lycée Charlemagne, 86, 254*n*3
Lycée Henri IV, 87
Lycée Impérial, 254*n*3
lycées, 42, 59, 82, 83, 86, 87, 254*n*3, 255*n*6
Lyons, Lord, 189

Maas, Myrtil, 255*n*8
MacMahon, Patrice, 213
Mainz Commercial Court, 53
Maistre, Joseph de, 71
Malino, Frances, 27
"Le Manifeste des étudiants à Bucharest," 223, 276*n*65
manual trades, 63, 131, 163, 181
Manuel, Eugène, 152, 161, 264*n*64
Maronite Christians. *See* Syrian Christians
Marpon and Flammarion (publishers), 219
marriage, 86, 90, 212. *See also* divorce; intermarriage; polygamy
Marrus, Michael, 276*n*1
Marseilles Consistory, 60, 128, 129
Marx, Karl, 275*n*39

maskilim, 72, 73
Masons. *See* Freemasons
Maury, Abbé, 23
Mayer, Julie, 71
Mayer-Dalmbert, Simon, 59, 72
Mémoire en faveur des israélites de l'Orient, 193–94
Mémoire sur la science de l'homme (Saint-Simon), 99
Mendelssohn, Abraham, 85, 87, 95
Mendelssohn, Bethsy, 87
Mendelssohn, Félix, 87
Mendelssohn, Moses, 72, 74
Mèndes France, Pierre, 226
Ménilmontant (France), 87, 90, 99
Merchant of Venice (Shakespeare), 108
merit (vs. inheritance), 62, 76–77, 94, 254*n*3
Merville, M., 89
messianism (political), 2, 96, 115, 124, 172–73, 181–82, 196, 236; Ahasverus as symbol of, 89–91, 99–100; antisemites on Jewish, 202, 206. *See also* peace
Metternich, Klemens, 189
Metz (France), 21, 46–47, 49, 71
Mévil, Mardochée, 62
Meyer, Arthur, 219
Meyerbeer, Giacomo, 102, 106
Michelet, Jules, 83, 97, 100–101, 106, 113, 125, 154, 174
Middle East: Alliance Israélite Universelle chapters in, 163–64; d'Eichthal's vision for, 144–45; French intervention in, 10; Jews in, 2, 117, 118. *See also specific Middle Eastern countries*
Mikveh Israel, 161
Miliana (Algeria), 208
military service, 248*n*33
Millaud, Edouard, 217
Ministry of Worship (France): as consistories' supervisor, 37, 68; and French colonial policy in Algeria, 127, 131, 132, 134, 213
Mirès, Jules, 151, 178
Mohammed (prophet), 124, 145
Moldavia, 184, 186, 187, 189

Le Monde (newspaper), 220
money lending (usury): Assembly of Jewish Notables on, 35–36; ban on, in eastern France, 31, 36, 43, 49–52, 244*n*37; by Catholic Church, 46; vs. charity, 35, 36; Christians' concerns about, 22–23, 30, 31–32, 52; consistories' discouragement of, 63; Jews' association with, 95; Jews restricted to, 20; Napoleon on, 17. *See also* bankers, businessmen, and financiers; credit; debts; *more judaïco*
Monier de la Sizeranne, Henri, 126
montagnards, 175, 176
Montefiore, Moses, 1, 120, 122
Montenegro, 139
Montpellier (France), 74
Mont-Tonnerre Consistory, 53
morality: Alliance Israélite Universelle's work as upholding, 169, 180, 182, 183, 195; Bible as basis of, 29, 34, 153, 192; charity's role in transforming, 136; different races as having different, 100–101; Foa's, 103–4, 108–9, 111–16; Judaism as expressing universal, 10, 13, 24, 29, 30, 40–42, 70–75, 84, 92, 99, 102, 103–4, 108–16, 124–25, 135, 137, 177, 189, 235; question of Judaism's, 17, 22, 52, 121, 128–29, 201. *See also* justice; regeneration; religion(s)
more judaïco (Jewish oath), 43, 51–56, 202, 248*n*32. *See also* equality (legal)
Morocco, 108, 163, 164, 213
Mortara, Edgardo, 148, 206
Moselle Prefecture, 48
Moses (biblical figure), 74, 170
Mostaganem (Algeria), 209
Mount Lebanon, 151
Muelsch, Elisabeth-Christine, 259*n*56
Munk, Salomon, 268*n*27
murders: accusations of ritual, 120, 121, 125, 201; of Jews, 120; of Syrian Christians, 151. *See also* torture; violence
Muslims, 120, 140, 141, 150, 153; in Algeria, 129, 133, 208, 210–13; in the Balkans, 194; Catholic Church's desire to convert, 129, 263*n*55. *See also* Arabs; Islam

Musset, Alfred de, 103
mysticism (Jewish), 169–71, 181, 201
myths: defined, 202; of Jewish world domination, 202–29; of Jews as a separate nation, 21–22, 48, 50, 75, 133, 201, 202, 204, 229; of Jews having invented credit, 94–95

Nancy (France), 29, 86
Napoleon Bonaparte, 12, 221; citizenship under, 45–46; education under, 132; hierarchical structures of, 57–58; interest rate set by, 65; Jewish citizenship reaffirmed under, 17–20, 29, 40, 43, 73; on Jewish traditions, 39; Judaism linked to state ideology under, 19, 30–38; secularism's origins under, 20–21, 31, 34, 44. *See also* First Empire; French Revolution; imperialism; Napoleonic Code
Napoleonic Code, 51, 52, 176, 230
Napoleon III, 119, 147, 206; capture of, 207; and Crimean War, 138, 140; opposition to, 159, 176, 177, 183; and Romania, 185, 186, 191. *See also* Second Empire
Napoléon III et les principautés roumaines (Lévy), 186
Narbonne (France), 61
Nathan the Wise (Lessing), 110
National Assembly (France), 23, 26, 104, 211
National Assembly (Romania), 188
National Convention (France), 47
National Guard (France), 24
national identities: and Alliance Israélite Universelle, 162–63, 167, 168–69, 191–92; antisemitism and, 204; Jewish identity as compatible with, 4–7, 12, 17, 18, 21–24, 29, 32, 38–39, 72, 168, 229–30, 255*n*3; Jewish identity as incompatible with, 4, 14, 52, 276*n*1; as a process, 5; as racial, 97–101; in Romania, 184–86; and solidarity, 177. *See also* citizenship; sovereignty
"Nation Portugaise," 23
Netherlands, 164
Netter, Charles, 161, 166
Nîmes (France), 46, 49, 54–55

Noachide laws, 34
Noah (biblical figure), 34
Nord, Philip, 158–59, 177
North Africa: Alliance Israélite Universelle in, 163, 165; commercial relations with, 129; Jews in, 2, 117. *See also specific North African countries*

oaths. See *more judaïco*
Observateur des Tribunaux (newspaper), 124
Octave de Bastard, Comte de, 214
October 24, 1870, decree (Crémieux decree), 202, 204, 207–8, 210–15, 217
Old Regime, 5, 48, 173; Catholic Church as spiritual foundation of, 76, 88; corporate bodies of, dissolved by French Revolution, 17, 38, 43; Jewish legal disabilities during, 6, 41, 43, 44–45, 47, 50, 52–53; remnants of, in Restoration period, 40–80; Saint-Simonians' rejection of values of, 87–88, 95. *See also* Catholic Church; *communautés*; corporatism; feudalism; inheritance; *lettres patentes*
Ollivier, Emile, 213
omnibuses, 82–83
L'Opinion Nationale (newspaper), 152, 161, 178, 188
Opportunists, 208, 215, 220, 221, 225
Oran (Algeria), 133–35, 166, 209, 210, 213, 215–17, 274n36
ordonnance (of 1823), 58, 62
ordonnance (of November 9, 1845), 133, 212
Le Organisateur (newspaper), 76, 77
The Origins of Totalitarianism (Arendt), 4
d'Orleans, duc de (Louis-Philippe), 105, 106
d'Orléans, Philippe, 46
Ottoman Empire, 13, 139, 196; breakup of, 184, 186; Christians in, 121, 140, 151; Jews in, 117, 120–26, 138, 140, 146, 147, 179. *See also* Muslims; Turks; *specific cities and countries of former*

Palestine: Alliance Israélite Universelle in, 164, 165; Jewish agricultural societies in, 161; as promised land for Jews, 21, 153.

See also Israel; Jerusalem; Zionist movement
Panama Canal, 219
Papal states (former), 46–47, 58, 247n16
Paris (France): Alliance Israélite Universelle based in, 160–63, 165, 167; Carmelites district of, 24; as center of "Jewish conspiracy," 216; elite Jews in, 21, 58–65, 71, 86, 95, 165, 177; Jewish citizenship granted in, 27; Jews in, during French Revolution, 24, 33; Sephardi Jews in, 66; synagogue donated to, 68. *See also* Central Consistory; Congress of Paris; Convention of Paris; Paris Consistory; Sanhedrin; *specific neighborhoods and institutions in*
Paris Commune, 24, 175, 221
Paris Consistory, 55, 65–67; composition of, 59, 62, 76, 138, 160, 178, 254n3; new synagogue for, 67–69, 91
Passover, 109
patriarchal tyranny, 105–9, 111–14
patriotism: Jewish solidarity framed as expression of, 3, 14, 214, 237; of Jews during French Revolution, 23–24, 32, 33–34
peace: Jewish solidarity as part of larger goal toward, 2, 3, 77, 79, 92, 93, 96, 98–102, 149, 150, 162–63, 168, 169–70, 181–82, 198–99, 230–31, 236, 237. *See also* messianism
peasants, 5
Peixotto, Benjamin Franklin, 191–92
Penslar, Derek, 94
Pereire, Emile, 178, 253n111; commercial affairs of, 66, 83, 94, 104, 167; as Saint-Simonian, 59, 76, 85, 94, 143
Pereire, Isaac (b. 1771), 59, 66
Pereire, Isaac (b. 1806), 178, 253n111; commercial affairs of, 66, 83, 94, 104, 167; as Saint-Simonian, 76, 85, 89, 94, 143
Pereire, Rachel, 66
Persia, 163, 165
Petit Africain (newspaper), 216
Petit Algérien (newspaper), 216
Petit Colon (newspaper), 216
Petit Constantinois (newspaper), 216

Petit Fanal Oranais (newspaper), 216
Le Peuple (Michelet), 174
philanthropy. *See* charity
Philippe (Foa), 103
philosophes, 105, 111–12
Picot, Emile, 189
Piette, Christine, 42, 250*n*58, 255*n*8
Pius VI (pope), 27, 31
Pius VII (pope), 71
Pius IX (pope), 142, 143, 145, 148, 155, 206
Plée, Léon, 150, 152
Poland, 126, 153, 166–67
Poliakov, Léon, 205, 218
polygamy, 33
Portugal, 23, 164
Posen (Germany), 223
poverty, 135–37, 165, 216
Prague, 166
Prague, Hippolyte, 218
prejudice (against Jews in nineteenth cen-
    tury): in Algeria, 118, 127–29, 137, 211,
    217, 231; antisemitism as building on tra-
    ditional, 201, 203–4, 211; in Damascus,
    120–21, 125; in France, 30, 31, 146, 155,
    156, 201, 206, 255*n*8, 269*n*48; interna-
    tional solidarity against, 161, 178, 180,
    196, 227; legal and occupational ramifica-
    tions of, 6, 47–53, 58, 82, 248*n*33, 255*n*8;
    in Romania, 185, 189–90; in Rome, 148,
    152, 206; in Switzerland, 149. *See also*
    antisemitism; violence
press (Algerian), 216
press (French): antisemitic, 203–8, 216–20,
    223, 224; on antisemitism, 228; Crémieux's
    reports in, 120–23; defamation of Ju-
    daism in nineteenth-century, 6, 8, 118,
    120, 121, 125, 128–29, 137, 158, 205; on
    Jewish solidarity, 177–79, 232, 263*n*55;
    liberal principles in, 162; on Ottoman
    Empire, 138, 151; on religious questions
    and French foreign policy, 140, 147–48;
    on Salvador's books, 74–75; on Syrian
    Christian campaign, 152–53. *See also*
    specific newspapers
press (Western), 2, 56

La Presse (newspaper), 141, 152
principe de nationalité, 185, 186
Le Producteur (newspaper), 76, 77, 86, 94
property rights: as backbone of feudalism,
    93; and credit, 36, 93; and Jewish law,
    133, 212; lack of, for Romanian Jews, 190,
    193; threats to Jewish communal,
    247*n*24. *See also* inheritance
Protestant religions (Huguenots), 34, 83,
    103, 132, 249*n*55; in Alsace, 52; vs.
    Catholic Church, 73, 145, 149, 205; con-
    sistories for, 31, 37, 41, 57; conversion
    of Jews and Muslims by, 263*n*55; and
    Crimean War, 140; and education, 40;
    in Nîmes, 55; no special taxes on, 60;
    prejudice against, 126, 152, 201, 205, 220;
    Romantic works on subject of, 106. *See
    also* Christianity
Protocols of the Elders of Zion, 204, 226–27
Proudhon, Pierre-Joseph, 88, 112, 174,
    275*n*39
Proust, Marcel, 105
Prugnon (French deputy), 28

"quarrel of the keys," 139
Quinet, Edgar, 89, 97, 101, 113, 125, 142–44,
    148, 154

Raba (Bordeaux notable), 66
race theory: antisemites' use of, 204,
    220–21; rhetoric of, 96–103, 115
Rachel (Elisa-Rachel Félix), 102
Rachel; ou, L'Heritage (Foa), 103
Radical Algérien (newspaper), 208
railroad development, 66, 145, 150, 166–67,
    269*n*48, 271*n*89
Ratti-Menton, Comte de, 120–22
regeneration (rehabilitation): as Alliance
    Israélite Universelle goal, 3, 159, 163, 181;
    antisemites' use of concept of, 226; con-
    sistories' support for, 63, 69; defined, 8,
    18; "Eastern" Jews' need of, 117–56, 186,
    190–91, 236; and Jewish citizenship, 20–22,
    29, 47, 214; and money lending, 36;
    rhetoric of, 18, 233; Romantics' view of

Jewish, 104, 113–15, 225; Saint-Simonians on Jewish, 91, 95–97, 99; of Syria and Europe, 144. *See also* civilization

Régis, Max, 209, 224

Regnault de Saint-Jean-d'Angély, Michel-Louis-Etienne, comte, 28

rehabilitation. *See* regeneration

religion(s): attempts to subordinate, to the state, 25–29, 31–34, 36–38, 43, 56–57, 84, 155; as divisive, 25–26; French Revolution as ushering in a new age in need of new, 76, 77, 114, 142, 144, 152, 235; as lacking in social utility, 25–26; law as forbidden to distinguish between, 12, 25–26, 40, 43, 44, 51, 54, 56, 64, 69; place of, in modern life, 42; as private matter, 54, 56, 78; rhetoric of, used to advance liberal interests, 88, 131, 152–55, 168–76, 179, 181, 234; state financial support for, 9, 26, 31, 37, 60, 64, 67, 68–69, 78; as support for state authority, 30, 34, 70; as a way to teach citizenship, 10, 12, 19, 28–38, 40, 41, 65, 70–74, 77–78, 131–33, 135, 137, 142–43, 165, 173–74, 179, 231, 235. *See also* Catholic Church; consistories; Islam; Judaism; morality; Protestant religions; religious freedom

religious freedom (liberty; tolerance): Alliance Israélite Universelle's support for, 161; Charte of 1814 as guaranteeing, 12, 44, 64, 71; as civilization component, 231; under Declaration of Rights of Man and Citizens, 25; France as champion of, 119–26, 129–30, 137, 147–48, 152–53, 177, 200; Guizot on, 73; Jews' advocacy of, 6, 41, 77, 84, 103, 105–6, 108, 113–15, 117–200, 207, 236; as liberal idea, 2, 10, 55, 75, 77, 139, 234; *more judaïco* used as example of, 53–55; under Napoleon, 17, 31; and Zionism, 228. *See also* religion(s); secularism

Rémusat, Charles de, 42, 75, 144

Renan, Ernest, 206

republicans: Algerian, 208; antisemites' use of language of, 206; in France, 6; Jewish alliances with, 7, 9, 14, 83, 118–19, 139, 142, 157, 159, 194–96, 198–202, 220, 225–26, 228–30, 232, 237; as part of "Jewish conspiracy," 14, 201–4, 212–17, 221–28; as part of Jewish tradition, 158; and rhetoric of international solidarity, 158–59, 168–84, 198–99, 214, 233, 237; Romanian, 185–88; and secularism, 11, 138, 159, 198–99, 218, 219–20, 225–26, 232. *See also* democracy; divine right vs. constitutional government; French Revolution; secularism; *specific French republics*

La République Démocratique et Sociale (newspaper), 175

Restoration France, 9, 40–80, 89, 94, 123, 156; Catholic Church as official state religion in, 41, 43, 44; corporatist remnants in, 12, 40–80, 131, 157

Résumé de l'histoire des juifs anciens (Halévy), 91–92

Résumé de l'histoire des juifs modernes (Halévy), 92

Reubell, Jean-François, 23, 27–28

Revolution of 1830, 74, 83, 94, 106, 119. *See also* July Monarchy

Revolution of 1848, 83, 166, 172, 174–76, 178–79

Revue encyclopédique (Leroux), 132

Revue Indépendante (Leroux and Sand), 174

Reynaud, Jean, 90

Rhineland. *See* Germany

Rhodes, 164

Riou de Kersalaun, François-Marie-Joseph, 48

Robespierre, Maximilien, 246n58

Rodrigue, Aron, 8, 18, 159, 163, 233

Rodrigues, Amélie, 76, 85

Rodrigues, Benjamin, 59, 66, 104, 105, 253n111

Rodrigues, Cécile, 105, 253n111

Rodrigues, Edouard, 76, 105, 253n111

Rodrigues, Eugène, 59, 76, 82, 85, 89, 93–94, 96

Rodrigues, Henry, 76, 105, 253n111

Rodrigues, Hippolyte, 253n111

Rodrigues, Isaac (b. 1765), 104, 253n111

Rodrigues, Isaac (b. 1771), 59, 76, 85–87, 94, 253*n*111

Rodrigues, Léonie, 104, 105, 253*n*111

Rodrigues, Mélanie, 76, 85

Rodrigues, Nancy, 259*n*57

Rodrigues, Olinde, 104, 253*n*111; as member of Generation of 1820, 59, 82; as Saint-Simonian, 76, 81, 85–87, 90, 92–94, 96

Rodrigues, Rachel-Herminie, 85, 253*n*111

Rodrigues-Henriquès, Isaac, 104, 253*n*111

rôle de réparation, 60–61, 65, 66

Romania: Alliance Israélite Universelle in, 164–66, 188–89, 191–92, 198; antisemitism in, 187–89, 192–93, 198, 204, 205, 218, 223; campaign for Jewish citizenship in, 158, 159, 179, 183–99, 201, 223; Christianity in, 185, 187, 192, 223; French trade agreements with, 11; Jewish citizenship in, 198; number of Jews in, 187, 270*n*66; restrictions on Jews in, 187–89, 192–93, 198, 199

Romano-European Antisemitic Congress, 224

Romans, 92

Romantic literature, 101, 102–16, 235

Rome: French clergy's tie to, severed, 26–27; kidnapping of Jewish children by papal authorities in, 148, 152, 206; religious intolerance in, 152; republicanism in, 142–43, 176. *See also* Catholic Church; Romans; Rome Campaign; *specific popes*

Rome Campaign (1849), 140, 142–43

Rosetti, C. A., 185–88

Rothschild, Alphonse de, 207, 227

Rothschild, James de, 95

Rothschild family, 201, 219, 221

Rousseau, Jean Jacques, 25, 74

Royer-Collard, Pierre-Paul, 69

Rural Laws (Romania), 187

Russia, 2, 139, 153, 165; antisemitism in, 204, 218, 226; and Romania, 185, 186, 188, 193, 197; and Turkey, 193–94

Said, Edward, 107

Sainte-Avoye neighborhood (Paris), 58, 67–69, 250*n*58

St. Esprit (France), 61, 243*n*17

Saint-Simon, Henri de, 76–77, 85–87, 90–91, 99, 174, 180. *See also* Saint-Simonians

Saint-Simonians, 172, 174; antisemites on, 221; goals of, 85; influence of, on later liberals, 138, 143–44, 178; internationalism of, 96–102, 158, 172, 235–36; Jewish elite among, 13, 81–82, 84–102, 255*n*3; new Christianity of, 10, 42, 75–78, 87–91, 95, 112, 115, 144, 172. *See also* Saint-Simon, Henri de

Salomons, David, 191

Salvador, Joseph, 42, 74, 75, 79, 92

Sand, George, 113, 132, 174

Sanhedrin: in ancient times, 33, 36; under Napoleon, 36–38, 51, 72–73, 76, 92, 109, 111, 233, 254*n*11

Sarreguemines (Lorraine region), 24, 33

Scandinavia, 149, 152, 164

Schechter, Ronald, 4, 10, 19–20, 24

Schwarzfuchs, Simon, 31, 245*n*38, 261*n*21

Scotland, 95

Scott, Walter, 96, 108, 110, 114

Scribe, Eugène, 106

Second Empire, 9, 10, 66, 119, 177; collapse of, 207, 213; French foreign policy in, 138. *See also* Napoleon III

secondhand goods trade, 63

Second Republic (of 1848), 9, 118, 140, 166, 174–76, 178

secularism (anticlericalism): analyzing construction of, 11, 229, 231–34; as not irreligious, 10–12, 38, 77, 84, 154–56, 172, 174, 180, 234–35; Jewish support for international, 184, 186–99, 203, 221–25, 231–32; Jewish support for state, in France, 7–13, 15, 34–36, 39, 41, 42, 70–80, 154–57, 203, 219–20, 231, 234–35; as legacy of French Revolution and Napoleon, 18, 25–27, 38–40, 97, 231, 236; as part of French imperialism's "civilizing mission," 11–13, 118–20, 123–56, 160, 195–96, 231–32, 235; as protecting Jews from antisemitism, 225–26; and republicans, 11, 101, 138, 159, 198–99, 218, 219–20, 225–26, 232; Saint-Simonianism's similarity to, 76–77. *See also* Catholic Church; religion(s); religious freedom

Seine Department, 68

self-defense strategies (of Jews): antisemitic attacks on, 199, 203, 204, 226–28, 230; citizenship as, 41, 43, 117–18, 138; international solidarity as, 13, 117–18, 121, 137, 138, 147, 156–58, 199, 203, 204, 226–30; secular emphasis as, 10. *See also* citizenship; secularism; solidarity

Seligman, Joseph, 270*n*83

Seligmann, Louis, 86

sénatus-consulte (of 1865), 210, 213

separatism (of traditional Judaism), 21–22, 84, 201, 203, 211. *See also* corporatism; Jews: as a separate nation

Sephardi Jews, 17, 23, 58, 62–63, 66, 255*n*3

Serbia, 11, 164, 165

settlers (in Algeria), 207, 209, 210, 216, 218

Sewell, William H. Jr., 5, 173, 183

Shakespeare, William, 96, 108, 114

Sibour, Marie-Dominique-Auguste, 140, 141, 145, 146, 154

Sicotière, Léon de la, 274*n*28

Le Siècle (newspaper), 150, 152, 188, 270*n*78

Silny, Louise-Amélie, 47

Simon, Jules, 143, 146, 150, 152, 161, 196, 221–22, 226

Singer, David, 62

Sintzheim, David, 51, 53

socialists (contemporary), 201, 204, 222

socialists (Jewish), 230

socialists (utopian), 112–13, 275*n*39; Jewish alliances with, 9, 83, 84–102; Jews as political symbols for, 12, 13, 79, 84, 85, 87–96, 115–16, 234; rhetoric of, 168–69, 233. *See also* Saint-Simonians

Société de la morale chrétienne (Guizot), 73

solidaire (as a term), 45–46, 172, 173, 177

solidarité: as collective oppression, 50, 51, 61, 78, 157, 176–77, 231, 232; as a term, 45–46, 48–50, 157, 176–77, 182–83, 232. *See also* solidarity

La Solidarité Républicaine (organization), 175–76, 179

solidarity (Jewish international): not abandoned under duress, 227–28; antisemitic attacks on, 4, 198, 200–230; as demonstrating fidelity to fellow Jews and fellow nationals, 4, 8, 230, 232, 237; French Revolutionary roots of, 12, 17–18, 117–19, 154, 172–76, 197, 231; goals of, 225; as growing out of Jewish integration into modern nations, 1, 4–8, 12–15, 84, 101–2, 116, 158, 168, 177, 200, 230, 233, 236; ideas associated with, 1, 6, 195, 225; and Jewish identity, 200, 230; Jewish tempering of, in face of antisemitism, 13, 198, 213, 226–28; Jews' reputation as wanderers and internationalists as contributing to, 14, 84, 89–92, 95, 99–101, 104, 116, 165–66; as part of larger goal to unite the world in peace, 2, 3, 77, 79, 92, 93, 96, 98–102, 149, 150, 162–63, 168, 169–70, 181–82, 198–99, 230–31, 236, 237; practices associated with, 1, 13–14, 157–99; as a religious duty, 2, 169–72, 182; as a rhetorical strategy, 6, 13–14, 17, 122–26, 157–99, 203, 225, 229–30; secularism's role in, 42, 79–80, 183–200; as a term, 157, 160, 172–83, 237. *See also* Alliance Israélite Universelle; citizenship; human rights discourse; integration; messianism; regeneration; self-defense strategies; *solidarité*; universalism

Solutions de la question d'Orient (Girardin), 143–44

South America, 2

Southern Railroad, 166

sovereignty (national), 25–27, 29, 32, 33. *See also* national identities; patriotism; *specific countries*

Spain, 23, 152, 166, 217–18. *See also* Inquisition

Spitzer, Alan, 83

Staël, Madame de, 103

Stanley, Lord, 191

Stern, Fritz, 197, 270*n*83, 271*n*89

Stoecker, Adolph, 224

Strasbourg Consistory, 61, 63

Sue, Eugène, 90

Sweden, 149, 152
Switzerland, 140, 149, 164, 165, 220
symbols: Jews as, in French left-wing political circles, 10–13, 20, 84, 85, 87, 88–103,
  115–17, 220, 226–27, 234–35; used by Alliance Israélite Universelle, 171
synagogues, 41, 51, 52, 60, 63, 65–69, 79,
  134, 135
syndics, 47
Syria, 141–42, 144
Syrian Christians (Maronite Christians),
  151–53, 179, 265*n*92
Szajkowski, Zosa, 44, 167, 267*n*9

Talmud, 2, 121, 171, 201, 206, 221
taxation: abolition of special, for Jews in
  France, 68; collection of, after dissolving
  of Jewish communal institutions, 30;
  consistories' role in Jewish, 41, 48, 59–61,
  63–64, 67, 78–79; on Jews in Algeria, 128,
  130; in Romania, 185; special, on Jews in
  France, 7, 40, 46–47, 63–67, 78, 79; in
  Turkey, 145. See also *communautés*
Le Temps (newspaper), 188
Ternaux family, 94
Tetuan (Morocco), 163
theocracy, 42, 71, 75, 138. See also Catholic
  Church: as official state religion
Théorie du pouvoir politique et religieux
  (Bonald), 71
Thierry, Amadée, 97–100
Thierry, Augustin, 97–100, 174
Thiers, Adolphe, 83, 121–22, 124, 126
Thiéry, Claude-Antoine, 21
Third Republic (France), 183, 196, 199,
  200, 234, 237; antisemitism in, 14,
  201–28; colonial policy in, 119, 130
Thomas (Capuchin friar), 120, 121
tikkun olam, 170, 181
Tlemcen (Algeria), 209
tolerance. See religious freedom; secularism
torture, 120, 122–23. See also Inquisition
Tours (France), 207
Toussenel, Alphonse, 174, 275*n*39
Treaty of Berlin, 197–98, 224. See also Con-
  gress of Berlin

Tunis, 152
Tunisia, 152, 164
Turin Appeals Court, 53
Turkey, 139, 141, 144, 145, 149, 196; Alliance
  Israélite Universelle in, 8, 164, 165; and
  Romania, 184–85; and Russia, 193–94
Turks, 130, 140, 145. See also Muslims;
  Ottoman Empire
tzedakah, 181. See also charity

ultramontane wing of Catholic Church
  ("clerical party"), 155, 235; anti-Jewish
  prejudice of, 121, 127; as authoritarian
  and intolerant, 13, 70, 89, 138, 142, 173,
  235; and French foreign policy, 119–21,
  138, 140, 141, 146, 148; as supporting
  Catholic Church's theocracy, 71, 75, 138
Union Générale (bank), 219, 221
United States, 2, 164, 191
Univers (newspaper), 121, 127, 206, 220
universalism, 146, 149, 232; antisemites on,
  205–7, 225–26; international solidarity
  based on ideology of Enlightenment,
  2–3, 15, 38–39, 168, 180; Jews as representing, 10, 13, 82, 84, 98–102, 151–52, 156,
  195–96, 198, 235; Judaism depicted as religion of, 34–35, 40, 42, 70–73, 108–10,
  189; Saint-Simonians on, 87, 89, 90, 92,
  96, 144, 152; as stemming from French
  Revolution, 118, 148, 155, 158, 161–62,
  172–73, 175, 179, 198, 215, 232, 233, 235–36.
  See also imperialism; liberalism; peace;
  religious freedom
L'Univers Israélite, 126, 145, 177, 205, 206
university system (France), 127–32, 139,
  142–43, 146, 220
Upper Rhine Consistory, 52, 53
Upper Rhine department, 51–52. *See also*
  Alsace
usury. *See* money lending
utilitarianism. *See* Saint-Simonians
utopians. *See* socialists (utopian)
Uzès (France), 54

vagrancy laws, 187–88
the Vaucluse, 48–49

Vaughn, William, 107–8
Veneziani, Emmanuel, 198
Vercelli (Italy), 164
Verdun (France), 3
Veuillot, Louis, 127, 140, 155, 206, 215
Vienna. *See* Austria
Vigny, Alfred de, 83
violence: against Jews, 6, 44, 165, 187–89,
    192–93, 198, 209, 224, 227; payments to
    prevent, against Jews, 46; against Protes-
    tants, 55. *See also* murders; torture
Le Visiteur du pauvre (Gérando), 136
Vital-Roux family, 94
La Voix des Femmes (newspaper), 175
Voltaire, 106

Waddington, William Henry, 194–96, 221,
    223–24

Wallachia, 184, 186
Walsin-Esterhazy, Jean-Louis-Marie, 210
War Ministry, 127–29, 131, 132, 207, 212–13
Weill, Alexandre, 102
Weill, Michel, 134, 135–36
Weissbach, Lee Shai, 136
Western Antilles, 164
White Terror of 1815, 55
women. *See* patriarchal tyranny; *specific
    women*
working class, 75, 93, 209, 215
world domination (myth of Jewish),
    202–29
Worms de Romilly, Olry, 59, 77, 85, 86, 94

Zionist movement, 2, 14, 228–30. *See also*
    Palestine
Zohar, 170